The Economics of the Oil and Gas Industry

Energy is a key resource for transformational development globally. Oil and gas continue to play a key role in this sector irrespective of the gradual transition towards renewables and will continue to do so in most developing and emerging economies in the near future. The industry is complex and highly capital intensive not only with significant risk, but also with significant benefits. Such a complex but important sector is generally not well understood both in academic and policy circles.

This book fills this void by serving as a comprehensive reference to the oil and gas sector, with a focus on emerging markets and developing economies (EMDEs). It offers in-depth coverage of the critical and contemporary issues in the economics of the oil and gas industry by carefully integrating the relevant theoretical underpinnings and practical policy issues across the value chain of the industry in relation to the development, fiscal arrangements, and the economic and financing aspects of the industry. These insights will significantly deepen the understanding of the industry and extend knowledge of the sector in ways that existing books do not.

The book includes relevant cases and, thus, will serve as a valuable resource for students taking courses in market analysis of the oil and gas industry, energy economics, development economics and finance, environmental and resource economics, the political economy of the extractive industry, and development studies. Researchers and practitioners working in these areas will also find the book to be a useful reference guide.

Joshua Yindenaba Abor is Financial Economist, Professor of Finance, and former Dean of the University of Ghana Business School. He is External Fellow at the Centre for Global Finance, SOAS University of London, UK, and Adjunct Professor of Development Finance at the University of Stellenbosch Business School, South Africa.

Amin Karimu is Associate Professor in Economics at the School of Economics, University of Cape Town, South Africa, and Visiting Scholar at the Centre for Environmental and Resource Economics at Umeå University, Sweden.

Runar Brännlund is Professor of Economics at the School of Business, Economics and Statistics, and former Director of the Center for Environmental and Resource Economics (CERE), Umeå University, Sweden.

Routledge Studies in the Economics of Business and Industry

Intellectual Property in Russia
Natalia M. Udalova and Anna S. Vlasova

A Market Process Theory of the Firm
An Alternative to the Neoclassical Model
Mateusz Machaj

The Rural Enterprise Economy
Edited by Birgit Leick, Susanne Gretzinger and Teemu Makkonen

The Evolution of Contemporary Arts Markets
Aesthetics, Money and Turbulence
Andrés Solimano

The Economics of Corporate Trade Credit in Europe
Julia Koralun-Bereźnicka and Dawid Szramowski

The Economics of the Oil and Gas Industry
Emerging Markets and Developing Economies
Edited by Joshua Yindenaba Abor, Amin Karimu and Runar Brännlund

The Professional Standards of Executive Remuneration Consultants
Calvin Jackson

International Trade and the Music Industry
Live Music Services from the Caribbean
Lisa Gordon

For more information about this series, please visit www.routledge.com/Routledge-Studies-in-the-Economics-of-Business-and-Industry/book-series/RSEBI

The Economics of the Oil and Gas Industry

Emerging Markets and Developing Economies

Edited by Joshua Yindenaba Abor, Amin Karimu, and Runar Brännlund

Routledge
Taylor & Francis Group
LONDON AND NEW YORK

First published 2023
by Informa Law from Routledge
4 Park Square, Milton Park, Abingdon, Oxon OX14 4RN

and by Informa Law from Routledge
605 Third Avenue, New York, NY 10158

Informa Law from Routledge is an imprint of the Taylor & Francis Group, an informa business

British Library Cataloguing-in-Publication Data
A catalogue record for this book is available from the British Library

Library of Congress Cataloging-in-Publication Data
Names: Abor, Joshua Yindenaba, editor. | Karimu, Amin, editor. | Brännlund, R. (Runar) editor.
Title: The economics of the oil and gas industry : emerging markets and developing economies / edited by Joshua Yindenaba Abor, Amin Karimu, and Runar Brännlund.
Description: 1 Economics. | New York, NY : Routledge, 2023. | Series: Routledge studies in the economics of business and industry | Includes bibliographical references and index.
Identifiers: LCCN 2022038633 (print) | LCCN 2022038634 (ebook) | ISBN 9781032324425 (hardback) | ISBN 9781032324449 (paperback) | ISBN 9781003315056 (ebook)
Subjects: LCSH: Oil industries—Developing countries. | Gas industry—Developing countries. | Renewable energy sources—Developing countries. | Capital investments—Developing countries. | Corporations—Developing countries—Finance.
Classification: LCC HD9490.D442 E36 2023 (print) | LCC HD9490.D442 (ebook) | DDC 338.2/7282/091724—dc23/eng/20221013
LC record available at https://lccn.loc.gov/2022038633
LC ebook record available at https://lccn.loc.gov/2022038634

ISBN: 978-1-032-32442-5 (hbk)
ISBN: 978-1-032-32444-9 (pbk)
ISBN: 978-1-003-31505-6 (ebk)

DOI: 10.4324/9781003315056

Typeset in Bembo
by Apex CoVantage, LLC

Contents

Tables

Figures

Contributors

Kevin Aanyu is Lecturer at the Department of Geology and Petroleum Studies, College of Natural Sciences, Makerere University, Kampala, Uganda.

Emmanuel Joel Aikins Abakah is Lecturer in Finance and Risk Management at the Department of Finance, University of Ghana Business School.

Abdul-Gafaru Abdulai is Associate Professor at the Department of Public Administration and Health Services Management, University of Ghana Business School, and an Honorary Research Fellow at the Global Development Institute, University of Manchester, UK.

Janet T. Abor is Associate Consultant with the Corporate Support Group, a management, financial, and economic consulting firm in Ghana.

Joseph Abor is Management and Financial Consultant, Managing Proprietor of Zuson Services, and Managing Director of Sap Oil Limited, an oil marketing company in Ghana.

Joshua Yindenaba Abor is Financial Economist, Professor of Finance, and former Dean, University of Ghana Business School. He is External Fellow at the Centre for Global Finance, SOAS University of London, London, UK, and Adjunct Professor of Development Finance at the University of Stellenbosch Business School, Bellville, Western Cape, South Africa.

James Atambilla Abugre is Doctoral Researcher at the Department of Finance, University of Ghana Business School and Senior Economic Development Planner, Ministry of Finance, Ghana.

Phillip Kofi Adom is Associate Professor of Economics at Ghana Institute of Management and Public Administration (GIMPA), a Senior Fellow of the Environment for Development (EfD) at University of Gothenburg, Sweden, and member of Steering Committee of Sustainable Energy Transition Initiative (SETI) at Duke University, Durham, North Carolina.

Michael Adusei is Associate Professor of Finance at the Department of Accounting and Finance, KNUST School of Business, Kwame Nkrumah University of Science and Technology, Kumasi, Ghana.

Elikplimi Komla Agbloyor is Associate Professor of Finance and Risk Management at the Department of Finance, University of Ghana Business School, Ghana.

Godwill Agordoh is Lecturer at the Department of Finance, University of Professional Studies, Ghana.

Benjamin Agyeman is Doctoral Researcher at the Department of Finance, University of Ghana Business School, Ghana.

Abdallah Ali-Nakyea is Senior Lecturer at the University of Ghana School of Law, Legon, Accra, Ghana.

Godfred Amewu is Senior Lecturer in Finance and Risk Management at the Department of Finance, University of Ghana Business School.

Mohammed Amidu is Professor of Accounting and Finance at the Department of Accounting, University of Ghana Business School.

Ebenezer Bugri Anarfo is Senior Lecturer in Finance and Economics at the Ghana Institute of Management and Public Administration, Ghana.

Gerald Emmanuel Arhin is PhD candidate at the University of Manchester and his thesis focuses on the comparative politics of oil and mining sector governance in Ghana.

Anastacia C. Arko is Consultant, Investment Analyst, and Wealth Manager. She currently provides technical advice to the Director of Securities and Exchange Commission, Ghana.

Thankom Arun is Professor of Global Development and Accountability at the Essex Business School, UK, and Professor Extraordinaire at the Stellenbosch Business School, South Africa.

Joseph Kwadwo Asenso is Head of Macroeconomic Research and Studies, ECOWAS Bank for Investment and Development, Lomé, Togo.

Simplice A. Asongu is Lead Economist and Director of the African Governance and Development Institute. He is also Research Associate at the Research NetworkAfrica, Botswana, and University of South Africa, South Africa.

Tov Assogbavi is Professor of Finance at Laurentian University, Canada.

Raymond A. Atuguba is Professor of Law and Dean of the University of Ghana School of Law, Legon, Ghana. He has been Visiting Professor of Law and the Henry J. Steiner Visiting Professor of Human Rights at Harvard Law School (2018–2019).

Lawrence M. Atuna is Senior Lecturer in Finance at the Department of Banking and Finance, School of Business, SDD-University of Business and Integrated Development Studies, Wa, Ghana.

Kannyiri Banyen is Senior Lecturer in Finance at the Department of Banking and Finance, School of Business, SDD-University of Business and Integrated Development Studies, Wa, Ghana.

Justice Nyigmah Bawole is Professor of Public Administration and Management at the Department of Public Administration and Health Services Management and Dean of the University of Ghana Business School, Ghana.

Runar Brännlund is Professor of Economics at the School of Business, Economics and Statistics and former Director of the Center for Environmental and Resource Economics (CERE), Umeå University, Sweden.

Daniel Domeher is Senior Lecturer in Finance at the Department of Accounting and Finance, KNUST School of Business, Kwame Nkrumah University of Science and Technology, Kumasi, Ghana.

George N. A. Donkor is President of the ECOWAS Bank for Investment and Development, Lomé, Togo.

Alex Donto is Professor of Accounting at the Stern School of Business, New York University, United States.

Vera Ogeh Fiador is Senior Lecturer in Finance at the Department of Finance, University of Ghana Business School, Ghana.

MacDonald Goanue is Director of Research and Strategic Planning of the ECOWAS Bank for Investment and Development, Lomé, Togo.

Khadijah Iddrisu is Doctoral Researcher at the Department of Banking and Finance, School of Business, SDD-University of Business and Integrated Development Studies, Wa, Ghana.

Anthony A. Idun is Senior Lecturer in Finance at the Department of Accounting Finance, University of Cape Coast School of Business, Ghana.

Zangina Isshaq is Senior Lecturer in Accounting and Finance at the Department of Accounting, University of Ghana Business School, Ghana.

Maxwell K. Kally is Senior Manager, Engineering and Maintenance of Ghana National Gas Company Limited, Ghana.

Amin Karimu is Associate Professor in Economics at the School of Economics, University of Cape Town, South Africa, and Visiting Scholar at the Centre for Environmental and Resource Economics at Umeå University, Sweden.

Paul Kibuuka is Associate Professor of Development Finance at the University of Stellenbosch Business School, Bellville, Western Cape, South Africa.

Nasir A. Mohammed is Senior Associate Consultant in charge of energy and extractive resource governance at Ali-Nakyea & Associates, a private law firm in Accra, and currently the Vice Chairman of the Public Interest and Accountability Committee (PIAC), Ghana.

Jabir Ibrahim Mohammed is Lecturer in Finance at the University of Professional Studies and Fellow at PFM-Tax NetWork Africa.

Freshia Mugo-Waweru is Senior Lecturer in Finance at Strathmore University Business School, Nairobi, Kenya.

Victor Murinde is AXA Professor of Global Finance and Director of the Centre for Global Finance at SOAS University of London, UK.

Betty Nagudi is Senior Lecturer at the Department of Geology and Petroleum Studies, College of Natural Sciences, Makerere University, Uganda.

Jonas Nanzoninge is Senior Manager, Enterprise Portfolio Management Office, MTN Ghana, Accra, Ghana.

Joseph Nyeadi is Senior Lecturer in Finance at the Department of Banking and Finance, School of Business, SDD-University of Business and Integrated Development Studies, Wa, Ghana.

Raphael Odoom is Senior Lecturer in Marketing at the Department of Marketing and Entrepreneurship, University of Ghana Business School, Legon.

Daniel Ofori-Sasu is Lecturer in Finance at the Department of Finance, Central University, Ghana.

Jephthah O. Osei is Research Assistant at the Department of Economics, Faculty of Liberal Arts and Professional Studies, York University, Toronto, Ontario, Canada.

Isaac Otchere is Professor of Finance at the Sprott School of Business, Carleton University in Ottawa, Canada.

Peter Quartey is Professor of Development Economics and Director of Institute of Statistical, Social and Economic Research (ISSER), University of Ghana, Ghana.

Ananth Rao is Emeritus Professor of Finance, former Dean Dubai Business School, and Ex-Chief Academic Officer (CAO) at University of Dubai, United Arab Emirates.

Olufemi M. Saibu is Professor of Economics at the Department of Economics, University of Lagos and Director of Institute of Nigeria-China Development Studies, University of Lagos, Nigeria.

Ruhul Salim is Professor of Economics and the Director of Graduate Research in the School of Accounting, Economics and Finance, Curtin University, Perth, Western Australia.

Emmanuel Sarpong-Kumankoma is Senior Lecturer in Finance at the Department of Finance, University of Ghana Business School, Ghana.

Ali Sheikhbahaei is Lecturer in Banking and Finance at the Monash Business School, Monash University, Australia.

Mohammed Aminu Sualihu is Assistant Professor of Accounting in the College of Business at Zayed University, United Arab Emirates.

Susana Yamoah is Assistant Lecturer in Risk Management and Insurance at the Department of Finance, University of Ghana Business School, Ghana.

Alfred Yawson is Professor in Corporate Finance at the University of Adelaide Business School, Australia.

Kemi Yekini is Professor of Accounting at the School of Finance and Management, SOAS University of London, UK.

Acknowledgements

Joshua Yindenaba Abor

To my wonderful wife, Dr Patience Aseweh Abor, and our lovely children, Ivana, Bastien, and Venka for their love, support, and encouragement. Also, to my parents, Mr Abor Ndobire and Madam Amina Tobga, for their inspiration and commitment throughout my education. I also wish to appreciate my co-editors, Amin and Runar, and co-authors of the various chapters.

Amin Karimu

I am eternally grateful to my awesome wife, Nasum, and my lovely children, Zaeem and Afnan, for the love and support throughout the entire process of the book. A special thanks goes to the entire members of the N-yo family for their wonderful support and encouragement. I would also like to appreciate the cooperation and support from my co-editors and co-authors of the various chapters contained in the book.

Runar Brännlund

Thanks to everyone involved with this book – especially my family; co-editors, Joshua and Amin; co-authors; the editing team; and the Publishing Manager.

General

We, the editors, would like to thank all contributing authors for the high quality of their chapters. We wish to thank the Carnegie Writing Centre, University of Ghana, for the excellent work in proof reading and language editing. We also thank all the reviewers of the various chapters as well as Dr Daniel Ofori-Sasu and Bright Oduro for providing editorial assistance.

Part I

Overview of the Oil and Gas Industry

1 Introduction to the Economics of the Oil and Gas Industry in Emerging and Developing Economies

Joshua Yindenaba Abor, Amin Karimu, and Runar Brännlund

1.1 Introduction

Oil and gas resources played a key role in the industrial revolution and continue to play a significant role globally in modern production, consumption, and distribution processes (of which transportation is a key sector). All developed economies achieved their respective economic transformation through industrialisation and value addition made possible by the availability of cheap energy, especially oil and gas resources. The experience from the Global North in terms of economic transformation driven by fossil fuels, especially oil and gas, suggests a development paradigm that emerging markets and developing economies (EMDEs) could emulate.

The current development paradigm is, however, heavily dependent on fossil fuels, the endowment of which is not evenly distributed globally. Second, these fossil fuels contribute significantly to climate change, and, third, they are non-renewable. For instance the volume of the global proven oil reserves in 2022 is about 1,661,905 (in millions of barrels) as indicated by EIA (2022). Out of this, the five top ranked countries (Venezuela, Saudi Arabia, Iran, Canada, and Iraq) account for close to 65.4% of this volume. This suggests, among other things, the potential energy security risk to which the world is exposed by depending on this energy source for growth and development. Furthermore, in the top ten ranked proven oil reserved countries, only two (Canada and the United States) are developed countries; the others are EMDEs, where geopolitical risk is also relatively high, suggesting the venerability of the world in depending heavily on oil. This venerability is not much different from that pertaining to the dependence on gas. The situation is highlighted by the recent Russia and Ukraine war and its consequences on oil and gas prices.

Data from British Petroleum indicate that in 2020, total daily production of oil was 88,391,000 barrels and daily consumption was 88,696,000 barrels, implying a slightly higher consumption relative to production, which will be equalised through price adjustment (BP, 2020). The more consumption overshoots production, the higher the upward price adjustment would be.

DOI: 10.4324/9781003315056-2

A study by Wu et al. (2018) suggests a superior decoupling between GDP growth and energy consumption by developed countries relative to that attained by developing countries, implying that after achieving some level of development, the advanced countries, due to many reasons such as CO_2 emission, energy security, and environmental concerns, managed to reduce the dependence of GDP on energy consumption. This is, however, not the case for EMDCs. One reason for this is that in EMDCs, the quest for growth and development is likely to be associated with an increased use of energy, especially oil and gas. The decoupling of GDP and energy consumption by the developed countries is driven largely by technical progress that promotes energy efficiency and by industrial structure, which is not the case in EMDEs.

These transitions are spearheaded by climate mitigation policies towards a net-zero emission scenario. The current clean energy and infrastructure investment required for a net-zero emission scenario for the global economy is significantly inadequate. Estimates by IEA (2021) indicate that in 2020, the investment in clean energy and infrastructure is 974 billion US dollars, but the amount required to achieve a net-zero emission scenario is 3,368 billion US dollars. This implies a huge investment gap of about 2,394 billion US dollars. Despite this gap, the estimated market size of clean energy technology industry (technology equipment) in a net-zero scenario is projected to be 1,200 US dollars in 2050, while that of oil is estimated to be 182 billion US dollars, suggesting a significant future opportunity for businesses and investors in clean energy industry (IEA, 2021).

The foregoing indicates three things that are currently happening in the energy sectors of the world. First, there is increasing consumption of oil and gas resources by the developing countries due to the quest for rapid economic growth and development and the quest to reduce poverty in most of the EMDCs, led by China and India.

Second, oil and gas resources are not renewable and therefore, given a high depletion rate, these resources would be economically unavailable for extraction over time. In this regard, sustainable management of these resources by converting some into financial and physical capital, as is the case in Norway, is mostly encouraged. Moreover, EMDEs are encouraged to chart a new, lower emissions path to growth that is centred on clean electrification and energy efficiency. The reason is to avoid the resource curse mostly associated with these resources and, at the same time, reduce the carbon footprint of the growth process.

Third, the high dependence on these fossil fuels generates significant environmental pressures, which are gradually driving global investors towards promising alternative energy sources which are friendly to the environment such as biofuel, solar, wind, and geothermal, among other renewable energy sources and technologies. Despite such a transition currently taking place, oil and gas resources will continue to be a significant energy source at least in the EMDEs in the medium term until the prices of renewable resources are competitive to oil and gas globally and the existing transportation, production, and consumption systems transformed and aligned with the low-carbon energy transition.

Despite the increasing interest in renewable energy globally, in recent years, there have been significant exploration and discovery of new oil and natural gas reserves in East and West Africa, as well as in the Eastern Mediterranean, the Caribbean, and the Asia-Pacific areas. These recent discoveries have added to the ranks of the world's oil- and gas-producing nations, and these oil and gas producers in developing economies have expressed a great interest in obtaining governance assistance. They are committed to avoiding the mistakes that have led to accountability failures among more established producers, and which have hindered certain producers from fully obtaining the economic benefits of their resources. Each stage of resource development from exploration through production to commercialisation brings a particular set of opportunities and challenges. Nevertheless, the supply of available oil and gas resources and the ability to attract foreign investment do not necessarily guarantee economic progress. The construction of proper institutions, methods, and regulations will guarantee that oil and gas incomes are used efficiently for long-term economic growth.

While rising oil and gas producers may benefit from the experiences of top national operators throughout the world, capacity restrictions frequently prevent them from implementing international best practices. Many new or emerging producers have little expertise managing petroleum and gas resources, and many are forced to make petroleum and gas policy choices without having a clear understanding of the magnitude of their resource base. Emerging producers are encouraged to pursue best practice standards, but it may be more beneficial for the practice, which acknowledges the realities of the national context; more effective practice, which seeks to achieve rapid results in a context of urgent need; or better practice, which seeks to incrementally improve governance processes through aspirational but achievable milestones.

Up until the 1980s, EMDEs' oil and gas companies mostly invested abroad to create trade support networks and get access to markets. Other major motivations were gaining access to natural resources overseas and avoiding bureaucratic limitations at home. Other emerging countries were the focus of investment (geographic, cultural, ethnic, and institutional).

These developments provide good motivation to understand the economics of the oil and gas industry in EMDEs. This book provides a comprehensive resource on the economics of the oil and gas industry. This is important in improving our understanding of the development and fiscal arrangement, economics, and financing issues of the industry. The oil and gas industry is a complex sector with a significant outreach in terms of providing the energy needs of the global economy and the security, environmental, and development consequences thereof on the well-being of humanity. In particular, the sector is extremely important for the growth and development of EMDEs.

1.2 Purpose of the Book

Energy is a key resource for transformational development globally, and oil and gas continue to play a key role in this sector irrespective of the gradual transition into renewables. The oil and gas sector will continue to play a key role in most EMDEs in the near future. The industry is complex and highly capital intensive not only with significant risk, but also with significant benefits. Such a complex but important sector is generally not well understood both in academia and in policy circles. This book volume seeks to fill this void by serving as a comprehensive material on the economics of oil and gas industry, with a focus on EMDEs for academia, policymakers, and practitioners.

This book examines the economics of the oil and gas industry with a focus on EMDEs. The book focuses on providing knowledge and a non-technical guide to practitioners and policymakers on development, fiscal arrangement, risk, the economics, and financing in the sector that can structure and reform the industry in ways that promote growth and development in EMDEs. Irrespective of the importance of the oil and gas industry to EMDEs, very few texts and research material exist, which target these regions of the world. This book provides comprehensive coverage of the critical and contemporary issues in the economics of the oil and gas industry by carefully integrating the relevant theoretical underpinnings and practical policy issues across the value chain of the industry in relation to the development, fiscal arrangement, economics, and financing aspects of the industry.

This edited book provides a comprehensive coverage of the resource development, fiscal development, economics, and financing of oil and gas resources in EMDEs. It is made up of contributions from scholars and practitioners in oil and gas finance and economics. The book provides a valuable resource for students taking courses in areas such as market analysis, energy economics, fiscal regime, project finance, and political economy of the oil and gas industry. Researchers and practitioners working in these areas will also find the book to be a useful reference material.

1.3 Overview of the Chapters

This book is composed of 20 chapters, and we provide an overview of the remaining chapters.

In Chapter 2, Jephthah O. Osei, Amin Karimu, Maxwell K. Kally, and MacDonald Goanue discuss the oil and gas industry in EMDEs. The authors provide a general overview of the oil and gas industry in EMDEs. The chapter covers important issues such as oil and gas in the global economy and the industry's players, such as independent players, integrated oil companies, and national oil companies. The chapter looks at nature and ownership structures and financing oil and gas projects in emerging and developing countries. It also covers the oil and gas value chain, including the upstream, midstream, and downstream, and discusses the risks in the oil and gas industry.

Chapter 3 presents an overview of oil and gas exploration and development and production in emerging and developing economies. In this chapter, Joseph Kwadwo Asenso, Betty Nagudi, and Kevin Aanyu discuss the two types of petroleum fiscal regimes and explain the processes investors go through to monetise their investments. They show that investors have the desire to maintain ownership of their resources, while investing relatively little compared to their partners, leading to various contracting regimes that discourage investment. They concluded that new exploration, findings, and field development activities are going on in quite a number of EMDEs, with the global oil and gas industry exhibiting increased efforts to develop cost-cutting state-of-the-art technologies to ensure the sustainability of oil and gas projects.

In Chapter 4, Abdallah Ali-Nakyea, Raymond A. Atuguba, Olufemi M. Saibu, and Nasir A. Mohammed explore the legal and fiscal arrangements in the oil and gas industry in emerging and developing countries. They focus on the prevailing genres of law and principles of resource ownership, how the prevailing challenges have been addressed by emerging and developing countries and ways in which this could be done better, and how industry actors can sustain their investments in the face of obvious legal, regulatory, and fiscal challenges in an ever-changing energy environment. They recommend that investors should always conduct comprehensive policy and legal due diligence to ascertain the applicable policy objectives, legal requirements, juridical nature, and institutional architecture when dealing with resource-rich emerging and developing countries.

Chapter 5 by Raphael Odoom, Runar Brännlund, Amin Karimu, and Jonas Nanzoninge looks at oil and gas energy security from the perspective of emerging and developing countries. The findings from their analysis suggest that oil-producing and exporting countries account for more than 50% of proven global oil reserves, and the top 16 fuel-exporting countries are all emerging or developing countries, with at least 80% of total merchandise exports made of fuel exports. They indicated that Africa has the least refining capacity globally, significantly creating vulnerabilities to refined products. Last, they provide evidence that the oil-producing countries are prone to geological risk.

In Chapter 6, Amin Karimu, Godwill Agordoh, Peter Quartey, and Runar Brännlund present an overview of the key economic aspects of oil and gas resources from the perspective of emerging and developing countries. Findings from their analysis suggest that the global oil and gas industry is an oligopoly by structure, with OPEC playing a key role. They reveal that emerging and developing countries (EDCs) are major players in both the supply and demand for these resources in general and OPEC's role in oil supply. They recommend that a careful management of oil and gas resources in the emerging and developing world is needed to lessen exposure to the resource curse threat in the region, reduce oil and gas dependency and risk exposure from such dependence, and to manage oil and gas trade effectively and efficiently within the developing regions of the world.

Chapter 7 by Khadijah Iddrisu, Phillip Kofi Adom, Jabir Ibrahim Mohammed, and Amin Karimu examines the various risks associated with the downstream oil and gas sector, the measurement of these risks, key resilient factors, and simulation and decision analysis of downstream oil and gas projects. They identify the associated risks in the downstream sector to include economic, political, environmental, technical, and energy transition risks. These are more pronounced in developing countries and are known to exert a negative effect on the sector's market share, capacity, and investment level. Further, the identified risks impede government revenue and affect the employment generation of the oil and gas sector. For the sector to remain competitive in the long term, they recommend the development of strategies to mitigate these risks in the oil and gas downstream sector.

Chapter 8 presents an overview of the market for crude oil. In this chapter, Ebenezer Bugri Anarfo, Joseph Abor, George N. A. Donkor, and Freshia Mugo-Waweru explore the formation of oil and crude oil prices and the nature of crude oil transactions, as well as the causes of oil price volatility and their effects on emerging and developing countries. They find that oil price volatility affects emerging economies' GDP growth (output), inflation, exchange rate, energy efficiency, and investment. Also, oil price volatility is influenced by the Organisation of Petroleum Exporting Countries (OPEC), demand and supply factors, natural disasters influencing oil production, political unrest in oil-producing countries, production cost, and storage capacity.

Chapter 9 provides an overview of financing oil and gas companies in EMDEs. Lawrence M. Atuna, Janet T. Abor, Ananth Rao, and Anthony A. Idun found that an optimal financing proposition should be the one in which the incidence of risk is assigned by a partner in a transaction that is best suited to control it, whether they are foreign private investors, indigenous companies, public sector or host governments, and multilateral institutions.

In Chapter 10, Joshua Yindenaba Abor, Benjamin Agyeman, and Paul Kibuuka discuss the project finance market in the oil and gas industry in EMDEs. They also examine the role of project finance, performance, and precedent projects of project finance in this industry. They show that project finance growth on the global, regional, and national levels depends on the quantum of appraised sovereign and project risks. Currently, hybrid financing is gaining more ground in the market, especially in the upstream fields. They concluded that employing project finance in the industry of oil and gas will go a long way to help governments channel their resources into developing other sectors of their economies.

In Chapter 11, Kannyiri Banyen, Daniel Domeher, and Joseph Nyeadi present an overview of investment appraisal for oil and gas projects. The chapter evaluates some capital investment decisions and challenges that firms face in implementing capital projects in the sector and provides evidence that the best possible evaluation of a project can be achieved by combining a number of techniques instead of relying on any of them in isolation – thus, helping firms to overcome the limitations associated with individual techniques when used in isolation.

In Chapter 12, Zangina Isshaq, Emmanuel Sarpong-Kumankoma, and Kemi Yekini show how to interpret the financial statements of firms in the oil and gas industry. They present an analysis of a typical oil and gas firm's financial statements considering profitability, efficiency, liquidity, and leverage. They show that financial ratios are only useful for financial information analysis, but other nonfinancial information can complement financial ratios when conducting analysis of performance to get a full picture.

Chapter 13 provides a general overview of financial planning and forecasting in the oil and gas industry. In this chapter, Mohammed Aminu Sualihu, Mohammed Amidu, Tov Assogbavi, and Alex Donto indicate that effective financial planning and forecasting assist oil and gas companies to formulate policies and strategies, plan for the future, and align their goals across the entire organisation.

In Chapter 14, Isaac Otchere, Michael Adusei, Joshua Yindenaba Abor, and Thankom Arun discuss the methods for valuing oil and gas companies including the asset-based approach, the market approach (Trading Multiples), and the income approach. Given the complexities in the methods of valuation, the chapter indicates that there is no single method for valuing oil and gas firms.

Chapter 15 by Anastacia C. Arko, Joshua Yindenaba Abor, Ali Sheikhbahaei, and Alfred Yawson examines mergers and acquisitions (M&As) in the oil and gas industry in EMDEs. The chapter shows how the aggressive tactical or cyclical M&A strategy of the past has made way for restrained, strategic, and environment-focused M&A deals in recent times. Despite some key M&A challenges identified in the sector, the chapter highlights that it is important for M&A oil and gas companies to prioritise capital discipline, strengthen their balance sheet, give shareholder distributions more importance than price-led growth and spending, and design a strong post-merger strategy to ensure a smooth consolidation of the two entities, post M&A.

Chapter 16 by Elikplimi Komla Agbloyor, Emmanuel Joel Aikins Abakah, and Susana Yamoah examines the enterprise risk management (ERM) practices in the oil and gas industry in Ghana. The study uses a single case study of GOIL Company Limited (GOIL) in investigating the ERM practices of the company. In order to establish ERM implementation and practices, the authors interviewed the risk officer of the company by using questions based on the conventional literature. The authors established that ERM practices in the oil and gas industry in Ghana are emerging and that the critical success factors for the effective implementation of ERM include top management commitment, culture, and risk appetite. The importance of promoting a safety culture through the adoption of a robust ERM strategy is significant. This, however, requires a good corporate governance that fosters an effective risk management strategy.

In Chapter 17, Godfred Amewu, Joshua Yindenaba Abor, and Victor Murinde explore the derivative for oil and gas transactions. They discuss in detail the potential risks associated with oil and gas transactions, as well as how these risks can be mitigated through the use of hedging, derivatives, and other risk-reduction techniques. Although the authors considered the functions and the trading strategies of derivative instruments, they indicated that investors can consider designing a specific product to meet their risk level, tolerance, and nominal amount.

In Chapter 18, James Atambilla Abugre, Joshua Yindenaba Abor, Ruhul Salim, and Daniel Ofori-Sasu examine how emerging and developing countries utilise and manage their petroleum wealth for the benefit of their citizens. The authors show that nations that have utilised petroleum wealth efficiently have improved the living conditions of their citizens, while those that mismanage petroleum wealth retrogress in their quest to seek development. The chapter highlights some challenges of petroleum exploitation and recommends that the maximisation of petroleum wealth in emerging and developing nations requires the adoption of best practices such as slow exploration of petroleum resources to cater for future needs, diversification of economic activities in critical sectors, equitable distribution of petroleum revenue, decentralisation of proceeds of oil sales, and instituting transparency and accountability mechanisms through legislation and policy direction to check mismanagement.

Chapter 19 is by Jabir Ibrahim Mohammed, Verah Ogeh Fiador, Amin Karimu, and Joshua Yindenaba Abor. The authors provide qualitative insights into the linkages among oil revenues, finance, and economic development. The study finds that oil-producing countries' ownership, especially for developing countries, is a mixture of international oil companies and the government where expected payments to the state are arranged through a fiscal regime. Additionally, the study found that the resource curse exists for both finance and growth; oil-producing countries smoothen their consumption for both current and future generations and against future fluctuations in oil prices. They recommend that a good management of oil revenues alongside solid institutional quality is needed to translate oil as a commodity and financial assets into financial and economic development in oil-producing countries.

Chapter 20 by Simplice A. Asongu, Gerald Emmanuel Arhin, Abdul-Gafaru Abdulai, and Justice Nyigmah Bawole explores the concept of the political-economy of oil and gas governance by focusing on the exploration, production, and revenue sharing in the hydrocarbon sector. Emphasis is placed on the extent to which oil and gas governance is shaped by geopolitics and interparty politics. The authors argue that the interests and ideas relative to the power of key stakeholders, such as political actors, multinational companies, the citizens and the state, are relevant to the understanding of the form and shape of the emergence and performance of the institutions governing the oil and gas sectors of emerging and developing countries.

1.4 Conclusion

The economics of the oil and gas industry in EMDEs covers various important themes on the oil and gas industry. Broadly, these issues include the economics of the oil and gas industry, legal and fiscal regimes of the oil and gas industry, various aspects of finance in the oil and gas industry, risk management in the oil and gas sector, petroleum wealth management, and the political economy of the oil and gas industry in EMDEs. These broad issues are covered by the 20 chapters contained in this edited book, written by various experienced authors from multidisciplinary backgrounds. The aim of each chapter is to serve as a relevant reference material for academic research in the broad thematic areas presented in this volume. The various chapters are also carefully written to be useful for practitioners and policymakers in the oil and gas industry, especially in EMDEs.

References

British Petroleum (2020, July). *Statistical review*. https://www.bp.com/en/global/corporate/energy-economics/statistical-review-of-world-energy.html

EIA (2022). *Crude oil production*. https://www.eia.gov/international/data/world

IEA (2021). World energy outlook. https://iea.blob.core.windows.net/assets/4ed140c1-c3f3-4fd9-acae-789a4e14a23c/WorldEnergyOutlook2021.pdf

Wu, Y., Zhu, Q., and Zhu, B. (2018). Comparisons of decoupling trends of global economic growth and energy consumption between developed and developing countries. *Energy Policy*, 116, 30–38.

Part II

Oil and Gas Development and Fiscal Arrangement

2 The Oil and Gas Industry in Emerging and Developing Economies

Jephthah O. Osei, Amin Karimu, Maxwell K. Kally, and MacDonald Goanue

2.1 Introduction

All areas of the global economy benefit from the oil and gas business. Transportation, heating and power fuels, lubricants, propane, and a variety of petrochemical commodities such as eyeglasses, carpets, and garments are all affected by the industry's final products. The industry has a significant impact on major geopolitics, international conflicts, security, elections, and other issues, making it the world's largest trade commodity. The transport sector is the largest consumer of crude oil and natural gas, the two major by-products of the industry. It consumes more than a third of global oil demand largely because of the reliance on motor spirits made from petroleum.

The Organization of Petroleum Exporting Countries (OPEC) forecasts that by 2045, the global oil products demand may reach not less than 109 million barrels per day (b/d). OPEC projects global oil product demand, especially for gasoline and diesel, to reach 109 million b/d by 2045, that is 30–40% higher than current demand. This sector suffers from several upheaval events including recent sanctions on Russia for invading Ukraine. Others include increased production of oil and gas in the United States, heightening of international relations, and striving in oil-exporting countries such as Iraq and Libya. This chapter provides an overview of the industry with much focus on developing economies. The chapter provides an overview of oil and gas supply, industry competition, value chain, and risk.

2.2 Oil and Gas and the Global Economy

The world economy relies heavily on oil and gas. The aggregate demand for crude oil and natural gas on the global market (including biofuels) stood at 91 million b/d in 2020 (BP, 2016) and at 96.5 million b/d in 2021. The International Energy Agency (IEA) expects this to increase by at least 1.5% each year on average through 2030. They also predict that countries outside the Organisation for Economic Cooperation and Development (OECD) will account for at least 80% of global demand growth. Oil, gas, and coal will continue to be the most popular products. Figure 2.1 shows oil production from 1998 to 2020.

DOI: 10.4324/9781003315056-4

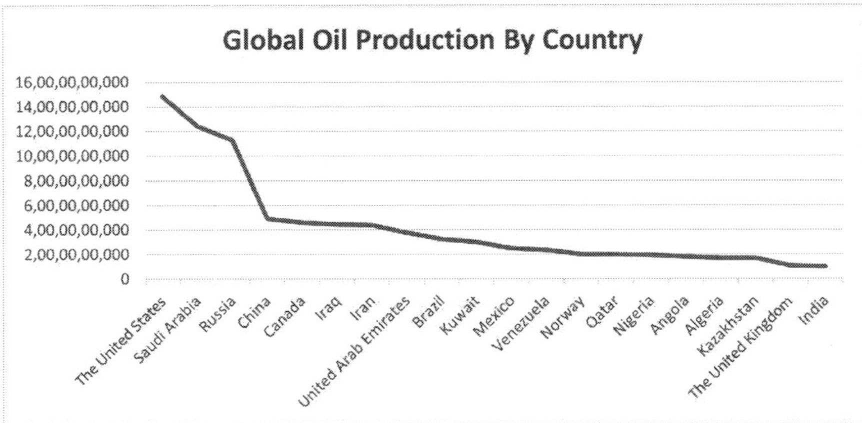

Figure 2.1 Global oil production from 1998 to 2020 (in million metric tons)

Source: Authors, using data from Statistica 2022[1]

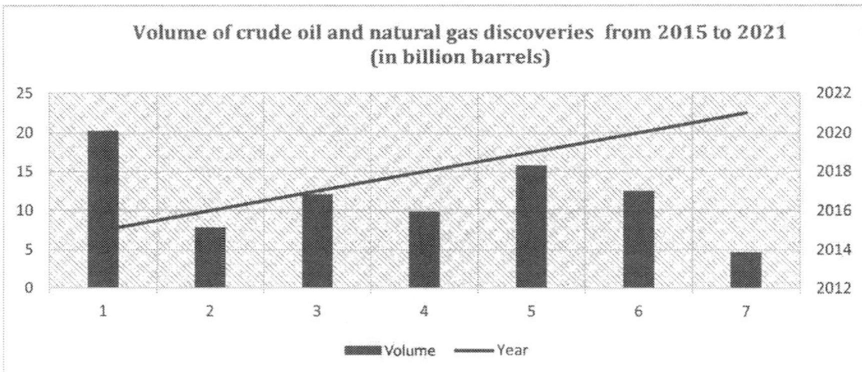

Figure 2.2 Volume of crude oil and natural gas discoveries from 2015 to 2021 (in billion barrels)

Source: Authors, based on data from Worldwide Rystad Energy, 2015 to 2021

According to statistics from 2021, oil and gas discoveries totalled roughly 4.7 billion barrels of oil. This is the lowest level in many years. In comparison to the previous year, Figure 2.2 shows a drop of around 166%. After peaking at roughly 20.3 billion barrels of oil equivalent in 2015 (see Figure 2.2), crude oil and natural gas discoveries have been declining since then. The Organization of Petroleum Exporting Countries (OPEC), which was founded in 1960 with the purpose of moving bargaining power from huge oil companies to producing countries, is a major cartel on the supply side. Currently, OPEC controls almost 82% of the world's proven oil supplies, which gives them some power to influence the global price of crude oil.

2.2.1 The Resource Curse Paradox

Oil and gas resources are supposed to be a blessing to any country with endowments as these are resources that the global economy depends on for its production, consumption, and distributional services. This is however not the case for several EMDCs, where such resources tend to be a curse. Most of the major oil and gas producers from EMDCs have relatively low development compared to countries in the Global North. The most highly ranked EMDC oil-producing country based on the human development index is the United Arab Emirates, which occupies the 31st slot in the world. Saudi Arabia occupies the 40th slot, Nigeria (161st), Angola (148th), Venezuela (113th), and Russia (52nd). This reality of the resource curse for some of the EMDCs is driven by many factors including poor Institutions, political capture, poor management, and a poor fiscal oil regime, among others.

2.3 The Industry Players

The oil and gas industry comprises many firms differentiated by their shapes, sizes, and production capacities. These players are identified and classified as given in the next sections.

2.3.1 Independent Players

Independent oil companies are those not owned by the government and are focused on either the upstream or downstream segment of the oil industry (Bacchetta and Van Wincoop, 2004). Most of these firms are major participants in the industry and are ranked in the upper 50 non-government-owned oil and gas companies. In terms of geography, goods, and technology, these companies have become increasingly important in some of the more high-risk and inventive oil and gas fields over the years. Globally, the biggest independent oil exploration and production firms are Occidental, Canadian Natural, Apache, Devon, OGX-Brazil, BHP-Billiton-Australia, and Woodside-Australia.

2.3.2 Integrated Oil Companies (IOC)

IOCs compete across national lines and are also known as international oil and gas companies. Integrated multinational firms dominate the oil and gas industry on a global scale. BP, ExxonMobil, and Shell are among these firms. Their operations are overseen by private investors with the purpose of earning the highest long-term profit. For their refineries, IOCs exchange crude oil and natural gas. They sell crude oil and natural gas to other businesses and buy completed goods from them. Because of the long product life cycles and significant capital expenditure required in the oil business, the huge IOCs are typically described as stodgy and conservative. The IOCs have learned how to deal with the oil and gas industry's significant financial and political dangers via experience.

2.3.3 National Oil Companies

These are national government-controlled corporations founded to handle a country's hydrocarbon resources. Many National Oil Companies (NOCs), including Gazprom, Petrobras, and Sinopec, are half held by private investors and partially controlled by the state. NOCs are normally part of a government ministry, such as the petroleum ministry or the oil and gas ministry. Some NOCs only operate in their native nation (e.g., PEMEX), whereas others compete globally in many industries, like IOCs (e.g., Gazprom, Petrobras, and Statoil). By a significant margin, the greatest oil and gas companies in terms of reserves are NOCs that are partially or entirely controlled by the government. NOCs control almost 90% of the world's oil and gas, and most fresh oil is likely to be discovered within their borders. Venezuela nationalised its oil industry in the 1970s and founded Petróleos de Venezuela (PDVSA). Examining the strategic aims of IOCs and NOCs is an important way to separate them. The degree to which larger oil and gas corporations are motivated by either shareholder maximisation or public policy aims is depicted in Figure 2.3.

Box 2.1 Venezuela's NOC

PDVSA developed a reputation for professionalism, competence, and comparative freedom from the corruption and cronyism that pervaded and continues to pervade many of the NOCs. By 1998, 36 foreign oil firms were operating in Venezuela, and PDVSA had ambitious expansion plans. The bitter strike in 2002 led to the company losing about two-thirds of the managerial and technical staff. The firm has seen a drastic decline in recent times after peaking at 2.9 million b/d in 1998. Production according to OPEC declined and was estimated at 2.3 million b/d, leading to PDVSA importing a significant amount of gasoline. Currently, PDVSA as a producing company is not distinguished from the state. Thus, the energy sector minister doubles as the chief executive officer (CEO) of the company. The statutory requirements are that the company spends 10% of its investment budget on social intervention programmes – for example providing low-cost heating to the poor.

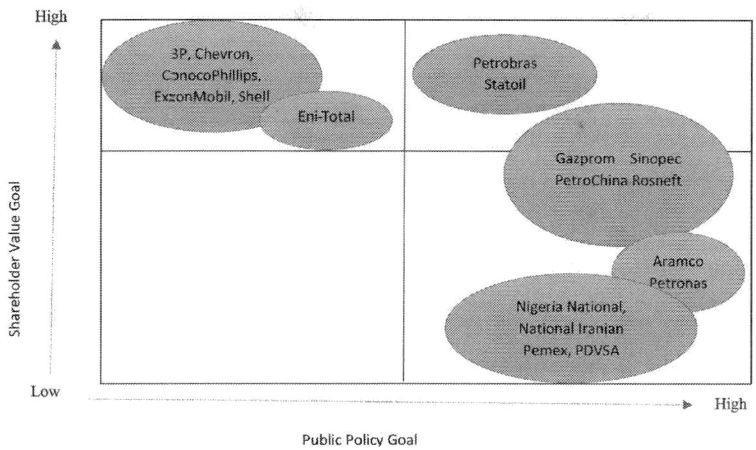

Figure 2.3 The strategic goals of NOCs and IOCs

Source: Inkpen and Moffett (2011)

2.4 Oil and Gas Industry in the Emerging and Developing Countries (EDCs)

The oil and gas industry in developing economies contributes immensely to economic growth. Activities of the sector provide employment opportunities for the host nation and citizens and enhance their economic living standards. The sector's contributions to the economy include taxes, royalties, foreign exchange reserves, power supply, and investments. Developing economies have recently recorded an increasing number of oil and natural gas discoveries. Oil fields are discovered in East and West Africa, the Eastern Mediterranean, the Caribbean, and the Asia-Pacific now and then.

2.4.1 Nature and Ownership Structures of the Oil and Gas Industry in EMDCs

The oil and gas landscape differs from country to country in the EDCs. Some are solely state-owned, while others are jointly owned by the public and private sectors.

2.4.1.1 The Russian Case

Russia is the world's third-largest oil producer, producing more than 12% of global crude oil output. The West Siberian and Volga–Ural oil and gas basins provide most of the country's energy resources. The oil business was privatised after the fall of the Soviet Union, but by the mid-2000s, it had mostly returned to be under government control. In terms of ownership, Gazprom, Lukoil, and Rosneft, all Russian oil firms, are among the world's most powerful energy companies. Rosneft is the domestic market leader, and its controlling holdings are held by Rosneftegaz, a Russian government-owned firm. Rosneft bought the stock of Yukos, which was formerly the country's largest oil producer but went bankrupt. Russian oil pipelines are operated by Transneft, a state-owned business.

2.4.1.2 The Case of Saudi Arabia

Saudi Arabia, officially the Kingdom of Saudi Arabia, is the world's second-largest crude oil producer, with 17% of proven reserves. With a current share of 22.4%, Saudi Arabia is a founding member of OPEC. Saudi Arabia lowered output in 2020 to rebalance the global oil market, as OPEC decided in 2005. In 2018, 2019, and 2020, the country produced 12.11, 11.47, and 10.85 million b/d of petroleum and other liquids, respectively. Saudi Arabia's total oil production was 12 million b/d in January 2022, according to the International Energy Agency (IEA). Aramco, based in Saudi Arabia, is one of the world's most valuable enterprises. The government owns oil and gas resources, according to the Kingdom's fundamental laws (enshrined in royal edict No. A/90 of 27/8/1412). The ministry in charge of energy, industry, and natural resource development supervises the implementation of the Kingdom's oil and gas policy and serves as its international representative.

2.4.1.3 The Case of China

China is one of the world's largest producers and users of energy. China was the only major economy that did not contract in 2020, and its oil production did not decrease. At 4.86 million b/d, it stayed unchanged. In 2021, production was 4.99 million b/d, while consumption was 15.27 million b/d. The Daqing Oil Province, in northeastern China's Songliao Plain, is the country's largest oil-producing region. China and Russia have been increasing their oil and gas commercial links in recent years. Early in February 2022, PJSC Rosneft Oil Company and China National Petroleum Corporation (CNPC) signed a 10-year agreement under which Rosneft will supply China with 100 million tonnes of oil via Kazakhstan. Most of China's largest crude oil firms such as China National Petroleum Corporation and Sinopec are publicly owned energy conglomerates. They operate globally through exploration, processing, storage, transportation, and other activities related to the oil and gas supply chain.

2.4.1.4 The Case of Nigeria

Nigeria is one of Africa's top oil and gas producers. The country produces over 2.5 million barrels of crude oil per day, making it Africa's and the world's sixth-largest oil producer. Currently, Nigeria has eight oil-producing states, and these states are mostly in the South-South and South-East geopolitical zones of the country (Ogunleye, 2015). The Nigerian Minerals and Mining Act of 2007 vests ownership rights to resources in the hands of the state. These ownership rights are vested in the hands of the government, and whether these resources are on-shore or off-shore is immaterial. In 2019, the mineral fuels, oils, and distillation products sector accounted for about 47 billion US dollars, which was almost 80% of Nigeria's export value. However, as a result of the COVID-19 pandemic, oil production and exports decreased. Data for 2020 reveals a significant reduction in the value of oil-related exports.

2.4.1.5 *Geopolitics and Its Economic Impacts*

On a worldwide scale, geopolitics has influenced how the oil and gas business operates. Geopolitics refers to several ongoing industry concerns, including security, the economics of the world, uncertainty in the market, fluctuations in the exchange rate, and diplomacy around the world. Many times, in history, geopolitics has had a significant impact on the oil and gas industry. Oil and geopolitics are intricately connected. Any loss of oil supplies due to geopolitical events such as wars has damaged the physical supply. In 1973, Israel and several Arab governments fought the Yom Kippur War. Because of the oil embargos imposed on countries that supported Israel, this War became recognised as the first official "oil crisis." This embargo, imposed by the OPEC, was dubbed an "oil weapon" since it significantly increased the price of crude oil per barrel. The second oil crisis occurred during the Iranian revolution from 1978 until 1981, shortly after the Yom Kippur War. This crisis doubled oil prices, putting them between $50 and $100 per barrel in the United States at the time of the conflict.

The disputes between Russia and Ukraine have an impact on the entire world, both directly and indirectly. The confrontations have kept recent world oil prices above $90. In terms of dollar payment platforms, Russia and China have been considering a scenario in which the two nations can build up non-dollar payment systems in their oil and gas trade to gain independence from dollar currency platforms that have previously been used by the United States in economic sanctions. On a larger scale, geopolitical power and control over Middle Eastern oil and gas resources are visibly moving, with the West (the United States and Europe) losing economic and political clout to a rapidly evolving Russia–China alliance.

2.4.2 *Financing Oil and Gas Projects in Emerging and Developing Countries*

Until the 1970s, foreign oil firms financed most petroleum projects in emerging and developing countries through internal cash generation. This began to alter in the 1970s, when governments became more directly involved in the petroleum business to maintain greater control over local reserves and, in the case of petroleum importing countries, to alleviate concerns about oil supply security (Huntington, 1994). As a result, funding for oil and gas projects came from government budgets and official borrowing, as well as foreign oil companies. In the early 1990s, when most governments reduced their involvement in budgetary commitments to the oil and gas sector, the focus shifted back to private sector finance. In 1995, the World Bank, in collaboration with member countries, international petroleum sector representatives, and other funding sources, re-evaluated its oil and gas financing policy. The Bank's new agenda which was developed in collaboration with the International Finance Corporation (IFC) and the Multilateral Investment Guarantee Agency, both members of the World Bank Group (MIGA), includes technical assistance, lending, and guarantees as follows:

1. Assist governments in creating regulatory frameworks that encourage private investment and efficiency.
2. Assist in the corporatisation, commercialisation, and privatisation of government-owned hydrocarbon companies.
3. Identify more efficient and environmentally friendly fuels and encourage people to cook with gas rather than with coal. According to recent studies in India, using modern fuels can help impoverished people climb the "energy ladder" to cleaner, more efficient cooking fuels than wood and agricultural waste.
4. Assist governments in decommissioning existing oil and gas facilities and implementing the standards and institutions required to monitor oil and gas projects' environmental consequences.
5. Encourage projects involving the facilitation of international trade (mainly gas pipelines but also oil pipelines). Because private investors regard gas pipeline projects to be risky ventures with long payback times, no other applications, and often unclear local markets, they may benefit from bank funding.
6. Fund urgent, economically viable oil development, processing, transmission, and distribution projects—but only if private sector funding is insufficient.
7. Provide risk insurance for important and environmentally sensitive projects.

2.5 The Oil and Gas Value Chain

Various actions must take place in every industry to transform raw resources, expertise, labour, and capital into final goods that buyers purchase. A value chain is a tool for identifying the industry's self-contained, economically viable sectors (Landes, 1969). The value chain aids in identifying the exact actions that create value throughout the chain, as value relates to what customers are prepared to pay for. The chain is the sequence of activities that are carried out in the upstream (exploring and drilling), midstream (storage and transport), and downstream (distribution and marketing) sectors. The oil and gas industry value chain consists of the listed segments[2] (see Figure 2.4) and are the essential identifier of industry activity in the oil and gas business.

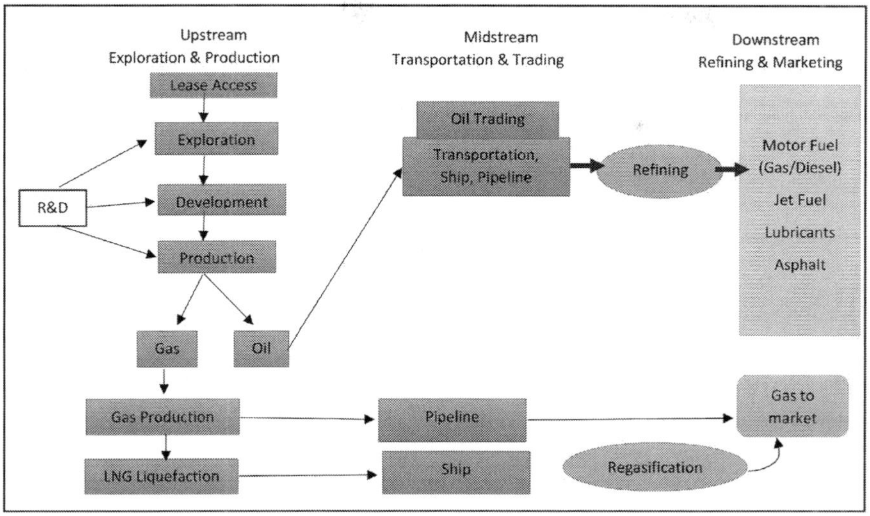

Figure 2.4 Global oil and gas value chain

Source: Inkpen and Moffett (2011)

2.5.1 The Upstream Segment

Exploration, development, and production are examples of upstream activities. Activities of upstream are such that oil and gas are discovered during exploration after obtaining a lease. The discovery requires development and production which are the long-term processes of extraction and drilling of oil wells. Oil and gas-producing companies operate within complex government policies and regulations regarding exploration and development. Most countries award private businesses oil and gas development rights through a negotiation or bidding procedure. ***Production-sharing agreements*** are the most common type of arrangements between oil firms and governments.

2.5.1.1 Production-Sharing Agreement (PSA)

The PSA is a globally progressive, egalitarian, and fair fiscal agreement for sharing oil and gas earnings. The host country gives a contract to an oil company or collection of enterprises known as the contractor(s) to explore a specific field for oil discoveries and extraction. The contract often bears the financial risk of exploration and production in most PSA agreements. Following a successful exploration, the contractor repays the government for royalties owed and uses the extra revenue to recoup capital and operational costs, often known as "cost oil." The money left over is referred to as "profit oil," and it is split between the government and the contractor. Over 75 emerging and developing countries (see appendix) produce oil and gas under this progressive fiscal system now. The

Netherlands-Indies Mining Law of 1899, as revised in 1919, was the catalyst for its acceptance (Taverne, 1999). Saudi Arabia and Kuwait have recently signed a PSA, making them the latest EMDCs to do so. Only Mexico and Turkmenistan are significant oil-producing countries that have switched to service-type contracts instead of PSA.

2.5.2 The Midstream Value Chain

Storage, trading, and transportation of oil and gas from the producing fields are all part of the midstream activity. The crude oil produced must be stored and transported from the well fields to a refinery, according to the value chain in the midstream. Natural gas must also be transported by pipeline or ship to markets. Crude oil has little or no value until it is processed into products like gasoline and diesel (Mitchell and Stevens, 2008). As a result, crude oil producers must sell and transport their goods to refineries. The most common routes of crude oil transportation are pipelines, tankers, and barges; however, trains and tank trucks are also used in different parts of the world. In recent decades, shipbuilding technology has evolved, allowing ships to become larger and safer. Pipeline technology has allowed oil and gas to be transported from remote producing areas to market centres (McGlade and Ekins, 2015). Pipeline construction and administration can take years, if not decades, because they are riddled with geopolitical intrigue. It is incredibly difficult to negotiate and build pipelines that span national borders. Countries have been known to use pipelines that cross their borders as bargaining chips. Terrorists routinely interrupt pipelines, and oil theft from pipelines, along with the associated environmental and safety risks, is common in several countries such as Nigeria and Iraq.

2.5.3 The Downstream Value Chain

In the oil and gas industry, downstream value chain activities include refining, distributing, and retailing petroleum products. This includes oil refineries, petrochemical plants, petroleum product wholesalers, and natural gas distribution companies. The downstream industry produces jet fuel, gasoline, diesel, synthetic rubber, plastics, pesticides, pharmaceuticals, natural gas, and propane. Various downstream petroleum activities have several negative environmental repercussions. Distribution activities may be heavily reliant on fossil fuels, resulting in higher greenhouse gas emissions. Pollutants emitted include carbon dioxide, sulphur oxides (sOx), and nitrogen oxides (nOx), as well as dangerous substances including solvents and groundwater contamination. According to 2013 estimates, the downstream oil and gas sector in advanced countries like Canada produced about 5% of sulphur oxide (sOx) emissions, 1% of nitrogen oxide (nOx) emissions, and 2% of volatile organic compound emissions. These figures are much lower than the upstream industry's emissions. Furthermore, because distribution is a component of downstream oil and gas, leaks are potential.

Box 2.2 Mainstream and Downstream Activities in Angola

Sonangol owns 22.8% of the LNG plant in Soyo, Angola's northwestern province, while Chevron owns 36.4% and Total, BP, and ENI each owns 13.6%. Bechtel and ConocoPhillips, both based in the United States, supplied engineering and construction services for the Soyo LNG complex, respectively. The factory began production in 2013, with a capacity of 5.2 million tonnes per year and a cost of approximately USD 10 billion. In 2015 and 2016, operations were momentarily halted owing to technical challenges but were reopened in early 2017. Brazil, China, South Korea, and France are among the countries that receive export shipments. Angola's downstream crude oil refinery and distribution remain below national demand. The major refinery plant with an installed capacity of 65000 b/d is jointly operated by the Italian Oil Company, ENI, and Sonangol. This joint venture was formed to boost production capacity and output levels by 45,000 b/d.

Source: Privacy Shield Framework (2020)

2.6 Risks in the Oil and Gas Industry

Risk is defined as a potential condition, element, event, or factor arising during project execution, which inhibits or negates the achievement of stated project function, scope, cost, schedule, or quality goals (Suda et al., 2015). The industry's growth potential is stable if oil and gas risk analysis is used at strategic stages. The risks associated with the oil and gas industry include political risk, geological risk, financial risk, environmental risk, and operational risk.

2.6.1 Political Risk

Politics can have a significant impact on the oil industry in terms of regulation. An oil and gas company typically operates under state rules regarding where, when, and how to extract products. These rules vary from country to country due to differences in political rulings. Most oil and gas producers in developing countries face political risk because of instability. In most cases, extracting companies prefer countries with stable political systems and track records of efficient contract awarding with a long-term lease.

2.6.2 Geological Risk

The lack of true visibility on the oil or gas reservoir creates a high degree of uncertainty about the viability of the reservoir to support oil and gas extraction in economic quantities (McGlade and Ekins, 2015). These dangers present themselves in the form of a poor reservoir resource rock, the absence of a reservoir rock, the non-existence of a cap rock, a faulted reservoir, and tight sand. Drilling into a reservoir containing all these characteristics carries a substantial risk of loss due to the high expense of exploration and drilling. Geologists in the oil and gas industry work hard to limit geological risk by testing often. They use the words "proven", "probable," and "possible" before reserve estimations to indicate their level of confidence in the findings.

2.6.3 Financial Risk

The business has long been concerned about price volatility, but the severity of the problem has worsened as extraction costs have increased, and political events influencing oil prices have become more common. An oil price collapse below $45 per barrel will cost significant recovery problems for many oil producers as the average cost of drilling per barrel ranges from $10 to $40, so that an additional cost of royalties, storage, and distribution will raise the price of oil supply far above $45 per barrel.

2.6.4 Environmental Risk

These are risks of pollution from oil and gas activities such as carbon dioxide emission and oil spillage that can affect marine ecosystems, risk of inattention to ecological surroundings, and gas flaring (Suda et al., 2015). All these contribute to both local and global environmental damage. The increased awareness of climate change has intensified environmental regulation, and environmental impact statements have now become a pivotal part of new projects, including detailed attention to the projects' carbon footprint.

2.6.5 Operational Risk

Oil and gas professionals conduct regular tests to ensure that estimates of accessible reserves are accurate, but geological risk also involves extraction obstacles, cost containment issues, and assuring safe drilling conditions as drilling has now migrated to less favourable environments. If the rules governing the operation are very stringent and drilling complicated, then the cost of operation may be high. However, most oil and gas companies compete fiercely to maintain skilled and professional employees during booms; as such there is a constant increase in payroll budget and hence operational cost. This characteristic explains why the sector is largely capital-intensive.

2.7 Conclusion

The oil and gas business, particularly in emerging and developing countries, offers more potential to provide financial and economic assistance for economic progress. Some of these smaller "independents" may have difficulty raising funds, but they can use their reserves, land, and pipelines as collateral to receive lower-interest loans. As the future of oil and gas markets looks dramatically different from the previous 15 years' experiences, many oil and gas producers, particularly in developing countries, will need to adjust their expectations and policy alternatives. At the peak of the commodity super-cycle, tremendous wealth is no longer a realistic expectation. Many grounds exist to believe that oil and gas will not necessarily be produced at the levels projected by many low- and middle-income countries, and that even if production does not disappoint, the resulting profits to governments will be illusory. At the very least, this will force them to reconsider how they manage their people's expectations, which have risen to ridiculous heights. It is largely common that many oil-rich countries are plagued by corruption and financial misappropriation, especially in EDCs. Authorities are therefore advised to make a conscious effort to intensify protection to efficiently operate the sector to minimise the fraudulent schemes. This is because when the sector is properly managed, it will lead to a boom in economic growth and development in the form of royalties, taxes, and bonuses for these emerging and developing economies.

Notes

1 See https://www.bp.com/content/dam/bp/business-sites/en/global/corporate/pdfs/energy-economics/statistical-review/bp-stats-review-2021-full-report.pdf

2 These terms have existed far longer than the value chain concept, which emerged in the 1980s.

References

Bacchetta, P., and Van Wincoop, E. (2004). *A scapegoat model of exchange rate fluctuations* (NBER Working Paper 10245). Washington, DC: National Bureau of Economic Research.

BP. (2016). *The statistical review of world energy 2016* (news item). London: BP. Available online at https://www.bp.com/en/global/corporate/energy-economics/statistical-review-of-world-energy.html

BP. (July 8, 2021). Oil production worldwide from 1998 to 2020* (in million metric tons) [Graph]. In *Statista*. https://www.statista.com/statistics/265229/global-oil-production-in-million-metric-tons/

Huntington, H. G. (1994). Oil price forecasting in the 1980s: What went wrong? *The Energy Journal*, 15(2). 1–22.

Inkpen, A. C., and Moffett, M. H. (2011). *The global oil & gas industry: Management, strategy & finance*. Tulsa, OK: PennWell Books.

Landes, D. S. (1969). *The unbound Prometheus: Technological change and industrial development in Western Europe from 1750 to the present*. Cambridge: Press Syndicate of the University of Cambridge.

McGlade, C., and Ekins, P. (2015). The geographical distribution of fossil fuels unused when limiting global warming to 2°C. *Nature*, 517(7533), 187–90.

Mitchell, J. V., and Stevens, P. (2008). *Ending dependence: Hard choices for oil-exporting states. A Chatham house report*. London: Chatham House.

Ogunleye, T. A. (2015). A legal analysis of production sharing contract arrangements in the Nigerian petroleum industry. *Journal of Energy Technologies and Policy*, 5(8), 1–10.

Privacy Shield Framework (2020) – Oil and gas Angola Privacy Shield (news item). https://www.privacyshield.gov/article?id=Angola-Oil-and-Gas

Rystad Energy. (2021, December 20). Volume of crude oil and natural gas discoveries worldwide from 2015 to 2021 (in billion barrels of oil equivalent) [Graph]. In *Statista*. https://www.statista.com/statistics/1291416/oil-and-gas-discovery-volume-worldwide/

Suda, K. A., Rani, N. S. A., Rahman, H. A., and Chen, W. (2015). A review on risks and project risks management: Oil and gas industry. *International Journal of Scientific Engineering*, 6(8), 938–943.

Taverne, B. (1999). *Petroleum, industry and government: An introduction to petroleum regulation, economies and government policies*. London: Kluwer Law International

Appendix

Emerging and Developing Countries Involved in Production-Sharing Agreement (PSA)

Angola, Nigeria, Cote D'Ivoire, Cameroon, Republic of Benin, Liberia, Sierra Leone, Mozambique, Niger, Chad, Togo, Sudan, South Sudan, Tanzania, Kenya, Egypt, Libya, Equatorial Guinea, Gabon, to mention a few in Africa producing under or signed on unto PSA; Brazil, Bolivia, Peru, Ecuador in South America; Trinidad and Tobago, Guatemala, Cuba, Belize in Central America and the Caribbean, Qatar, Jordan, Syria, Yemen Bahrain, Iraq, Iran in the Middle East, Indonesia, Malaysia, Philippines, East Timor, Vietnam, China in Asia, Albania, Bulgaria Croatia, Georgia, Romania, Azerbaijan, Russia, and Ukraine in Eastern Europe.

3 Oil and Gas Exploration, Development and Production in Emerging Markets and Developing Economies

Joseph Kwadwo Asenso, Betty Nagudi, and Kevin Aanyu

3.1 Introduction

For well over a century, many Emerging Markets and Developing Economies (EMDEs) and their partners have invested significant resources into exploration in a bid to find hydrocarbons and the enhanced revenue flows that come with hydrocarbons. The capital-intensive nature of the petroleum industry renders many of these countries incapable of venturing all by themselves, thereby requiring partnerships with International Oil Companies (IOCs). The multi-billion-dollar budgets for large projects in emerging markets and infrastructure requirements inhibit oil and gas exploration and development. That notwithstanding, IOCs have realised significant returns on their investments in EMDEs.

Increased environmental consciousness and global climate policies have mounted pressure on fossil fuel investments, putting long-term profitability in doubt. In effect, there is a race to produce new and existing resources in the near term to take advantage of current demand and avoid assets becoming stranded.

This chapter discusses oil and gas exploration, development, and production. It explains the processes investors go through to monetise their investments. The chapter has six sections. After the introductory section, the next sections discuss resource exploration, finding oil and gas, fiscal regimes, development, and production of oil and gas. The final section concludes the chapter.

3.2 Exploration of Oil and Gas

Oil and gas exploration is a high-risk, capital-intensive, time-consuming, and technologically intensive activity. Exploration methods vary from remote sensing to fieldwork, generation of geological and subsurface maps to locate suitable lithology and geological structures, geochemical and geophysical surveys, and wildcat drilling. The cost of exploration depends on the location of possible petroleum reserves (on land or in deep water), reservoir depth, field size, information, and the type and structure of the subsurface.

DOI: 10.4324/9781003315056-5

The global oil and gas industry is undergoing a period of uncertainty and a tremendous disruption caused by the growing pressure from the global energy shift (Herkenhoff, 2018; Staalesen, 2021). Exploration activities have been affected by the 2014 Paris Agreement on climate change, shale revolution, geopolitics and conflicts in the Middle East (Shin and Mahmudlu, 2020), and the current COVID-19 pandemic.

Geopolitics continues to dictate the pace with regard to oil and gas asset ownership and new investments (Herkenhoff, 2018), even though low prices have tended to discourage new investments. Conflicts in the Middle East have influenced exploration activities of oil and gas in EMDEs (Shin and Mahmudlu, 2020). Of late, Europe and North America have been searching for more secure and predictable sources in Africa.

Exploration of unconventional oil and gas is underway in many EMDEs, including China, Indonesia, Poland, Algeria, Libya, Argentina, Columbia, Venezuela, Russia, and Mexico. This includes huge natural gas exploration projects in Russia, Peru, Argentina, Brazil, the Middle East, North Africa, Tanzania, and Mozambique.

On the demand side, there was a general decline in fuel consumption as a result of COVID-19, particularly in 2020, with India's consumption collapsing by as much as 70%. This put a downward pressure on oil prices. The collapse of prices resulted in companies abandoning planned projects and scaling back on exploration activities, while ceasing high-cost operations.

The slowing oil demand vis-à-vis cheap oil supply from National Oil Company (NOC)-led markets and unconventional resources seems to make a long-term price recovery a remote possibility. The surge in oil and gas prices in the latter part of 2021 to the first half of 2022, mainly as a result of the build-up of Russian troops along the Ukrainian border in November 2021 and the subsequent war that ensued in February 2022, is expected to abate once the war is over. Some IOCs are therefore preparing for a 'lower-for-longer' future, as others brace themselves for a 'lower-forever' future (Waterworth and Bradshaw, 2018). Clearly, there is less room in the market for the high-cost, long-term projects traditionally owned by IOCs.

Apart from the uncertainty surrounding oil prices, a number of factors have led to low private interest in the upstream sector. In Africa, civil and political unrest, terrorism and kidnapping, oil piracy, and disputes between states have held exploration back (Adusei, 2015). Others include a lack of transparency, regulatory uncertainty and policy instability, infrastructure deficit, and delayed digitalisation of the sector (Botes et al., 2018). In most other countries, it may result from poor terms of investment, strong NOCs, rampant corruption, lack of incentives such as investment credit and tax holidays, as well as poor asset quality.

Nevertheless, oil and gas are expected to account for more than three quarters of global energy consumption by 2040 (Adusei, 2015), a situation that has sustained exploration activities in EMDEs. For example Sub-Saharan Africa accounts for 30% of all new discoveries worldwide, with more recent commercial discoveries in Uganda (see Box 3.1), Kenya, Ghana, Congo, Tanzania, and Mozambique (Olawuyi, 2018).

Box 3.1 Exploration of Oil in Uganda

The search for petroleum in Uganda commenced in the 1920s when oil seeps were reported along the shores of Lake Albert (Wayland, 1925). Aeromagnetic, gravity/magnetic surveys and geological mapping in the early 1990s identified five sedimentary basins with the Albertine Graben as the most prospective basin to date.

To date, over 30 seismic surveys have been made resulting in the acquisition of 7254.6 line kilometres of 2D and 1948.6 km^2 of 3D seismic data. In addition, 116 exploration and appraisal wells have been drilled, with 102 wells encountering oil and/or gas. However, Rhino Camp, Lake George-Edward, and Semliki basins have not had commercial discoveries yet. Three dry wells with no shows in Rhino camp, two dry wells with oil shows in Lake George-Edward basin and Semliki, and another well with natural gas heavily contaminated with carbon dioxide in Semliki basin have been drilled. Two other wells in Semliki basin were dry with no shows.

The acquired data led to some of the largest onshore discoveries in the world, estimated at more than 6.5 billion barrels of oil equivalent in place with 1.4 billion barrels recoverable and 500 billion cubic feet of gas (MEMD, 2014).

To date, only 40% of the Albertine graben has been explored. More finds/reserves could result from reinterpretation and integration of existing geologic shows and seismic data and by employing petroleum system migration models and play concept for the Semliki basin.

In 2021, China National Petroleum Corporation and Sinopec discovered 16 billion tons of oil and gas reserves in China (Global Times, 2021). In some countries, exploration companies have adopted the coopetition (cooperative competition) model by sharing data, information, and equipment to reduce costs and find the most prospective/sweet spots (Waterworth and Bradshaw, 2018). IOCs, service companies, and NOCs such as Petrobras and PEMEX working on offshore projects such as pre-salt that are capital intensive have been sharing expertise and international experience to reduce costs.

3.3 Finding Oil and Gas

For a long time, the oil and gas industry has been focusing on developing methods that establish the amount of oil and gas still remaining in basins and identifying the best methods that have been employed by different companies in finding it. Petroleum exploration techniques have thus evolved at a rapid pace. However, finding oil and gas has always been difficult and risky (Dolson, 2016). For oil, the search began by finding oil seeps at the surface and then collecting it. However, this has since evolved into a highly technical task. This search combines first principles, computing technology, software, and diverse disciplines to find new oil. Despite all this, the success rate remains low, and new ideas and techniques are therefore needed to find new oil pools by explorers.

For example advanced technology and very sophisticated drilling systems and evaluation techniques have been employed to find new and sometimes giant oil fields in various places, including areas without any surface manifestations of seeps (Dolson, 2016).

Currently, oil and gas shows in wells are playing a huge role in finding the resource. Although recognizing oil and gas in cuttings becomes increasingly difficult due to suppression by drilling mud in the rocks around the wellbores, the assessment of the shows has greatly improved with use of wireline logging. Wireline measures several electrical properties (resistivity and conductivity), density, radioactivity, and porosity of the subsurface to detect lithology and fluid content.

In tight wells, oil shows are likely to be from a waste zone in the up-dip part of the trap. It is advisable to go down-dip of a tight oil show and look for a better rock. This requires correct mapping of the facies and use of the show and petrophysical information to understand the trap. This reduces drilling of dumb wells that may make a basin to be statistically mature and therefore mistaken to have very little oil and/or gas left to find. Some basins, once considered a driller's graveyard, have since undergone a renaissance of drilling for unconventional resources and other more difficult reservoirs using new ideas and new technology, for example in China, Brazil, and Mexico.

It is also important to pay attention to key details regarding fluids in rocks. A difference in fluid phase in two wells is an indication of a barrier between them. Dry and/or uneconomic wells are difficult to avoid but are a good lead. For any success, therefore, it is important to understand the petrophysical, rock and fluid analysis more quickly and develop better ways of integrating, visualizing, and interpreting subsurface data. Most of this information can be obtained from only one or two wells, as long as they have cuttings or cores to look at and good well log suites and test information. Detailed studies of these can unveil most of the information about the petroleum system of a basin.

Finding oil and gas also requires a clear understanding of the basin drilling history, its regional stratigraphic and structural framework, the rock properties, and oil and gas shows at the very beginning of the interpretive process (see Box 3.2). Maps that fully explain the oil and gas shows and reservoir properties in an area, including the geometry of the seals, individual traps, and lateral and vertical migration from the source rock, guide the best location for drilling. This approach has led to the discovery of giant fields in the deep-water Nile Delta. Huge reserves of oil and gas have also been found in basins with expiring lease acreages in several EMDEs.

Box 3.2 Finding Oil and Gas in Mexico

In Mexico, the opportunity for finding oil and gas will arrive when some of the PEMEX (NOC) fields are sold out to other companies. Some of these have billions of barrels in place. Some giant fields with very low recovery (5% to 20%) provide good investment opportunities, especially for IOCs with experience in the Gulf of Mexico. Geologically, Mexico is a rich structural environment with a world-class petroleum system (Special Report, 2016).

Recently, Mexico made carbonate discoveries at great depth and with high pressure. This carbonate play is very well understood, and the same source rock in carbonate rocks has been drilled before, and 61 billion barrels were found. However, PEMEX has less experience with deep drilling. It has only produced using shallow drilling and has never drilled subsalt or explored the pre-salt. But in the Santos Campos basin in Brazil, there have been record-breaking pre-salt fields. There are indications of similar potential structures and potential plays in Mexico. Spectrum has also improved its seismic imagery of the region by carrying out full integrity broadband surveys, with PSTM (post stack time migration) data, which is showing more detail in the subsurface.

Optical satellite oil slick data have also been used to confirm the existence of an active petroleum system with producible oil. These data sometimes also indicate the absence of an effective seal. However, Cantarell field, one of the biggest oilfields in the world, was originally discovered because of extremely clear oil slicks in the waters above it. In addition, more analogue ergs which are extensive (up to 50,000 km^2 in places) when found will also provide additional oil and gas resources in Mexico. In general, there exists a huge opportunity of finding more oil and gas when IOCs co-invest with PEMEX.

Successful exploration companies employ the play concept instead of prospects. Since prospects rely on proven exploration techniques, they are cheaper and easier to generate. However, only one well can be drilled. The play concept, on the other hand, requires 'out-of-the-box' thinking and a break from traditional exploration methods. Plays contain several prospects, and many wells can then be drilled. Therefore, companies are more interested in finding new and big plays instead of prospects in any basin of interest. However, finding oil and gas requires teamwork and sharing of information and ideas as well as proper integration of the acquired data.

To reduce time wastage in finding oil and gas, differentiation of residual oil shows from continuous-phase shows found within a viable trap is essential. Residual shows may be found in a 'swept' oil field, along migration pathways, or paleo-oil accumulations that have been lost due to later uplift. The oil–water contacts and the base of the trap at the free-water level should be clearly differentiated because oil–water contacts easily change across a field with a change in lithology. Therefore, workstation-generated maps, with rock/lithology and fluid details, capillary pressure data (to determine the position of the oil show from the free-water level), and explanation of migration and entrapment processes can guide economic decisions. These decisions may force a company to wind up and abandon the area or farm-out a prospect considered high risk. Notably, successful companies use all the acquired data, including negative results and the play concept, to determine what to do differently and avoid abandoning good ideas prematurely (Dolson, 2016).

For example quantitative show assessment close to or at old dry wells or production wells that had been abandoned by some companies has led to successful production of oil and gas from shales (China, Democratic Republic of Congo, Morocco, Brazil, Mexico, Argentina, and Jordan). However, conventional reserves have been discovered in Angola. These are places that had been written off, but proper interpretation of the oil and gas shows led to the discovery of new plays.

In some EMDEs, the data are missing or not good enough to understand the subsurface. This implies that there are chances of finding more oil and gas in new plays and old mature ones in these countries with the right data and technical staff with new ideas. Most of these countries do not have the technology, skilled technical staff with new ideas, good data, infrastructure, and the capital to find oil and gas resources and develop them fully to support their economies (IEO, 2016).

Seismic survey is the only tool that allows relationships between wells to be visualised directly, giving information about faults, facies, and seal geometries, using procedures that include 3D projection and 4D modelling. In some cases, oil, gas, or water can be detected using Direct Hydrocarbon Indicators (DHI), which are seismic anomalies highlighted by changes in seismic amplitudes arising from changes in the rock's elastic properties, thus finding hydrocarbons directly. DHI can greatly reduce risk, although many seismic features interpreted as DHI could be caused by lithology changes and not necessarily fluids (Dolson, 2016), thus underscoring the need to recognise and understand the pitfalls of DHI analysis/interpretation.

Petroleum system migration modelling has also been employed to increase chances of finding oil and gas. Building a good model requires data inputs including accurate structural maps; facies models with seal integrity and reservoir properties including subsurface environments (P, T, water); knowledge of the source rocks (age, geochemistry, and thermal maturity); and timing of oil and gas migration. This model displays traps along migration pathways (Dolson, 2016).

Regardless of the growing advancement in building good migration and entrapment models to improve success rates of finding oil and gas, other methods such as use of oil and gas shows data, surface seeps, and rock geochemical information will remain critical in understanding and calibrating migration and trap models. In addition, because of the growing use of software manipulation with 3D seismic and petroleum systems software, application of basic principles to determine the potential and limitations of these tools is key in finding oil and gas.

3.4 Oil and Gas Licensing/Fiscal Regimes

Oil and gas licensing systems or fiscal regimes constitute rules, laws, regulations, and agreements governing the incomes derived from petroleum exploration and exploitation and are key to avoiding the resource curse. Although fiscal regimes tend to be hybrids of the various agreement types, different fiscal regimes offer different levels of control, payoff structures to the developer, and degrees of NOC involvement.

Governments aim at maximizing petroleum revenues, while providing sufficient incentives to IOCs. Olawuyi (2008) opines that governments consider diverse factors when selecting fiscal regimes and arrangements for their countries, including:

1. level of participation by the state (whether solely as a regulator or as commercial participant),
2. nature of returns expected (whether purely royalties or focus on share of petroleum produced),
3. pick-up location of proceeds (wellhead or export point),
4. timing of revenues (early or late production stages),
5. risk-tolerance or neutrality of the state (quota of risk allotted to the state and IOC),
6. transparency expectations,
7. national content and accountability, and
8. willingness to attract IOCs by reducing tax obligations and other fiscal incentives.

In selecting new opportunities, investors, on the other hand, consider political stability, state-intervention in setting the environment for granting instruments and overall business climate, robustness of legal systems, infrastructure, and geological promise, among others (Pereira et al., 2017).

3.4.1 Types of Fiscal Regimes

Petroleum licensing systems or fiscal regimes are categorised either as a concessionary system or as a contractual system, including all production sharing contracts (PSCs) or service contracts (Alfarsi, 2018). Thus, IOCs are concessionaires under a concession and contractors under a contractual system.

3.4.1.1 Concessionary System

Concession agreement is a type of contract between a state and a company, which provides the latter with the right to operate a business within the jurisdiction of the former based on negotiated terms and conditions (Alfarsi, 2018). Under concession, the state transfers its ownership of subsurface resource to a commercial entity (concession holder) that is granted exclusive rights to extract hydrocarbons from defined concession areas for defined periods. The concessionaire receives all of the petroleum produced from the field but pays royalties and taxes to the state (Olawuyi, 2008).

The company provides capital and exploration capacity; develops, produces, and processes petroleum, thereby absorbing all financial risks, especially where no economically viable hydrocarbon reserves are found. The primary benefit to the company is the ownership of the reserves, while benefits to the host country are realised from taxes and royalties derived from production. In essence, depending on the type of concession, the IOC owns all the hydrocarbons produced from the territory of the agreement, with the exception of the share to be paid to the state or NOC (Inkpen and Moffett, 2011; Olawuyi, 2008).

3.4.1.2 Contractual Agreements

Contractual frameworks, on the other hand, take the form of PSCs, joint venture contracts, service contracts, and participation agreements (e.g. farmout contracts, polling and unitisation contracts). This section focuses on PSCs and service contracts.

3.4.1.2.1 PRODUCTION SHARING CONTRACT

Olawuyi (2008) defines PSC as an agreement between a host country and a contractor, where the contractor bears all exploration risks and production and development costs in return for a share of profit from production. It defines the processes and procedures for sharing and recouping production costs, bonuses, royalty oil, and profit oil, among others. The state retains ownership of the hydrocarbons produced, subject only to the contractor's entitlement to its share of production, with the contractor having the option of participating in different aspects of the exploration and development process.

A standard PSC holds detailed terms on the sharing formula, contract tenure, place of delivery, provisions on default, termination, dispute resolution, and the governing law. This contract-based regime grants a private investor or a consortium the right to explore for and produce hydrocarbons in specified acreage and timeframe (Olawuyi, 2008).

3.4.1.2.2 SERVICE CONTRACT

A service contract requires the holder to develop a contract area by providing exploration, extraction, and processing capacities. The company receives payments from the state for providing the contracted services, and such income is subject to a corporate income tax and a special tax arrangement (Alfarsi, 2018). A service contractor receives a fixed sum payment and does not participate in the sharing of the petroleum output or profits.

Service contracts are often seen as the ideal choice in circumstances characterised by nationalism since they afford the greatest deal of control over resources to the host government. Nonetheless, the provision of services as mere contractors without opportunities for future shareholding can adversely affect contractor productivity (Olawuyi, 2008). This gives little incentive to the contractor to be innovative and efficient. Although the state bears significant financial risks under this contract, it is less attractive from an IOC perspective (Olawuyi, 2008).

There are three main types of service contracts, namely pure service contract, risk service contract, and technical assistance contract.

In a **Pure Service Contract**, the state bears all the risks while the contractor receives remuneration for the performance of a specific service. In this contract, the contractor has the option to acquire an interest in the output. These agreements, which have been utilised mainly in Middle Eastern countries, are rare in Africa (Olawuyi, 2008).

Under **Risk Service contract (RSC)**, the risk of exploration is borne by the contractor, who obtains cash remuneration if commercially exploitable resources are identified. The contractor can also become a part owner of the business or receive a discounted price on a given percentage of the total production (Olawuyi, 2008). RSCs are used extensively in South America and Latin America.

In a **Technical Assistance Contract**, the contractor gets paid for the services rendered, with no scope to acquire any interest in the project. It differs from a pure service contract because the company is engaged to provide technical services, without any interest in the oil at any time, with its remuneration consisting solely of a specified and pre-agreed fee (Olawuyi, 2008).

3.5 Developing Oil and Gas Projects

After the discovery and evaluation of petroleum deposits, 5 to 10 years of the field's life is spent on field development, during which subsurface and surface facilities are designed and implemented to enable safe and efficient hydrocarbon production. Thus, field development creates a producing asset out of a discovery that is deemed viable after investment appraisal (Inkpen and Moffett, 2011). It encompasses activities on environmental impact, geophysics, geology, reservoir and production engineering, infrastructure, well design and construction, completion design, surface facilities installations, project economics, and risk assessment.

The decision-making and project development processes conceptually involve project sponsors evaluating qualitative and quantitative risks; assessing project economics; identifying the source of capital; creating contractor supply chains managing the project design, construction, and execution; handing the project over to the operators; and integrating the project into a larger organisation.

3.5.1 Field Development

There are four stages of project development: feasibility and appraisal, selection, definition, and execution. The first two stages require several specialist teams that perform feasibility studies to ascertain the optimal development plan for the field by defining costs, schedule, and project economics in order to reach a Final Investment Decision (FID). With the FID reached, field construction/execution follows. At each stage, project documents are prepared and findings presented with recommendations to a decision board to move the project to the next stage.

Specialist knowledge and input are required from geologists, geophysicists, and reservoir engineers to formulate a field development plan that establishes the number of wells to be drilled to achieve production objectives, recovery techniques to extract the reservoir fluids, the type and cost of installations needed, the separation systems for gas and fluids, and the treatment systems needed to preserve the environment.

Approval of field development plans is proceeded by detailed design of the facilities, procurement of construction materials, facilities' fabrication, facilities' installation, and commissioning of plants and equipment. Drilling engineers, reservoir engineers, and geologists decide on the optimal placement and design of production/injection wells. On the other hand, production engineers, reservoir engineers, and facilities engineers decide on the optimal production facilities required for proper processing of hydrocarbons before treatment and/or delivery to refinery or customer. Logistics engineers decide on the best transportation options and efficient export routes for the oil and/or gas. That notwithstanding, upstream sector success, particularly, demands highly sophisticated engineering and hardware technologies.

Development of a petroleum field may cost hundreds of billions of United States dollars, onshore development being comparatively much cheaper than offshore development. Field development typically lasts 5–10 years, depending on field location, size and complexity of necessary facilities, and the number of wells required to achieve the economic and production targets. It entails seismic reservoir identification (1–2 years), drilling of production and injection wells (at least 1–2 years), well completion works (about 1 year), and infrastructure development (at least 2–3 years).

Both physical extractive infrastructure (rail, roads, ports, bridges, pipelines, refineries, gathering systems) and associated infrastructure (such as telecommunications, electricity, logistics, and the institutions) are required to extract, produce, refine, transport, store, and distribute extractive resources across the extractives industry value chain (Olawuyi, 2008).

Given the magnitude of activities involved, several key factors impact field development, including field location, geologic complexity, politics, environmental concerns, land/mineral rights, access to pipelines, and the projected price of the oil. Sensitive environments require approvals by different government agencies, lengthening the time required for field development. Sometimes, the supply of oil field specialists cannot keep up with the demands, which leads to delays. Inkpen and Moffett (2011) observed that taking upstream development projects from concept to completion is never a challenge-free straightforward linear process from onset to on-time and on-budget finish but rather involves time delays, partner disputes, government approval holdups and manpower, material, and technological shortages.

3.6 Oil and Gas Production

3.6.1 Subsurface Processes

The production of oil and gas is made possible by pre-installed facilities, which may vary according to the characteristics of the field. Conventional onshore facilities include sucker rod pumps (donkey pump), with less sophistication when it comes to transportation, depending on production size and distance to delivery points. This section focuses on offshore production, which is predominant in EMDEs.

The scale and complexity of infrastructure required for offshore production depend on the resource (oil, gas, or condensates), depth of the reservoir, and distance from onshore facilities and delivery points, among others. Production facilities include production and injection wells, wellhead structure (Christmas tree), risers and riser platforms, processing and accommodation platforms, gravity bases, compliant towers, floating production and storage facilities, and onshore transportation and processing facilities.

Production begins in earnest once the subsea infrastructure is installed and the wells completed. Some wellheads are not production wells but injection wells through which water and/or gas is injected to maintain reservoir pressure to enable the resource to reach the surface. Manifolds and gathering systems then collect the resource and transmit it through risers to the surface. Oil wells typically require the installation of artificial lifts, which are necessary for periods of low reservoir pressure, while this may not be needed for gas and condensate wells, given that they rise naturally to the surface due to their light weight. If the pressure in the reservoir as well as gas and water injection fail to increase reservoir pressure to transmit oil to the surface, then an artificial lift becomes necessary.

3.6.2 Surface Processes

The resource undergoes a critical process of separation into oil, gas, water, condensates, and contaminants. The separated oil is then sent to a coalescer for a further reduction of water content, usually to below 0.1% (Devold, 2009), and for removal of any excess salt by an electrostatic desalter.

One of the essential elements of the production process is metering, which is necessary for determining the actual production, partner offtake, invoices, and tax obligations, among others. Fiscal metering takes many forms, from manual process to metering equipment. Some metering equipment comes with analyser components, giving information about the water content, viscosity, pressure, density, and temperature. Gas meters measure the energy value, hydrocarbon content, temperature, and pressure (Devold, 2009).

Depending on the architecture, some oil and gas projects have transportation pipelines that supply the commodity to onshore storage tanks, while others do not. Many African countries do not have adequate refining capacity and therefore sell their oil overseas without the need to send the commodity onshore. They also have Floating, Production, Storage, and Offloading (FPSO) vessels onsite to store the commodity. Depending on the distance to the market, shuttle tankers or very large crude carriers are deployed to offtake the oil from the FPSO or other storage facilities onsite. Gas transportation is quite complicated, especially if it is not done by pipelines. The sales gas is liquefied in order for vessel transportation to be possible. On delivery to the point of destination, it is re-gasified before it is put to use.

Natural gas is processed to remove pollutants and to meet transporters' and offtakers' specifications before it becomes sales gas. During the processing, natural gas liquids (NGLs) are produced as by-products. NGLs are for industrial use, and by-products such as isopentanes, in particular, are used as fuel for power production.

3.7 Conclusion

Oil and gas exploration is capital intensive, making it difficult for most EMDEs to venture into it all by themselves. The desire to maintain the ownership of the resource, while investing relatively little compared to their partners, has led to various contracting regimes that have discouraged investment. The global shift from fossil fuel to green options has further reduced investor appetite.

In spite of the green revolution, there is the belief that oil and gas will not be phased out in the near future, given that demand has remained high, save the 2020 COVID-19-induced global demand plunge. More attention should be directed towards energy security/energy poverty, economic development, and affordability imperatives. New exploration, findings, and field development activities are going on in quite a number of EMDEs, with the global oil and gas industry exhibiting increased efforts to develop cost-cutting state-of-the-art technologies to ensure the sustainability of oil and gas projects. Brent crude oil price rose to $86 per barrel in December 2021; however, given the projected decline in demand in the coming years, prices may eventually decline, making the industry less profitable.

References

Adusei, L. A. (2015). 'Threats to the exploration, production and supply of Africa's energy resources', *South African Journal of International Affairs*, 22(1), 43–65. https://www.tandfonline.com/doi/abs/10.1080/10220461.2014.1001432?journalCode=rsaj20.

Alfarsi, H. (2018). *Fiscal regimes: Three major types of oil and gas agreements*. https://www.profolus.com/topics/types-oil-and-gas-agreements/

Botes, A., Lane, A., and Edinge, H. (2018). The new frontier: Winning in the African oil and gas industry. *Deloitte Insights Feature*. https://www2.deloitte.com/content/dam/insights/us/articles/za22455_the-new-frontier/DI_The-new-frontier.pdf (accessed 14 November, 2021).

Devold, H. (2009). *Oil and gas production handbook: An introduction to oil and gas production*. Oslo: ABB Oil and Gas.

Dolson, J. (2016). *Understanding oil and gas shows and seals in the search for hydrocarbons*. Switzerland: Springer International Publishing.

Global Times. (2021, June 19). *Global Times: 1-billion-ton oil and gas field discovered in Xinjiang's Tarim Basin*. https://www.globaltimes.cn/page/202106/1226540.shtml.

Herkenhoff, L. (2018). *A profile of the oil and gas industry: Resources, market forces, geopolitics, and technology*. 2nd ed. New York: Business Expert Press, LLC.

Inkpen, A., Moffett, H. M. (2011). *The global oil and gas industry: Management, strategy and finance*. Tulsa, OK: PennWell Corporation.

International Energy Outlook (IEO) (2016). https://www.osti.gov/servlets/purl/1296780.

Ministry of Energy and Mineral Development (MEMD) (2014). *Progress of implementation of the national oil and gas policy for Uganda*. Phoenix, AZ: MEMD

Olawuyi, S. D. (2008). Extractive sector infrastructure. In *Extractives industry law in Africa* (pp. 56–80). New York: Springer .

Olawuyi, S. D. (2018). *Extractives industry law in Africa*. New York: Springer International Publishing.

Pereira, G. E., Gregio, F., and Amorim, L. (2017). The Brazilian pre-salt case: Governmental interference and challenges for potential joint ventures. *Journal of Energy & Natural Resources Law*, 35(4), 451–461 .

Shin, S. Y., and Mahmudlu, C. (2020). Global oil-market strategies of Saudi Arabia and Iran. *Middle East Policy*, 27(1), 102–114.

Special Report Finding Oil in Mexico and the Caribbean. (2016, October 21). *Special report finding oil in Mexico and the Caribbean*. London: The Geological Society, https://www.google.com/url?sa=t&rct=j&q=&esrc=s&source=web&cd=&ved=2ahUKEwjN6Yum0az3AhUuPewKHSGzD0QQFnoECAcQAQ&url=http%3A%2F%2F83a7383a5e33475eed0e-e819cda5edf0a946af164bb0b2f2ae3c.r0.cf1.rackcdn.com%2FFPMexicoreport.pdf&usg=AOvVaw0W8uFTUI5KpL0dZsUFDskL

Staalesen, A. (2021, May 6). *Russian Arctic oil races against time*. https://thebarentsobserver.com/en/industry-and-energy/2021/05/russian-arctic-oil-races-against-time

Waterworth, A., and Bradshaw, M. J. (2018). Unconventional trade-offs? National oil companies, foreign investment and oil and gas development in Argentina and Brazil. *Energy Policy*, 122, 7–16.

Wayland, E. (1925). Petroleum in Uganda. *Nature*, 115, 980.

4 Legal, Regulatory, and Fiscal Arrangements in the Oil and Gas Industry in Emerging and Developing Countries

Abdallah Ali-Nakyea, Raymond A. Atuguba, Olufemi M. Saibu, and Nasir A. Mohammed

4.1 Introduction

The recognition of oil and gas as important energy sources is not without basis. The world's population is expected to double by the middle of the 21st century, and economic development needs to continue, particularly in the global south (Nakicenovic et al., 1998). Crude oil and natural gas are precious substances that are both 'critical to national strategies and crucial to international politics – they are indispensable to the economic progress and prosperity of all countries, no matter what their level of development might be' (Gao, 1994).

A cursory study of the extant literature suggests that the oil and gas industry is the chief economic mainstay of many emerging and developing countries (KPMG, 2017; US Energy Information Administration, 2013). The African continent accounts for an important allocation of global oil and gas production and supply (UNECA, 2011). Among other emerging and developing economies, most African countries are, no doubt, hugely endowed with oil and gas resources (Heringshaw, 2004). For example while Nigeria, Libya, Algeria, Egypt, and Angola are historical giants in oil-producing countries in Africa, others, including Ghana, Côte d'Ivoire, Liberia, and Uganda, continue to attract sizeable investment and income from oil and gas resources in recent decades. For instance since the early 2000s, Ghana has signed 18 petroleum agreements with various international and local oil companies. Although Ghana has recently terminated a few of these agreements, exploration efforts under the existing agreements have resulted in the country's only producing fields: Jubilee, Tweneboa-Enyenra-Ntomme (TEN), and Sankofa-Gye Nyame (SGN).

Olawuyi (2018b at p. 5) has observed that the revenue generated from the oil and gas industry has been the cornerstone of development financing in most African states. This would seem to be the case in Nigeria, Angola, Libya, Algeria, Egypt, Gabon, Cameroon, Tunisia, Equatorial Guinea, the Democratic Republic of the Congo, Cote d'Ivoire, and Ghana, among others.

DOI: 10.4324/9781003315056-6

Despite prevailing 'resource curse' and climate change/energy transition concerns, most emerging market and developing resource-rich economies are responding to the current energy crisis through the banner of 'Energy Progression'. On 'resource curse', Stiblitz and Spiegal (2007) and Auty (1993) indicate that many developing countries, such as Africa, have been unable to enhance the economic, sustainability of their rich hydrocarbon resource endowment. At the heart of the 17 Sustainable Development Goals (SDGs) adopted by the world's governments in September 2015 is SDG 13 which requires urgent action to combat climate change and its impacts. This is currently influencing how the world is approaching the economic advancement of its oil and gas resources towards achieving a viable and established oil and gas industry. Nalule (2020) and Nalule and Acheampong (2021), in discussing 'Energy Progression', advocate that sustained investments in fossil fuels and other energy sources, especially in resource-rich developing countries, are a sine qua non to achieving global energy justice. The past decade has seen a groundswell of research and debate in this regard. Although the rationales for "Energy Progression" remain largely uncrystallised, the many legal, regulatory, and fiscal arrangements across the value chain, which evokes largely similar approaches among resource-rich developing countries, are helping to shed light on the path ahead for these countries.

This chapter attempts a deeper exploration of these legal, regulatory, and fiscal arrangements, highlighting how the challenges have been, and could be better, addressed by emerging and developing countries and how industry actors can sustain their investments in the face of obvious legal, regulatory, and fiscal challenges in an ever-changing energy environment.

The chapter is organised into four sections. Following this introduction and drawing comparative examples mostly from Africa and the developed world, Section 4.2 explores the genres of law and the fundamental concept of ownership of oil and gas in their natural state, and how these affect the management and regulation of oil and gas in developing countries. Section 4.3 discusses the legal, institutional, and regulatory arrangements and regimes across emerging and developing countries with a view to identifying and addressing the challenges for both state and industry actors. A similar approach is adopted in Section 4.4 to consider the fiscal arrangements across emerging and developing countries. Section 4.5 is the concluding section.

4.2 Genres of Law and Fundamental Principles

4.2.1 Nature and Scope of Legal Principles

The nature and scope of oil and gas law are often difficult to define, due principally to its all-embracing containment and application of different principles of law, including those of property law, law of contract, tax law, constitutional and administrative law, environmental law, international law and general principles thereof, and African customary law. The list is not exhaustive. The diverse applicable legislation, institutions, and frameworks in the oil and gas industry in Africa and other developing countries are underpinned by a whole gamut of sources and legal principles and maxims emanating from these areas of law. Generally, five key sources of oil and gas law are identifiable, namely, international law, domestic legislation, common law, judicial decisions, and scholarly publications (Olawuyi, 2018b, at pp. 109–140). The remainder of this chapter is discussed within the specific context of the applicable legal principles.

4.2.2 Ownership and Control of Oil and Gas Resources in Their Natural State

The juridical nature and essence of ownership and control of oil and gas resources in their natural state among the various African countries are well documented (Olawuyi, 2015). Subject to existing contestations (Njotini, 2017; Bouckaert, 1990), the ownership of oil and gas denotes the ultimate residual bundle of rights and interests that are available to a person, and over which the person can exercise sole dominion over and above every other person in relation to the resource (Olawuyi, 2018a at pp. 88–89). The rights include such rights as the right and incidentals to use and enjoy the resource as the owner pleases, including the right to possess, exclude others, or alienate the resource (Omorogbe, 2001; Omorogbe and Oniemola, 2010).

Depending on the history, socio-political aspirations, legal tradition, and existing regulatory arrangements in a given country, ownership rights over oil and gas resources may take a peculiar form different from what applies in other jurisdictions. Following the dominal as opposed to the non-dominal system of resource ownership, all African and developing resource-rich countries have, through their national constitutions and other principal industry laws, vested the entire ownership and control of all oil and gas resources in, under, or upon any lands within their respective jurisdictions on the state (Omorogbe and Oniemola, 2010 at p. 115 and 118).

Also known as the 'Ad Coelum theory of ownership', the non-dominal system of resource ownership recognises and allows private ownership of oil and gas by the surface land owner. Canada and some states of the United States of America subscribe to this system. In Texas Company v. W. H. Daugherty et al., 107 Tex. 226 (Tex. 1915), the US Court held that the person who owns the land owns the oil and gas beneath the surface of the earth, in keeping with the Latin maxim, '*cuius est solum eius usque ad coelum et ad inferos*', meaning 'whomsoever owns the soil, owns up to the sky and down to the depths'.

Similarly, developing countries from the Middle East such as Kuwait, Qatar, Iran, United Arab Emirates, and Saudi Arabia are all dominal jurisdictions (Olawuyi, 2018b). There is, generally, no recognition of private ownership of land and natural resources in both Africa and the Middle East (Olawuyi, 2018a at p. 92).

The dominal system of resource ownership is where the ownerships of oil and gas resources are vested in the state, whether unitary or federal, where the oil and gas are located. Other concepts of ownership include the 'Islamic perspective' and the 'regalian' and 'US' concepts which have been exhaustively discussed in Duval et al. (2009, at pp. 13–20). These are, however, outside the scope of the present work. Developed out of the 'regalian doctrine', this dominal ownership right of the state is true and absolute in Ghana (Article 257(6) of the 1992 Constitution of Ghana), Nigeria, and in many other emerging market and developing economies, subject of course to surface landholders' entitlement to private property and incidental rights recognised by law (Constitution of the Federal Republic of Nigeria, 1999; Laws of the Federation of Nigeria 2004, c 23). Also, s.1 of the Petroleum Industry Act, 2021 (ACT No. 6) stipulates that the property and ownership of oil and gas within Nigeria and its territorial waters, continental shelf, and exclusive economic zone are vested in the government of the Federation of Nigeria.

Although there have been initial contestations over the applicability of Article 257(6) of the 1992 Constitution of Ghana to oil and gas in light of the use of the word 'mineral', this legal conundrum was subsequently cured by Section 3 of the Petroleum (Exploration and Production) Act, 2016 (Act 919) which reproduced almost verbatim a similar provision in the repealed Petroleum (Exploration and Production) Act, 1984 (PNDCL 84).

This 'regalian doctrine' originates from Roman law and is anchored on the principle that the king or state is the owner of all conquered lands, waters, and mineral resources, with power to authorise the criteria for granting rights and privileges over public lands and natural resources and the terms associated with the grant (Davies and Fouracre, 1995).

It is on the basis of this ownership regime that emerging and developing countries develop legal, institutional, and regulatory frameworks to govern oil and gas operations, including setting the conditions for foreign investor participation in the development of these resources within their jurisdictions. This is in sync with successive United Nations resolutions on the sovereign rights of states to ownership of natural resources within their jurisdiction. The first, Resolution No. 626 (VII), was adopted in 1952 and provides that: "The right of peoples freely to use and exploit their natural wealth and resources is inherent in their sovereignty". A decade later in 1962, the General Assembly adopted Resolution No. 1803 (XVIII) entitled 'Permanent Sovereignty Over Natural Resources', which emphasises both the welfare of the host nation's people to resource development and the right of host nations to nationalise or expropriate private investments (both domestic and foreign), subject to the payment of appropriate compensation in accordance with domestic law and consistent with international law. Other General Assembly Resolutions on the subject include No. 2158 (XXI) of 1966 and No. 3281 (XXIX) of 1974. For a detailed examination of these Resolutions, see Duval et al. ((n 19) at pp. 21–23).

An important issue that borders on the question of ownership of oil and gas in their natural state is the additional requirement for formal prior parliamentary approval of all categories of authorisations in most African countries as opposed to Western jurisdictions like Canada. In Ghana, for example

Parliament has the mandate under Article 268(1) of the country's 1992 Constitution to ratify all natural resource agreements, save those it exempts under Article 268(2). Article 268(2) provides: 'Parliament may, by resolution supported by the votes of not less than two-thirds of all members of Parliament, exempt from the provisions of clause (1) of this article any particular class of transactions, contracts or undertakings'. Additionally, Parliament has the mandate to form natural resource commissions for the 'regulation and management of the utilisation of the natural resources concerned and the co-ordination of the policies in relation to them' (1992 Constitution of Ghana, Article 269(1)). It is under this provision that the establishment of Ghana's Petroleum Commission may have constitutional backing. At its good judgement and convenience, Parliament may also authorise any agency of government other than the Commissions referenced to in Article 269(1) to 'approve the grant of rights, concessions or contract in respect of the exploitation of any mineral, water or other natural resource of Ghana' (1992 Constitution of Ghana, Article 269(2)).

The effect of the dominal system of ownership is that in most emerging and developing resource-rich countries, the extent of rights over and interest in oil and gas in their natural state and how they can be exploited are codified in specific country constitutions. Other provisions include laws affecting the industry and other laws of general application. The nature and character of the authorisations granted the investor are also spelt out. Investors must therefore be wary of dealing with entities rather than dealing directly with the governments or national oil companies of emerging and developing countries when seeking to enter and acquire oil and gas authorisations in such jurisdictions. Proper due diligence, including understanding the nature, extent and scope of rights and interests acquired under applicable laws and authorisations and mastering the art of negotiating protective contractual provisions, is a sine qua non to investing prudently, as is avoiding legal and political risks in the oil and gas industry in emerging economies and the developing world (Olawuyi, 2015).

4.3 Legal and Regulatory Framework

4.3.1 Snapshot

In addition to the question of ownership of oil and gas in their natural state is the complex matrix of other legal and regulatory issues of utmost importance to emerging and developing resource-rich countries. This matrix encompasses a network of oil and gas policies, legislation, contractual arrangements, fiscal systems, and the government's management of the extraction of oil and gas resources (Hunter, 2009 at p. 45). These issues have generated compelling discussions and reviews in the economic and regulatory space over the years (Olawuyi, 2018a at p. 8).

While the geographies of the various emerging and developing countries vary considerably, approaches to these frameworks are largely similar. The existing complication associated with the regulatory frameworks, institutions, and legal instruments governing the industry will help appreciate the nature and development of the industry among emerging and developing countries.

4.3.2 Overview of Policy Environment

As with their resource-rich developed counterparts, the development of oil and gas resources in a given developing country is often anchored on a unique national energy policy. Such a policy determines the strategy and structure under which the country plans to foster exploitation of its oil and gas, among other natural resources. This foundational policy is often undergirded by principles of law inherent in the dominal system of ownership and the concept of permanent sovereignty over natural resources.

For example Ghana's comprehensive National Energy Policy (National Energy Policy, February 2010) demonstrates fidelity to these principles. This Policy is currently under review by the government. However, the review process has not been completed. In the policy, the goal of the oil and gas sub-sector is stated to be this: 'to sustain and optimise the exploitation and utilisation of Ghana's oil and gas endowment for the overall benefit and welfare of all Ghanaians, present and future' (National Energy Policy, 2010, at p.16). While a foundational oil and gas policy is often a unique document, its legitimacy is sometimes rooted in the constitution itself, as pertains in Papua New Guinea, or in other legislative enactments such as Norway (Duval et al., 2009 at p. 26.), or a combination of both, as pertains in Ghana (Article 257(6) of the 1992 Constitution of Ghana; and Section 3 of the Petroleum (Exploration and production) Act, 2016 (Act 919)) and Nigeria (the 1999 Constitution of the Federal Republic of Nigeria, Laws of the Federation of Nigeria 2004, c 23; and Section 1 of the Petroleum Industry Act, 2021 (Act No. 6)). Goals 3 and 4 of the Independent State of Papua New Guinea expressed in the preamble to the country's Constitution are to the effect that the country be: 'politically and economically independent, its economy be self-reliant, and its natural resources and environment be conserved and used for the collective benefit of the nation' (Constitution of the Independent State of Papua New Guinea, n.d.).

In virtually all resource-rich developing countries, policy objectives on oil and gas are structured to define the broad but substantive contractual and regulatory requirements of the industry, including the host country's control of the rate and extent of exploration or exploitation, the nature of state participation, institutional architecture, local content, revenue streams and management, environmental and social issues, as well as identified challenges and ways of redressing them (see e.g. Ghana's National Energy Policy, February 2010). Policies are also sometimes made to address specific objectives such as Ghana's 2010 petroleum local Content and Local Participation policy, the Gas Masterplan and a Client Service Charter, Nigeria's Oil and Gas Content Development Act of 2010, and the National Content Policy for the Petroleum Subsector in Uganda (2008).

4.3.3 Overview of Legislative Framework

Generally, oil and gas activities are regulated under one or more or a combination of three legislative systems, namely the fixed content system, the agreement system, or the flexible content system. The fixed content system is where the laws and regulations are fully detailed, the agreement system provides broad negotiating room for licensing rounds or direct negotiation while the flexible content system is a hybrid of the fixed and flexible content systems. For a detailed explanation of what these systems entail, see Duval et al. (2009 at pp. 26–29). The dominant system in emerging and developing resource-rich countries is the flexible system.

In Ghana, for example the law (section 10 of Act 919) requires the state (including the national oil company) to execute petroleum agreements with investors, despite that the regulatory requirements of the industry are fully detailed in primary legislation and regulations. These are generally contained in the Petroleum (Exploration and Production), 2016 (Act 919) and its accompanying regulations. Ghana's 1992 Constitution, as well as other laws of specific and general application to the oil and gas industry in the country, provides for these. The specific industry laws would include: the Ghana National Petroleum Corporation Act, 1983 (P.N.D.C.L 64); the Petroleum Revenue Management Act, 2011 (Act 815) as amended; and the Petroleum Commission Act, 2011 (Act 821), together with their accompanying legislative instruments. The laws of general application would include the Income Tax Act, 2016 (Act 896), particularly Part VI thereof and the environmental and labour laws of Ghana. Similar approaches are adopted in Nigeria, Equatorial Guinea, Egypt, Angola, and across the African continent.

4.3.4 Overview of Institutional Framework

4.3.4.1 Ministry Responsible for Oil and Gas Resources

Generally, the ministry responsible for oil and gas resources is the main government body that oversees oil and gas policy formulation, implementation and general management of the operations of the oil and gas industry. Save some few exceptions, virtually all emerging and other resource-rich developing countries have dedicated supervisory ministries for regulating the oil and gas industry. These few exceptions include Algeria (Ministry of Energy and Mining), Zambia (Ministry of Energy and Water Development), Equatorial Guinea (Ministry of Industry, Mines & Energy), and South Africa (Minister for Mineral Resources), where both petroleum and mining activities are handled by the same ministry. To this list can be added Ghana, given that the country's Ministry of Energy which oversees the oil and gas sector also oversees the policy and regulatory environment for the power sector. In Libya, for example, the ministry is designated as Ministry of Oil and Gas. Similarly, in Nigeria, it is the Federal Ministry of Petroleum Resources which is further segregated into the Department of Petroleum Resources ('DPR') and the Department of Gas Resources (DGR) for the ease of regulation.

In Ghana, Nigeria, and most countries in Africa, the ministry responsible for oil and gas is often a cabinet-level ministry with overall regulatory powers to implement, enforce, and ensure full compliance with petroleum legislation. The Minister is responsible for granting rights for the exploration, extraction, and production of oil and gas through different categories of authorisations. In the case of Ghana, the Minister has power to grant oil reconnaissance licenses and negotiate petroleum agreements on behalf of the state (see ss. 9 and 10 of the Petroleum (Exploration and Production), 2016 (Act 919)). Similarly, the Minister in Nigeria has the power to grant oil exploration licenses, oil prospecting licenses, and oil mining leases (see Petroleum Industry Act, 2021 (ACT No. 6), s.3(1)(g),(h)). For a comprehensive overview of the powers of the minister in the respective jurisdictions, see the various oil and gas codes in the applicable jurisdiction, particularly Act 919 of 2016 for Ghana and ACT No. 6 of 2021 for Nigeria.

4.3.4.2 The National Oil Company

In addition to dedicated sector ministries, most emerging and developing countries establish separate agencies and national oil companies (NOCs) for the oil and gas industry. For example the Nigerian National Petroleum Corporation (NNPC) and the Ghana National Petroleum Corporation (GNPC) are NOCs established by these countries as initial institutional vehicles through which their countries could ensure adequate state participation in their respective oil and gas industry Examples of other African NOCs include Sonatrach of Algeria, Grupo Sonangol of Angola, GEPetrol Equitorial Guinea, Societe Nationale des Hydrocarbures du Gabon, National Oil Corporation of Kenya, National Oil Corporation of Libya, and PetroSA of South Africa. Some African countries also have dedicated national gas companies such as the Ghana Gas Company Limited.

The underlying rationale for the establishment of national NOCs is to maximise economic efficiency and the generate social and economic benefits to citizens of resource-rich countries. In the particular case of Ghana, the GNPC was established as a corporate body for the commercial objects of undertaking 'exploration, development, production and disposal of petroleum' (see Ghana National Petroleum Corporation Act, 1983 (PNDCL 64), ss. 1, 2(1)) for and on behalf of the state. Originally, GNPC was also to execute related regulatory (see PNDCL 64, s. 2(2)) and advisory (see PNDCL 64 (n 51), s. 2(3)) functions.

The regulatory functions included promoting the exploration and the orderly and planned development of the oil and gas resources of Ghana, ensuring that Ghana obtains the greatest possible benefits from the development of its oil and gas resources, obtaining the effective transfer to Ghana of appropriate technology relating to oil and gas operations, ensuring the training of citizens of Ghana and the development of national capabilities in all aspects of oil and gas operations, and ensuring that oil and gas operations are conducted in such a manner so as to prevent adverse effects on the environment, resources, and people of Ghana.

The advisory functions include advising the Minister of Energy on matters relating to petroleum operations; engaging in petroleum operations, either alone or in association with others; entering into petroleum exploration and production agreements and other petroleum contracts; providing for the assistance, participation, or co-operation of contractors in connection with petroleum operations, either alone or in association with others; buy, sell, trade, store, exchange, import, or export petroleum, and, for this purpose, acquire or operate any installations, facilities, or means of transportation; engage in research and development programmes related to petroleum; and engage in such other activities, either alone or in association with others, as may be necessary or desirable for the carrying out of petroleum operations. Some of these original advisory functions have now been ceded by GNPC to the Petroleum Commission on the coming into force of the Petroleum Commission Act (n 41). The GNPC has since ceded its original regulatory powers to the Petroleum Commission (see Petroleum Commission Act, 2011 (Act 821), s. 24(2)) and is now a purely commercial venture of the state for oil and gas operations.

4.3.4.3 Ancillary Institutions

Emerging and developing countries have also established other supervisory institutions to superintend specific mandates and functions in their respective oil and gas industries. In Ghana, for example, the Petroleum Commission was established to regulate and manage the utilisation of petroleum resources and to coordinate the policies in relation thereto (see Petroleum Commission Act, 2011 (Act 821), ss. 1(1) and 2).

Similarly, the Public Interest and Accountability Committee (PIAC) was established (see Petroleum Revenue Management Act, 2011 (Act 815), s. 51) in Ghana to promote transparency and accountability in the management of oil and gas revenues.

In the case of Nigeria, the Nigerian Content Development and Monitoring Board was established for, among others, developing procedures that will guide, monitor, coordinate, and improve the requirements of substantive law (Sections 4 and 69(1) of the Nigerian Content Act). In Ghana, local content and participation, including job creation through the use of local expertise, goods and services, business, financing in the oil and gas industry value chain, and value retention, are all coordinated by the Petroleum Commission pursuant to the Petroleum Commission Act (n 41) and the accompanying Petroleum (Local Content and Local Participation) Regulations, 2013 (L.I. 2204). Similar and more specialised institutions exist in Nigeria, Ghana, Tanzania, Angola, and other emerging and developing countries.

4.3.4.4 Ministry or Department Responsible for the Environment

Environmental regulation of oil and gas activities is integral to the broader regulation of oil and gas operations in resource-rich countries. Emerging and developing countries are not excepted. Accordingly, to ensure compliance with environmental protection and continuous advancement, ministries or departments responsible for implementing government policy on these areas have been established in virtually every resource-rich African country and across the developing world, as detailed by Olawuyi (2018a, pp. 155–156).

In Ghana, the primary institution established to ensure environmental protection is the Environmental Protection Agency (EPA), established by the Environmental Protection Agency Act, 1994 (Act 490), which operates under the overall supervisory Ministry of Science, Environment and Innovation. Through the Environmental Assessment Regulations, 1999 (L.I. 1652), the EPA has the general obligation to prevent damage to the environment in the course of operations (including oil and gas operations) of a business enterprise. These Regulations not only contain the policy direction of the EPA, but, together with their enabling legislation, also empower the Agency 'to manage, control and monitor compliance of environmental regulations by specific industries', including the oil and gas industry (see generally L.I. 1652).

4.4 Overview of Contractual Arrangements and Fiscal Systems

The fiscal regimes adopted across emerging and developing countries are broadly categorised into two, concessionary and contractual, subject to industry-wide considerations, such as:

- i Determining the degree of willingness of a state to attract oil and gas investment (which is brought about by reduced tax obligations and other fiscal incentives).
- ii The nature and character of state or national oil company participation (depending on whether solely as regulator or as commercial participant as well).
- iii Nature of returns expected (this could be purely royalties or focus on share of oil, gas, or minerals produced).
- iv Risk allocation, local content, and expectations on transparency and accountability in revenue collection and related matters.

Although fiscal regime procedures are often spelt out in the constitution and primary laws of most of these countries, the fine details are considered within the framework of contractual arrangements between the state and the investor community (Olawuyi, 2018a at p. 192). A concession is a right granted by the state to an IOC to search for, win, explore, extract, and develop oil and gas resources from a defined area of land over a stipulated time period, and, if oil and gas was discovered, to produce and market or export the resource, subject of course to specific privileges (Olawuyi, 2018a at p. 200).

In sum, the central organizing principle underlying concessionary fiscal regimes is that the host country (HC) grants the IOC ownership over all oil and gas production, subject to the possible reservation of royalty (in cash or kind) which is a share of production, payable to the HC (Duval et al. (2009) at p. 57). Accordingly:

> [T]he IOC may book all the corresponding oil and gas field reserves, with the possible exception of any royalty taken in kind. However, the HC is and remains the sole owner of the petroleum when it is in the ground (*in situ*) prior to production. The HC's revenues generally consist of a royalty paid by the concessionaire, either in kind or in value, an income tax on the IOC's net profits earned in the HC, and other fees and taxes, possibly including a special petroleum tax on 'excess' profits. These features are so common to concession agreements that these agreements are often referred to as tax and royalty contracts, an apt characterisation. Concession agreements are also known as license agreements, and called *licenses* and *concessions* for short.
>
> (Duval et al. (2009) at p. 57)

Whether in its traditional or modern form, and subject to contextual peculiarities, the concessionary fiscal regime has been applied in countries such as Kuwait, Oman, Iraq, Nigeria, South Africa, Ghana, Namibia, Mozambique, Algeria, and Cameroon. Olawuyi (2018a at pp. 193–205) discusses the evolution of the concessionary fiscal regime, including its traditional and modern dimensions.

In contra-distinction to the concessionary regime, contractual fiscal regimes are agreements that seek to balance the allocation of rights and interests in resource extraction between the HC and the IOC. Common issues addressed in contractual regimes include modalities for sharing control over the financing, exploration, production, and marketing of oil and gas resources based on clear, comprehensive, and negotiated terms and conditions.

Among others, the variants of contractual fiscal regimes include production sharing, joint venture, joint operating and service, assignment and participating interest, and oil sales agreements. Olawuyi (2018a at pp. 191–232) provides a comprehensive study of the concessionary and other contractual regimes. The contractual system, in its varying arrangements, has been practiced across emerging and developing countries. Countries that subscribe to contractual fiscal regimes include Nigeria, Angola, and Ghana, all of which operate these contractual fiscal arrangements alongside concessionary arrangements (Olawuyi, (2018a at p. 205). By way of illustration, Box 4.1 gives a vivid account of Ghana's current upstream oil and gas fiscal regime.

Box 4.1 Ghana's Current Fiscal Regime

Ghana began oil production in commercial quantities in 2010 after discovering oil in 2007. Before then, Ghana had been conducting exploration for the discovery of oil but had not been successful. Due to this, the upstream oil sector has had a number of legal frameworks to help guide the exploration and exploitation of oil and gas. The first Act was enacted in 1984 known as the PNDC Law 84. In August 2016, this law was repealed and replaced by the Petroleum (Exploration and Production) Act 2016 (Act 919). The object of this Act as stipulated is 'safe secure, sustainable and efficient petroleum activities to achieve optimal long-term petroleum resources and exploitation and utilisation for the benefit and welfare of people of Ghana'. This law provides the fiscal regime of Ghana which comprises royalties, carried interest, income taxes, additional oil entitlement, and other taxes. The Ghana National Petroleum Corporation (GNPC) determines the concessionaires in the oil and gas sector in Ghana.

Prior to the development of the Jubilee field, GNPC only practised the concessionary system where only royalties were collected from International Oil Companies (IOCs). It now practises a hybrid system of royalties and taxes. This system is unique because it has a mixture of concessionary systems and taxes such as corporate income tax, state participation, and profit-sharing. Thus, the general principle of taxation and petroleum taxation is applied in Ghana. This means that the fiscal regime practised in Ghana gives a piece of general information about the sharing of petroleum wealth between the state and the IOCs. The 2016 Petroleum Exploration Act (Act 919) proposes the following fiscal regime arrangements for Ghana:

- **Royalties:** Ghana charges a royalty rate between 5% and 12.5% of the oil extracted by the IOCs. This rate varies depending on the oil field or bloc and the depth of the water matter in the royalty rate determined for an IOC. However, a 35% royalty rate is charged for natural gas.
- **Carried Interest:** The state is entitled to 10% of any field discovered without any costs to be incurred. That is what the state carries throughout the development stages of the oil bloc.
- **Additional Interest:** Within 60 days of discovery, the state through GNPC can opt for an additional interest of 3.75% in the Jubilee field, and this varies from bloc to bloc. Ghana has the option to obtain up to 15% of additional interest.
- **Income Tax on Petroleum:** The old law provides a corporate tax of 50%, but this can be altered which is currently at 35% for the Jubilee field and other fields in Ghana.

- **Additional Oil Entitlements (AOE):** The state can seek additional oil entitlements if after royalty and after-tax inflation-adjusted Rate of Return (RoR) exceeds 12.5% in progressivity. The following rate will be applied subsequently:
    - 15% is applied for more than 12.5% but less than 17.5%.
    - 20% is applied for more than 17.5% but less than 22.5%.
    - 22.5% is applied for more than 22.5% but less than 27.5%.
    - 27.5% is applied for more than 27.55 but less than 30%.
- **Other Taxes:** The law also allows for taxes such as surface rent, training fees, and withholding taxes. The surface rent is a charge of US$30 for sqkm/year. This price is subject to increment by the law as the IOCs continue to extend. However, during the development stage, surface rental is US$100/sqkm/year.

Conclusion

This fiscal regime constitutes the amount of oil and gas revenues Ghana raises from its petroleum wealth. The amount raised is spent through an arrangement by the Petroleum Revenue Management Act 2011 and as amended in 2015. The spending is smoothened between current consumption and future consumption.

4.4.1 Authors' Construct, 2022

Others such as Azerbaijan, Senegal, Mozambique, Libya, Kenya, Angola, and Cameroon all apply the contractual fiscal regime either alone or in hybrid with the concessionary fiscal regime. Olawuyi (2018a at pp. 193–199) provides a comprehensive matrix of countries applying these fiscal regimes either alone or alongside others, using the case of Azerbaijan on p. 207.

According to Duval et al. (2009, at p. 57), while contractual fiscal regimes are more often used in developing countries, concessions are somewhat more commonly used in industrialised countries. However, Olawuyi (2018a, at p. 200) has maintained that the most widely used fiscal arrangement in African extractive industries is the concession. This raises a major concern for investors who may be wary when entering into the oil and gas industry in any emerging or developing country, especially in Africa.

4.5 Conclusion

The oil and gas industry is witnessing rapid reforms in emerging and developing countries. While the rationale for reforms is hardly contested, the many arrangements across the value chain evoke similar but diverse approaches among resource-rich emerging and developing economies, which require crucial attention by the investor community. This chapter explored the evolving legal, regulatory, and fiscal arrangements and provided information on the institutional frameworks, key processes, and actors in the oil and gas industry in these countries. The essential industry challenges that investors usually face in developing countries are identified, including questions of resource ownership and control, risk mitigation, as well as transparency and accountability in revenue and fiscal regimes.

To address the challenges identified in this chapter, investors are advised to always conduct a comprehensive policy and legal due diligence to ascertain the applicable policy objectives, legal requirements, juridical nature, and institutional architecture when dealing with resource-rich emerging and developing countries.

References

Auty, R. (1993). *Sustaining development in mineral economies: The resource curse*. London: Routledge.

Bouckaert, B (1990). What is property? *Harvard Journal of Law and Public Policy*, 13, 781.

Constitution of the Federal Republic of Nigeria. (1999). Laws of the Federation of Nigeria 2004, c 23.

Constitution of the Independent State of Papua New Guinea (n.d.). http://www.parliament.gov.pg/images/misc/PNG-CONSTITUTION.pdf

Constitution of the Republic of Ghana, 1992.

Davies, W., and Fouracre, P. (eds) (1995). *Property and power in the early middle ages*. Cambridge: Cambridge University Press.

Duval, C., et al. (2009). *International petroleum exploration and exploitation agreements: Legal, economics & policy aspects*. 2nd ed. New York: Barrows Inc.

Environmental Assessment Regulations, 1999 (L. I. 1652).

Gao, Z. (1994). *International petroleum contracts: Current trends and new directions*. London: Graham & Trotman

Ghana's Income Tax Act, 2016 (Act 896).

Ghana National Petroleum Corporation Act, 1983 (P.N.D.C.L 64).

Ghana's Petroleum Commission Act, 2011 (Act 821).

Ghana's Petroleum Revenue Management Act, 2011 (Act 815), as amended.

Heringshaw, V. (2004). 'Natural Resources – curse or blessing?' *New Economy*, 174.

Hunter, T. (2009). 'Comparative law as an instrument in transnational law: The example of petroleum regulation. *Bond Law Review*, 21(3), 42 at 45.

KPMG. (2017). *Oil and gas in Africa: Africa's reserves, potentials and prospects*. https://www.resourcedata.org/hr/document/rgi-oil-and-gas-in-africa-africa-s-reserves-potential-and-prospects.

Nakicenovic, N., Grubler, A., and McDonald, A. (eds). (1998). *Global energy perspectives*. 1st ed. Cambridge: Cambridge University Press.

Nalule, V. R. (2020). Transitioning to a low carbon economy: Is Africa ready to bid farewell to fossil fuels? In *The Palgrave handbook of managing fossil fuels and energy transitions* (pp. 261–286). Basingstoke: Palgrave Macmillan.

Nalule, V. R., and Acheampong T. (2021). Energy transition indicators in African countries: Managing the possible decline of fossil fuels and tackling energy access challenges. *The Journal of Sustainable Development, Law and Policy*, 12(1), 1–48.

National Content Policy for the Petroleum Subsector in Uganda (2008). https://pau.ug/uploads/NATIONAL_LOCAL_CONTENT_POLICY_FOR_THE_PETROLEUM_SUBSECTOR_IN_UGANDA.pdf

National Energy Policy (2010, February). https://www.energymin.gov.gh/policies.

Nigeria's Petroleum Industry Act, 2021 (ACT No. 6).

Njotini, M. (2017). Examining the 'objects of property– rights' - Lessons from the Roman, Germanic and Dutch legal history. *De Jure*, 50(1), 136–155.

Olawuyi, D. S. (2015). Legal strategies and tools for mitigating legal risks associated with oil and gas investments in Africa. *OPEC Energy Review*, 39(3), 247–265.

Olawuyi, D. S. (2018a). *Extractives industry Law in Africa*. Doha: Springer Nature Switzerland AG.

Olawuyi, D. S. (2018b). *Regulation of upstream oil & gas*. Lexis Nexis: Gulf Legal Advisor.

Omorogbe, Y. (2001). *Oil and gas law in Nigeria: Simplified*. Lagos: Malthouse Press Limited.

Omorogbe, Y., and Oniemola, P. (2010). Property rights in oil and gas under dominial regimes. In A. McHarg, B. Barton, A. Bradbrook, & L. Godden (Eds.), *Property and the law in energy and natural resources*. Oxford: Oxford University Press.

Stiblitz, J. E., and Spiegal, S. (2007). *Escaping the resource curse*. New York: Columbia University Press.

The Nigerian Oil and Gas Content Development Act of 2010. https://resourcegovernance.org/sites/default/files.pdf

UNECA. (2011). *Minerals and Africa's development: The international study group report on Africa's mineral regimes*. Addis Ababa: UN Economic Commission for Africa.

US Energy Information Administration. (2013). *Oil and natural gas in Sub-Saharan Africa*. https://www.eia.gov/pressroom/presentations/howard_08012013.pdf.

5 Oil and Gas Energy Security

Raphael Odoom, Runar Brännlund, Amin Karimu, and Jonas Nanzoninge

5.1 Introduction

Several strands of academic and public discourses uphold weighty concerns regarding energy security across the globe. This is largely because energy is an essential element in the provision of fundamental human needs and services, as well as a vital contributing component of efforts aimed at poverty reduction and sustainable development. Accordingly, energy (such as natural gas, electricity, crude, fuel, coal) is strongly linked to socio-cultural, environmental, and, ultimately, economic development (Martchamadol and Kumar, 2012; Hughes and Lipscy, 2013; Valdés, 2018). Evidently, the world's energy consumption keeps mounting each year due to growth of the global population, whose demand for energy access seems ever-increasing. It is also reported that within the last decade, the Energy Transition Index (ETI) indicates that over 80% of countries realised improvement in their energy systems, although additional effort is required to put an end to the global energy-related menace (World Economic Forum, 2018).

From the early 2000s, the relevance of energy security as a public discourse has been growing along with other concerns among academics and policymakers. The quick depletion of some energy reserves across the globe, increasing volatility in energy prices, inadequate fossil fuels, the quest to decarbonise energy systems, and geopolitical supply pressures (Bielecki, 2002; Hughes and Lipscy, 2013) are among the key drivers of the mounting problems with energy security. Quite profoundly, energy security is currently a persistent central topic in the politics of energy among many nations, largely due to energy supply as well as its strong connection with other energy-related matters like the mitigation of climate change and equitable access to contemporary energy (Goldthau, 2011). In the 1970s, however, concerns of energy security mainly emphasised the stable distribution of economical oil due to price manipulation by exporters and the threat of embargoes (Yergin, 1988).

Irrespective of its level and size of progress, every country requires an energy system that is reliable for meeting the demands of its energy end-usage. Such a system evolves over time, and the changes in it in most cases have significant and comprehensive consequences for the users of energy within the country

DOI: 10.4324/9781003315056-7

as well as other stakeholders. Liberalisations in the energy market as well as the integration of technology in securing and managing various forms of energy in recent times, therefore, mean that the usage and concerns about the term energy security will constantly evolve in the coming years. Therefore, actions and policies to be designed in response to the future dynamics of energy security within and among nations should be continually improved and upgraded. Notably, there is a strong consensus among both scholars and policymakers on the need for energy plans to be congruent with environmental and economic objectives. Consequently, this has become a major commitment for several countries that are aiming to transform their energy systems.

The rest of the chapter is structured as follows: Section 5.2 explains what energy security is; Section 5.3 discusses energy security in a global perspective; Section 5.4 presents and analyses energy security in emerging and developing countries; and finally Section 5.5 concludes the chapter.

5.2 What Is Energy Security?

Energy security (ES) is usually described as a concept that accounts for nations' ability to successfully meet their energy needs. Even though defining energy security is difficult, various descriptive perspectives have been spawned, and researchers and policymakers have provided many definitions. However, it is worth noting that the meanings assigned to energy security, to a very large extent, are context dependent. Ang et al. (2015) suggest that specifics such as level of economic development, a country's special circumstances, prevailing geopolitical matters, perceptions of risks, and the strength of its energy system make energy policy polysemic and multi-dimensional. Consequently, some streams of research focus mainly on the security of the supply part, such as energy prices and availability, in defining energy security (see, Jamasb and Pollitt, 2008; Winzer, 2012; Cherp and Jewell, 2014). On the other hand, there appear to be a number of studies, which define the term in a more inclusive way that comprises downstream outcomes like the impact on social and economic welfare (Vivoda, 2010; Le and Nguyen, 2019).

Following from the point made, it appears that the definitions and properties of energy security are dynamic and change with prevailing conditions over time. The emergence and advancement of energy technologies, for example, have triggered an increase in climate change consciousness and other sustainability-related issues, thereby reshaping the pertinent dimensions of energy security. In fact, countries such as South Africa and Senegal consider the 'fight against poverty' as part of their definition of energy security (Martchamadol and Kumar, 2012). According to the Asia Pacific Energy Research Centre (2007), 'the ability of an economy to guarantee the availability of energy resource supply in a sustainable and timely manner with the energy price being at a level that will not adversely affect the economic performance of the economy' is what constitutes energy security. Other criteria have been used to define energy security, such as obtaining energy supply for social endeavours, defence, and other purposes. Other schools of thought describe the term as the availability of good-quality energy resource that is timely and sustainable enough without harming the environment but accessible by all citizens.

Ultimately, defining energy security involves more than asking around (Cherp, 2012). Given the disparities in economic contexts, the definition for energy security provided for advanced countries covers a robust energy scheme and securing at satisfactory prices the quantity of energy that will be required for people's livelihood, social and economic activities, defence, and other goals (Murakami et al., 2011). Likewise, a general definition of energy security touted for developing countries encompasses the availability of adequate energy supply – both in quantity and quality. This is, at all times, expected to meet all requirements for citizens at stable and reasonable prices that also result in sustained economic performance, better quality of life, and poverty alleviation without any harm to the environment (Martchamadol and Kumar, 2012). The obvious implication from these economically differentiated definitions is that varied measurements and indicators will also be used in quantifying energy security in these settings.

Notwithstanding these perspectives, current and future definitions of ES are most likely to depict the continuous accessibility of energy in varied forms (reliability), in adequate quantities (adequacy), and at reasonable prices (affordability). In other words, it is access to sufficient (adequacy), reliable energy resources (reliability) at affordable prices (affordability) for the predictable future, which is free from grave risk of key disruptions or service. The key elements in the definition of energy security are: *Reliability* (short-term physical equilibrium), *Adequacy* (long-term economic equilibrium), and *Affordability* (social equilibrium and economic access). It is important to note that different energy sources pose different security challenges. Non-renewables for instance pose the security concern of inadequacy, whereas renewables pose the challenge of intermittency.

5.3 Global Perspective of Energy Security

From historical accounts, energy security has been mainly linked with the supply of oil. This is due to the first oil crisis that hit the world in 1973 and which led to high-oil-import-dependent countries such as the United States and most of Western Europe to start thinking of energy security issues. This led to the establishment of the International Energy Agency (IEA) to act in response to such crises. In recent years, energy security is not limited to oil but to all energy sources due to the increasing complexity of energy systems. Globally, more than 90% of transport energy in many countries is from oil products. As a result, interruptions in oil supplies could have disastrous impacts across mobility, production, and distribution of food; medical services; national security; and manufacturing, among others. Conventional oil resources are ever more clustered in just a few regions, thereby creating high import dependency among countries that rely extensively on natural gas. Consequently, price fluctuations and supply disruptions are normally the most crucial energy security issues in such countries (Johansson et al., 2012).

Across the globe, the subject of energy security may be considered as one that is interminable, given some dynamics posed by energy demand and supply. From the energy security debates over the years, hints of external political and security pressures on energy suppliers, for instance, are assuming a growing relevance. In 2014, Poland's former Prime Minister (who later became EU President) tabled the creation of an Energy Union as a mechanism to fortify policy and expand measures and goals to meet gas supply concerns (Austvik, 2016). Prior to and after this proposition, security risks to energy supply as well as energy infrastructure were often quoted as a source of alarm in public debates, especially on Europe's energy relationship with (North) Africa (Lacher and Kumetat, 2011; Tichý, 2019). Indeed, there have been key developments in most developed economies which have led to a high system performance and readiness in energy transition, resulting in an enhancement of sustainable environment (World Economic Forum, 2018).

In a study by Wang and Zhou (2017), the results showed that most countries are struggling to develop a comprehensively secure energy system. From their study, only 1 country out of 162 achieved an 'Excellent' score, and 37 countries achieved a 'Good' score. These, together, accounted for almost a quarter of the sampled countries. The researchers aver that the spatial discrepancy in the global performance of national ES is highly crucial. It was identified that the 'Good' and 'Excellent' groups were domiciled in North America and Western Europe, while the 'Limited' group are concentrated in Europe, Asia, and the Middle East. Africa and Asia had the largest concentration of the 'Weak' and 'Poor' groups. Meanwhile, sufficient global energy supplies, at both micro and macro levels, are critical for sustainable development, appropriate functioning of economies, and human welfare.

In Europe, Baran (2007) opined that the lack of dependable and sustainable European access to energy signifies an obvious threat to the continent's security, citing that if the situation continued, the EU faces imminent further danger, as its dependence left it indebted to Russian interests. Such dependency highlights anxieties about the security of energy supplies, especially those emanating from contexts with the likelihood of geopolitical or social-economic conflicts (Hasanov et al., 2020). Over the last decade, however, there have been many revisions to the narratives within the energy sector. Notable among them are the dramatic changes in the global energy landscape, which have been triggered by the rise of new technologies and the help of policies favouring renewable energy sources (Franki and Višković, 2015). It is noticeable that the right combination of technologies and policies on energy security has fuelled economic growth; countries that effectively await energy developments are deriving significant advantages on the global market while those which fail to recognise the essence of innovative trends run the risk of making unfortunate policy and investment choices.

Given that it is the largest energy-consuming country in the world (Wu, 2014), possibly due to its population, China's energy policies, for instance, have affected Asia's energy security situation in various ways as the Chinese government has implemented appropriate policies to better various dimensions of energy security. As reported by Yao and Chang (2014), the country has taken two key measures to reverse the downward outlook in energy security by implementing the 'going out' strategy and the 'cap-and-trade' policy. Moreover, in Latin America, there have been propositions for variable renewable energy – particularly, the use of hybrid power generation systems that combine multiple sources of energy by utilising their matching features to neutralise the variability of energy production. Viviescas et al. (2019) indicate that given the renewable energy potentials, Brazil, for example, could offer an important role regarding renewable energy integration in Latin America.

As a subject that has become a significant concern in many regions across the globe, there has been a particular emphasis on the alarming rate of energy security in emerging and developing countries in recent times. Batidzirai and Johnson (2012) aver that for many aid-dependent, oil-importing countries in (southern) Africa especially, the abilities to meet a growing demand for energy are top economic priorities. Indeed, disruptions in oil supply, fuel shortages, power blackouts, and high and/or volatile oil prices are hinted to be some of the key issues triggering the concerns about energy security in the region. Yet, these are issues that appear to have been surmounted in most developed countries. Consequently, it has been suggested that energy security studies of evolutions in developing countries should be given more profound consideration. This is because they are unlikely to simply transplant available frameworks from their sources to their different implementation contexts (Hansen et al., 2018).

5.4 Energy Security: Emerging and Developing Countries' Perspective

Energy security in the emerging and developing countries is analysed on the basis of oil and gas dependency, political risk of major oil-producing countries, domestic refining capability, and diversity in source of supply.

5.4.1 Oil and Gas Dependency

OPEC is the major oil-producing group in the world, contributing about 41% of total oil production in 2019 (IEA, 2021). The share is much higher for OPEC+,[1] about 60%. This highlights the significance of OPEC in influencing the global oil supply and price movements. Most of the oil-producing countries are in emerging and developing countries, and since oil and gas reserves are not uniformly distributed globally, it creates the dependence of countries without such resources on a few countries that have them. The global economy depends on only 13 countries for about 41% of total oil needs, creating some vulnerability of the non-producing countries to disruption of oil production in these 13 countries, as highlighted by some energy crises such as those that occurred in 1973, 1979, and 1990 and their implications on oil prices, and ultimately on the world economy, especially oil-importing countries.

One key metric to determine the level of a country's dependence on oil and gas resources is how reliant the country is on oil and gas as an export commodity and as a share of GDP. Available statistics from the World Bank suggest that about 15 countries have at least 80% of their merchandise exports made up of fuel exports over the period 2000 to 2019. The topmost ranked country is Iraq (98.5%), followed by Algeria (97.7%), Angola (96.2%), Libya (94.2%), and Brunei Darussalam (94.1%) (see, Figure 5.1). Saudi Arabia, the de facto leader of OPEC, only occupies the twelfth position. All the top ten

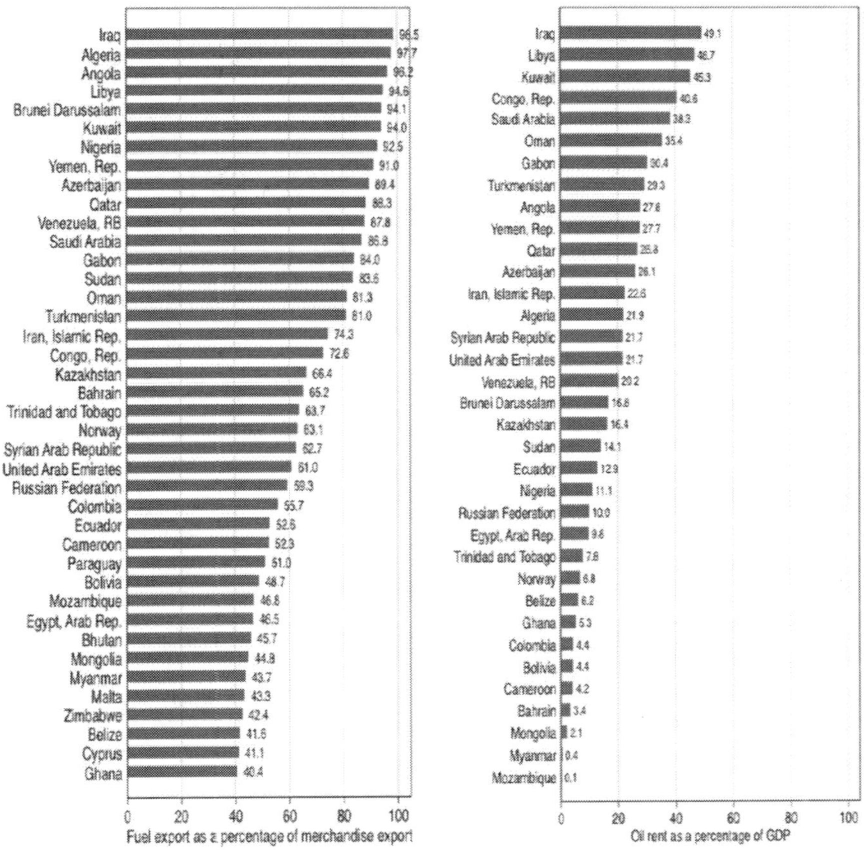

Figure 5.1 Fuel exports as a percentage of merchandise exports and oil rent as a percentage of GDP for oil-producing countries

Source: Authors' computation based on data from World Bank (2022), World Development indicators

countries on the list are emerging and developing countries, suggesting the significant reliance of these countries on oil and gas resources. The topmost ranked developed country in terms of export dependence is Norway (63.1%) which only occupies the twenty-second position in the global ranking. It appears that despite having significant oil endowment, Norway managed to diversify her exports relative to some of the oil- and gas-rich countries in developing countries such as Angola. Furthermore, Norway is the only developed country among the list of countries with at least 50% of their merchandise exports contributed by fuel exports; all the other countries are emerging and developing countries.

In the case of Angola, only less than 4% of her exports constitute non-oil commodities such as small quantities of diamonds, coffee, sisal, and fish, suggesting a less diversified export sector of the country and high external risk exposure to the global oil market, as any disruption in the oil market that affects prices will significantly affect Angola's export earnings. Furthermore, most of the exports do not include manufactured products. In comparison, Norway has more export products beyond oil, which include electrical and electronic equipment, machinery, nuclear reactors, boilers, optical and medical apparatus, aluminium, ships, and boats, among others, that help diversity her export risk. The situation in Angola is not different from the top oil-exporting countries in the emerging and developing countries such as Iraq and Algeria.

Furthermore, considering the contribution of oil rent to GDP, Iraq (49.1%), Libya (46.7%), Kuwait (45.3%), DR Congo (40.6%), and Saudi Arabia (38.3%) are the top five countries in the world. The only developed country in the list is Norway, which is ranked the twenty-sixth with oil rent contributing only 6.8% of its GDP. The top 25 countries on the list are all emerging and developing countries, with the top 3 from the Middle East and North Africa (MENA) sub-region. The two indicators (fuel exports as a share of merchandise exports and oil rent as a share of GDP) both suggest a significant dependence on oil and gas resources by the emerging and developing countries, both for export earnings and contribution to growth via GDP, making this group of countries very reliant on oil and gas resources for growth and development.

5.4.2 Political Risk of Major Producing Countries

The oil and gas industry faces several significant risks along its value chain activities that include economic risks such as price risk, geological risk, environmental risk, and political risk. The significance of these risks on any country in relation to energy security will depend to a large extent on whether the country is a net exporter or importer. One key factor that is used in assessing potential risk of disruption of global oil production is geopolitical risk, a key factor that accounted for several of the historical energy crises the world has experienced, starting from the 1973 energy crisis. Data from a British Petroleum (BP) statistical review, 2022, suggest that in 2020, the top ten oil-producing countries accounted for about 73% of global oil production, of which the United States

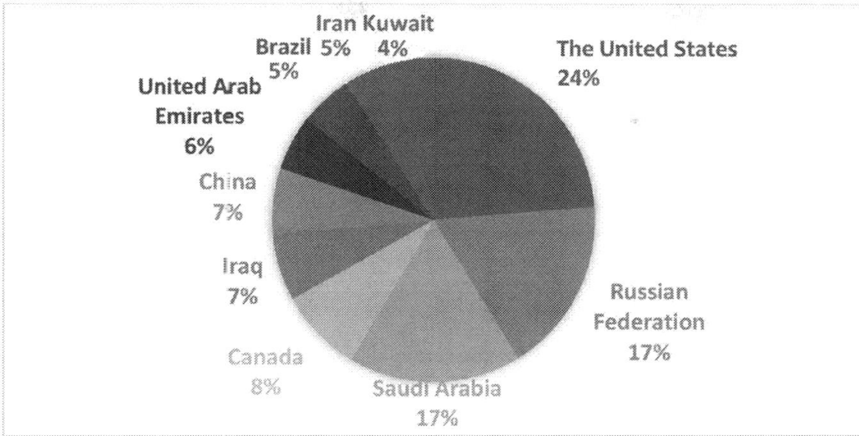

Figure 5.2 Share of oil production among the top ten oil producers in 2020

Source: Authors' computation using data from BP Statistical Review (July, 2020)

(24%) is the top producer, followed by Russia (17%) and Saudi Arabia (17%) as shown in Figure 5.2 (British Petroleum, 2020). This highlights the potential vulnerabilities of the global economy with respect to oil because any significant disruption in production in these countries creates significant price pressure on oil products globally, as the recent Russian invasion of Ukraine has demonstrated.

Furthermore, the relationship between oil production and degree of political risk, as shown in Figure 5.3, supports the observation that high geopolitical risks in key oil-producing countries have the potential to disrupt global oil production.

The linear line fit for the relationship between oil production and political risk, using data from ten key oil producers over the period 1984 to 2011, shows a positive association between the two. Thus, high political risk is associated with low production, and low political risk is associated with high oil production. The political risk variable is taken from the PRS Group's International Country Risk Guide (2012), where the index is computed using three components: internal conflicts, external conflicts, and military involvement in politics in the top ten oil-producing countries, as reported in Figure 5.2. Of all the countries on the list of top ten oil-producing countries, only two are developed countries. Despite the emerging and developing countries being highly represented on the list (eight countries), they comprise less than 2% of all the emerging and developing countries. This suggests that a significant number of the emerging and developing countries are also susceptible to geopolitical risk consequences as they may well depend on the few countries that are net exporters of oil.

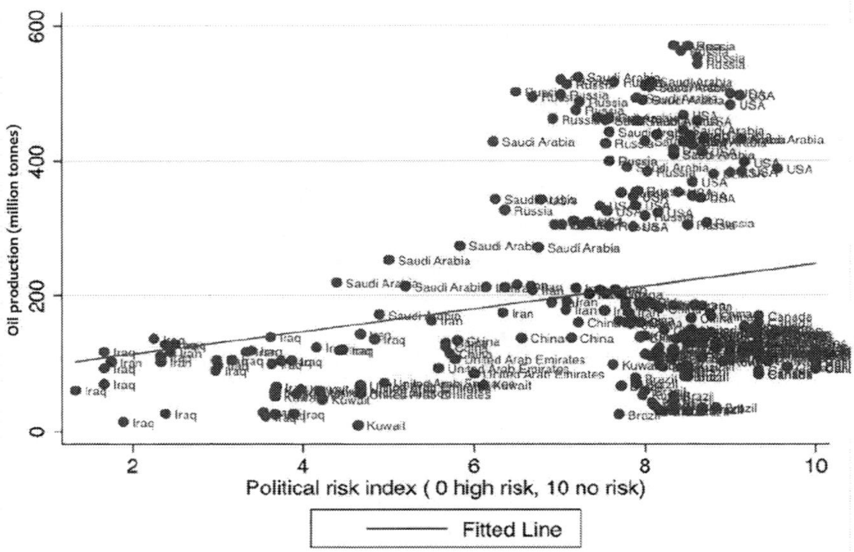

Figure 5.3 Relationship between political risk and oil production for top ten oil-producing countries (1984 to 2011)

Source: Authors' computation

5.4.3 Domestic Refining Capacity

Refining capacity highlights the countries that have the capacity to serve the domestic oil consumption requirement and partially reduces the countries' domestic vulnerability to refined oil products. Figure 5.4 shows the distribution of global refinery capacity for the year 2020. Only two countries, China and the United States, have refinery capacity in the region of 10,143 barrels or more per day. Russia has the third-largest refining capacity globally (6,736 barrels per day), followed by India, Saudi Arabia, and Iran in that order.

In the case of Africa, the country with the largest size of refining capacity is Egypt (795 barrels per day), followed by Algeria, South Africa, and Nigeria (460 barrels per day). The country with the largest oil production in Africa (Nigeria, 26%) is only ranked fourth in refining capacity in Africa. The daily production in Nigeria in the year 2020 was 1,798 barrels per day, whereas the refining capacity in that year was only 460 barrels per day. This suggests that a significant amount of Nigerian oil is exported to other countries (especially China) to be refined, given the low domestic capacity in Nigeria, reducing the value chain employment and revenue-generating potentials for the refining segment of the Nigerian oil industry.

Figure 5.4 Distribution of global oil refining capacity for 2020

Source: Authors' computation using data from BP Statistical Review (July, 2020)

5.4.4 Diversity in Source of Supply

In the emerging and developing regions, China and India are the two leading importing countries. China's total crude oil imports in 2020 were about 22 times the total of Africa's imports. China's major oil suppliers are Saudi Arabia, Russia, South and Central America, West Africa, and Iraq and other Middle East countries. In total, China imports oil from 17 different countries and regions, but with a significant concentration on the top 5 countries listed (they account for about 65.5% of the total oil imports). The top five oil supply sources for India are Iraq, Saudi Arabia, UAE, West Africa, and South and Central America as shown in Table 5.1. These five countries account for about 71% of India's total oil imports in 2020.

Africa's major importing countries and regions include Saudi Arabia which occupies the topmost spot, followed by West Africa, Kuwait, Iraq, and UAE. Total imports in Africa in 2020 were about 25.5 million tonnes, the second least oil-importing developing region. South and Central America is the least oil importing region among the emerging and developing group of countries in 2020.

Global gas movements based on the top three countries that supply the various regions in the world are presented in Table 5.2. The data in the table show that across all the regions, the top three supplying countries account for at least 60.9% of their total gas supply. In some regions (South and Central America), the share of the top three supplying countries is as high as 87%. The major sources of gas imports for Middle East and Africa are Qatar (3.2 billion cubic metres), Nigeria

Table 5.1 Crude Oil Import Sources in the Emerging and Developing Countries

Crude (Million Tonnes)	*To*					
From	*South & Central America*	*Middle East*	*Africa*	*China*	*India*	*Other Asia Pacific*
Canada	0.5	†	†	3.2	1.0	0.3
Mexico	0.1	0.1	–	0.4	8.0	7.0
The USA	8.5	1.9	0.2	19.8	10.7	26.9
South & Central America	–	1.2	0.6	72.0	16.0	5.2
Europe	0.7	0.5	0.4	18.8	1.6	2.9
Russia	0.4	0.1	0.1	83.4	2.6	10.6
Other CIS	0.1	7.1	0.9	6.3	3.6	6.9
Iraq	0.3	1.0	1.4	60.1	47.3	13.6
Kuwait	–	†	3.6	27.5	9.9	37.5
Saudi Arabia	2.9	10.6	8.4	84.9	37.6	79.5
UAE	†	†	1.1	31.2	22.2	34.6
Other Middle East	†	5.7	0.1	53.1	12.9	15.3
North Africa	1.0	0.9	†	3.4	4.5	4.7
West Africa	3.3	4.3	8.1	71.8	21.4	16.0
East & South Africa	†	†	†	2.1	0.6	0.3
Australasia	†	0.2	†	1.4	0.1	5.6
China	†	†	†	–	0.1	0.7
India	†	†	†	–	–	†
Japan	†	–	†	–	–	†
Singapore	†	†	†	–	†	1.5
Other Asia Pacific	†	0.4	0.5	17.8	4.0	–
Total imports	**17.8**	**34.0**	**25.5**	**557.2**	**203.9**	**269.0**

Source: Authors' compilation from BP Statistical Review (July, 2020)

Note: - denotes that data is available, but the country is not among the top three supply countries to the reference region. † Denotes that the data is less than 0.005.

(1.5 billion cubic metres), and the United States (1.3 billion cubic metres). These three countries cumulatively account for 65.2% of total gas supply to the Middle East and Africa. In the case of South and Central America, the three major supplying countries to the region are the United States (7.1 billion cubic metres), Trinidad and Tobago (4.2 billion cubic metres), and Qatar (0.9 billion cubic metres).

5.5 Conclusion

Globally, oil and gas resources are not evenly distributed on the basis of natural endowment. Only 13 countries that constitute the Oil Producing and Exporting Countries (OPEC) accounted for 79.4% of proven global oil reserves (OPEC, 2019). In addition, the world's economic activities depend significantly on oil

Table 5.2 Global Gas Import from the Top Three Countries in 2022

Billion Cubic Metres	*From*								
To	*US*	*Trinidad & Tobago*	*Nigeria*	*Qatar*	*Russia*	*Australia*	*Malaysia*	*Total*	*Top 3 Share of Total*
North America	0.9	2.5	0.4	–	–	–	–	4.6	82.6%
South & Central America	7.1	4.2		0.9				13.9	87.8%
Europe	25.6	–	–	30.2	17.2	–	–	114.8	63.6%
Middle East & Africa	1.3	–	1.5	3.2	–	–	–	9.2	65.2%
Asia & Pacific	–	–	–	71.8	–	106.0	32.8	345.4	60.9%

Source: Authors' compilation from BP Statistical Review (July, 2020)

Note: - denote that data is available, but the country is not among the top three supply countries to the reference region.

and gas resources, creating significant security risk for countries that depend on other countries for these very important resources for modern production and consumption processes. All the 13 OPEC members are emerging and developing countries (EDC), but they constitute only about 7% of the total EDC in 2022. This suggests that the majority of EDCs significantly depend on a few oil-producing and exporting countries for their oil and gas needs.

Oil and gas are the most consumed fossil fuels in the emerging and developing region, driven partly by population growth, demands for rapid economic growth and transformation, an increasing middle class, and the associated personal transportation needs. Despite the increasing demands by various policymakers for a transition to a low carbon economy due to the impacts on climate change, reliance on oil and gas by developing countries in their quest to grow and develop their respective countries will increase in the short-to-medium term.

The evidence from key indicators for energy security such as oil and gas dependency, diversity in source of supply, political risk of major producing countries, and domestic refinery capability showed some level of energy security, especially for oil-importing developing countries in South and Central America, Africa, Southeast Asia, and some countries in Asia and the Pacific. In terms of refinery capacity, Africa is the most vulnerable region, with the least capacity to produce refined products domestically.

Furthermore, evidence suggests that significant geopolitical risks exist for the top ten oil-producing and exporting countries, suggesting the vulnerability of the global economy to disruption of oil supply, due likely to both internal and external political tensions such as the current Russian invasion of Ukraine and its impact on oil supply and consequently on prices.

Note

1 A new group formed in 2016 that includes the original 13 OPEC members along with Azerbaijan, Bahrain, Brunei, Kazakhstan, Malaysia, Mexico, Oman, Russia, South Sudan, and Sudan.

References

Ang, B. W., Choong, W. L., and Ng, T. S. (2015). Energy security: Definitions, dimensions, and indexes. *Renewable and Sustainable Energy Reviews*, 42, 1077–1093.

Asia Pacific Energy Research Centre. (2007). *Quest for energy security in the 21st Century: Resources and constraints*. Tokyo: Asia Pacific Energy Research Centre.

Austvik, O. G. (2016). The Energy Union and security-of-gas supply. *Energy Policy*, 96, 372–382.

Baran, Z. (2007). EU energy security: Time to end Russian leverage. *Washington Quarterly*, 30(4), 131–144.

Batidzirai, B., and Johnson, F. X. (2012). Energy security, agro-industrial development, and international trade: The case of sugarcane in southern Africa. In A. Gasparatos and P. Stromberg (Eds.), *Socio-economic and environmental impacts of biofuels: Evidence from developing nations* (pp. 254–277). New York: Cambridge University Press.

Bielecki, J. (2002). Energy security: Is the wolf at the door? *The Quarterly Review of Economics and Finance*, 42(2), 235–250.

British Petroleum (2020, July). *Statistical review*. https://www.bp.com/en/global/corporate/energy-economics/statistical-review-of-world-energy.html

Cherp, A. (2012). Defining energy security takes more than asking around. *Energy Policy*, 48, 841–842.

Cherp, A., and Jewell, J. (2014). The concept of energy security: Beyond the four As. *Energy Policy*, 75, 415–421.

Franki, V., and Višković, A. (2015). Energy security, policy and technology in South East Europe: Presenting and applying an energy security index to Croatia. *Energy*, 90, 494–507.

Goldthau, A. (2011). Governing global energy: Existing approaches and discourses. *Current Opinion in Environmental Sustainability*, 3(4), 213–217.

Hansen, U. E., Nygaard, I., Romijn, H., Wieczorek, A., Kamp, L. M., and Klerkx, L. (2018). Sustainability transitions in developing countries: Stocktaking, new contributions, and a research agenda. *Environmental Science and Policy*, 84, 198–203.

Hasanov, F. J., Mahmudlu, C., Deb, K., Abilov, S., and Hasanov, O. (2020). The role of Azeri natural gas in meeting European Union energy security needs. *Energy Strategy Reviews*, 28, 100464.

Hughes, L., and Lipscy, P. Y. (2013). The politics of energy. *Annual Review of Political Science*, 16, 449–469.

IEA. (2021), *World Energy Outlook 2021*. https://iea.blob.core.windows.net/assets/4ed140c1-c3f3-4fd9-acae 789a4e14a23c/WorldEnergyOutlook 2021.pdf; https://www.eia.gov/finance/markets/crudeoil/supply-opec.php

Jamasb, T., and Pollitt, M. (2008). Security of supply and regulation of energy networks. *Energy Policy*, 36(12), 4584–4589.

Johansson, T. B., Patwardhan, A. P., Nakićenović, N., and Gomez-Echeverri, L. (Eds.). (2012). *Global energy assessment: Toward a sustainable future*. Cambridge: Cambridge University Press.

Lacher, W., and Kumetat, D. (2011). The security of energy infrastructure and supply in North Africa: Hydrocarbons and renewable energies in comparative perspective. *Energy Policy*, 39(8), 4466–4478.

Le, T. H., and Nguyen, C. P. (2019). Is energy security a driver for economic growth? Evidence from a global sample. *Energy Policy*, 129, 436–451.

Martchamadol, J., and Kumar, S. (2012). Thailand's energy security indicators. *Renewable and Sustainable Energy Reviews*, 16(8), 6103–6122.

Murakami, T., Motokura, M., and Kutani, I. (2011). An analysis of major countries' energy security policies and conditions. *IEEJ Energy Journal*, 6(1).

OPEC. (2019). OPEC. *Annual Statistical Bulletin Report*. https://www.opec.org/opec_web/static_files_project/media/downloads/publications/ASB_2019.pdf

PRS Group (2012). *International country risk guide*. Liverpool, NY: PRS Group

Tichý, L. (2019). The Islamic State oil and gas strategy in North Africa. *Energy Strategy Reviews*, 24, 254–260

Valdés, J. (2018). Arbitrariness in multidimensional energy Security indicators. *Ecological Economics*, 145, 263–273.

Viviescas, C., Lima, L., Diuana, F. A., Vasquez, E., Ludovique, C., Silva, G. N., . . ., and Paredes, J. R. (2019). Contribution of variable renewable energy to increase energy security in Latin America: Complementarity and climate change impacts on wind and solar resources. *Renewable and Sustainable Energy Reviews*, 113, 109232.

Vivoda, V. (2010). Evaluating energy security in the Asia-Pacific region: A novel methodological approach. *Energy Policy*, 38(9), 5258–5263.

Wang, Q., and Zhou, K. (2017). A framework for evaluating global national energy security. *Applied Energy*, 188, 19–31.

Winzer, C. (2012). Conceptualizing energy security. *Energy Policy*, 46, 36–48

World Bank. (2022). *World development indicators 2022*. Washington, DC: The World Bank.

World Economic Forum. (2018). *Fostering effective energy transition: A fact-based framework to support decision making*. https://www.mckinsey.com/~/media/mckinsey/industries/oil%20and%20gas/our%20insights/a%20framework%20for%20fostering%20effective%20energy%20transitions/fostering-effective-energy-transition.ashx

Wu, K. (2014). China's energy security: Oil and gas. *Energy Policy*, 73, 4–11.

Yao, L., and Chang, Y. (2014). Energy security in China: A quantitative analysis and policy implications. *Energy Policy*, 67, 595–604.

Yergin, D. (1988). Energy Security in the 1990s. *Foreign Affairs*, 67, 110.

Part III

Oil and Gas Economics and Finance

6 The Economics of Oil and Gas Resources

Amin Karimu, Godwill Agordoh, Peter Quartey, and Runar Brännlund

6.1 Introduction

The oil and gas industry is an important one for the growth and development of the global economy as modern economic and social activities depend heavily on energy. Oil and gas are major energy resources consumed globally. Available statistics and projections from ExxonMobil (2019) suggest that oil and gas will contribute about 56% of global energy demand in 2040.

Despite the importance of oil and gas resources, especially to the growth and development of the emerging and developing countries (e.g. Barnes and Floor, 1996; Barnes et al., 2003; Toman and Jemelkova, 2003), their endowment is not uniformly distributed across the globe. The Organization of Petroleum Exporting Countries' OPEC (2019) indicates that OPEC member countries accounted for 79.4% of proven global oil reserves. All the OPEC member countries, according to the UN (2019) country classification, are under the emerging and developing country grouping. This suggests that these resources are predominantly located within the emerging and developing regions of the world. It is however important to note that these resources are non-renewable in nature. Therefore, care must be taken in extracting them in order not to completely deplete and prevent future generations from benefiting from such resources.

Furthermore, the renewable energy transition is underway, creating significant competition between renewable and non-renewable resources, particularly oil and gas. Such a competition from renewables puts significant pressure on oil- and gas-producing countries and firms to diversify their investment portfolios and promote effective and efficient practices in the management of such resources to promote their sustainable extraction and to improve intergenerational welfare at least in jurisdictions where these resources are located.

The key objective of this chapter is to present the economic fundamentals of the oil and gas industry such as the supply of oil and gas and the demand (consumption) profile for these resources to highlight trade oil security implications and to determine the market structure of the industry and its implications for price movements, particularly in the context of emerging and developing countries.

DOI: 10.4324/9781003315056-9

The structure of the chapter is as follows: The next section presents a brief overview of global oil and gas supply and that from emerging and developing economies. Section 6.3 presents the demand profile of oil and gas globally and that from emerging and developing economies, whereas Section 6.4 deals with the market structure of the oil and gas industry to understand the quantity and pricing strategy of the global oil and gas industry. Section 6.5 presents the conclusion of the study.

6.2 Global Oil and Gas Supply

Oil and gas are energy resources heavily relied upon by economies to propel and boost economic activity. Available statistics from the International Energy Agency (IEA) show that oil and gas made up about 53.5% and 54.6% of all global primary energy supplied in 2010 and 2019, respectively, compared to 57.3% in the year 2000 (IEA, 2021). Moreover, available projections estimate that oil and gas supply will be about 56% in the year 2040 (Exxon Mobil, 2019). Evidently, this shows that oil and gas resources will continue to provide more than 50% of all global energy to meet future demand.

6.2.1 Oil Supply from Emerging and Developing Countries

Consistently, the production of world oil has largely been driven by non-OECD countries which are predominantly emerging and developing countries. Available statistics from the Statistical Review of World Energy (2021) show that non-OECD countries currently supply three times as much oil as OECD countries as seen in Figure 6.1. Countries that drive the high level of production from non-OECD countries include Saudi Arabia, Russia, Iraq, Iran, China, United Arab Emirates, Kuwait, and Brazil, which are within the UN classification of emerging and developing countries.

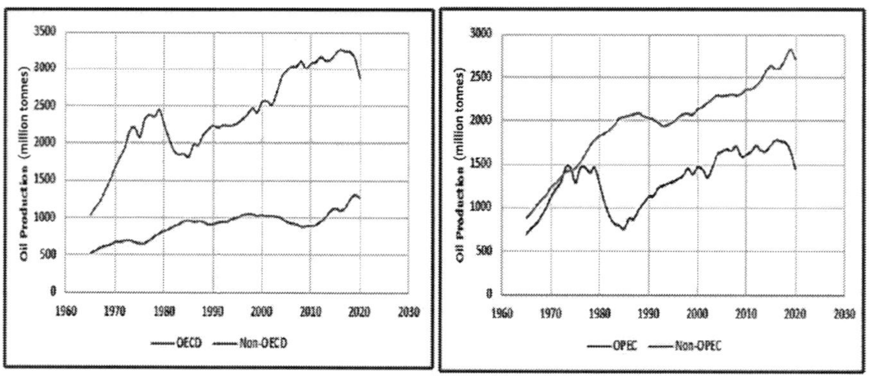

Figure 6.1 OECD and non-OECD and OPEC versus non-OPEC oil production in million tonnes

Source: Authors' computation based on data from BP Statistical Review of World Energy, 2021

Table 6.1 Oil Production by Region (2000–2018)

Year	*2000*	*2005*	*2010*	*2015*	*2016*	*2017*	*2018*	*% Change (2018–2000)*
Europe	7,098	5,961	4,403	3,716	3,742	3,692	3,666	−48.4%
Russia and Central Asia	7,864	11,700	13,414	13,950	13,120	14,223	14,477	84.1%
Middle East	23,510	25,588	25,366	29,831	31,674	31,278	31,720	34.9%
Africa	7,814	9,906	10,243	8,337	7,810	8,206	8,366	7.1%
Asia-Pacific	7,929	7,994	8,367	8,285	7,988	7,724	7,594	−4.2%
North America	10,726	10,118	11,084	17,394	16,980	18,083	20,686	92.9%
Central America	10,268	10,894	10,306	10,403	9,930	9,443	8,644	−15.8%

Source: Authors' own computation based on data from ENI (2019) world oil review

Further, non-OPEC countries currently produce more than 55% of global oil, with the United States driving this supply with the shale revolution.[1] Although OPEC countries currently produce less than half of global oil, they have about 79.4% proven crude oil reserves as earlier stated, which offers a huge influence on international oil prices.

Table 6.1 showcases the oil production pattern by regions of the world to better appreciate which regional bloc has been driving production since the year 2000. The percentage change over the period suggests that beyond North America, growth in oil production is driven by Russia and Central Asia (84.1%), the Middle East (34.9%), and Africa (7.1%), as juxtaposed to Europe (−48.4%).

6.2.2 Gas Supply from Emerging and Developing Countries

Gas resources are geographically and geologically diverse. They play a crucial role in satisfying energy needs of consumers worldwide while simultaneously mitigating the risks of climate change. From the early 1970s, OECD countries produced about 74% of gas, whereas non-OECD countries produced about 24%. Around the mid-1980s, non-OECDs seemed to have caught up with OECD countries in the production of gas and subsequently exceeded their production levels as seen in Figure 6.2. This is partly due to the increase in demand from industrial customers and a 45% increase in worldwide gas use (IEA, 2021). To this end, trade in LNG more than doubled to respond to rising demand from developing economies, led by China.

Conventional gas represents the major production of current gas; however, it is projected to decline to 70% in 2040, from the current 80% (IEA, 2021). Interestingly, almost two-thirds of production growth comes from the Middle East and Russia. However, gas supply is increasingly becoming underpinned by unconventional gas production, which is led by the United States. According to the IEA (2021), the United States will account for most of the growth

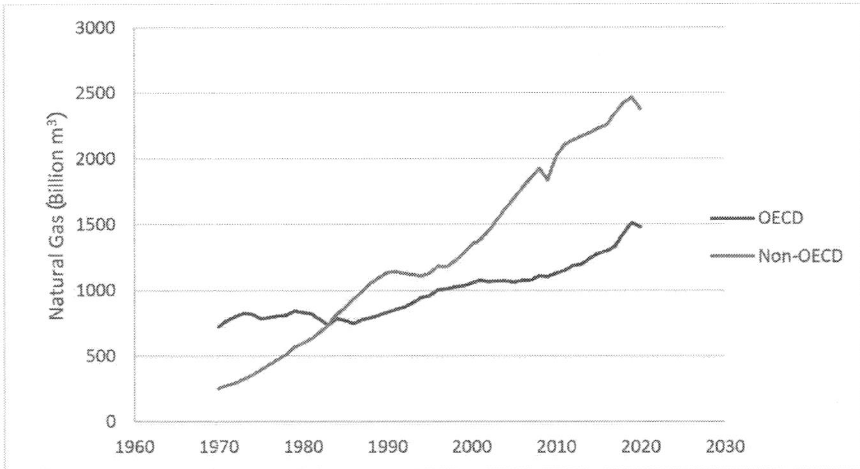

Figure 6.2 Share of OECD and non-OECD in gas production

Source: Authors' computation based on data from Statistical Review of World Energy, 2021

to 2025 through shale gas production, with other countries such as Canada, China, and Argentina following suit.

6.3 Global Oil and Gas Demand

Oil and gas are currently the dominant energy resources demanded globally. According to available statistics by ExxonMobil (2019), oil and gas share of world primary energy consumption was 59.2% in 2000 and 55.6% in 2010. Further, it was projected to be 56% by 2040. These numbers clearly show the dominant role of these two fuels in the global energy demand, a trend which will continue despite the increasing interest in renewables, partly driven by the transport sector over the years, and increasing demand for economic activity in emerging economies such as China and India, as highlighted by Karimu and Dramani (2020).

6.3.1 Oil Demand in Emerging and Developing Countries

Over the years, the developed countries have played a dominant role in the demand for oil and gas resources. Available statistics from the US Energy Information Administration (EIA, 2021) suggest that the share of the Organisation for Economic Co-operation and Development (OECD) of global demand in 1980 was 66.2%, suggesting that less than half of global oil demand comes from non-OECD countries. Figure 6.3 clearly shows the dominance of OECD in oil consumption, relative to non-OECD countries, driven by the developed countries in the OECD country group. The dominance of OECD started to decline in 2000 as demonstrated by the narrowing gap between OECD and

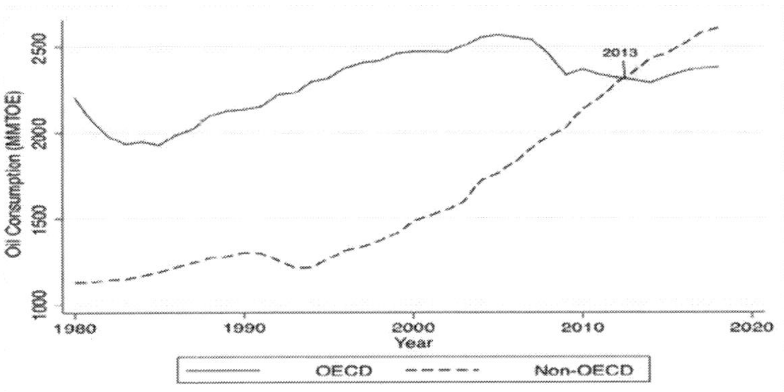

Figure 6.3 Share of OECD and non-OECD oil consumption in million tonnes of oil equivalent (MMTOE)

Source: Authors' computation based on data from EIA, 2021

Table 6.2 Oil Consumption by Region (2000–2018)

Year	*2000*	*2005*	*2010*	*2015*	*2016*	*2017*	*2018*	*% Change (2000–2018)*
Europe	16,475	17,137	15,948	14,952	15,177	15,516	15,542	−5.7%
Russia and Central Asia	3,243	3,303	3,375	4,137	4,050	4,064	4,232	30.5%
Middle East	5,011	6,206	7,529	8,747	8,714	8,729	8,666	72.9%
Africa	2,466	2,928	3,548	4,208	4,255	4,279	4,314	74.9%
Asia-Pacific	20,889	24,177	27,293	31,957	32,933	33,850	34,574	65.5%
North America	22,007	23,494	21,856	22,257	22,470	22,718	23,259	5.7%
Central America	7,053	7,398	8,539	9,052	8,844	8,793	8,753	24.1%

Source: Authors' own computation based on data from ENI (2019) world oil review

non-OECD oil consumption thereof. After 2013, non-OECD consumption surpassed that of OECD, driven significantly by demand from China, India, and the African continent, which is partly due to economic growth, growing prosperity, and population growth.

Table 6.2 highlights the consumption patterns of the various regions of the world since the year 2000. The percentage over the period 2000–2018 suggests that the highest growth in consumption comes from the emerging and developing regions led by Africa (74.9%), relative to developed Europe (−5.7%) and North America (5.7%). This suggests that in the last two decades, growth in oil demand was significantly influenced by demand from emerging and developing countries.

In the last 20 years, Europe has made significant efforts in gradually decoupling economic growth from oil via energy efficiency, uptake in electric vehicles, and promotion of renewable energy, compared to the rest of the regions. Oil and gas still dominate Europe's energy mix. For instance a report by the European Commission (EC, 2020) suggests that in 2020, oil and gas constituted about 60% of the European Union's energy demand.

6.3.1.1 Oil Trade by the Emerging and Developing Countries

Trade in oil resources predominantly flows from non-OCED countries to OECD countries, as revealed in Figure 6.4. The figure depicts negative net exports for each year for the OECD and positive net exports for the non-OECD country group.

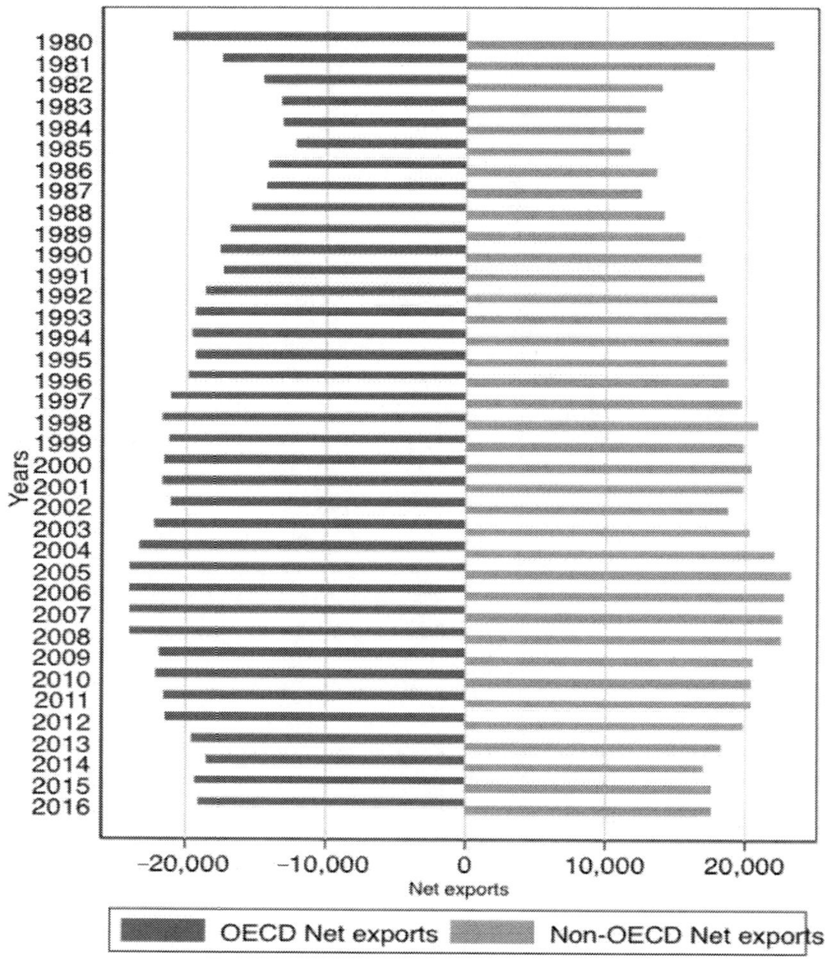

Figure 6.4 Net oil exports by OECD and non-OECD country groups

Source: Authors' own computation based on data from ENI (2019) world oil review

The top ten exporting countries in the world are Saudi Arabia, Russia, Iraq, Canada, the United Arab Emirates, Iran, Kuwait, Nigeria, the United States, and Angola (ENI, 2019). Most of these countries are emerging and developing countries and are generally among the major oil-producing countries in the world. In contrast, the top ten oil-importing countries are China, the United States, India, South Korea, Japan, Germany, Spain, Italy, the Netherlands, and Thailand, most of whom are developed countries. Only three out of the ten countries are emerging and developing countries.

6.3.2 Gas Demand in Emerging and Developing Countries

Global gas demand in the early years was dominated by OECD countries. For instance in 1995, OECD share of global gas demand was 55.5%. In 2000, it increased further to 56.6%, and in 2005, it increased by 52.5% as presented in Table 6.3. The table further indicates a reversal in global gas demand dominance from OECD to non-OECD since 2010. This is driven by increasing demand for gas in electricity generation, in transportation, and for cooking in the non-OECD countries. This growth in demand for gas is facilitated by population growth, economic growth, and an increasing middle class in the emerging and development countries such as China and India.

6.3.2.1 Gas Trade by the Emerging and Developing Countries

Gas trade in the world follows a similar pattern as that of oil. Thus, it flows predominantly from non-OECD countries to OECD countries as revealed in Table 6.4. The net export values for OECD countries are negative for each of the years, whereas those for the non-OECD countries are positive. Key exporting countries include Russia, Qatar, the United States, Norway, Australia, Canada, Algeria, the Netherlands, Nigeria, and Indonesia.

Table 6.3 Natural Gas Demand, OECD versus Non-OECD

Year	*OECD Gas Consumption*	*Non-OECD Gas Consumption*	*OECD Gas Consumption % Share*	*OECD Gas Net Export*	*Non-OECD Gas Net Export*
1990	946.4	946.7	50.0	−152.7	164.2
1995	1138.5	910.9	55.6	−194.6	193.0
2000	1279.0	979.0	56.6	−260.9	266.5
2005	1358.6	1227.1	52.5	−336.7	336.1
2010	1489.8	1519.6	49.5	−384.8	355.3
2015	1547.0	1730.2	47.2	−350.4	339.0
2016	1586.4	1757.6	47.4	−357.5	340.3
2017	1602.2	1850.4	46.4	−357.9	338.5
2018	1681.6	1939.3	46.4	−340.7	338.9

Source: Cons denotes consumption. Authors' own computation based on data from EIA (2021)

6.4 Market Structure of the Oil and Gas Industry

6.4.1 Overview of Market Structure

The structure of any market can be categorised into perfect competition, oligopoly, monopolistic competition, and monopoly as shown in Figure 6.5. Each structure has some unique characteristics that distinguish it from the others.

Table 6.4 highlights the key characteristics of each of the structures. For instance in the case of a monopoly, a single firm produces and supplies the

Table 6.4 Characteristics of the Different Market Structures

Characteristics	*Perfect Competition*	*Monopolistic Competition*	*Oligopoly*	*Monopoly*
Number of firms competing	Large number	Large number	Small number	Single firm
Nature of the product	Homogeneous	Differentiated	Undifferentiated or differentiated	No close substitutes
Entry	No restrictions	Few barriers	Many barriers	Blocked
Information availability	Complete	Relatively good	Asymmetric	Asymmetric
Firm's control over price	None Firm is price taker	Some	Some	Substantial Firm is price maker

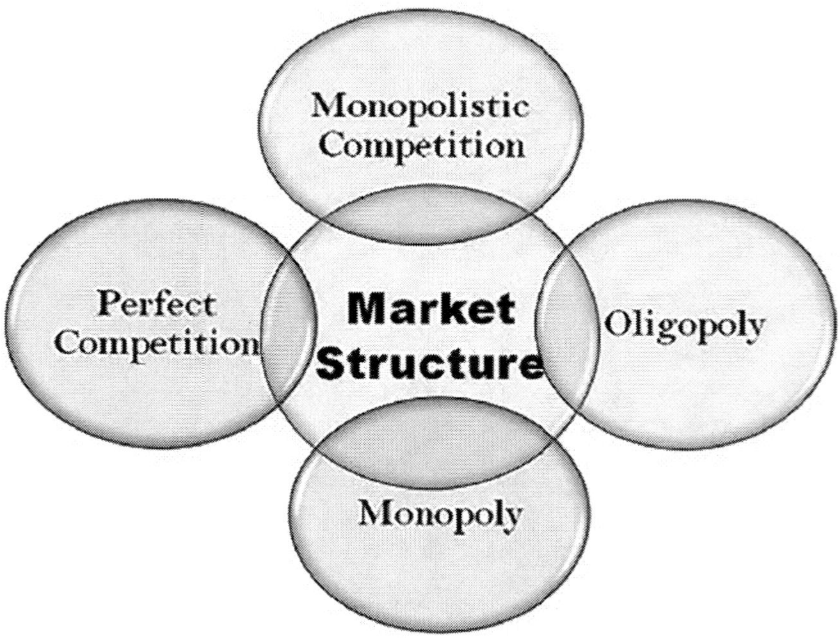

Figure 6.5 Market structure

entire market, whereas in the case of a perfectly competitive structure, there are many firms so that no single one has an influence on the market price of the good or service they are providing. Monopoly and perfect competition are the extreme market structures at both ends. In between, there is oligopoly, which is close to that of monopoly in terms of market power (ability to influence market price), and monopolistic competition, which is close to perfect competition in terms of number of firms in the industry.

Oligopoly firms can easily collude, especially if they produce and supply undifferentiated goods or services. This makes it possible to have a significant market power such that they can control the market, an example being the airline industry. It is also clear from Table 6.4 that in the case of oligopoly, there should be significant barrier(s) to entry such as initial capital outlay to start producing goods and services in the industry, which ultimately will serve as a barrier to many other firms wishing to enter the industry (Dahl, 2015). For instance the capital requirement to produce aircrafts for sale is substantial; therefore, few firms can afford to operate in the industry. This, therefore, provides them some unique feature to operate an oligopoly market structure relative to a competitive market structure.

A key importance of market structure is to guide the market players on strategic behaviour in pricing and output control to maximise profits and promote market share in the industry. Given the structure of the industry, firms will understand how their output decisions may influence market price if they are operating as monopolistic competition, oligopoly, or monopoly, whereas in the case of perfect competition, they will understand that their unilateral output decision will not influence market price but drive customers away if it is higher than the market price or make losses if it is lower than the market price.

6.4.2 Oil and Gas Market Structure

Prior to the formation of OPEC in 1960, the oil and gas industry was dominated by seven oil companies, popularly referred to as the 'Seven Sisters'. The Seven Sisters comprise five American companies (Gulf Oil; Standard Oil of California; Standard Oil of New Jersey, later Exxon; Standard Oil of New York, later Mobil; and Texaco), one British (Anglo-Iranian Oil Company, now British Petroleum) and one Anglo-Dutch company (Royal Dutch Shell). These seven companies controlled the world oil and gas resources in terms of output and pricing of the products.

The seven companies competed against each other to get a greater share of the market but also realised the need to work together to protect their collective interest of maximising profits and circumventing government regulations. Even though they did not formally and openly coordinate their activities to control the price of oil and gas products, they nevertheless did so behind closed doors in a manner that attracted the term 'clumsy cartel' as suggested by Adelman (1993).

World price for oil and gas products declined following the end of the Second World War, when demand fell because of cuts in demand of fuel fighter aircrafts, tanks, and war machinery. This was further compounded by the new oil discoveries in Libya and Algeria. The fall in oil prices led a group of major oil-producing nations to form OPEC in 1960. The aim of OPEC was to have control in the determination of oil prices to make profit for its members. Levy (1982) indicates that the aim of OPEC is 'to gain a voice and, possibly, even control over posted prices for crude oil'.

6.4.2.1 Membership of OPEC

OPEC membership has increased over the years, relative to when it was formed in 1960. In the early years of its formation, there were only five member countries, namely the Islamic Republic of Iran, Iraq, Kuwait, Saudi Arabia, and Venezuela. These five countries are now regarded as the founding members of the organisation. OPEC distinguishes between two membership statuses: founder member and full member. Founder member countries are those who formed the organisation in 1960, whereas any other member country that was accepted after 1960 obtains a full member status.

Over the years, new countries joined the organisation and stayed, while others joined and later left for diverse reasons. In 2020, total membership was 13, all of which are emerging and developing countries by the United Nations (2019) country classification. OPEC membership in terms of regional distribution is dominated by African countries (seven), followed by Western Asia (four); there is one South Asian country and one Latin America and Caribbean country. Table 6.5 presents the 13 OPEC member countries and their regional distribution.

In 2016, ten major non-OPEC oil-producing countries agreed to join OPEC, culminating in the OPEC+. The OPEC+ members include the 13 OPEC members plus Azerbaijan, Bahrain, Brunei, Kazakhstan, Malaysia, Mexico, Oman, Russia, South Sudan, and Sudan.

Table 6.5 OPEC Membership as of 2020 and Its Regional Distribution

Country	*Region*	*UN-Classification as of 2020*
Algeria	Africa	Developing
Angola	Africa	Developing
Congo	Africa	Developing
Equatorial Guinea	Africa	Developing
Gabon	Africa	Developing
Iran	South Asia	Developing
Iraq	Western Asia	Developing
Kuwait	Western Asia	Developing
Libya	Africa	Developing
Nigeria	Africa	Developing
Saudi Arabia	Western Asia	Developing
United Arab Emirates	Western Asia	Developing
Venezuela	Latin America and the Caribbean	Developing

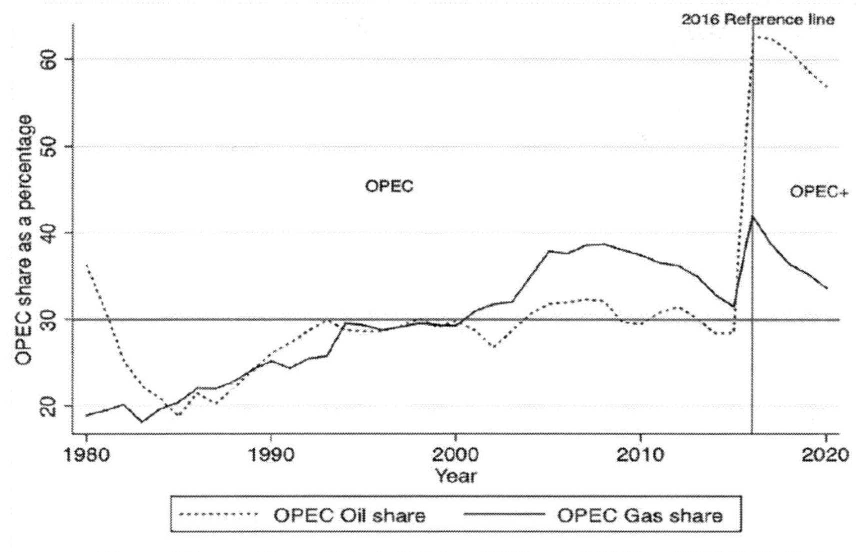

Figure 6.6 OPEC and OPEC+ share of global oil and gas production

Source: Authors' computation based on data from EIA, 2021

OPEC+ was formed to respond to the highly dynamic economic and geopolitical developments that have a potential impact on the oil and gas industry, particularly prices. They generally make changes to their production capacities in a manner that will affect oil prices.

OPEC as an organisation has had a significant market share of the oil and gas industry and, therefore, has had over the years some significant influence on world supply of oil and gas products and oil price movements. In the 1980s, OPEC's share of global oil production was around 36%, as shown in Figure 6.2. From 1982 to 1997, production reduced and accounted for below 26% for most of the years within this period. The share of global production picked up and hovered around 30% after 1997. In the period starting from 2016, the share of OPEC's output was between 55% and 60%, because of the addition of the ten new members, culminating in OPEC+. The picture is not very different in the case of natural gas production, as depicted Figure 6.6.

6.4.2.2 OPEC Market Share of Global Oil and Gas Industry

Furthermore, when export shares are considered, the market shares are much more significant, accounting for between 65.7% (the lowest) and 77.8% the highest. Figure 6.7 presents the export shares of OPEC over the period.

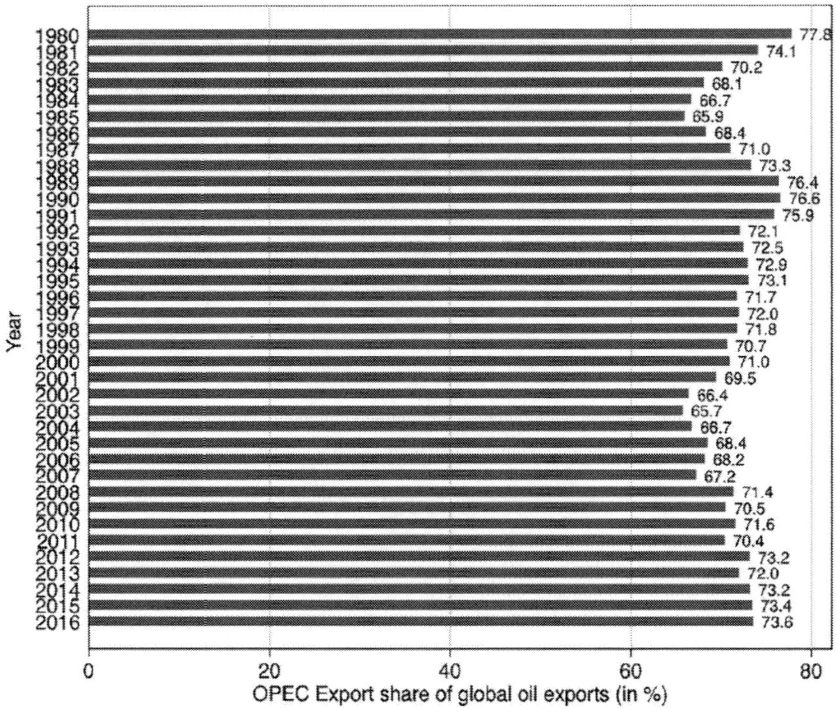

Figure 6.7 OPEC share of global oil exports

Source: Authors' computation based on data from EIA (2021)

Moreover, OPEC[2] member countries (excluding the additional ten that joined in 2016) have the largest share of proven crude oil reserves in the world, as shown in Figure 6.8. Their share constitutes about 79.4% of the world's total oil reserves as of 2018, with Venezuela (25.5%) and Saudi Arabia (22.4%) having the largest reserves. The other top five ranked countries in OPEC in terms of crude oil reserves are Iran (13.1%), Iraq (12.2%), and Kuwait (8.5%).

The foregoing discussion regarding OPEC's cartelisation of oil and gas and its market share in terms of production, exports, and proven reserves all points to a market structure where a few players exist, driven by endowment and the specialised and capital-intensive nature of the industry. More importantly, the few players have a common interest and therefore could coordinate their activities to influence the market in a direction that benefits them. This suggests that the oil and gas industry has an oligopolistic characteristic, as outlined in Table 6.4.

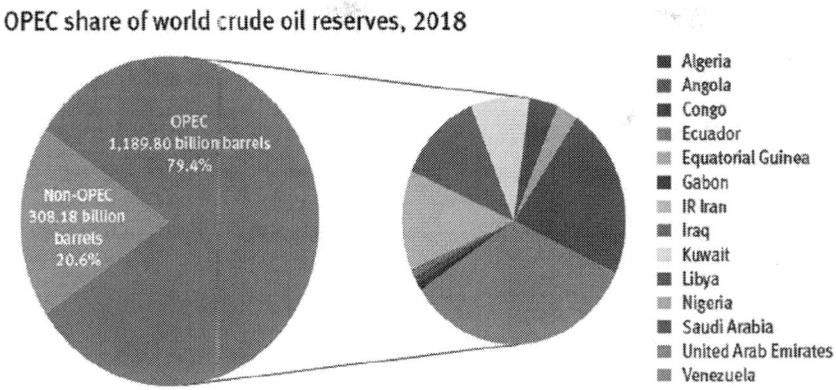

OPEC-proven crude oil reserves, at the end of 2018 (billion barrels, OPEC share)

Venezuela	302.81	25.5%	Kuwait	101.50	8.5%	Algeria	12.20	1.0%	Gabon	2.00	0.2%
Saudi Arabia	267.03	22.4%	UAE	97.80	8.2%	Ecuador	8.27	0.7%	Equatorial Guinea	1.10	0.1%
IR Iran	155.60	13.1%	Libya	48.36	4.1%	Angola	8.16	0.7%			
Iraq	145.02	12.2%	Nigeria	36.97	3.1%	Congo	2.98	0.3%			

Figure 6.8 Proven crude oil reserves as of 2018 – OPEC versus non-OPEC

Source: OPEC Statistics (OPEC, 2019)

6.4.3 OPEC Oil Production and Oil Price Movements

To consider OPEC as a true oligopoly, its activity should have an influence on global oil and gas price movements. Figure 6.9 presents the association between OPEC's spare capacity and WTI crude oil price (real price) from the first quarter of 2001 to the fourth quarter of 2022. Clearly, there is a negative association between OPEC's spare capacity and crude oil price, as with a decrease in spare capacity from 4.5 million barrels a day to 3 million barrels a day, crude oil prices increase from about 25 dollars to 100 dollars a barrel. In particular, the extent to which OPEC member countries utilised their production spare capacity determines the extent to which they could influence oil prices. Saudi Arabia historically kept 1.5–2 million barrels per day as spare capacity for market management (EIA, 2021). The implication from this is that the larger the spare capacity, the easier it is for OPEC member countries to respond positively to oil demand by adjusting production levels, which does have implications for crude oil price movements.

Furthermore, a line graph of spare capacity and real price of crude oil in the same graph (Figure 6.10) confirms the negative association between spare capacity and price of crude oil. For example in the first quarter of 2002, crude oil price was 25.9 US dollars per barrel, while the OPEC spare capacity was 6 million barrels per day. In the first quarter of 2008, when the spare capacity reduced to 1.5 million barrels per day, the price of crude oil was about 100 US

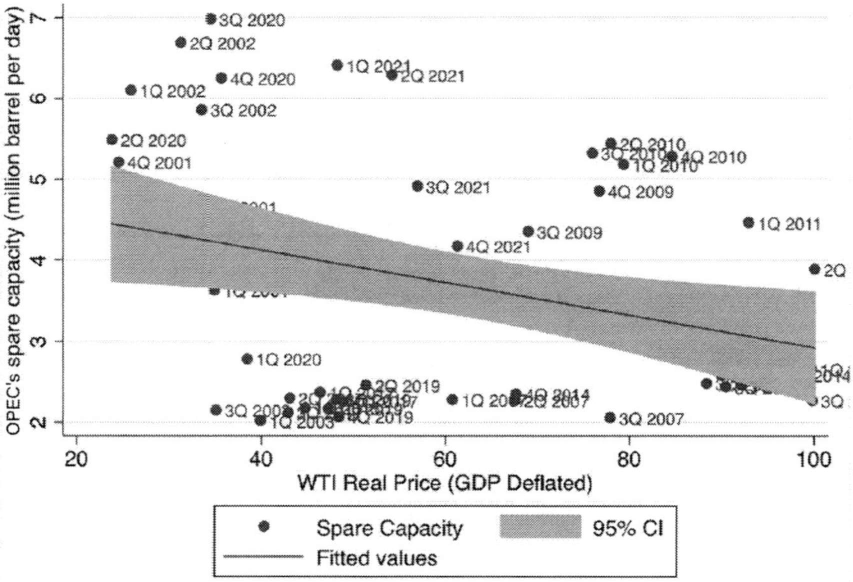

Figure 6.9 OPEC's spare capacity and crude oil price movements

Source: Authors' computation using data from the EIA (2021)

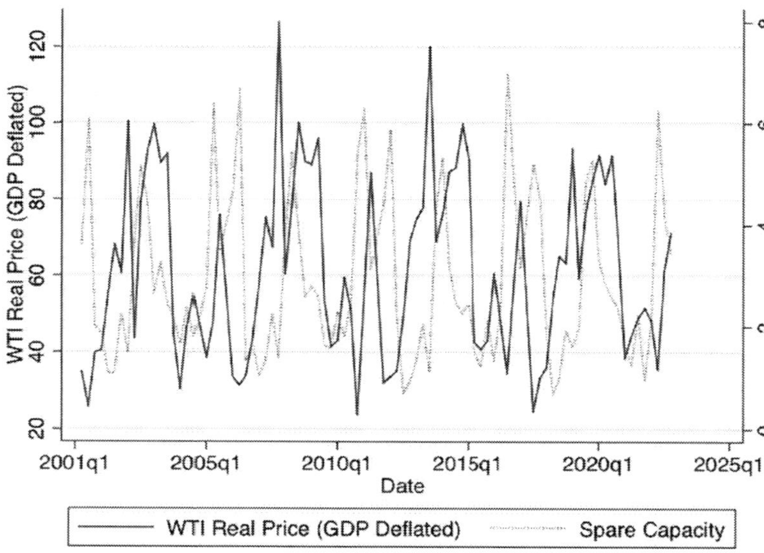

Figure 6.10 Line graph of OPEC's spare capacity and crude oil price

Source: Authors' computation using data from the EIA (2021)

dollars per barrel. This highlights the role of spare capacity in the management of crude oil supply in response to demand and the likely effect of the supply and demand balance on crude oil price build up.

6.4.4 Non-OPEC Oil Production and Oil Price Movements

Though non-OPEC countries in total have the largest share of global oil and gas production (about 60%) prior to 2012, they have had less contribution since then, contributing about 40% of global oil and gas production. In terms of exports, non-OPEC member countries contributed less than 30% on the average. More importantly, the non-OPEC members' activities are not coordinated, and, therefore, they do not have a unified production target; rather, individual countries make their production decisions. This, among other things, implies that they have relatively smaller market shares, are often dominated by international oil companies (IOCs), and are therefore likely to have less influence on global market price, and hence on market power relative to OPEC, especially OPEC+. Figure 6.11 shows a marginal positive association between non-OPEC oil production and crude oil price for the period 2001 to 2020, suggesting less influence on oil prices by non-OPEC production changes relative to OPEC during that period.

Considering all the characteristics shown by OPEC over the years in terms of the number of member countries, market share, and influence on prices,

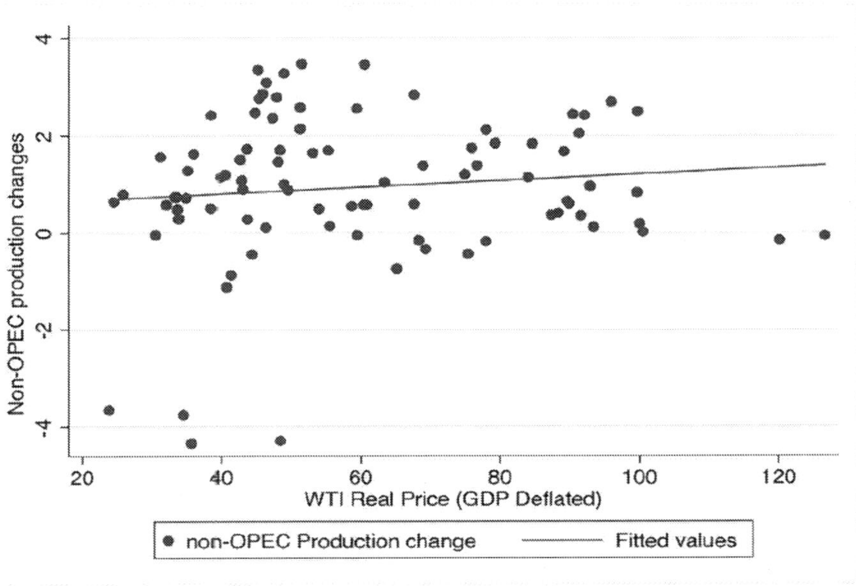

Figure 6.11 Association between non-OPEC oil production and oil prices (2001–2020)

Source: Authors' computation based on data from EIA (2021)

the oil and gas market is generally an oligopoly by structure, irrespective of the increasing number of non-OPEC oil-producing countries.

6.5 Conclusion

Most of the proven reserves of oil and gas resources are in emerging and developing economies. A recent report by ENI (2019) indicates that ten countries control about 83.9% of global proven reserves. Of these, eight are classified by the UN as emerging and developing countries, which account for 80% of the 83.9% share of global proven oil and gas reserves. Furthermore, OPEC's share of global proven oil and gas reserves is about 79.4%, and all the countries that constitute OPEC are classified by the UN as emerging and developing countries.

Despite the predominantly high oil and gas reserves within the emerging and developing regions, coupled with the high production from these regions, energy poverty in terms of oil consumption per capita is the worst here relative to the developed countries. For instance in Africa, oil consumption per capita in 2018 was about 1.38 barrels and that of Asia and Pacific was 3.05 barrels, compared to Europe's 8.34 barrels. This suggests that irrespective of the developing regions being rich in oil and gas resources, the domestic use of these resources for economic and social activities is low, relative to the developed regions. This, among other things, has implications for the growth and development of the developing regions due to the importance of energy in modern production, transportation, and consumption processes.

Oil and gas are the most consumed fossil fuels in developing regions, and these fuels are projected to grow significantly soon due to an expanding middle class, increasing needs for economic growth, and population growth in emerging and developing countries.

Evidence from the various data presented in the chapter reveals that the global oil and gas industry is an oligopoly in structure and has predominantly been organised as a cartel over the years, led by OPEC. The impact of OPEC on global oil production during crisis periods and on global oil and gas price is still significant. These characteristics point to a cartelisation of the industry, which was started by the 'Seven Sisters' prior to the formation of OPEC in the 1960s.

The evidence from the oil and gas structure, reserves, production, demand, and trade all point to a careful management of oil and gas resources in the emerging and developing world to reduce exposure to the resource curse threat in the region, reduce oil and gas dependency and risk exposure from such dependence, and manage the oil and gas trade effectively and efficiently within the developing regions of the world.

Notes

1 The 'Shale Revolution' refers to the combination of hydraulic fracturing and horizontal drilling that enabled the United States to significantly increase its production of oil and natural gas, particularly from tight oil formations, which now account for 36% of total US crude oil production.

2 Ecuador suspended its membership in 2020 and is no longer a member of OPEC. Its share of proven crude oil reserves as of 2018 is small (0.7%) relative to the total OPEC share.

References

Adelman, M. A. (1993). *The economics of petroleum supply. Papers by M.A. Adelman, 1962–1993*. Cambridge, MA: MIT Press.

Barnes, D., and Floor, W. M. (1996). Rural energy in developing countries: A challenge for economic development. *Annual Review of Energy and Environment*, 21, 497–530.

Barnes, D. F., Peskin, H., and Fitzgerald, K. (2003). The benefits of rural electrification in India: Implications for education, household lighting, and irrigation. In *Draft paper prepared for South Asia Energy and Infrastructure*. Washington, DC: World Bank.

Dahl, C. (2015). *International energy markets: Understanding pricing, policies & profits*. Tulsa, OK: PennWell Books.

EIA. (2021). *What drives crud e oil prices?* https://www.eia.gov/finance/markets/crudeoil/supply-opec.php

ENI. (2019). *ENI annual report 2019*. https://www.eni.com/assets/documents/eng/reports/2019/Annual-Report-2019.pdf

European Commission. (2020). *EU energy in figures: A statistical pocketbook*. https://op.europa.eu/en/publication-detail/-/publication/87b16988-f740-11ea-991b 01aa75ed71a1/languageen?WT.mc_id=Searchresult&WT.ria_c=37085&WT.ria_f=3608&WT.ria_ev=search

ExxonMobil. (2019). *Outlook for Energy: A perspe ctive to 2040*. https://corporate.exxonmobil.com/-/media/Global/Files/outlook-for-energy/2019-Outlook-for-Energy_v4.pdf

IEA. (2021). *World Energy O utlook 2021*. https://iea.blob.core.windows.net/assets/4ed140c1-c3f3-4fd9-acae 789a4e14a23c/WorldEnergyOutlook2021.pdf

Karimu, A., and Dramani, J. B. (2020). Energy consumption patterns in Africa: The role of biomass fuels for cooking and fuel use in the transportation sector. In *Sustainable Consumption and Production, Volume I: Challenges and Development* (p. 315). New York: Springer Nature.

Levy W. J. (1982). *Oil strategy and politics, 1941–1981*. Boulder, CO: Westview.

OPEC (2019). *Annual Statistical Bulle ting*. https://www.opec.org/opec_web/en/publications/202.htms

Statistical Review of World Energy (2021). *Reviewing energy data for 70 years*. https://www.bp.com/content/dam/bp/business-sites/en/global/corporate/pdfs/energy-economics/statistical-review/bp-stats-review-2021-full-report

Toman, M. T., and Jemelkova, B. (2003). Energy and economic development: An assessment of the state of knowledge. *The Energy Journal*, 24(4).

United Nations. (2019). *World economic situation a nd prospects*. https://www.un.org/development/desa/dpad/wp-content/uploads/sites/45/WESP2019_BOOK-ANNEX-en.pdf

7 Economics of Downstream Oil and Gas Project, Risk, and Decision Analysis

Khadijah Iddrisu, Phillip Kofi Adom, Jabir Ibrahim Mohammed, and Amin Karimu

7.1 Introduction

The downstream oil and gas sector plays a critical role in the socio-economic transformation of economies. As the sector that connects end users to refined products, the downstream sector drives major activities in homes, industries, and businesses. For example it plays a special role in the agriculture sector as it provides pesticides, fertilizers, and fuels needed for agricultural equipment such as tractors. Also, the products of the downstream sector have a lot of influence on some of the products and equipment used by the health sector. In addition, the downstream sector contributes significantly to employment and revenue generation. The sector directly employs about 6 million people and indirectly creates more than ten times this number of jobs.[1] In 2021, total revenue generated from the oil and gas sector amounted to US$2.1 trillion (IBISWorld, n.d.). In Ghana, the downstream sector contributes about 6% to GDP, which is US$3.9 billion.[2]

The operations of the downstream sector provide some benefits to the oil industry. For example they increase the profit margin when oil prices fall. This happens because when crude oil prices fall, refining margins typically grow (Sar, 2017). This sector has a lot of opportunities due to the availability of technological advancement and communication systems. For example the sector often uses different supply chain solutions in times of uncertainty, from crude oil selection to retail distribution (Balasubramanian, 2010). This industry has ten players including petroleum and coal products' manufacturing, petroleum refineries, asphalt paving mixture and block manufacturing, asphalt shingle and coating materials manufacturing, petroleum lubricating oil and grease manufacturing, all other petroleum and coal products manufacturing, petroleum bulk stations and terminals, fuel dealers, petroleum and petroleum products merchant wholesalers, and petroleum brokers (wholesale trade agents and brokers).

Despite the numerous benefits the sector professes, it suffers from several risks which threaten the long-term competitive nature of the sector. These associated risks continue to threaten the market share, investment, and capacity levels in the downstream oil and gas sector. This chapter examines the

DOI: 10.4324/9781003315056-10

associated risks, conducts a measurement of those risks, and provides simulation and decision analysis of energy projects in the downstream sector.

7.2 Overview of Downstream Oil and Gas

All over the world, oil and gas and their constituents are important resources for economic activities. Without energy, the comfort of lives and leisure would be difficult to satisfy, and industrialization would essentially stop. Over the past century, the expansion of oil and gas interests has become one of the most important exchanges in the business world, and the industry has become a cardinal one that truly controls the economy (Aryeetey, 2016). The oil and gas industry includes the global processes of exploration, extraction, refining, transportation,[3] and marketing of petroleum products. There are three major sectors in the oil and gas industry, namely the upstream, midstream, and downstream (Energy Institute, 2019). The upstream oil and gas sector drives and drills exploration wells to search for potential underground (or underwater) crude oil and gas deposits and then drills and operates wells to extract oil and gas. The midstream oil and gas sector is only responsible for the transportation and storage of oil and gas (Appiah et al., 2018). The downstream segment of the oil and gas industry, which is the final stage of the production process, constitutes refining, distributing, and marketing refined products (Kramer, 2022). The refinery activities entail transforming crude oil and raw gas into liquefied natural gas, lubricants, antifreeze, fertilizers, gasoline, heating oil, synthetic rubber, plastics, pesticides, and others (Lewin, 2003; Wamono et al., 2012; Appiah et al., 2018; Chen, 2021). As of 2020, there were about 359 refineries operating in EMDCs out of the over 600 refineries that existed globally. North Asia dominates in terms of the number of refineries, driven by China (86). Africa is the region in the EMDCs with the least number, with about 42 refineries (Mckinsey, 2022). Examples of some of the companies in the refinery industry include Marathon Petroleum Corporation (MC) and Phillips 66 (PSX) which deal in oil refinery and are part of the leading US oil refineries (Franco, 2019). In Ghana, Tema Oil Refinery (TOR) and Bulk Oil Storage and Transport (BOST) are examples of the downstream oil and gas sectors (Appiah et al., 2018).

The sector is also seen as the final processing stage to purify or modify a hydrocarbon in a chemical process and then distribute and offer it to consumers.[4] The transformation process depends on the end product that the sector seeks to obtain. For example when synthetic rubber and plastics are needed, hydrotreating will be used to remove unwanted elements, which will be cracked to produce synthetic rubber and plastics.[5]

The marketing activities of the downstream oil and gas sector include bulk supplies and brokering of fuel oil, transportation of fuel oil, and direct trade in the form of wholesale and retail of fuel oil, gas, and petrochemicals (Wamono et al., 2012; Appiah et al., 2018). The products and activities of the downstream oil and gas sector suggest that the sector is engaged in the provision of services to other sectors.

7.3 Downstream Oil and Gas Projects

7.3.1 Refinery

An oil refinery is an industrial plant that converts and purifies oil into useful products such as gasoline, diesel oil, kerosene, liquefied petroleum gas, asphalt base, fuel oil, thermal fuel oil, and petroleum naphtha (Speight, 2006; Leffler, 1985). Other products are obtained from the by-products of the refining process, referred to generally as petrochemical feedstocks. Key petrochemical feedstocks include naphtha, ethylene, and propylene that the petrochemical industry depends on for producing a menu of products from polyvinyl chloride (PVC) for PVC pipes to athletic shoes and various rubber, coating, wire, and cable components of automobiles. Gudde (2018) argues that modern petroleum refining involves a complicated system of interrelated chemical reactions that produce a wide variety of petroleum-based products. These chemical changes require precise temperature and pressure parameters. Refineries are usually large industrial complexes with wide pipelines that transport fluid flows between large sections of chemical processing, such as distillation columns (Bhende and Patil, 2014).

In the refinery industry, the key processes can broadly be classified into separation, conversion, and purification. Any refinery activity involves one or more of these processes, each of which can be carried out using varied techniques and technologies. A typical refinery is designed to be able to perform all three activities. An example of the first category of the refining process is crude oil distillation, a process that will result in separating crude oil into various refined products such as petrol, diesel, and kerosene. The residue after the distillation process can be further utilised by the petrochemical industry to produce rubber and chemical and pharmaceutical products.

There are many refinery companies, but we present some popular ones in the world[6] in terms of the production of oil (barrels per day). These oil refineries include Sinopec, China National Petroleum Commission (CNPC), Jamnagar refinery, Paraguaná Refinery Complex, SK Energy Ulsan refinery complex, GS Caltex Yeosu refinery, S Oil Ulsan refinery, Exxon Mobil Singapore refinery, Baytown refinery, Ras Tanura refinery, Baton Rouge refinery, and BP Texas city. Table 7.1 presents the top oil refineries in 2020 and their daily capacity and country of origin.

Data from British Petroleum (BP) indicate that in the year 2020, the world's oil refinery capacity amounted to 101,947,000 barrels per day, of which the share of non-OCED countries was 56.1% and that of OECD countries was 43.9% (BP, 2021).

7.3.1.1 Steps Involved in Refining Crude Oil

There are various chemical processes used in refining crude oil. However, we adopt the Marsden Point refinery process which provides three main processes for refining crude oil. These processes include separation, conversion, and purification.

Table 7.1 Top Ten Oil Refineries in 2020

Rank	*Name of Refinery*	*Capacities (Barrels of Oil Per Day)*	*Country of Location*
1	Jamnagar refinery	1,240,000	India
2	SK Energy Ulsan refinery	1,120,000	South Korea
3	Paraguaná Refinery Complex	971,000	Venezuela
4	GS Caltex Yeosu refinery	730,000	South Korea
5	S Oil Ulsan refinery	669,000	South Korea
6	Exxon Mobil Singapore refinery	605,000	Singapore
7	Baytown refinery	572,500	The USA
8	Ras Tanura refinery	550,000	Saudi Arabia
9	Baton Rouge refinery	503,000	The USA
10	BP Texas city	467,720	The USA

Source: Statista (2021)

Table 7.2 Crude Oil Breakdown to Various Products Based on Different Boiling Ranges

Hydrocarbon Boiling Range	*Products*
Less than 85°F	Butane and Lighter products
85–185°F	Gasoline blending components
185–350°F	Naphtha
350–450°F	Kerosene, jet fuel
450–650°F	Diesel, heating oil
650–1050°F	Heavy gas oil
Greater than 1050°F	Residual fuel oil

Source: Authors' computation from information from EIA (2012)

7.3.1.1.1 STEP ONE: SEPARATION

Crude oil constitutes different hydrocarbons, and the purpose of this step is to separate the various hydrocarbons into their broad categories (fraction). The process involves heating the crude oil, which is transferred to a distilling column, where different hydrocarbons boil off and are recovered at different temperatures. Table 7.2 presents the different hydrocarbons that constitute crude oil and their respective boiling points and products.

7.3.1.1.2 STEP TWO: CONVERSION

After the crude oil has been separated into the six main grades, the next step is to treat (since the various grades have some level of sulphur except for refinery gas) and convert these grades into final products. This is done through various chemical processes. For instance the desulfurization conversion process involves the removal of sulphur compounds from gasoline, kerosene, and diesel oils. Furthermore, a catalytic reforming process converts the desulphurised naphtha molecules into higher-octane molecules to generate reformate. This reformate has a higher content of aromatics and cyclic hydrocarbons which may be gasoline or petrol.

7.3.1.1.3 STEP THREE: PURIFICATION

The final stage deals with generating the end product from the oil. In this stage, the hydrogen produced is purified to remove the carbon oxides. In Step 1, the hydrogen sulphide from the processing plant gas is converted to sulphur and sold to liquid fertilizer producers in liquid form.

7.3.2 Distribution

The second project of the downstream oil and gas sector is distribution which entails the storage and marketing of refined crude oil.

7.3.2.1 Storage of Final Product

The storage of oil and natural gas helps to eliminate supply and demand errors. Companies save more when costs are lower than they would like and export more when costs are higher. The cheapest method is storage in an underground space, such as a *depletion reservoir*.[7] This technique is mainly used for natural gas; refined oil products shall not, according to the regulations, be placed in underground natural spaces. Surface tanks are used for crude and refined oils, refined petroleum products, and natural gas. In retail outlets, such as gas stations, containers are placed underground for convenience. Larger shipping vessels are used for short-term storage when ground storage is limited, making them the most expensive option (Downey, 2009). In 2020, the coronavirus (COVID-19) pandemic decisively decreased the demand for oil, which was combined with an oversupply because of Saudi Arabia expanding oil creation and OPEC and non-OPEC nations neglecting to come to a settlement on lessening oil production.[8] This implied that storage tanks were close to the limit. Accordingly, oil storage organizations radically expanded their storage rates. For instance tankers were charging around $25,000 each day in February of 2020; by April, the rate had increased to $300,000 per day.[9] Examples of oil storage companies include BOST, Vista Energy, and Logistics Ghana Limited.

7.3.2.2 Marketing of Refined Crude Oil

Marketing is the wholesale and retail distribution of refined petroleum-based products to businesses, industries, governments, and the public. Large volumes of crude oil and oil-based raw products flow to the business sectors that provide the most benefits to suppliers, which are the closest markets in the first place in terms of lower transportation costs and higher service provider net income. In practice, this marketing chain may not follow this example due to various elements, such as sophisticated design, mixed product demand, and product quality characteristics. Gasoline service stations handle the heft of public consumer deals, and oil organizations sell their oil-based commodities straightforwardly to production lines, power plants, and transportation-related ventures. Natural gas deals are equally split between modern consumers, electrical suppliers, and private and commercial heating plants.

7.4 Risk Analysis of Downstream Oil and Gas

The oil and gas industry is exposed to many risk factors that can generally be classified into four. These are – environmental, economic, political, and geological risks. Beyond the risk, the development of oil and gas projects often requires large amounts of capital. For instance the cost of an oil vessel is about 100 million dollars or more with a life span of 40–50 years. Therefore, addressing the financing difficulties for oil and gas projects in the midst of significant risk is one of the most important issues (Kim and Choi, 2019). In the downstream oil and gas sector, three of four classified risks are encountered – that is economic, environmental, and political. These risks for the downstream oil and gas sector are pronounced in emerging markets and developing countries. They include price risk, geopolitical risk such as nationalisation of integrated oil majors, and technical risk.

7.4.1 Economic Risk

Economic risk in the downstream oil and gas sector includes price risk and market risk. In most oil refineries, crude oil is purchased 30 days in advance, implying a significant time lag between the input for the refinery and the output of refining products. This time lag and the volatile nature of crude oil prices and refining products create significant price risk for the refining companies, especially independent refineries which depend entirely on open market purchase of crude oil relative to integrated majors which depend on the crude produced by the upstream segment. This type of risk is more pronounced in EMDCs due to less developed futures and forward commodity markets that could help hedge some of these risks to some extent.

Another economic risk factor for the downstream oil and gas sector is the nature of the market in which the refined products are sold. If the market is protected or the refineries have some market power, relatively high prices for the refined products can be charged to generate a significant gross refinery margin (a key measure of the profitability of a refinery) and therefore reduce the risk of negative return for the refinery. Other economic risks include the likely future uptake of electric mobility in EMDCs currently being promoted and supported in developed countries. This is made possible through the rapidly developing battery technology (Vynakov et al., 2016; Greenblatt, 2016).

7.4.2 Environmental Risk

Refining activity will always produce some secondary products that are waste products, and some of these include sulphur contaminants, carbon dioxide, contaminated water, and volatile organic compounds. These waste products can pollute and damage the environment. Besides the waste products, the operations of the refineries can also pose environmental risks via leakages from storage tanks, accidents, gas emissions, and fires that can create serious environmental risks. These environmental risk factors are relatively high in EMDCs relative to the developed countries due to poor regulatory frameworks, corruption, and inefficient environmental and safety standards.

7.4.3 Technical Risk

The gross refinery margin (GRM) for a refinery is greatly influenced by the technical configuration of the refinery. The configuration determines the ability of a refinery to convert crude oil into lighter products such as gasoline, diesel, and jet fuel, which have significant value relative to fuel oil. This implies that a refinery that has a greater ability to convert crude to light products would likely make a greater margin. Typically, the simple configuration can produce 50% light products from crude oil, complex configuration 65% and deep conversion configuration a 95% conversion rate. Based on available statistics from BP (2021), Africa has the least refining capacity in the world, followed by South and Central America as shown in Table 7.3. Possible reasons for this include political risk, lack of capital to invest in refineries, and the poor experience in terms of refining margin for the existing refineries in these regions.

7.4.4 Political Risk, Pandemic, and Shocks

A key risk factor for the downstream oil and gas sector is a political risk which can be in the form of changes in royalty and tax structure. Depending on how strong the rule of law and other good governance institutions are, renegotiation of economic terms, the risk of nationalization of independent oil refineries, the role of geopolitical tensions and conflicts, among others, can impose significant risk for refining activities. A key recent example is the Russian–Ukraine war and the difficulty it has imposed on refining activities in the region and others that depend on Russian crude oil for refining operations. Available data from

Table 7.3 Regional Share of 2020 Refinery Capacity

Region	*Share of 2020 Refining Capacity (%)*
North America	21.40
South and Central America	6.10
Europe	15.30
CIS	8.2
Middle East	10
Africa	3.3
Asia and Pacific	35.8

Source: Authors' computation based on data from BP (2021) Statistics

PRS Group, International Country Risk Guide (2022) indicate a significant level of risk for oil-producing countries located in EMDCs. For instance the composite political risk recorded for Iran in 2022 is 64.5% compared to 79.75% in Canada (high values indicate less political risk). Also, the value for Brazil is 68.5%, while that of the United States is 71.75%.

COVID-19 also created significant changes and risks for the downstream oil and gas sector. The average annual demand for oil in 2020 decreased by about 9.2 mbl/d as compared to 2019 (Bahmanyar et al., 2020). For example in 2020, jet fuel production's profit margin was negative when compared with the Dubai Oil Index. Also, there was a reduction in the end product of crude oil for the petrochemical industry (Norouzi, 2021). The EIA estimates that the world's consumption of oil and other liquid fuels in 2020 declined about 9 per cent relative to the previous year.[10] In the first 9 months of 2020, Sinopec, one of the largest refinery companies, had a decrease in its refinery capacity by 6.3 per cent due to declining demand during the COVID-19 crisis.

7.4.5 Energy Transition Risk

Other risk factors that the downstream oil and gas sector faces are due to current ongoing energy transition into renewable energy sources driven by climate change and energy security concerns. For instance the 2030 plan of the UK is to stop selling gasoline/diesel-powered vehicles. The European Union (EU) strongly supports the transition to a low-carbon, more resource-efficient, and sustainable economy and has been at the forefront of efforts to build a financial system that supports sustainable growth. For example in 2009, policies designed to reduce the emission of greenhouse gases inevitably reduced the use of oil in transport, which created 23% of all estimated CO_2 emissions from fuel usage. This suggests that environmental concerns will gradually compel refiners to provide a higher quality fuel with lesser pollution and higher production cost. In addition, to protect the environment, environmental agencies and regulatory costs keep on increasing. This may have a negative impact on the production cost of refiners and the demand for these fuels globally. These transition processes will have serious consequences on demand for oil and gas in the EMDCs in the long run, as in the short-to-medium term, there will be an increase in demand for oil and gas for transportation, electricity generation, and to grow the economy. This is because the existing systems and structures in the EMDCs will take a long time to align with the new energy sources that will result from the transition process.

7.5 Measurement of Risk Factors and Building Resilience

The downstream oil and gas sector is confronted with numerous risks as classified before. It is, however, important to provide a guide on how some of the risk factors and ways could be measured to build resilience towards them. These are summarised in Table 7.4, where information is provided for the

Table 7.4 Risk Factors, Measurement, and Building Resilience

Risk Factor	*Indicator*	*Measurement*	*Risk*	*Resilience Building*
Economic and market risks	Oil price volatility in global markets. Diversity of source of crude oil and level of competition for refined product	Quarterly variance of oil prices. Herfindahl diversity index.	Exposure to changing market prices of crude and refined products. Concentration of source of crude oil and loss of market power for refined products due to competition.	Participation in oil market hedging to reduce price and exchange rate risk. Diversify source of crude for refining activities. Also, join forcing competing refineries to create market power within the law.
Environmental risk	Emissions from oil and gas refineries	Carbon footprint of a barrel of refined products. % of emissions from the refining process per barrel of refined products.	High emission levels per barrel of refined products. Exposure of the refinery plant to emission leakages.	Keep to current technology in the refinery industry. High standards in maintenance culture. Strick adherence to environmental regulation and standards.
Technological risk	Number of light products processed from the refineries	% of light products or % of fuel oil from a barrel of crude oil. Complexity index.	Exposure to low gross refinery margin. Negative profitability margins.	Support investment in modern technology and increase refining capacity. Invest in having complex and deep conversion configurations.
Political risk	Lapses in good governance and institution. Rule of law and contract enforcement challenges. Corruption.	Political risk index. Quality of institutions index.	Exposure to changes in tax structure at will. Possibility of a nationalisation policy. Likelihood of non-enforcement of contracts.	Diversify the jurisdiction of the refinery. Encourage shareholding by local partners to diversify the political risk

indicator of risk for each of the risk factors, how much risk could be measured, the risk exposure associated with the risk factor, and how to build resilience for the risk. In the case of economic and market risk, two key measures are the variance of oil prices to assess the volatility of the price changes and the Herfindahl diversity index to assess the level of competition and related market power of the refineries in the market.

In building resilience to price and market risk, it is suggested that refiners use market hedging techniques to reduce exposure to price risk. Furthermore, refiners are advised to diversify the source of supply of crude oil and cooperate with other refining companies to build some market power for refining products to have some control over product prices.

Similarly, technological risk factors can be measured by the percentage of light products produced from a barrel of crude oil in a refining process or the complexity index of the refinery. Using these measures, the technological risk associated with the refinery can be determined. After determining and measuring technological risk, a refinery can build reliance on the exposure to this risk by investing in either current refining technology to increase refining efficiency and capacity or in a complex refining configuration that increases the production of light products from crude oil.

7.6 Risk Simulation

This section highlights how the identified risk factors and their respective measurements can be modelled to promote efficient decision-making in the context of the risks. As indicated in Table 7.4, there are many risk factors that can broadly be classified into four or five (if we include the risk posed by energy transition). This suggests that any downstream oil and gas risk simulation model must accommodate these multi-risk factors and their probabilities of occurring. Furthermore, given the complex systems in the downstream oil and gas sector, especially the refining segment, there will likely be a significant level of uncertainty regarding the probabilities of the various risk factors. This suggests, among other things, that some level of sensitivity analysis must be applied to the risk simulation models' estimates to provide a range that will reflect the true value relative to a point estimate. The specific model, parameters, and software for risk simulation in the downstream oil and gas sector are outside the scope of this chapter, and therefore will not be presented and discussed here.

7.7 Decision Analysis of Downstream Oil and Gas Projects

The following are decision analyses of downstream oil and gas projects:

- New manufacturing materials and methods: the sector can engage in the production of new products such as polymer 3D printing, which is expected to grow to $180 billion by 2035, presenting challenges and opportunities to the refinery business models.

- The sector should plan very well to reduce energy consumption and free up working capital – for example through the efficient calculation of the refineries' material balance closure.
- There should be long-term transformation projects to shift future production profiles to build resilience against the disrupted, fast-changing transportation fuel market.
- The sector should embark on environmental projects to achieve a lower carbon footprint and pollution cost in compliance with environmental laws and focus.
- The downstream sector should create value through precision, limiting product exceedances of minimum quality requirements by improving product-demand forecasting, blending processes, and using in-line measurement tools.

7.8 Concluding Remarks

The downstream oil and gas sector is seen as the final processing stage of purifying or modifying a hydrocarbon in a chemical process and then distributing it at that time and offering it to consumers. The sector mainly focuses on purchasing raw crude and transforming it into refined products for use by economic agents in a country. Due to the nature of the projects this sector undertakes, it requires some level of initial capital and is confronted with a series of risks. Hence, we examined the nature of the projects in the sector. We found that the sector basically engages in refinery projects which include the manufacturing of the final products of oil such as fuel oil, gasoline, kerosene, light and heavy diesel, and residues (asphalt, fertilizer, synthetic rubber, plastics, pesticides, among others). Furthermore, the sector undertakes distribution, which incorporates storage (storing of the products after distribution) and marketing of products.

Various risk factors were identified, and suggested measurements for the risk factors were provided. Moreover, measures for building risk resilience for the identified risk factors were provided. It was clear that such risk factors are more pronounced in EMDCs relative to developed countries. Despite the risks and their consequences, the world will still need the downstream oil and gas industry in the short-to-medium term, especially for EMDCs, as it will take some time to transform the current production, consumption, and distribution systems to align with a low carbon economy.

Notes

1 https://www.ilo.org/inform/online-information-resources/research-guides/economic-and-social-sectors/energy-mining/oil-gas-production/lang--en/index.htm
2 https://theenergyyear.com/articles/ghanas-dynamic-downstream-sector/#:~:text=We%20plan%20to%20ensure%20a,to%20around%20USD%203.9%20billion
3 Transportation is often through oil tankers and pipelines.
4 https://www.schedulereader.com/blog/oil-and-gas-industry-overview/
5 https://guides.loc.gov/oil-and-gas-industry/downstream

6 https://www.offshore-technology.com/analysis/largest-refining-companies-in-the-world/
7 https://guides.loc.gov/oil-and-gas-industry/midstream/storage
8 https://crsreports.congress.gov/product/pdf/IN/IN11246
9 https://www.wsj.com/articles/oil-traders-are-scrambling-to-book-tankers-for-storage-11587502041
10 https://www.eia.gov/todayinenergy/detail.php?id=46596

References

Appiah, K. M., Possumah, B. T., Ahmat, N., and Sanusi, N. A. (2018). External environment and SMEs investment in the Ghanaian oil and gas sector. *Economics and Sociology*, 11(1), 124–138.

Aryeetey, M. (2016). *Introduction to Ghana's oil industry: History and fut ure trends.* http://ugspace.ug.edu.gh/handle/123456789/32488

Bahmanyar, A., Estebsari, A., and Ernst, D. (2020). The impact of different COVID-19 containment measures on electricity consumption in Europe. *Energy Research & Social Science*, 68, 101683.

Balasubramanian, K. (2010). *Supply chain management in oil downstream distribution business: A perspective on IT alternatives and issues.* http://www.infosys.com/supplychain/white-papers/Documents/SCM-oil-downstream-distribution.pdf

Bhende, S. G., and Patil, K. D. (2014). Modeling and simulation for FCC unit for the estimation of gasoline production. *International Journal of Chemical Sciences*, 5(2), 38–45.

British Petroleum (2021, July). *Statistical r eview.* https://www.bp.com/en/global/corporate/energy-economics/statistical-review-of-world-energy.html

Chen, J. (2021). *Downstream.* https://www.investopedia.com/terms/d/downstream.asp

Downey, M. (2009). *Oil 101* (Vol. 600). New York: Wooden Table Press.

Energy Information Administration (EIA) (2012). Crude oil distillation and the definition of refin ery capacity. https://www.eia.gov/todayinenergy/detail.php?id=6970

Energy Institute. (2019). *Oil and gas.* https://www.energyinst.org/exploring-energy/topic/oil-and-gas

Franco, G. (2019). *Big oil facing energy transition: Implications, corporate strategies and role as incumbent regime companies* (Master's thesis, University of Twente).

Greenblatt, N. A. (2016). Self-driving cars and the law. *IEEE Spectrum*, 53(2), 46–51.

Gudde, N. J. (2018). Adaptation of oil refineries to make modern fuels. *Proceedings of the Institution of Mechanical Engineers, Part D: Journal of Automobile Engineering*, 232(1), 5–21.

IBISWorld. (n.d.). *Global oil & gas exploration & production market size 2005–2025.* https://www.ibisworld.com/global/market-size/global-oil-gas-exploration-production/

Kim, S. T., and Choi, B. (2019). Price risk management and capital structure of oil and gas project companies: Difference between upstream and downstream industries. *Energy Economics*, 83, 361–374.

Kramer, L. (2022, March). *Upstream vs. downstream oil and gas operations: What's the difference?* https://www.investopedia.com/ask/answers/060215/what-difference-between-upstream-and-downstream-oil-and-gas

Leffler, W. L. (1985). *Petroleum refining for the nontechnical person.* Tulsa, OK: PenWell Books

Lewin, G. (2003). Managing the downstream oil supply chain: A customer-led strategy. *World Energy*, 10, 22–25.

Mckinsey (2022). *Energy insights.* https://www.mckinseyenergyinsights.com/resources/refinery-reference-desk/refining/

Norouzi, N. (2021). Post-COVID-19 and globalization of oil and natural gas trade: Challenges, opportunities, lessons, regulations, and strategies. *International Journal of Energy Research*, 45(10), 14338–14356.

Sar, A. K. (2017). Competitive advantage and performance: An analysis of Indian downstream oil and gas industry. *Academy of Accounting and Financial Studies Journal*, 21(2), 1–7.

Speight, J. G. (2006). *The chemistry and technology of petroleum*. London: CRC press.

Vynakov, O. F., Savolcva, E. V., and Skrynnyk, A. I. (2016). Modern electric cars of Tesla Motors company. *Автоматизация технологических и бизнес-процессов*, 8(2), 9–18.

Wamono, R. N., Kikabi, P., and Mugisha, J. (2012). *Constraints and opportunities for SMEs investment in Uganda's oil and gas sector*. Dakar: Investment Climate and Business Environment.

8 The Market for Crude Oil

Ebenezer Bugri Anarfo, Joseph Abor, George N. A. Donkor, and Freshia Mugo-Waweru

8.1 Introduction

> The Future looks like gasoline . . . crude oil . . . is the future before it has been refined. It is like a dream of the future, really, and like any dream, it ends with a rude awakening.
>
> —Chris Cleave

Crude oil is a non-renewable naturally occurring mineral resource. It is a combination of natural-source hydrocarbons that range in colour from yellow to black and vary in density and viscosity. It is extracted and distilled into different products such as gasoline, diesel, jet fuel, and heating oils.

The modern-day oil business dates back to Baku in the year 1837. It was in the same year that commercial oil refinery was established to distil oil into paraffin. In 1846, the first modern oil well was drilled. Thereafter, commercial oil wells were drilled in Bóbrka, Poland, in 1854; Bucharest, Romania, in 1857; Pennsylvania, the United States, in 1859; and Ontario and Canada in 1858, prompting a "black gold" rush in many of these areas. Iran, Kuwait, Iraq, Venezuela, and Saudi Arabia established the Organization of Petroleum Exporting Countries (OPEC) in the 1960s in Baghdad, Iraq, with the goal of suppressing competition and controlling prices among their economies. They were supposed to be the Organization's founding members. Qatar, Indonesia, Libya, the United Arab Emirates, Algeria, Nigeria, Ecuador, and Gabon were among the first group of countries to become members of OPEC after its establishment in the 1960s.

Economic and political situations, fluctuations in the growth of the petroleum sector, and technological breakthroughs are some of the factors that have determined the price of crude oil throughout its history. These factors continue to impact oil prices today (Zweifel et al., 2017). Tables 8.1 and 8.2 show the world's leading producers and consumers.

Global markets determine the price of crude oil. Oil price hikes can have a variety of impacts on the real price of oil, and this depends on the fundamental cause of the rise in price. The main factors that influence the real price of oil are divided into three categories: shocks to current availability of crude oil

DOI: 10.4324/9781003315056-11

Table 8.1 World Oil Producers and Number of Barrels Per Day (2022)

Country	*Estimated Oil Reserves (Barrels Per Day, in Millions)*
Russia	10.58
Saudi Arabia	10.13
The United States	9.352
Iran	4.469
Iraq	4.454
Canada	3.977
China	3.383
United Arab Emirates	3.174
Kuwait	2.753
Brazil	2.622

Table 8.2 World Oil Leading Consumers and Number of Barrels Per Day (2022)

Country	*Estimated Oil Reserves (Barrels Per Day, in Millions)*
The United States	19.69
China	11.75
India	4.489
Japan	4.026
Russia	3.594
Saudi Arabia	3.237
Brazil	3.018
South Korea	2.63
Germany	2.41
Canada	2.379

(oil supply shocks), shocks to recent demand for crude oil caused by changes in the world business environment (oil demand shocks), and shocks caused by changes in precautionary demand for oil (precautionary demand shocks).

The rest of the chapter is structured as follows: Section 8.2 gives an overview of the oil market in emerging and developing countries, Section 8.3 looks at crude oil price formation, Section 8.4 examines crude oil transactions, Section 8.5 explores the effect of oil price volatility on emerging and developing economies, and finally Section 8.6 concludes the chapter.

8.2 Overview of the Oil Market in Emerging and Developing Countries

Countries all over the world desire and pursue measures that propel economic growth that is geared towards improving the living standard of its citizens, as well as guaranteeing stability in its macro-economic environment. Macroeconomic stability has the potential of fostering and promoting the smooth running of businesses. The earnest desire by countries to achieve economic growth can be attributed to the varied benefits it provides, some of which may include improved government revenue, better infrastructure, lower unemployment, higher incomes, increased life expectancy, better education, stability in the macroeconomic environment, poverty reduction, and various forms of public and private investments. Economic growth is basically explained as a rise in the real GDP of a country over a period of time. It is therefore highly imperative to explore the various factors that could contribute to achieving this all-important macroeconomic goal with a particular focus on the role of oil markets within the context of emerging and developing countries.

The oil market involves the trading of oil and gas products. Oil products are in the form of either unrefined oil or refined oil. The unrefined oil, also known as crude oil, is the raw form of oil and is defined by the Britannica dictionary as a mixture of relatively volatile liquefied hydrocarbons; it also contains some nitrogen, sulphur, and oxygen. It is the key raw material processed in a refinery. The crude oil is the main input for obtaining the various kinds of refined petroleum products. Crude oil varies in colour, consistency, and composition and is broadly grouped as heavy or light and sour or sweet, resulting in the production of different kinds of refined petroleum products. Gasoline, LPG, kerosene, naphtha, jet fuel, fuel oils, lubricants, etc., are therefore some of the various types of refined petroleum products that are obtained from the processing of crude oil. The price of crude is therefore a major determinant of the price of the refined petroleum products. Crude oil prices, however, are largely determined by global supply and demand. It is worthy to note that the economic growth of emerging and developing countries is a major factor which affects the demand for oil.

The oil sector is categorised into three segments: downstream, midstream, and upstream. The upstream sector, popularly called the exploration and production (E&P) sector, encompasses activities and processes that are undertaken to find and extract crude oil. Well drilling starts in the upstream sector. The midstream serves as a critical link between producing areas and urban areas. The midstream sector's primary assets include field gathering, processing plants, and transmission pipelines, and it is dependent on both strong upstream supply and consumer demand.

The downstream component of the oil market is in charge of refining, transporting, and selling refined petroleum products derived from crude oil. Its main functions are oil refining, supply and trade, and marketing of oil products. The downstream sector is distinguished by the fact that it provides goods to end users.

8.2.1 The Oil Market in Ghana

Oil market in Ghana is highly regulated so as to enable a systematic and fair business environment. Whereas the upstream is regulated by the GNPC, the downstream is regulated by the National Petroleum Authority (NPA). Ghana currently has oil companies that operate in the upstream sector and also those that operate in both the upstream and downstream sectors. The following sections will consider them in turn.

8.2.2 The Upstream Oil Market in Ghana

Ghana licensed international companies such as Tullow Oil and Kosmos Energy in 2004 to engage in offshore oil exploration and production. Ghana's first crude oil was discovered in the Western Region of the country in July 2007. The second major crude oil discovery, named the Tweneboa Field, was made in March 2009, and since then, Sankofa-Gye-Nyame fields and other wells have also been discovered. The surge in Ghana's crude oil production has resulted in the country being a net exporter. The crude is sold to international refineries at benchmarked prices to enable adequate generation of foreign currency into the country since crude oil prices are quoted in United States Dollars. The upstream operation in Ghana is however very limited and therefore is unable to offer a lot of job opportunities to the citizenry. The institution responsible for the issuance of upstream license is the Petroleum Commission of Ghana.

8.2.3 The Downstream Oil Market in Ghana

The downstream sector of Ghana's petroleum companies is licensed by the NPA. The various downstream licenses issued include the Bulk Oil Distribution and Export Company (BIDEC), the Oil Marketing Company (OMC), the Liquefied Petroleum Gas Marketing Companies (LPGMS), and the Bulk Road License and the Terminal Construction License. All licensed companies which provide petroleum services to the citizenry are termed Petroleum Service Providers (PSPs). The NPA regulates the activities of PSPs and ensures that oil products are made available to consumers at all times. Prior to 2015, part of the Authority's responsibility was to regulate prices by PSPs, but from July 2015, the industry was price deregulated apart from premix fuel and residual fuel oil (RFO). A significant benefit of the establishment of these companies in the oil market is their contribution to the creation of more jobs in the Ghanaian economy.

8.2.4 The Oil Market in Nigeria

Just like Ghana, the Nigerian oil market encapsulates both the upstream and downstream sectors. However, there are remarkable differences in their modus operandi, especially in the area of the downstream activities. The Nigerian National Petroleum Corporation (NNPC) is the body which issues licenses to service providers in the petroleum sector in PSPs of Nigeria.

8.2.4.1 The Upstream Oil Market in Nigeria

Nigeria is the largest producer of oil in Africa, and, since 1971, it has been part of the Oil Producing and Exporting Countries (OPEC). The country thus has a very vibrant upstream sector. Several types of crude oils were discovered in Nigeria, but the crude of interest in this chapter is the Bonny Light crude. This crude is sweet and also largely free of sulphur. The major concern, however, is Nigeria's over dependence on its oil for the country's economic growth. The US market was the largest consumer of the Nigerian Bonny Light up until July 2014. Currently, it is the Indian market that is the biggest importer of the Nigerian crude oil.

The major concern however is the economy of Nigeria being over-dependent on its oil product since 1956. The oil industry in Nigeria accounts for over 95% of the country's export earnings and about 40% of its government revenues, according to the International Monetary Fund. This indeed poses a major threat to the soundness of the Nigerian economy. It makes the Nigerian economy more vulnerable to external shocks in the global oil market.

8.2.4.2 The Downstream Oil Market in Nigeria

The downstream sector deals with trade in only refined petroleum products, and these products are fully imported. The downstream operation of the oil market in Nigeria is completely different from that of Ghana, but similar to that of Namibia, Burkina Faso, and Mali. The modus operandi is in the form of a state tendering process, where the NNPC controls the entire process. The Authority decides on periodic basis, the amount of refined petroleum products that must be supplied in order to meet the needs of the country for the refined petroleum products. Negotiations are then made with various refineries in any part of the world, and, upon agreement, the Authority acquires the amount of the refined products needed by the economy.

A tender is then opened after the product acquisition to the various licensed oil marketing companies in the country to bid for product allotment. Successful tenderers are awarded allotments of the product to trade within a specified period. One important feature of this model is the ownership right of the state over the refined product and also the fact that PSPs are not operating in a free market. The Authority further enforces price regulation among the PSPs.

8.3 The Formation of Oil Prices

Private oil majors stopped being vertically integrated after the emergence of national oil businesses in the 1970s, resulting in a large growth in international oil trading. The wholesale oil markets consist of two types of merchants.

Firms that have taken a long position are the net suppliers who sell more crude oil than they could actually produce or refine, resulting in a crude oil surplus. National oil businesses, for example, lack not only processing capacity but also access to consumer market because the oil majors continue to control the majority of filling station networks. Companies which have a short position are the net demanders who rely on crude oil purchases to fill their filling station networks and use their refining capacity. Typically, they are the oil majors, who have lost a large number of oil fields and extraction rights.

The development of wholesale oil markets is aided by this framework. One has to differentiate spot markets (for physical delivery), forward markets (ultimately for physical delivery), and financial derivatives markets. On spot markets, the contract is signed, the delivery is made, and the payment is made all at the same time. Settlement in the oil business is often delayed due to logistical issues, but it seldom takes more than 2 weeks. With regard to forward markets, the delivery and payment are due in months, if not years, after the contract has been signed. Volumes and prices are established ahead of delivery, allowing the party less capable of bearing risk to shift the risk (of a price change in particular) to the party who is better able to bear it because its activities are more diversified.

Physical quantity contracts, such as futures and options, are exchanged on derivative markets rather than on exchanges, and payment is financial instead of physical. The derivative markets are open to merchants who are outside the oil industry, such as financial markets and institutions.

Another distinction is between contracts executed on an energy exchange and those made outside of such an exchange. Those contracts that are made outside of the energy exchange are called over-the-counter contracts—in short, OTC markets. Because of counterparty risk, energy exchanges are used instead of over-the-counter markets. Each contracting party faces the possibility of the counterparty defaulting, for example due to bankruptcy. While this risk increases as time passes until the contract is settled, it can be avoided if the energy exchange acts as the counterparty. Because it maintains a large number of contracts, the exchange is better positioned to resist this risk, minimizing the likelihood of many defaults.

Clearing houses, on the other hand, insulate themselves from business and financial risk by letting their members present collateral security. This collateral is adjusted to reflect new market developments – that is "marking to market". The cost of counterparty insurance can result in high transaction costs for traders. Another benefit that energy exchanges provide is that sellers and buyers do not need to know the identity of their counterparty. The two most important crude oil exchanges are the International Commodity Exchange (ICE) in London (formerly called the International Petroleum Exchange) and the New York Mercantile Exchange (NYMEX). Each one develops a "benchmark crude" to describe the quality of the product. West Texas Intermediate (WTI) trades in Cushing, Texas, and North Sea Brent trades in Europe. Dubai Crude has just been established as the benchmark crude for the Persian Gulf.

8.4 Prices of Crude Oil and Crude Oil Transactions

Oil prices, unlike most other commodities, are not solely determined by supply, demand, and market perceptions of the product itself. Instead, oil futures contracts, which are commonly traded by speculators, are driven by supply, demand, and the attitude of market participants towards the commodity. Crude oil prices are influenced on a global scale by supply and demand. Economic growth is a major factor determining petroleum product and consequently crude oil demand. Energy consumption rises as economies expand, notably for transporting commodities and resources from producers to consumers.

8.4.1 Prices of Crude Oil Futures

Derivatives markets can emerge once spot markets that are liquid for benchmark crudes have been created. Oil futures markets are traded on energy exchanges and are the most important derivatives. Futures are standardised contracts with 1,000 barrels as benchmark oil that are settled at defined prices and delivered over a set period of time (middle of the month). While physical quantity settlement is possible, it is more common to settle on a financial basis. If the spot price is higher than the price agreed upon in the future, the exchange pays the difference to the contract buyer, while the seller must pay the difference to the exchange. If the spot price is lower than the future price, the contract buyer must make up the difference, while the seller is paid.

The operator of a refinery with excess capacity is a common example. One option is to purchase crude oil on the spot market and store it for use months later. This approach has a "cost of carry" that includes insurance and storage charges and the interest savings on the capital invested. A future contract with the right maturity T can likewise be purchased by the operator. There is a possibility for arbitrage as long as the two options differ in price, which the refinery operator can use to reduce its sourcing expenses. In contrast, if there is no room for arbitrage at trade date *t,* the market equilibrium is achieved, which suggests the following link between spot price P_t and future price $P_{F,t}(T)$ (Hull, 1999; Kaldor, 1939):

$$P_{F,t}\left(T\right) = P_t.e^{(i+c)(T-t)} \tag{8.1}$$

Thus, the price of the forward contract must be equivalent to the spot price accrued for interest *i* and the carrying cost of *c* during the time Periods $(T - t)$, provided *c* does not vary but is constant. Eq. (8.1) stands for a cointegration equation of degree one, which suggests that the two time series, cannot diverge permanently. Eq. (8.1) therefore becomes

$$\lim_{t\to T} P_{F,t}\left(T\right) = P_t \tag{8.2}$$

$$P_{F,to}\left(T\right) > P_{F,t1}\left(T\right) > P_t \text{ for } t_1 > t \tag{8.3}$$

The no arbitrage condition predicts four things. With regard to Eq. (8.1), (i) as long as the spot price increases, all things being equal, the future price should rise over time; (ii) based on Eq. (8.2), the forward price contract for any given time *T* should approach the spot price as time *t* goes on; (iii) the forward price should always be greater than the spot price in view of the inequality (8.3); and

(iv) this excess should decline over time since the difference $(T - t)$ goes to 0, again in view of inequality (8.3).

8.4.2 Wholesale Prices of Oil Products

Crude oil wholesale price is equivalent to the sum of the purchase price paid by refineries and the cost of the refinery plus a margin. The spread margin is different from the cash margin when calculating refinery margins. The spread margin is the difference between the oil product's sale price and the crude's purchase price; it is crystal clear since it can be determined using publicly available price data. The difference between oil sales and oil production cost is the cash margin. Its estimate necessitates the insider knowledge of refinery operating costs, which is not available to the general public. Due to the unavailability of data on refinery products and their costs, calculating the spread is difficult, so the calculation is done on the basis of the use of simplified assumptions. For determining the crack spread of refineries, the following formula is frequently used:

$$Crack\ Spread = (2.P_{gasoline} + P_{fuel\ oil}) / 3 - P_{crude} \tag{8.4}$$

The difference in price between a barrel of crude oil and the petroleum products processed from it is referred to as a crack spread. It is a form of gross processing margin that is unique to a given industry. The phrase "crack" refers to the process of dissolving crude oil into its constituent products, which include gases such as propane, heating fuel, and gasoline; light distillates such as jet fuel; intermediate distillates such as diesel fuel; and heavy distillates such as grease. Refiners employ futures to hedge the crack spread in order to reduce pricing risks. The crack spread can also be used to hedge other assets or speculate on expected price fluctuations in oil and refined petroleum products by futures and options traders. The refiner buys oil futures and offsets the position by selling gasoline, heating oil, or other distillate futures that they will be generating from those barrels, according to the conventional crack spread strategies.

8.5 Impact of Oil Price Volatility on Emerging and Developing Economies

Over the past years, oil prices have witnessed series of shocks, leading to high volatilities in prices and uncertainties in the oil market. Oil consumption has also increased over the years due to growth in productive capacities. However, it is worth noting that the increased consumption of oil has largely been the case for emerging and developing markets. This could be attributed to their rapid economic growth and the fact that most of these markets are net importers of oil. It is therefore important to understand the extent to which such economies are impacted by oil price fluctuations and volatility.

A vivid example of a negative effect of oil price shocks on emerging markets is the drastic increase in price of petroleum products due to the Russian-Ukraine war that broke out on 24th February 2022. While the world witnessed a sharp increase in the oil prices, developing countries like Ghana witnessed over 30% jump in their oil pump price. Two major factors that have accounted for such a drastic impact are the hikes in the oil price and the depreciation of the Ghana cedi against the dollar. Oil prices either from Brent or West Texas Intermediate (WTI) are usually spot prices, and they experience changes daily. Also, oil traders buy futures contracts that enable them to buy quantities of oil for a specific price on a particular date in the future, which results in either contango or backwardation.

When the spot price of oil is lower than the forward price of a futures contract, the market is said to be in contango, whereas with backwardation, the forward price of the futures contract is lower than the spot price. Oil businesses in Ghana, for example, modify prices approximately every 2 weeks.

Aside the rapid shocks of oil prices due to the volatile nature of the oil commodity, the prices are denominated in US Dollars, and therefore unstable exchange rates of emerging markets also contribute to the volatilities. Oil price volatility refers to the fluctuations in oil prices over a period of time, creating a measure of uncertainty in the oil markets. The highly volatile nature of oil prices tends to make oil prices see larger fluctuations and uncertainties compared with other commodities. Oil price volatility can however be low or high, where low volatility will occur when oil prices are relatively stable over a period of time, while high volatility of oil prices occurs when there is a continuous rise in the oil price over shorter periods of time. The following are some factors that could account for the continuous changes or volatility in the oil prices:

8.5.1 The Role of OPEC

OPEC is made up of Algeria, Angola, Congo, Ecuador, Equatorial Guinea, Gabon, Qatar, Iran, Iraq, Kuwait, Libya, Nigeria, Saudi Arabia, United Arab Emirates, and Venezuela. OPEC's principal purpose is to ensure fair and stable oil prices by coordinating and harmonizing policies on petroleum production and output among its member countries. One of its major foci is to control oil output in order to influence prices, as they control the world's largest supply of oil reserves and set production levels to meet global demand for oil. The strategies adopted by OPEC at any given time, especially with respect to oil availability, have a direct impact on oil prices. If, for any reason, OPEC is unable to supply to meet global demand, oil price will soar, and vice versa.

8.5.2 Capacity Utilisation

Another important factor which contributes to changes in oil prices is capacity utilisation. When capacity utilisation is low, a rise in oil demand can be met with a little extra cost. The oil supply curve in a market diagram is perfectly elastic (practically horizontal). When capacity utilisation is high, the only way to meet additional demand is to work longer, faster, and hire more people, all of which can boost marginal cost (haste makes waste, as the proverb goes). Because the supply curve has a high slope, every rise in demand will result in a price increase. In the long run, capacity is modified by introducing new machinery that combines technical advancements and thereby lowers marginal cost. The supply curve shifts out, resulting in a decrease in price only if demand does not rise continually. Many analysts distinguish between OPEC and non-OPEC countries in terms of capacity utilisation. Large spare capacity in non-OPEC countries, in particular, limits the cartel's ability to raise oil prices. Spare capacity in OPEC countries, on the other hand, may be meaningless if cartel discipline among OPEC members is high.

8.5.3 Natural Disasters

Natural disasters such as earthquakes, hurricanes, and flooding that occur in major oil-consuming and oil-producing countries can affect oil prices. A shortage of oil supply could arise when an oil-producing country suffers some disaster, and this could lead to an increase in the oil price since demand will outpace the supply. On the other hand, oil price can fall when a natural disaster hits a major oil-consuming country and therefore limits the country's ability to import oil, resulting in over supply.

8.5.4 Political Instability

Political unrest in oil-exporting and -importing countries has a significant impact on oil price volatility. Due to turmoil and consumer panic over wars in Afghanistan and Iraq, the price of a barrel of oil hit $128 in July 2008. And currently, the war between Russia and Ukraine has resulted in oil price changes. This indicates that political instability in a country that supplies the majority of the world's oil has a significant impact on price fluctuations.

8.5.5 Production Cost

Brazil's oil production costs nearly $49 per barrel. In Canada, a barrel of oil costs roughly $41. Production expenses in the United States are $36 per barrel, which is still less than the market price. The costs of operating and maintaining oil wells and related facilities per barrel of oil equivalent are known as the production cost of oil. Oil prices rise when production costs rise, and vice versa.

8.5.6 Cost of Storage

Surplus oil is stored in oil storage facilities such as oil tanks. Surplus oil could arise when supply outweighs demand for oil. There are, however, limits as to the quantity of oil that can be stored. Hence, as the storage tanks fill up, concerns about the surplus oil impact heavily on oil prices. A vivid example was when oil price became negative for the first time in the early part of 2020 due to the tightening of oil-storage capacity amid the COVID-19 pandemic that led to a dramatic fall in oil futures.

8.5.6.1 Impact of Oil Price Volatility—Theoretical and Empirical Evidence

Oil prices volatility may have a number of adverse effects on governments, firms, and consumers in emerging economies. The following section reviews some of the empirical literature on the effects of oil price volatility on emerging economies.

Rafiq and Salim (2014) carried out a study on six major emerging countries in Asia using quarterly GDP and oil price data from 1986 to 2013. According to the study, oil price volatility has a negative effect on output growth in China, Malaysia, and Thailand. In India and Indonesia, oil price volatility negatively affects GDP growth as well as inflation, but it affects only inflation in the Philippines.

Kuboniwa (2014) used quarterly real GDP and nominal Brent oil prices to compare the impact of oil prices on three growing oil-rich economies: Russia, Indonesia, and Malaysia, from 1995Q1 to 2011Q4. The link between economic growth and oil prices in emerging economies was examined using two channels: terms of trade and energy efficiency. The author identified a link between output (GDP) and oil prices, as well as between GDP and energy efficiency. The article also looked at the effect of oil prices on output growth via the terms of trade and energy efficiency channels. The author discovered that while oil prices improve energy efficiency in all three economies, they also enhance terms of trade.

The structural vector autoregressive approach was used by Cheng et al. (2019) to examine the dynamic impact of international crude oil price uncertainty on the Chinese economy. Using data on GDP, investment, and government spending from 2000 to 2015, they discovered that larger oil price shocks tend to lower real GDP and investment, whereas lower oil price volatility increases the macro economy. The Chinese government, however, concentrated on and stabilised the economy through expansionary fiscal and monetary measures.

Wilson et al. (2014) utilised a multivariate model to investigate the causal link between oil prices and important macroeconomic indicators in Nigeria from 1980 to 2010. Inflation, interest rate, exchange rate, and real gross domestic product (GDP) were the macroeconomic factors studied using a Granger causality model to assess the impact of oil prices on the macroeconomic indicators. They discovered a positive, although not statistically significant, link between oil price volatility and Nigeria's GDP. To ensure data stationarity, the Granger causality test was used, and the results demonstrated that oil price volatility has no effect on GDP in the short run. The study's findings in Nigeria, however, could be a unique case of the Dutch Disease, in which a country's apparent good fortune turns out to be harmful to its economy in the long run.

Schubert and Turnovsky (2011) investigated the effect of oil price volatility on a small emerging economy. Specifically, the study looked at how the economy's internal production structure and access to the global financial market influence the impact of oil price shocks. They discovered that, in the long run, the impact of oil price volatility is much more dependent on the economy's internal production structure than on financial market access. Three important metrics for summing the long-run consequence were the relative proportion of oil in output, the elasticity of substitution in production, and the sensitivity of the influence of the oil price to the elasticity of substitution.

8.6 Conclusion

This chapter discussed the oil market in emerging and developing countries, the formation of oil prices, and transactions of crude oil. It also examines the causes and impact of oil price volatility on emerging and developing economies. Oil price volatility has the potential of influencing emerging markets' GDP growth (output), inflation, exchange rate, energy efficiency, and investment. There is the need to implement policy measures and reforms in emerging economies and developing countries in order to address the negative impacts of oil price volatility on their respective economies. This will help ensure some stability in oil prices in these countries. Some of the measures they could pursue include macroeconomic stability, proactive measures that reduce natural disasters influencing oil production and curbing political unrest in oil-producing countries. Other measures include reducing oil production cost and increasing storage capacity.

References

Cheng, D., Shi, X., Yu, J., and Zhang, D. (2019). How does the Chinese economy react to uncertainty in international crude oil prices? *International Review of Economics & Finance*, 64, 147–164.

Hull, J. C. (1999). *Options, futures, and other derivative securities*. 4th ed. Englewood Cliffs, NJ: Prentice-Hall.

Kaldor, N. (1939, October). Speculation and economic stability. *Review of Economic Studies*, 7, 1–27.

Kuboniwa, M. (2014). A comparative analysis of the impact of oil prices on the oil-rich emerging economies in the Pacific Rim. *Journal of Comparative Economics*, 42, 328–339

Rafiq, S., and Salim, R. (2014). Does oil price volatility matter for Asian emerging economies? *Economic Analysis and Policy*, 44(4), 417–441.

Schubert, F. S., and Turnovsky, J. S. (2011). The impact of oil prices on an oil-importing developing economy. *Journal of Development Economics*, 94, 18–29.

Wilson, A., David, U., Inyiama, O., and Beatrice, E. (2014). Oil price volatility and economic development: Stylised evidence in Nigeria. *Journal of Economics and International Finance*, 6(6), 125–133.

Zweifel, P. Z., Praktiknjo, A. P., and Erdmann, G. E. (2017). *Energy economics: Theory and applications*. New York: Springer.

9 Financing Oil and Gas Companies in Emerging and Developing Economies

Lawrence M. Atuna, Janet T. Abor, Ananth Rao, and Anthony A. Idun

9.1 Introduction

Energy products in the form of oil and gas contracts have gained traction lately due to their risk/return behaviour (Creti and Nguyen, 2015). As opportunities in oil and gas businesses in advanced markets are diminishing, the attention of industry players is turning to developing countries (Razavi, 1996). This increased attention does not come as a surprise since most of the proven resources can be located in these regions. Thus, international oil companies (IOCs), investors, and service providers are re-allocating their investments to regions in the developing world rather than Europe or North America.

Despite the opportunities that the oil and gas sector presents in these regions, new projects hardly take off due to challenges in securing adequate financing. Projects in the sector are generally capital intensive, long-term, and risky in nature. Considering the nature of the sector, financial institutions in these regions generally lack the capacity to finance large projects due to their weak capital base and the risk-averse nature of their portfolio investments. Oil and gas projects also have difficulty attracting external financing due to weaker regulatory frameworks to monitor and protect the interest of foreign lenders, a difficult operating environment, challenges with accountability and transparency, and the lack of credible institutions in most parts of these regions.

The prospects of proven resource endowments in developing countries and a new wave of stable political climate and positive engagements with the rest of the world present opportunities in the oil and gas sector. In the past, oil and gas projects were financed by IOCs. However, this situation changed in the 1970s with increased involvement of governments, especially in oil-importing countries, to secure control of their reserves. Projects were funded through government budgetary support, official borrowing, and, to some extent, IOCs' funds. The experience of state involvement left much to be desired, hence attention shifted to private financing in the 1990s with reduced state activity. In the last two decades, the traditional model of financing oil and gas projects has collapsed; international companies finance less of projects, creating a huge gap in financing, and there is no consensus on a new appropriate model.

DOI: 10.4324/9781003315056-12

Lenders for projects in developing countries increasingly demand local participation from both public and private indigenous oil companies to drive local participation and sharing of risk in contracts. Though public and private enterprises are markedly different, it is becoming a growing trend for state-owned entities to tap into commercial markets for private bonds, bank loans, and sale of equities traditionally employed by private companies to fund projects, and for private companies to apply for official sources, mostly with government guarantees, and enter joint venture agreements. State involvement may influence access to capital base depending on the nature of the project and the business climate of the country. It is argued that investors tend to fund projects in the upstream and refineries when they are private business led. For infrastructure projects, a larger role for the state is normally justified. Where projects have an appropriate ownership mix, it influences the range of financing opportunities including access to multilateral institutions (Razavi, 1996).

The chapter discuses financing of oil and gas companies. It examines recent developments in oil and gas financing in emerging and developing economies and the financing needs of oil and gas companies. It also discusses the nature of oil and gas financial markets and funding for oil and gas companies.

9.2 Recent Developments in Oil and Gas Financing in EMDEs

The attractiveness of energy markets in developing countries can be associated with the regions' recent growth-oriented policies and initiatives, liberalised business environment, fast-paced economic growth and development, increasing regional collaboration, and positive engagement with multilateral agencies, buttressed by political stability (Songwe, 2014). This changing environment presents opportunities for international investors to diversify portfolios. Four factors can largely explain the recent developments in the oil and gas sector in developing countries, namely the increase in demand for natural gas for both domestic and industrial use in line with cleaner energy mechanisms, changes in energy markets globally, repositioning of state involvement, and the global demand of energy sustainability.

In the last two decades, natural gas has been identified as a cheaper alternative for power generation. This efficient and economic consideration has increased the demand for gas as a popular energy source. It is reported that annual natural gas consumption in developing countries has increased by 6% in the last two decades (Razavi, 1996). Closely linked to this is the success in the development of the combined gas-based cycle plants which run on both gas and steam to produce more electrical energy from the same fuel source than traditionally produced by a simple-cycle plant. The residual heat generated from the gas turbine is routed to a steam turbine which generates additional power. It is estimated that an additional 50% of power can be produced from this hybrid scheme.

Changes in the political and economic environments in Africa and most developing countries have had a marked impact on the oil and gas industry globally. The period between the 1970s and 1980s was characterised by heightened uncertainties in the petroleum sector in general and the energy prices in particular (Zhang, 2018). Though these concerns still persist, since the 2008 global financial crisis, energy markets globally have exhibited more financial characteristics and a strong correlation with financial markets (Zhang, 2018). Energy commodity assets have been critical factors that have largely driven the so-called "commodity bubble" in the post-crisis era (Zhang and Ji, 2018; Creti and Nguyen, 2015). Thus, these assets are now viewed as associated risk with financial products and the development of derivative markets through the financialisation of commodity assets, mainly oil and gas. The emphasis is now to trade energy assets through cost-effective means on international markets and for local products in developing markets to be priced on an international competitive basis.

Prominent on the global agenda are issues of the environment and climate change. Oil and gas projects often pose a threat to environmental safety and sustainability which need to be examined and addressed. Projects in industrial countries come with clear safety standards at the design and implementation stage. In developing countries, the need for transparency and safety standards for the oil and gas sector has gained steam, unlike in the past. The emergence of more private players in the hydrocarbon industry has heightened the demand for environmental standards since most private players operate at sub-optimal standards, posing a threat to the environment. Following the development of Emission Trading Scheme (ETS) in Europe, developing countries are designing their own schemes. In response to the increasing demand to reduce greenhouse emissions, China has established its own ETS. The attendant challenges these schemes pose are issues of carbon pricing and carbon financing.

Hydro carbon markets, green finance, and investment are now an important trend since the introduction of the carbon fund in April 2020 by the World Bank (Zhang, 2018). Globally, China offers the largest market for "green bonds" which offer opportunities for players in the renewable energy space. The establishment of a system of financing green (renewable) projects has influenced further development of the carbon market by monetary authorities and commercial banks in facilitating the financing of low-carbon emissions projects (Campiglio, 2016).

In developing countries, the experience of state involvement in the industry has helped largely to redefine their roles. Most governments in developing countries are reducing their involvement in direct oil and gas operations since they do not make good entrepreneurs, focusing instead on policy and regulation of markets. Most policies are targeted at increasing local content in a bid to crowd in indigenous private oil companies and allow freely the forces of demand and supply to determine the most efficient ways of supplying products and services.

9.3 Financing Needs of Oil and Gas Companies

The oil and gas industry is made up of several players: independent companies, majors, international oil companies (IOCs), and national oil companies (NOCs). These players are concentrated on an array of segments and geographical areas. As a result, there are variations in the risk profiles and financial requirements of these players. In financing the oil and gas developments, the lenders will study key features such as the strengths; financial, managerial, and technical capabilities of the project sponsors and service company contractors; and several other factors such as political risks and project economics.

It is expected that the financing needs of the industry will be highly enormous, varying from one player to another. Moreover, the probability of the oil majors meeting their financial needs through their own equity funds and internal cash flow complemented by international bond markets is very high. On the other hand, where joint venture partners are incapable of meeting the project development expenditure, they may fall on international banks to raise limited recourse project finance. It is important to note that the internal finances of most NOCs alone cannot help them meet their funding needs, hence the need for various forms of debt finance. Fortunately, raising project finance from the international banks has not been difficult for the majority of NOCs since they have the needed skills and experiences to do so, but the costs of such debt will vary as a result of the differences in the credit rating of the respective countries. Moreover, the international bond market will possibly be a very good competitive alternative to the international bank market for countries with quality or higher credit rating (investment grade). Interestingly, the bond investors usually have a high desire for attractive oil and gas assets.

The success story of oil and gas discoveries in commercial quantities and viable reserves has been good for smaller independent companies. For instance recently, there have been a number of discoveries in East and West Africa. Over the years, the capitalisation and managerial resources of the companies were less compared to the costs of developing such oil and gas reserves. Therefore, there is the need for smaller players to seek funds from private equity providers since they may not be able to finance the operations from their own internal resources. This is imperative because the equity capital will help them finance their exploration before they can get other external supports from either public bonds or private placement. They can also gain project financing in the form of reserve-base lending from banks for their future activities. The inability of the smaller players to get the right finance providers and equity investors will create some challenges for them at all levels of their operations, which can give an opportunity to other companies to take over their operations (companies).

It is important to note that IOCs will face tougher competition for funding new developments, especially in areas with high risks, as NOCs gain more ground in the various host countries. Notwithstanding these challenges and changes in the oil and gas industry such as the bank-financing environment, the financing needs of the oil and gas companies must be met in the future if they are able to combine the various sources of funding (Martin, 2014).

NOCs in countries that produce on a large scale may have access to enormous resources due to their scale compared to those in their early phases; for start-ups, their financial position is far from being ideal. NOCs backed by allocations from government budget continue to suffer financially due to inadequate transfers while those able to retain earnings from sales upstream can easily access finance to execute capital expenditure projects. Companies in the middle of the road, such as GNPC, can retain a defined percentage of revenue from sales and transfer the balance to the state. Though such companies are usually constrained financially, they benefit from a greater predictability for planning purposes. The common challenge is ensuring a balance, as too much independence for NOCs can lead to agency problems (abuse of funds for pet projects). On the other hand, state control inhibits their commercial drive and ability.

Large producers' objectives will be harmed in a period of persistently low oil prices. Governments may lack the patience to invest in the petroleum sector during the downturn due to a diminished revenue stream and other pressing budget considerations. This has implications for NOCs that keep their earnings: the government may request higher dividends. Even in good times, most NOCs have had to augment their revenue through joint ventures with foreign oil firms and financial market transactions, where they compete with private oil corporations. Finding the correct balance between the necessity for governmental supervision over NOC finances and a degree of operational spending autonomy is a major concern for NOCs in the production phase. NOCs that receive government budget allocations usually suffer financially, whereas NOCs that are able to keep earnings from upstream sales can more readily secure the level of capital required for capital-expenditure programmes.

The drop in oil prices, combined with the stalling of exploration programmes, has made it difficult to fund NOC budgets. Many of the NOC's aspirations have had to be curtailed. Spending should be closely aligned with the company's objectives. Lower oil prices also provide a chance for NOCs to achieve new levels of efficiency, focus on their mandate, and improve their overall performance.

9.4 The Nature of the Oil and Gas Financial Markets

For modern economic systems, oil and gas play a pivotal role, and several studies have explored their impact on economic performance extensively. The traditional view held that oil and gas rents (prices) were influenced by demand and supply forces in international markets. Fundamentally, economic factors were adequate in explaining energy prices in the pre-crisis period, but failed afterwards. On the turn of the global crisis in 2008, the failure of the upsurge of global demand to influence supply and price called for a new attention to the drivers of energy markets (Hamilton, 2009). The dynamics in energy markets cannot simply be explained away by fundamental factors (demand and supply). Globally, energy markets and financial markets are now closely linked, and energy prices mimic financial asserts. The energy and finance nexus is inherently interdisciplinary, aimed at exploring linkages. Given the importance of energy and environmental challenges globally, there exists a renewed interest by investors and policymakers in understanding this twin concept (energy finance). Zhang (2018) elaborates on some broad themes in the area.

9.4.1 Energy and Financial Markets

In assessing the impact of oil price risk on stock markets, Chen et al. (1986) do not support a separate role for oil. Sadorsky (1999) suggests a link between energy and stock markets when they employ the price of oil futures as an energy market indicator. These pioneering works have stimulated empirical works exploring the dynamic connectedness of energy and financial markets. In discussing the transmission mechanism of price uncertainty of energy to stock markets, Broadstock et al. (2014) propose both linear and nonlinear relations when they use a capital asset pricing model. Fluctuations in volatility at different times show that there are structural changes and that energy prices have been largely influenced by news from international financial markets since the global crisis (Zhang, 2017).

9.4.2 Pricing Mechanisms

Valuation of oil and gas products has always been a critical issue in energy markets. Most often, price movements largely affect economic output. The key question is – how are products valued? Oil and gas are special commodities, so naturally, fundamental factors are considered relevant in their pricing. Recent evidence of financialisation of energy products has challenged the standard pricing mechanism (Cheng and Xiong, 2014). The characteristics of oil and gas products appear to resemble those of financial assets. The trend now is to incorporate these characteristics into the valuation of energy products (Weiner, 1991; Zhang and Ji, 2018).

9.4.3 Energy Corporate Finance

Understanding the financing and investments decisions in oil and gas projects is a recent breakthrough in energy corporate finance. This development has been shaped by the standard literature in corporate finance, albeit with the notion that oil and gas projects are peculiar and should be independently studied from that perspective. Energy companies tend to hold huge volumes of funds and to invest in low or negative NPV projects (Jensen, 1986). Jensen (1986) proposes the popular Free Cash Flow (FCF) problem that stimulates the agency problem discourse. Empirically, Griffin (1988) and Lamont (1997) examine the FCF hypothesis and conclude that oil price volatility is consistent with Jensen's (1986) hypothesis. In Asia, Zhang et al. (2016a, 2016b) show that energy companies do not take optimal investment decisions and this leads to overinvestment at a cost to stockholders.

9.4.4 Energy Risk Management

Since oil and gas products mimic financial assets, they are prone to uncertainty. For economic and policy reasons, the control and management of risks are crucial. Oil firms must take positions against future price uncertainty, and public authorities must guarantee energy security. Energy market security has received attention empirically (Andriosopoulos et al., 2017; Sadeghi and Shavvalpour, 2006). Results in all these studies indicate that risk contagion has significant implications for market participants. Examining price fluctuations at different times, Ahmad and Rais (2018) further confirm earlier theses on oil and gas financialisation, reinforcing the significant implications for energy risk management.

9.4.5 Energy Derivative Markets

Perhaps oil and gas financialisation gained impetus through the emergence of energy derivative markets. Though critics argue that the activities of speculators impact further uncertainty in spot markets, the primary role of derivatives is as a vehicle in managing risk. Though evidence of the role of energy derivatives is mixed, Haigh and Holt (2002) confirm that futures contracts significantly lower volatility. In periods of financialisation, market instability largely cannot be put down to speculative trading; indeed, the activities of speculators can positively improve price discovery in markets through information sharing (Kim, 2015).

9.5 Funding for Oil and Gas Companies

Increased funding is necessary at all stages of the operations of the oil and gas companies across the globe. The financial crisis of 2007 and 2008 has put lenders and investors in a position that can make it difficult to secure the capital that companies need for their operations. Oil and gas companies can meet their financial needs through a number of ways.

Profits, customers, and suppliers can help the businesses fulfil some of their financial needs internally. Internal finance comes from profit management and distribution. Retained earnings can be used to boost capital, which can then be utilised to fund corporate expansion. Current and fixed asset costs might be compensated by retained profits during inflationary periods. Companies can sell some fixed assets in favour of a less costly alternative in order to generate cash. Companies can raise money from their customers by expediting collections from them. This is done through encouraging partial payments on long-term projects, where appropriate, and by putting an aggressive credit collection policy into effect. Suppliers' credit is an excellent source of low- or no-cost funds. With a good established relationship, suppliers will extend interest-free credit on purchases of goods or services to these companies.

Receivable factoring and project financing are two other ways for oil and gas companies to get money. Factoring is a highly convenient way to finance working capital shortfalls, and it is often an appealing option for a new business with a significant increase in sales that has to be funded. Upon the completion of the work, this technique allows for an advance of up to 90% of the accounts' receivable amount. Project finance is treated in more detail in the next chapter.

Oil and gas businesses can fund their operations through a Technical Assistance Agreement (TAA) or a Joint Venture Contract (JVC). Under a TAA, a country hires an IOC with the necessary technical skills and experience as a contractor to perform a specific duty in an upstream petroleum operation. The project's whole budget is provided by the host country. In exchange for services done, the contractor is only entitled to a cash payment. Two or more corporations make a specific contribution to a project under the JVC (involving the exploration and production of oil for the purpose of making a profit). It has been regarded as a method of risk sharing because each stakeholder contributes unique and valuable abilities to the project. Joint ventures with giant IOCs are the most popular way for developing countries to finance oil and gas projects. Smaller exploration or production businesses and large IOCs frequently create joint ventures.

Leasing and participation bonds can both help oil and gas businesses finance some of their operations. Leasing entails the use of fixed assets rather than their ownership in exchange for a monthly lease payment. Companies' capital funding requirements are reduced, and cash resources can be freed up for more successful business and working capital provision. Companies can utilise participation bonds to finance the construction of commercial/industrial property or to borrow against commercial/industrial property they hold for up to 20 years. Within the first 5 years, just the interest is paid. Following that, the loan is repaid in annual instalments.

Oil and gas firms can also use the capital market to raise funds. This entails issuing equity and bond instruments in order to raise funds for the project. The sale of ordinary and preference shares in the capital market is referred to as equity stock sale. If this is the first time the company is selling shares, it is referred to as an Initial Public Offering (IPO). They can also use the capital market to raise debt financing by issuing bonds. Commercial banks, the World Bank Group, and other regional and national development banks can also provide senior or subordinated loans.

Box 9.1 Turbulent Funding Environment of Oil and Gas

Following the commodity shock of 2014, African oil-exporting countries are under pressure due to a fall in oil prices and the impact of the global pandemic, most recently, as investors liquidate their investments in bond markets. Low prices and global demand are pushing oil and gas balance sheets to the brink. Many key projects depend on a break-even crude oil price of more than $45 per barrel – a far cry from the current value of benchmark commodity Brent crude, which is about $30 per barrel. Raising traditional debt remains a challenge that requires projects to restructure. Oil and gas companies are tapping into alternative sources such as Private Equity investors, hedge funds, distressed debt funds, direct lending, and sovereign wealth funds to see out the down turn. It is estimated that 33% of capital expenditure (US$ 10 billion) of upstream developments could not be carried out across the continent in 2020 as energy firms exercised prudence. Oil and gas companies have to institute robust measures to control and manage cash in a low-price environment as other infrastructure needs are competing with oil and gas projects for the attention of investors and lenders.

Source: Mackenzie (2020)

9.6 Conclusion

Conventional wisdom holds that energy is an indispensable input for socio-economic development. Developing countries are a home of vast natural resources including both fossils and renewable energy endowments. It is also a blessing that the world's frequent and major oil and natural gas discoveries occur in most of these locations. Reserves (oil) grew approximately by 25% and gas by 100% in Africa. The continent's proven oil fields and prospects for further finds have transformed it as a significant player and key "target" in oil production and extraction globally. Despite the prospects of the energy industry in developing countries, its continued development and growth are constrained by financing. The scale of investment required for financing energy projects is enormous. The 2008 global crisis resulted in stringent bank regulations, and as climate sustainability debates heat up around the world, institutions are shying away from fossil fuel investments. On the other hand, developing countries are also pushing for the development of cleaner energy mechanisms to create a balance. Fewer commercial institutions are lending to oil and gas projects in developing countries. Deficit financing is now covered by private equity funds, trade-based lending, and non-bank lenders and, more recently, from investors in both debt and equity.

In developing economies, the "business as usual" model will not be adequate to meet project financing needs. Countries must open up energy sectors to private investment. This can be done through independent power projects (IPPs) and in some cases sector privatisation. Project financing offers many advantages, but to crowd in investment including domestic investors, there is the need for reorganisation within the sector. External finance for oil and gas projects from

IOCs will play a critical role for developing countries. For private capital to play a key role in scaling up investment in developing countries, host countries must establish legal, regulatory, socio-economic, and environmental conditions which are attractive to private investors. The augmented role of private capital should be encouraged in the midst of the changing roles of the public sector of host countries and official assistance.

References

Ahmad, W., and Rais, S. (2018). Time-varying spillover and the portfolio diversification implications of clean energy equity with commodities and financial assets. *Emerging Markets Finance and Trade*, 54(8), 1837–1855.

Andriosopoulos, K., Galariotis, E., and Spyrou, S. (2017). Contagion, volatility persistence and volatility spill-overs: The case of energy markets during the European financial crisis, *Energy Economics*, 66, 217–227.

Broadstock, D. C., Wang, R., and Zhang, D. (2014). Direct and indirect oil shocks and their impacts upon energy related stocks, Economic Systems, 38(3), 451–467.

Campiglio, E. (2016). Beyond carbon pricing: The role of banking and monetary policy in financing the transition to a low-carbon economy, *Ecological Economics*, 121, 220–230.

Chen, N., Roll, R., and Ross, S. A. (1986). Economic forces and the stock market, *Journal of Business*, 59(3), 383–403.

Cheng, I., and Wei Xiong, W. (2014). Financialization of commodity markets, *Annual Review of Financial Economics*, 6(1), 419–441.

Creti, A., and DucKhuong Nguyen, D. K. (2015). Energy markets' financialization, risk spillovers, and pricing models. *Energy Policy*, 82, 260–263.

Griffin, J. M. (1988). A test of the free cash flow hypothesis: Results from the petroleum industry. *The Review of Economics and Statistics*, 1, 76–82.

Haigh, M. S., and Holt M. T. (2002). Crack spread hedging: Accounting for time-varying volatility spillovers in the energy futures markets. *Journal of Applied Econometrics*, 17(3), 269–289.

Hamilton, J. D. (2009). Understanding crude oil prices. *The Energy Journal* 30(2), 179–207.

Jensen, M. C. (1986). Agency costs of free cash flow, corporate finance, and takeovers. *The American Economic Review*, 76(2), 323–329.

Kim, A. (2015). Does futures speculation destabilize commodity markets?, *Journal of Futures Markets*, 35(8), 696–714.

Lamont, O. (1997). Cash flow and investment: Evidence from internal capital markets. *The Journal of Finance*, 52(1), 83–109.

Mackenzie, W. (2020). *How will Africa be affected by the oil industry's capita l investment cuts?* https://www.nsenergybusiness.com/features/oil-investment-africa-coronavirus/

Martin, J. (2014). *Innovative financing for upstream oil and gas, 21st world petroleum congress.* http://firstforum.org/DownloadSpecialistPublicationDetail.1913.ashx

Razavi, H. (1996). Financing oil and gas projects in developing countries. *Finance & Development*, 33(2), 2–5.

Sadeghi, M., and Shavvalpour, S. (2006). Energy risk management and value at risk modelling. *Energy Policy*, 34(18), 3367–3373.

Sadorsky, P. (1999). Oil price shocks and stock market activity. *Energy Economics*, 21(5), 449–469.

Songwe, V., and Africa Growth Initiative. (2014). Africa's capital market appetite: Challenges and opportunities for financing rapid and sustained growth. *Foresight Africa*, 13–17.

Weiner, R. J. (1991). Is the world oil market. One great pool? *The Energy Journal*, 12(3).

Zhang, B., Han Q., Zhang-Ming C., and Bin C. (2016b). Growth in embodied energy transfers via China's domestic trade: Evidence from multi-regional input–output analysis. *Applied Energy*, 184, 1093–1105.

Zhang, D. (2017). Oil shocks and stock markets revisited: Measuring connectedness from a global perspective. *Energy Economics*, 62, 323–333.

Zhang, D., and Ji, Q. (2018). Further evidence on the debate of oil-gas price decoupling: A long memory approach. *Energy Policy,* 113, 68–75.

Zhang, W., Ke L., Dequn Z., Wenrui Z., and Hui G. (2016a), Decomposition of intensity of energy-related CO2 emission in Chinese provinces using the LMDI method. *Energy Policy,* 92, 369–381.

Zhang, Y. (2018). Investigating dependencies among oil price and tanker market variables by copula-based multivariate models. *Energy*, 161, 435–446.

10 Project Finance for the Oil and Gas Industry in Emerging Markets and Developing Economies

Joshua Yindenaba Abor, Benjamin Agyeman, and Paul Kibuuka

10.1 Introduction

Two of the key sources of energy in the world are oil and gas. The demand for oil and gas keeps on growing steadily with significant financial demand. In this regard, the International Energy Agency (IEA) has predicted that the petroleum industry needs US$1 trillion each year to meet the global energy demand in the next two decades. It is a challenge to finance oil and gas projects in a number of countries, especially the emerging markets and developing economies (EMDEs), given that project development activities entail a lot of capital, time, and a high level of risk. For instance in the gas industry alone, there is the need for Africa to mobilise about US$721 billion by 2035 to be in a position to finance its operations.

How do the EMDEs meet the funding needs of the oil and gas industry? Project finance can be used to partly meet this demand. The financing of a number of infrastructure projects in most sectors in these economies including oil and gas has to date been done through the use of project finance. In project finance deals, the lenders look up to the projected cashflows generated from the intended project to repay debt rather than the project sponsor's balance sheet (Clews, 2016). Thus, lenders provide debt to the intended project without recourse to the financial standing of the project sponsor. Understanding this concept assists in raising funds for commercially and economically viable projects with a high level of risk and long-term capital requirements, symptomatic of the oil and gas industry. The complexity can partly be explained by the numerous parties involved in the transaction and the fees that are paid to the third-party participants such as lawyers, insurers, and financial advisors including the cost of monitoring the progress of the project. Notwithstanding this, theoretically, the project finance approach is feasible for any project in most sectors of the economy.

Projects generally have sector- and region-specific characteristics and risks, making it difficult to have a general project finance format for all types of transactions irrespective of the nature of sector or country. Admittedly, there is no exact definition for project finance. Different authors have defined it to suit

DOI: 10.4324/9781003315056-13

their aims and objectives. However, what is provided next is considered a broad project finance definition:

> Project finance is generally used to refer to a nonrecourse or limited recourse financing structure in which debt, equity and credit enhancement are combined for the construction and operation, or the refinancing, of a particular facility in a capital intensive industry, in which lenders base credit appraisals on the projected revenues from the operations of the facility, rather than the general assets or the credit of the sponsor of the facility, and rely on the assets of the facility, including any revenue-producing contracts and other cash flow generated by the facility, as collateral for the debt.
>
> (Institute of International Project Finance)

The definition contains two key terms: nonrecourse and limited recourse. Nonrecourse simply indicates that only the cashflows that will be generated from the project will be used to service the debt secured (Hoffman, 2008; Ahmed and Fang, 1999), while limited recourse means the lenders can in some special situations use some resources from the project sponsor or parent company sponsor of the project to reclaim the capital invested (Ahmed and Fang, 1999). There is a positive relationship between risks associated with predicted cashflows and the level of recourse to be given to the lenders. Another important aspect is that under the tenets of project finance covenants, the borrowing company is seen as the special purpose vehicle (SPV). The Special Purpose Vehicle is allowed as per the covenants to develop, operate, and maintain the project (Kensinger and Martin, 1988).

This chapter discusses project finance in the oil and gas industry. Section 10.2 discusses the project finance market. Section 10.3 examines the role of project finance in the oil and gas industry. Section 10.4 focuses on structured and hybrid finance in the oil and gas industry. Section 10.5 concludes the chapter.

10.2 Project Finance Market

Funding of projects in the oil and gas sector can be obtained from different sources. Previously, host countries financed these projects through budgetary allocation and international oil companies (IOCs). However, given that host governments have to attend to a number of national sector priorities, they sometimes lack the required technology, capital, expertise, and the latitude to solely finance developments in the oil and gas industry. Therefore, there is the need for both domestic and foreign funding. As a result, most oil-producing countries in EMDEs have allowed for foreign investments in the upstream sector developments of the industry. This has created room for the entry of large international companies to capture the oil resources in Africa. In contrast, there is limited access, opportunities, and incentives for investors among major reserve holders in the other regions of the world. Before international institutions commit to finance oil and gas projects either through equity or debt, they undertake due diligence to determine risks, the borrower's credibility, and the trends in the oil price. Given in the next section are some of the funding sources for oil and gas projects in EMDEs.

10.2.1 Equity

Equity can be raised through public offering or private placement.

Public Offering involves companies raising funds for their projects through the issuing of specific financial instruments in the financial markets. Financial markets are composed of capital and money markets. The money markets encompass trade in short-term debt, while the capital market deals in long-term assets. These markets are made up of the primary and secondary divisions: "a primary market is where securities are created, while the secondary market is where securities are traded". Ordinary and preference shares are equity securities, and company shares issued for the first time to raise capital in the market are called Initial Public Offering. Subsequent issues are called public offerings. The stock exchange helps companies to raise funds. Those companies in the businesses of oil and gas products listed on the stock exchange have easier access to public funds through higher corporate governance compliance than those that are not listed. Independent indigenous oil companies involved in exploration and production activities list on the stock exchanges to raise capital for project development. The various bond markets in the respective countries also provide financial support for project development.

With **Private Placement,** private investors with interest in project development also fund project sponsors for financial and developmental returns in bankable projects. Institutional investors in the developed economies have done more in the oil and gas industry than their counterparts in the EMDEs. These institutions are risk averse to fund the petroleum industry in regions where country, completion, and commodity price risks are considered to be high.

10.2.2 Project Finance Debt

The traditional role of commercial banks in the project finance funding process cannot be underestimated. These banks, through loan syndications, are able to raise capital from the local and more especially the international markets to finance a number of projects.

Commercial Banks (local and foreign): aside their traditional functions of taking deposits, providing loans, and offering other payment services, the structuring of project finance transactions has been another key role of commercial banks. They have been at the forefront of lead arranging deals in the oil and gas industry's project finance projects. For instance in 2009, US$265 million was raised by eight Nigerian banks as a refinancing deal for ExxonMobil and the Nigeria National Petroleum Corporation. The financing of projects in the oil and gas industry by the international banks is linked to a number of factors including: Is the project viable?

Does it have a strong sponsor and is it located in a country with strong macro-economic fundamentals? What is the level of security of the project, and will the cashflows generated be sufficient to service the loans on time? The financing costs of these projects in EMDEs are normally higher than those in the developed economies due to underperformance in the factors mentioned.

Export Credit Agencies: exporters receive support from their governments through export credit agencies (Clews, 2016). This support is provided through various financing schemes in project finance, mainly guarantee structures or credit insurance (Clews, 2016). They cover the export of goods and services that are eligible. Each export credit agency through the respective government provides support according to their own methods and procedures. In general, export credit agencies have played some roles in funding oil and gas projects though project finance. The Exports Credit Guarantee Department and Multilateral Investment Guarantee Agency are some of the outstanding export credit agencies in the world. Part of the merits of using export credit agencies in project financing includes the following:

- Loans guaranteed by an export credit agency can be booked as a sovereign credit risk to be borne by the HC of the export credit agencies.
- Currently, there is zero-rated credit risk for government-backed export credit agencies in OECD countries.
- Political risks are covered by the export credit agencies.
- Commercial banks have a shorter repayment period as compared to that of the export credit agency, which is over 10 years, enabling the project to record an increase in the return on equity.

Box 10.1 Export Credit Agency Supported Project in Nigeria – Nigerian Liquefied Natural Gas (NLNG)

"Nigerian Liquefied Natural Gas" was expanded with the introduction of two additional trains in 2002 through the "Nigerian Liquefied Natural Gas Plus project". This expansion made the project the highest project finance deal in Nigeria. Additionally, it was considered the highest project value financed through private sector participation in the whole Sub-Saharan Africa then and was titled "the African oil and gas deal of the year for 2002". The cost of the project was valued at US$620 million for a period of 8 years. Some of the participants in the deal included the African Development Bank as well as six banks from Nigeria. It was agreed that in case of default export, credit agencies would be responsible for buying debt from the banks as well as the loan recovery. Fortunately, by December 15, 2010, the loans had been fully settled.

10.2.3 Multilateral Agencies and Development Finance Institutions

These are institutions owned by national and regional governments, which are responsible for promoting development. They are normally involved in co-lending with commercial banks. On the other hand, some MLAs offer equity, advisory, and other services to governments relating to specific projects. The World Bank Group has provided a lot of assistance to projects in EMDEs. International Bank for Reconstruction and Development, International Monetary Fund, International Finance Corporation, and Multilateral Investment Guarantee Agency are key agencies of the World Bank.

International Bank for Reconstruction and Development (IBRD) – the IBRD came into existence in 1944. It was called the World Bank. It provides support for long-term finance to countries with favourable sovereign rating for infrastructural development projects in the form of loan guarantees to cover political and economic risks (Gatti, 2018). Other World Bank loan products are in the form of direct lending to the project company whereby the host country serves as a guarantor or the loan is granted to the host country by the World Bank and the host country in turn re-lends it to the project company. In 2019, Morocco and Angola were among countries that received assistance from this organisation amounting to US$1830 million and US$1380 million respectively.

Multilateral Development Banks – developing countries mostly receive a lot of support in the form of technical assistance and finance from multilateral development banks. They target promoting private sector growth and crowding it into development through encouraging privatisation policies and funding. Countries in the EMDEs with significant political risks also receive financial assistance from these organisations.

International Finance Corporation (IFC) – the IFC is one of the main agencies of the World Bank Group. It came into existence in 1956. Globally, it is the largest development organisation that functions mainly in the developing countries with emphasis on private sectors of the various economies. It provides long-term loans, guarantee equity finance, advice, and risk management support through project finance in the oil and gas projects. Under a project finance transaction, the main role of the International Finance Corporation is to ensure that the participants from the private sector are not disadvantaged by mitigating political risks. In 2018, Ghana and India were among the countries that received the highest assistance from this organisation: US$336 million and US$1474 million respectively.

Multilateral Investment Guarantee Agency (MIGA) – the MIGA came into existence in 1988. It is one of the agencies of the World Bank Group formed to assist developing countries to receive foreign direct investment against political risks and investors' protection management in the member countries of the World Bank, especially those with low ease of doing businesses, among other things (Gatti, 2018). The oil and gas political risks are covered by the Multilateral Investment Guarantee Agency.

10.2.4 Regional Development Banks

These play similar roles as the agencies under the World Bank Group but targeted at specific geographical regions. They include:

The African Development Bank (AfDB) – the AfDB commenced operations in 1966 after its establishment in 1964 with a mandate to promote economic and public growth of the regional states in the areas of infrastructural and private sector development (Gatti, 2018). The shares of the total stock of the bank held by regional and non-regional members are 60% and 40%, respectively. Both public and private sectors including some oil and gas projects in Africa receive technical assistance, advisory services, and financial assistance from this organisation. For instance, in 2010, the oil and gas field development project in Tunisia was financed by this entity with a US$150 million corporate loan. Senegal, Morocco, and Kenya received U$638 million, U$632 million and U$349 million loans, respectively, in 2019.

The African Finance Corporation (AFC) – in its quest to offer funding for infrastructure, power, telecommunications, natural resources, and transportation needs of the countries of the continent, the African Finance Corporation was established by African countries in 2007. West African countries currently form its membership. The Seven Energy firm received a sum of US$20 million from this organisation as part of its US$200 million equity and debt raised for the development of a gas reserve in Nigeria's Niger-delta state. Second, it invested US$80 million in 2011 in Neconde Energy. In the US$150 million senior debt syndication loan agreement, African Finance Corporation was a lead arranger with Access Bank.

Asian Development Bank (AsDB) – the AsDB was established with 31 member countries in 1966. It now has a membership of 68, of which 49 are from Asia-Pacific while 19 are non-regional member states. It was established to be of an Asian character and to bring about cooperation as well as act as an agent for economic growth in a region which is among the poorest in the world (Gatti, 2018). During the 1960s, this entity focused much on food production and rural development. It now funds a number of projects in many sectors in its region as well as in other EMDEs. In 2020 alone, the commitments Asian Development Bank made in the various forms amounted to US$31600 million.

10.2.5 Leasing and Lease Finance Market

The type of funding method where there is separation of ownership and usage is referred to as lease finance. The asset is financed by the lessor and for the lessee to have full permission to use the asset; the lessee then pays rent to the lessor. There are certain terms that govern this kind of arrangement. Under project finance, for instance, there can be a lease agreement between the project sponsor and a financial institution. Lease finance is normally used to finance specific assets instead of the whole project. Leasing is employed by some companies in the petroleum sector. Typical examples of assets procured through lease finance arrangements include the lease of floating production storage and offloading vessels during the extraction and production activities. Tankers and ships can be leased to deliver liquefied natural gas products to another country or company. One advantage of lease finance is that it brings about important competences through specialisation.

10.3 The Role of Project Finance in the Oil and Gas Industry

The upstream, midstream, and downstream sectors are where all the respective activities in the oil and gas industry take place. For instance the exploration and production activities happen in the upstream sector, the transportation and storage of crude oil takes place in the midstream area, while the refining of crude oil and natural gas into finished products is carried out in the downstream sector. A lot of capital is needed in the various sectors, but the quantum of the capital depends on the kind of activities that are carried out in a particular sector of the industry. The industry has largely been using structured corporate finance. The industry's annual investment is very high, but project finance used is less than 10% of the total investment. This is so because the organisation and implementation of project finance deals in the industry are considered to be expensive, time consuming, and burdensome. Second, project finance is more difficult for lenders to assess in this industry than in others. In this section, we consider the benefits of project finance markets to the oil and gas industry, and the performance of project finance.

10.3.1 The Benefits of Project Finance to the Project Sponsor

Project finance strategy can be used to raise a high level of debt to fund specific risk profiles of projects. It has therefore become an alternative source of funding for sponsors who are unable to meet the funding needs through corporate funding. National oil and gas companies in EMDEs rely heavily on project finance for their development projects, thereby reducing the pressures on states' funding. The information given next is about some benefits of project finance to the project sponsors and the host country.

Box 10.2 Benefits of Project Finance to the Project Sponsor and the Host Country

Project finance assists sponsors to attain high levels of gearing since more debt is pushed into the project.

It helps in sharing almost all forms of risks with other participants. For example the transfer or sharing of political and economic risks is very attractive in EMDEs.

The sponsors have numerous sources of funding for proposed projects. They can use project finance, a hybrid, conventional, or structured approach in raising the needed capital for project development.

The sponsors are free not to put their corporate balance sheet at risk since the project will pay its own debt.

Advantages to Host Country

- The host country is able to receive foreign capital.
- There is the transfer of technical know-how and experience from the developed world to the host country.
- It helps the host country to reduce borrowing by the public sector due to the engagement of the private participants in the project's development.
- Projects which would not have been developed due to lack of resources are likely to be undertaken. Local people get more trained and educated by receiving more skills for work.

10.3.2 Performance and Precedent Projects of Project Finance

Project finance has a relatively small market share in relation to the global debt market and the oil and gas industry, forming about 10% of the transactional value. In 2019 and 2020, for instance, the global project finance value was around US$301 billion and US$278 billion, respectively, of which the share of the oil and gas sector was respectively US$73 billion and US$64 billion. From the regional point of view, the Americas recorded US$95 billion and US$88 billion, Asia Pacific/Japan US$90 billion and US$64 billion, Europe US$100 billion and US$82 billion, EMENA US$126 billion and US$127 billion, while Africa/Middle East/Central Asia recorded US$25 billion and US$43 billion respectively over the same period, 2019 and 2020 (Refinitiv, 2021). It is seen that there were reductions in the volumes globally and at the regional level except EMENA and for that matter Africa that saw an increase in volumes in 2020. The variation would be due to the ravaging nature of the COVID-19 pandemic that brought most activities in the various economies to a standstill. Africa and other developing countries did not experience the ravaging nature of COVID-19 to the extent to which the developed world did. Asia/Japan is seen as the hub of most active project finance activities as it accounts for 32% of the global project finance volumes or market. Africa, on the other hand, could account for about 12% of the project finance transactions. Tables 10.1 and 10.2 and Figure 10.1 give global information about project finance volumes.

Table 10.1 Global Project Finance Volumes for the Period 2009–2020 (US$million)

Year	*Global*	*Americas*	*Asia-Pacific/ Japan*	*Europe*	*EMENA*	*Africa/Middle East/ Central Asia*
2009	138,468	19,277	56,421	44,447	62,768	18,321
2010	206,615	24,357	97,510	66,015	84,746	18,731
2011	214,506	38,305	91,317	67,443	84,883	17,440
2012	197,526	39,397	88,199	46,298	69,929	23,631
2013	204140	51,368	62,762	52,715	90,010	37,295
2014	262,463	93,191	76,679	70,466	92,592	22,126
2015	277,475.9	91,819.4	76,237.9	76,679	109,418.7	32,739.7
2016	267,416.1	55,682.8	59,397.6	90,898.7	152,335.6	61,436.9
2017	229,638.2	64,431.3	80,380.6	57,988.2	84,826.3	26,838.1
2018	282,684.8	96,043.1	76,531.6	90,767.2	110,110.1	19,342.9
2019	301,346.8	94,589.8	90,256.5	100,430.8	125,500.5	25,069.7
2020	277,613.4	88,337.7	63,632	82,213.1	125,631.9	43,418.8
Total	2,859,893.2	756,799.1	919,324.2	846,361	1,192,751.1	346,390.1

Table 10.2 The Oil and Gas Industry Project Finance Volumes from 2005 to 2020 (US$million)

Year	*Global/All Sectors*	*Oil and Gas Industry (OGI)*	*Others*	*Share% for OGI*	*Others (%)*
2005	76,319.5	31,001	45,318.5	40.6	59.4
2006	100,783.7	46,631	54,152.7	46.3	53.7
2007	153,311.5	42,725	110,586.5	27.9	72.1
2008	214,201.1	51,836	162,365.1	24.2	75.8
2009	138,468	28,437	110,031	20.5	79.5
2010	206,615	37,257	169,358	18.0	82.0
2011	214,506	43,450	171,056	20.3	79.7
2012	197,526	64,652	132,874	32.7	67.3
2013	204,140	50,281	153,859	24.6	75.4
2014	262,463	77,195	185,268	29.4	69.6
2015	277,475.9	56,050.1	221,425.8	20.2	79.8
2016	267,416.1	45,992	221,424.1	17.2	82.8
2017	229,638.2	37,665.2	191,973	16.4	83.6
2018	282,684.8	54,068.8	228,616	19.1	80.9
2019	301,346.8	73,227.3	228,119.5	24.3	75.7
2020	277,613.4	64,237.7	213,375.7	23.1	76.9
Total	2,859,893.2				

There have been significant levels of fluctuations in the last two decades in the oil and gas project finance market volumes globally as indicated in Figure 10.2. The 2009 value of US$ 28 billion was the global lowest value, while the highest value of US$ 77 billion was recorded in 2014. The number of significant transactions influence the level of activity each year. For instance the years 2014 and 2019 with values of US$ 77 billion and US$ 73 billion, respectively, were seen as the best years. The market share of oil and gas project finance was very high in 2005 and 2006 with 40.6% and 46.3%, respectively. The market shares started reducing and reached lower scores of 17.2% and 16.4% in 2016 and 2017, respectively.

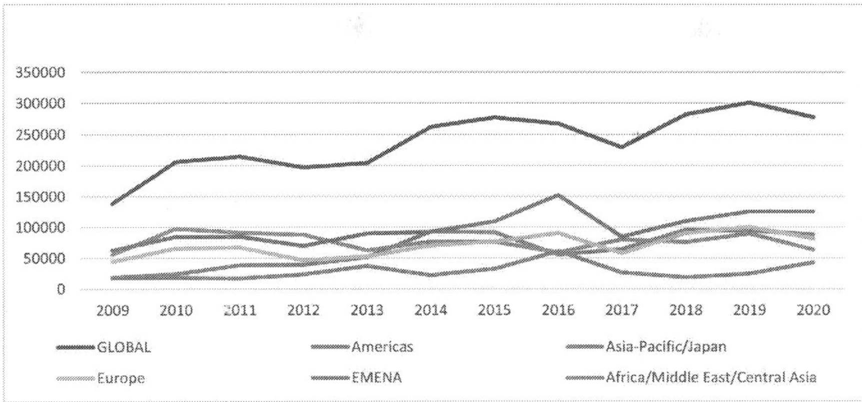

Figure 10.1 Regional project finance volumes 2009–2020 (US$million)

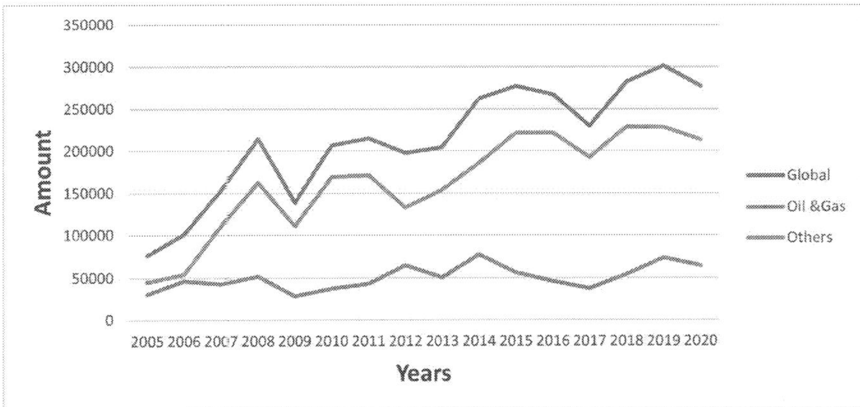

Figure 10.2 Sectoral representation of project finance volumes 2005–2020 (US$million)

Box 10.3 Sudan and China's relationship in the oil and gas industry

China's National Petroleum Corporation established an oil outpost in 1995 in Sudan after successfully gaining exploration rights. The United States was not happy about this and in 1997 imposed sanctions on Sudan. The oil industry in Sudan was established with maximum support from China such as technology and other expertise. Additionally, China invested heavily in that sector. Sudan started oil production in 1999. As a result of its heavy investment, the National Petroleum Corporation of China holds the largest share in the energy sector of Sudan. Five percent of China's total oil imports come from Sudan which accounts for more than half the oil Sudan exports. China has so far invested US$ 15,000 million in Sudan's 932-mile oil pipeline. Source: Looy (2006).

Box 10.4 China and Africa's oil and gas industry

Why is China busy investing so much in the upstream sector of the oil and gas industry in Africa? It is doing so probably due to the following reasons: it wants to be one of the biggest players globally in the petroleum industry, given the surge in its local demand for energy and the fact that its reserves are drying up quickly. Currently, China is significantly investing in this industry via 20 African countries through its National Oil Companies. For instance it is undertaking a contract which will enable it build as well as operate the project upon completion in Benin. This is a crude oil pipeline of about 1,980 km that will connect Niger to Benin. Moreover, it spent US$ 2.3 billion in 2006 to attain 45% stake in Nigeria's oil mining lease deal and also managed to take a majority stake in the upstream activity in Guinea Bissau that was in the hands of FAR Ltd of Australia. China is investing close to US$ 15 billion in the upstream sector alone in Africa over the period 2019 to 2023.

Source: Africa Oil Newspaper (October 7, 2019) Chinese investment in Africa's oil and gas industry. *Africa Oil Newspaper and Author's modifications.*

Box 10.5 Yemen Liquefied Natural Gas Project (Yemen LNG) – Project Finance Deal

In 1995, Yemen LNG was established. The Gas Development Agreement was ratified in March 1997 by the parliament of Yemen. Thereafter, an agreement was signed between Total & Power Ltd and Yemen LNG on sales and purchase in August 2005 to enable it to develop its gas reserve. The construction of the plant and pipelines started in September 2005. The available resources were not enough, so Yemen LNG took a US$ 2,800 million project finance debt from a consortium of international banks in May 2008. These banks were from Japan, Europe, and South Korea. This amount corresponds to 58% of the total project cost and is the highest project finance deal in Yemen. By May 2008, a 320-km gas pipeline was in place, and by November 2008, the first gas had arrived at Balhaf. The project was fully inaugurated with both trains operating in June 2010. This field also helped Marib power plant in generating electricity for the country by feeding the plant with gas. The project directly and indirectly employs 5,000 people, and it is boosting the economy of Yemen.

Source: Yemen LNG Company Corporate Brochure (2009) and author's modifications

10.4 Structured and Hybrid Finance for the Oil and Gas Industry

Operations in the value chain of this industry are capital intensive especially for the EMDEs, as development of oil and gas products takes a national view. Second, the governments of these countries do not normally have the resources to meet the operational cost and expertise required and, hence, may rely on others to undertake such operations. Companies need to invest heavily in the upstream subsector in order to find new fields or reserves. There is the need for continuous capital investment in the industry so as to replace depleted fields. There is a positive relationship between the price of oil and gas and capital spending. A price fall can lead to a reduction in capital investment and cessation of project development, especially in the developing countries. The funding needs of the industry can be met in diverse ways. This section categorises these sources into the structured and the hybrid.

10.4.1 Structured/Conventional Finance for the Oil and Gas Industry

The companies in this industry have the option of choosing from using internally generated funds, debt, or equity to meet their funding needs traditionally. When selecting an option to employ, factors such as most efficient capital structure, funding with lowest cost, liquidity, and dividend policy are taken into consideration. The large integrated multinationals, the medium sized, and small independent companies and others do not have the same levels of gearing ratios. For instance the large integrated multinationals have traditionally been maintaining a gearing ratio below 40%. The three funding options available to project sponsors include internally generated funds (IGF), corporate debt borrowing, and equity funding in terms of public and private equity.

10.4.2 Hybrid Finance for the Oil and Gas Companies

The financial instrument that shares some features of debt as well as equity is referred to as hybrid finance. This will give the investor a combination of the positive aspects of both instruments. The two extremes of financial instruments are debt and equity. Hence, hybrid finance is between these two extremes. Equity holders have ownership rights – the right to vote and to be voted for to join the board, when necessary – wield some sort of control over the management and are entitled to receive dividends. Debt holders, on the other hand, do not have control over the management but receive a fixed interest as well as the principal. Some of the reasons why hybrid finance is used include to make room for unusual cashflow profiles, to optimise tax, and to ensure special accounting treatment of cashflows. Some of the hybrid finance categories that are employed in this industry include the following:

- **Technical Assistance Agreement (TAA) and a Joint Venture Contract (JVC)**: under TAA, there exists a contract agreement between an IOC and a country. This IOC serves as a contractor who has the technical knowhow with the needed experience to undertake a particular assignment in any of the sectors in the industry. The funds for the intended assignment are provided by the HC. The HC pays the contractor cash for the task undertaken. The contractor works solely under the instruction of the management of the NOC. Under the JVC, two or more companies jointly finance a project (involving the exploration and production of oil, which lead to profit making).
- **Leasing and Participation bond (PB):** leasing reduces capital funding requirements of companies. Thus, companies use some fixed assets of others at a fee instead of buying themselves at a higher cost. The saved cash from this kind of arrangement could be used to support the working capital or other activities that are likely to bring in profits. Companies can finance an asset for a minimum of 20 years by using participation bonds. Under this strategy, only the interest is paid during the first 5 years. The loan is repaid in annual instalments thereafter.
- **Borrowing Base Facilities (BBF):** a borrowing base is an amount of loan that a lender is prepared to grant a company which is based on the collateral or portfolio of the company. For example the reserves in this industry that are valued based on their NPV of future production will serve as the borrowing base. In fact, BBF has been one of the key methods of financing in the upstream project in the petroleum sector in a number of oil-producing countries in the world. Some lenders feel very comfortable using the BBF because loans are made against some specific assets, and the BBF can be adjusted downward to protect them. For instance the credit limit drops as the value of the collateral declines.
- **Mezzanine:** when companies want to expand their ongoing existing business or management buyouts, or acquisition, they employ this kind of financing. It is hybrid finance. It is principally a debt capital. It can sometimes be converted into equity interest when there is a tendency of breaches as a result of non- or late payment of loans (Clews, 2016; Szczetnikowicz et al., 2018).
- **Production Loans (PL) and Forward Purchase Facilities (FPF):** companies can take some debt facilities from lenders in exchange for lenders having access to some reserves in the industry (Cuthbert, 2004). The repayment of the loan with the accrued interest is done through the sales of the products. This kind of deal is termed a production loan. Under the FPF deal, there is an agreement between a lender and a borrower (special purpose company) whereby the amount of loan that will correspond to a

certain quantity of oil or gas is paid upfront to the borrower before production is done. The quantity of oil or gas is given to the lender to sell to repay the loan. The FPF has the advantage of reducing the supply lead time, improving production delivery, and saving cost.

- **Pre-Export Financing:** this takes place when funds are advanced to a borrower on the basis of proven orders from buyers. The borrower uses this fund to produce and supply the goods. Thus, cash made from the export sales is used to repay the loans, which is in line with the agreed terms. The lender receives the payment of the goods directly from the buyer. All charges as well as interest on the loan are deducted from the money received by the lender before the borrower receives the remaining amount through its account. This means that the security of the export contract and cashflows are under the control of the lender. This type of financing is different from project finance because it funds existing production under a very short tenor rather than funding the project development costs.
- **Inventory Financing:** this technique helps companies with loans to acquire products to sell at a later date. This is a short-term loan. Thus, this kind of loan assists companies to take security over some stocks. In this industry, the petroleum products serve as collateral for the loans (Szczetnikowicz et al., 2018). This kind of loan is important in times of serious cashflow fluctuations. This will obviously help the companies to sell more, have more stocks for use on request, and eventually raise more capital.
- **Islamic Finance**: asset-based financing is done by adopting the terms as enshrined in Islamic law (Sharia). There are great similarities between the structures of this funding technique and that of the Islamic financial institutions. It has very flexible terms with regard to pricing and tenor (longer tenor). The sukuk instrument ensures that return or interest coming to it must be in tandem with the risks and project performance of the ownership of the project or assets (Clews, 2016; Szczetnikowicz et al., 2018). For instance the US$ 20 billion Sadara mega petrochemical plant project in Saudi Arabia which began in 2011 and started operations in 2017 was financed through the Sukuk financial structure.

10.5 Conclusion

In this chapter, we discussed project finance in the oil and gas industry in EMDEs. Project finance was explained as a funding technique that raises more capital to fund very capital-intensive project portfolios, which otherwise could not be financed using the ordinary corporate finance method. Under project financing deals, the cashflows made through the project itself are used to service the debt that were used to undertake the project. The global project financing system involves a large number of different financing methods by a wide range of entities, including the traditional, the hybrid, and those that are specifically for project financing. The various markets for project finance in the oil and gas industry were covered, focusing on equity and debt markets and the sources of funding including commercial banks (both local and foreign ones), IMF, Export Credit Agencies, IFC, MIGA, AfDB, and AFC in addition to leasing and lease finance markets. The study also discussed the role of project finance in the oil and gas industry, highlighting not only the significant contribution of project finance, but also the structured and hybrid forms of finance for the industry.

In conclusion, it emerged that project finance growth on the global, regional, and national levels depends on the quantum of appraised sovereign and project risks. Currently, hybrid financing is gaining more ground in the market, especially in the upstream fields. There is an indication that a significant number of national oil companies are working towards securing an upper hand in the global activities in the industry. As it stands, close to 85% of the top 20 companies in the industry globally are national oil companies based on proven oil and gas reserves. This means that international oil companies control only about 5% of these reserves globally. Although the project finance market has shown some weakening globally in recent years due to cost, tenure, and complexity, it remains the best funding option for the EMDEs, since they do not have the required capital and capacity for project development in this industry. Last, employing project finance in the oil and gas industry will go a long way in helping governments to channel their resources towards developing other sectors of their economies.

References

Africa Oil Newspaper (2019, October 7). Chinese investment in Africa's oil and gas industry. *Africa Oil Newspaper.* https://africa-oilweek.com/articles/understanding-chinese-investment-in-african-o

Ahmed, P. A., and Fang, X. (1999). *Project finance in developing countries* (Vol. 7). New York: World Bank Publications.

Clews, R. J. (2016). Project finance for the international petroleum industry. London: Academic Press.

Cuthbert, N. (2004). *A guide to project finance.* London: Denton Wilde Sapte, Londres, Inglaterra.

Gatti, S. (2018). Project finance in theory and practice: Designing, structuring, and financing private and public projects. Amsterdam: Elsevier.

Hoffman, S. (2008). *The law and business of international project finance: A resource for governments, sponsors, lenders, lawyers, and project participants.* Cambridge: Cambridge University Press.

Kensinger, J. W., and Martin, J. D. (1988). Project finance: Raising money the old–fashioned way. Journal *of Applied Corporate Finance*, 1(3), 69–81.

Looy, J. V. D. (2006). *Africa and China: A strategic partnership?* (ASC Working Paper Series, 67). Leiden: African Studies.

Refinitiv (2021). *Global project finance review/project finance/managing underwriters.* https://thesource.refinitiv.com/TheSource/getfile/download

Szczetnikowicz, S., Dewar, J., and Finance, P. L. (2018). *Financing options in the oil and gas industry.* London: Milbank, Tweed, Hadley & McCloy LLP and Practical Law Finance and Thompson Reuters.

Yemen LNG Company Corporate Brochure (2009). www.yemenlng.com.

11 Investment Appraisal for Oil and Gas Projects

Kannyiri Banyen, Daniel Domeher, and Joseph Nyeadi

11.1 Introduction

The contribution of the oil and gas industry to the global economy cannot be overemphasised. Despite growing competition from alternative energy sources, the oil and gas industry remains the greatest source of energy for most firms and households. In fact, several petroleum firms make it to the Fortune's Global 500 list each year, and more petroleum firms make it to the fortune's 500 list in several countries each year (Fortune, 2022). For instance China National Petroleum and Sinopec Group Limited ranked fourth and fifth places in terms of revenue generation on the 2021 Fortune's Global 500 list (Fortune, 2022). Over the last decade, improvements in technology and advocacy for energy efficiency and energy substitution for renewable energy have posed a threat to oil and gas firms globally. The COVID-19 pandemic further reduced the demand for oil and gas products, reducing prices and profits for many firms. The effect has seen an increase in stockpiles of crude and other petroleum products and a reduction in capital expenditure (capex).

However, rising urbanisation in emerging economies among other factors is expected to stabilise demand overtime, especially as countries get back on their feet following the COVID-19 pandemic. According to US Energy Information Administration's International Energy Outlook (2021), the demand for petroleum will be largely driven by steady economic growth in especially non-OECD economies, and this is expected to rise overtime (Figure 11.1). The US Energy Information Administration (2021) projects that OPEC petroleum production will rise by nearly 2.7 million barrels per day (b/d) in 2022, the biggest year-over-year rise in Organization of Petroleum Exporting Countries' (OPEC's) production since 2004. The continuous rise in demand for oil and gas products requires substantial capital investments to ensure adequate production to meet global demand and maintain market stability.

These capital investment decisions require oil and gas firms to make judgements on the best way to allocate limited resources for optimal gain to relevant stakeholders. However, the oil and gas industry consists of a miscellany of institutions, regulations, agreements, networks, and players that facilitate the

DOI: 10.4324/9781003315056-14

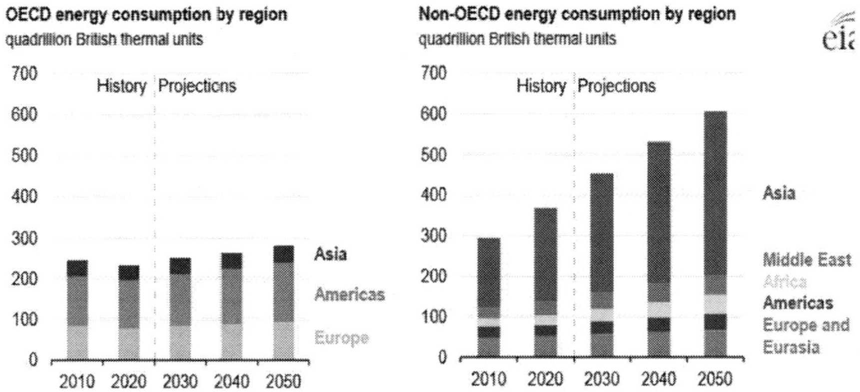

Figure 11.1 Energy consumption projections by region

Source: US Energy Information Administration (EIA), International Energy Outlook 2021 Reference Case

production and distribution of petroleum products in domestic and international markets in and equitable and socially responsible manner.

The complexity of oil and gas contracts and the competing demands of different supply and demand-side stakeholders among other issues increase the risk of oil and gas projects. This makes investment appraisal and decision-making in the industry a bit more challenging than most other industries. Besides, OPEC has international standards that all firms in member states must conform to, and these regulatory frameworks transcend national legal requirements and firm expectations. Additionally, in preparing oil and gas projections for each project, firms must often leave room for deviations from estimated production levels overtime in seeking capital and production rights. The capital expenditure required often cover both exploration and development costs as well as spending on maintenance of existing capital stock and purchase of new tangible and intangible fixed capital for business activities. Therefore, oil and gas investment decisions are guided by the firm, industry, and macroeconomic factors that influence the cost and risk of operations.

The foregoing discussions highlight the need for a continuous evaluation and proper documentation of the investment appraisal processes and capital investment decision strategies employed in oil and gas projects. As the global oil and gas industry continues to evolve in response to shifting paradigms in global energy supply and demand markets, the effect of these dynamics on the success or failure of oil and gas firms also need to be evaluated to inform investment decision-making. These details will guide appropriate methodology selection and decisions and action initiatives by policymakers, oil and gas firms, managers, and other practitioners, which will ensure an optimal allocation of oil and gas investment capital and the natural resource. This chapter therefore seeks to examine the investment decision processes in the oil and gas industry in recent times, with the view of providing guidance to existing firms and new entrants on best practices that will lead to an optimal usage of investment capital in the industry. The chapter therefore provides a broad scrutiny of the extrinsic and intrinsic considerations, capital investment requirements, and other dynamic issues that influence investment appraisal and capital budgeting decisions in the oil and gas industry.

The rest of the chapter is outlined as follows: Section 11.2 provides an outline of the capital investment requirements in the oil and gas industry. Section 11.3 discusses the factors that influence capital investment decisions of oil and gas firms, while Section 11.4 reviews literature on the formulation of capital investment proposals in the industry. Section 11.5 discusses the various capital investment techniques used in the industry, while Section 11.6 examines the capital decision-making process. Section 11.7 concludes the chapter.

11.2 Capital Investment Requirements in the Oil and Gas Industry

In this section, we review the literature on the capital investment requirements in the oil and gas industry. This is meant to help readers appreciate the varying dimensions of thought and considerations that go into funding a typical oil and gas project. Global oil and gas supply derives from the investment decisions of individual firms and a mosaic of factors ranging from the political decisions of governments in OPEC countries to supply chain system dynamics that affect pricing, OPEC policy, geopolitics, inventory levels, exchange rates, and even resource availability.

Generally, oil and gas exploration and development are highly volatile and capital-intensive ventures, with expensive lease agreements, intricate tax rules, complex trade-offs between risk and return, and long payback periods. The initial cost of prospecting and acquiring leases and licenses for exploration before a firm even quantifies the oil reserves to determine economic viability is enormous. A typical oil and gas project requires millions, sometimes billions, of US dollars to commence, with no actual guarantees of breaking even or yielding profits. However, the key component of investment is to have reasonable belief in getting returns for invested capital. However, in oil and gas projects, reserves could turn out to be of a lesser quantity and quality than geologic details suggest and may turn out to be of lesser quality and quantity than estimated. Meanwhile, the firm would have invested millions into the project in hope of gaining some reward for the investment. Typically, the capital investment requirements for an oil and gas project are guided by the exploration, construction, operations, production, and processing demands of each phase of the project as well as the risk involved in these activities. It also depends on whether a company is investing in the upstream or downstream sector.[1]

According to McMonigle et al. (2021), both OPEC and the International Energy Agency foresee a slow recovery in oil and gas demand after

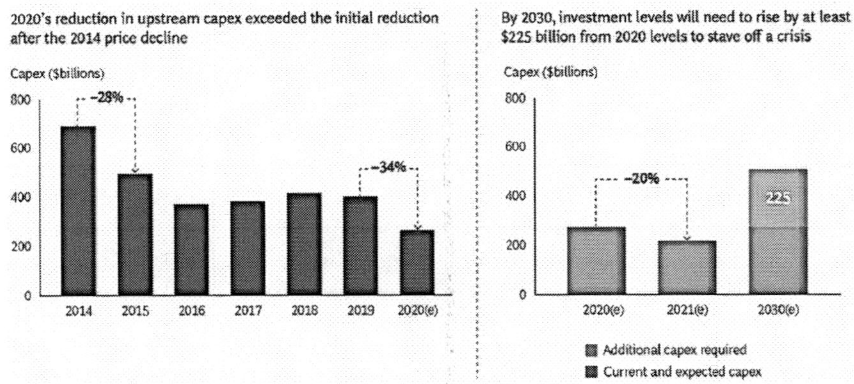

Figure 11.2 Risk of peak investment in oil and gas

Source: IEA, Rystad, BCG Analysis.

Note: The 2030 estimated figures assume that demand will return in the 2022 time period. (e) = estimated

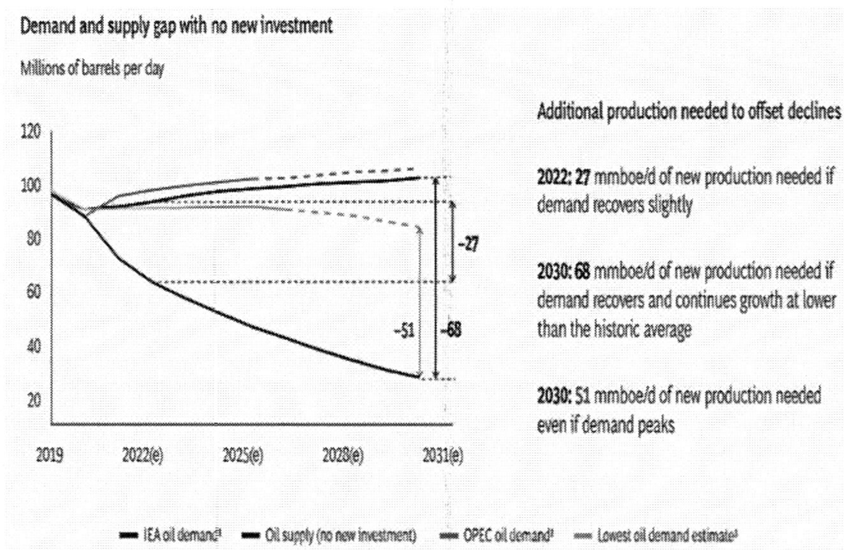

Figure 11.3 Oil and gas demand and supply projections (2022–2030)

Source: IEA, OPEC, BP.

Note: Dotted lines connect organizations-provided period forecasts. (e) = estimated; mmboed = million barrels of oil equivalent per day

the COVID-19 pandemic though there is still a global shortage of oil and gas which requires significant investments between now and 2030 to stabilise the market. Figure 11.2 shows that investments in oil and gas need a significant rise to increase supply levels globally. Also, Figure 11.3 shows that about 27 to 68 million barrels of oil equivalent (mmboe) are required during the period 2022–2030 to ensure global stability in the oil and gas market.

11.3 Factors Influencing Capital Investment Decisions

This section examines the factors influencing capital investment decisions of firms. These factors could be classified into generic factors applicable to all firms and the factors specific to the oil and gas industry. These factors could also be divided broadly into the external and firm-specific factors. The external factors, unlike the others, are out of the control of the firm. Examples include the socio-economic and political environment or conditions. Internally, factors such as internal finance, liquidity, cash flow, and leverage have also been identified as having an influence on firm investment decision. In the oil and gas industry, capital investment decisions involve investment in long-lived assets such as gas liquefaction plants and natural gas pipelines, among others. The wide range of factors influencing how and where oil and gas companies invest are discussed in subsequent sections.

11.3.1 Government Policies and Regulations

Government's regulations tend to change over time as the economy grows and becomes more open (Abor, 2017). Regulation among several things creates a level playing ground for competing firms and puts the activities of profit-oriented firms in check. Changes in environmental protection regulation and those related to climate change could have serious consequences on returns for firms investing in related industries. As these regulations change over time, it may have cost implications for firms. For instance changes in taxes and royalties may render upstream projects less profitable and deter related investments. Governments might defer investment to preserve hydrocarbon resources and revenues for future generations (Reynolds, 2005). This could be a legitimate policy for a country with relatively high GDP per capital and no pressing need for additional oil revenue to fund infrastructure or social programmes.

11.3.2 Economic Expectation

This refers to investors' anticipation of the performance of the economy as a whole going into some future time period. The performance of a given investment project will depend on its ability to generate income over time into the future (Kuuskraa, 2008; Phan and Nguyen, 2020). The overall health of the economy directly or indirectly impacts on a given project's potential to generate income to pay for its cost over a set time (Dhochak and Sharma, 2016). When investors are generally bullish in their expectation of the economy, it affects positively their forecast of the income stream to be generated by the project. All things equal, this may yield a favourable net present value and hence a decision to invest in the project. The reverse is true under conditions of bearish economic expectations. The performance of the macro economy reflects partly in the level of interest rates.

11.3.3 Risks

Risk refers to the possibility that actual outcomes will deviate from the expected. In the context of investment decisions, it implies the likelihood that the expected project cash flows/returns arrived at based on forecasts conducted will substantially vary from the actual cash flows when the project eventually becomes operational. Explorations in the oil and gas sector require huge initial capital outlay and could go without revenue prospect for up to 10 years. In this sector, it is believed that risk is the most critical factor influencing investments in related activities (Kaiser and Pulsipher, 2007). Firms are faced with the difficult decision to invest an amount today for returns which are uncertain in a given future time period. When investing in exploration activities, oil firms are not certain of finding oil reserves in commercial quantities. It is estimated that for every successful strike of oil, there are about nine empty oil wells drilled. On completion of an oil or gas project, economic conditions may change significantly. This can vary the underlying demand and supply. Changes in demand and supply could affect the prices in a way that will make the project less profitable or completely unprofitable. Investors must thus subject their cash flow estimates to various risk events, scenario analysis, and stress testing. A firm can more confidently defend its decision to invest in a project if the net present value remains positive after subjecting the cash flows to risk analysis.

11.3.4 Oil and Gas Price Expectation and Volatility

The price of hydrocarbons is probably the single most important factor in the Exploration and Production (E&P) industry (Coopersmith et al., 2000). For companies that produce oil and gas, price and income are closely related: when the price of oil and gas is high and expected to remain so for a significant period, it may entice firms to acquire fixed assets needed to drill or explore and further produce the oil. Coopersmith et al. (2000) note that drilling activities and related investment are lowered when there is a sustained downward pressure on oil prices. In addition, firms may shut down high-cost wells and delay further development activities and risky ventures. High prices, on the other hand, tend to stimulate investments as returns tend to be more enticing. While the stock of oil gas may still be sufficient, meeting long-term oil and gas demand could be a big challenge unless prices stay at a level high enough to induce the requisite investments. In a high-risk and capital-intensive industry like E&P, investment decisions are usually based on forecasted long-term prices, full-cycle project economics, strategic rationale, and portfolio decision-making.

11.3.5 Availability of Funds

Oil and gas companies create value by investing in those projects for which the market value of cash inflows exceeds the required investment outlays (Kaiser and Pulsipher, 2007). The purpose of drilling is to discover reserves, but it costs money to identify, acquire, and interpret seismic data and drill wells. If the resources found are not adequate to make a sufficient return on capital, then the E&P industry in the region will drop and shift investment where the return is acceptable. The extent to which a firm can access funds to invest is critical to the investment decision-making process. This will vary across firms; smaller firms, unlike the larger ones, have limited access to financial markets and very often rely on internal sources to meet their funding requirements. Larger firms with limited internal funds are able to access funding through capital markets. This is mostly not possible with the smaller firms. Hence investment decision will vary across firms depending on the availability of funds. From the perspective of the free cash flow theory, the firm's financial status, particularly with reference to the level of cash flows, will hugely affect the decision on whether to invest or not and how much to invest.

11.3.6 Financing Decision

How a firm chooses to finance its activities to a large extent could impact its investment decision. In making investment decisions, it thus matters whether a firm decides to use debt or equity to fund the proposed project (Kaiser and Pulsipher, 2007). The financing decision has taxes and issuance cost implications for the firm. This can alter the cost of capital, depending on whether the firm chooses internal or external financing. Hence, the incentive to go for certain projects may change depending on the financing decision taken.

11.4 Formulation of Capital Investment Proposals in the Oil and Gas Industry

This section seeks to guide the formulation of project proposals for the oil and gas industry. The key consideration when preparing project proposals for investment in the oil and gas industry is providing investors and other stakeholders with concise, sound, and convincing outline of what the project entails; financing requirements; its commercial viability financing strategies; operational structure; risk analysis, among others.

According to CTI Private Financing Advisory Network (2014), the essential elements of a project proposal should be to provide reviewers with a sincere, factual, and realistic understanding of the costs and benefits of the proposed project and its commercial viability. Though the format of an oil and gas investment proposal may differ from firm to firm, there are various common sections and details that need to be outlined. First, the proposal should start with an executive summary that provides reviewers with a brief understanding of the project purpose and scope, where it is located, who is involved, and the commercial rationale for the project. The executive summary should also capture project timelines, summary of investment requirements, and possible exit strategies for external investors.

Second, the proposal should clearly state the value offers and business model for the project. This should capture the business model, project structure, and commercial rational for the project, providing details on market opportunities the project is intended to exploit, the kind of contracts that need to be signed, the stakeholders involved, input requirements, project development and implementation plan, growth strategies, and exit strategies. The next thing an oil and gas investment proposal should provide is the management and manpower as well as the technological plan for the project. This section should clearly outline the organogram of the project and give clear but concise statements of roles and responsibilities for task completion and project execution. The choice of technologies and supplier information is critical at this stage of the proposal formulation. The proposal should also capture the commercial impact of the technology choice, its benefits, costs, and reason for choosing that technology over others.

The proposal should also have a detailed market analysis that captures the commercial viability of the project including an analysis of the market potential, the competitive environment, and other environmental factors that affect the project. A section of the proposal should also be dedicated to the financing requirements and financing structure of the project. Reviewers should be provided with details on the ask amount, the type of financing required, cost of capital for each funding source, and how these funds are to be used in the project implementation. The proposal should also capture the cash flow and risk analysis of the project. Adequate financial forecast is required to convince investors to invest in any project. The project proposal should, therefore, contain adequate and non-complex financial analysis that highlights the economic attractiveness of the project. This should capture capital expenditure (capex), operating expenditure, revenue, production volume assumptions and forecasts as well as the risk involved in the project and how these may affect project execution, cash flows, and other elements of the project. Last, the proposal should capture and quantify the non-financial impacts of the project such as environmental and social effects of the project. The conclusion of the proposal could then capture the key strengths and benefits of the proposed project and attempt convincing investors to invest in the project.

11.5 Investment Appraisal Techniques Used in the Oil and Gas Industry

The primary objective of investing is the creation of wealth. But the investor is faced with two broad constraints: a limited budget and the possibility of not making the expected return due to some risk exposure. Investors must, therefore, select projects that optimise the use of limited capital. This is even more critical for oil and gas firms as the initial capex is often very high, and the price of wrong decisions is catastrophic. Investment appraisal is all about assessing the income streams against the cost of investment among other variables. In this chapter, rather than reproducing literature on the common investment appraisal techniques used in the general investment appraisal literature such as the payback period,[2] net present value (NPV), accounting rate of return (ARR),[3] and the internal rate of return (IRR),[4] these techniques are briefly discussed in the context of the oil and gas industry and referred to in the discussion of the practical techniques commonly employed by oil and gas firms in appraising capital projects in the industry. These are discussed in the subsequent sections.

11.5.1 Net Present Value (NPV)

One of the most common investment appraisal techniques used by oil and gas firms is the NPV estimation. For every investment, we have cash inflows and cash outflows. The NPV is the difference between the discounted cash outflows and the discounted cash inflows. In other words, it is the present value of what is being obtained (benefits) minus the present value of what is being given out. Mathematically it is defined as

$$\begin{aligned} NPV_p &= \sum_{i=1}^{n} \frac{NCF_i}{(1+r)^i} - I_0 \\ &= \left(\frac{NCF_1}{(1+r)^1} + \frac{NCF_2}{(1+r)^2} + \frac{NCF_3}{(1+r)^3} + \cdots + \frac{NCF_n}{(1+r)^n} \right) - I_0 \end{aligned} \tag{11.1}$$

where *NCFi* is the net cash flow at time *i*, *r* is the cost of capital (discount rate), and I_0 is the initial investment.

Under these criteria, the rule is to accept projects that either break even or produce a positive NPV (NPV ≥ 0). Typically, oil and gas projects have long payback periods, and so projects with positive NPVs are viewed as good projects that are expected to attract investors. However, the NPV techniques must be tested for sensitivity to changes in underlying assumptions. This method, however, has certain limitations that make absolute reliance on its estimates inadvisable (Domnikov et al., 2017). For instance the sensitivity analysis varies one determinant after the other when in reality these variables are related, and changes could occur concurrently. Also, the method assumes that the analyst knows the value of input variables with certainty which is a flawed assumption, and therefore incorporating some degree of uncertainty and risk into the project helps improve the reliability of the analysis.

11.5.2 Expected Market Value (EMV)

Another commonly used investment appraisal technique in oil and gas projects is the expected monetary value (EMV) estimation which combines the net present value technique with decision tree analysis to generate act forks that guide investors on whether to proceed with a project or not. This method is widely used in the industry as it combines profitability estimates of risk and uncertainty to generate risk-adjusted values that guide the investment decision-making. The underlying principle in the EMV method is that when an investor

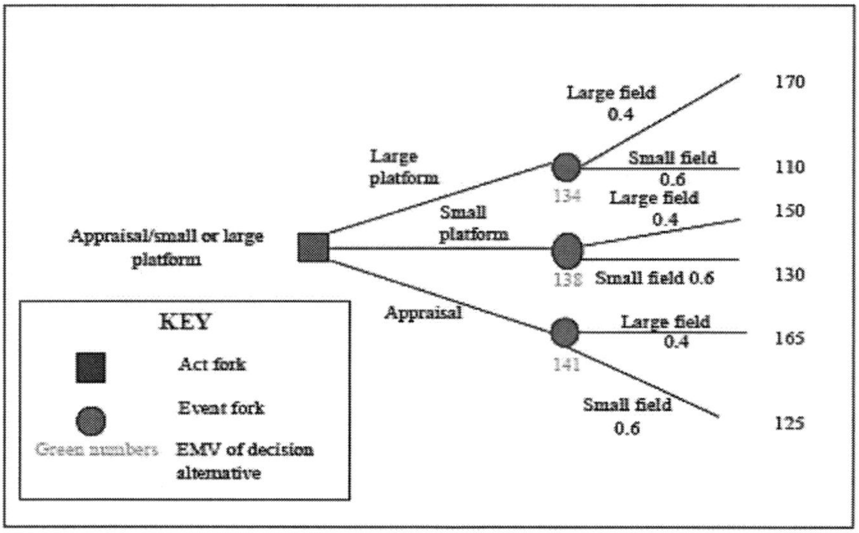

Figure 11.4 Demonstration of a simple EMV analysis presented on a decision tree

Source: Macmillan (2000)

is faced with choosing among several mutually exclusive project decision alternatives, s/he should accept the alternative that maximises the average monetary value (EMV). However, this method is criticised for being difficult as assigning probabilities to variables used in the analysis can be challenging. Besides, the method is criticised as failing to incorporate in any quantitative form, the particular attitudes and feelings the investor or manager associates with money.

For instance, Figure 11.4 shows a simple decision tree and forecasted NPVs and related EMVs associated with each event fork (Macmillan, 2000; Domnikov et al., 2015, 2017). These EMVs inform investor choices at each phase of the project. In Figure 11.4, decisions are represented by the blue square, called the act fork while each branch is a possible decision with related NPVs and EMVs. For instance the firm could decide to immediately install a large platform or a small platform or assess the two before a final decision is arrived at. Each red circle is an event fork representing the uncertainty of the quantity of reserves in the field (large field or small field). The end nodes are the resulting NPVs. The EMV is therefore computed for each decision alternative by multiplying the probability of discovering a large field or small field by its NPV. For instance for the middle branch, EMV = (0.4 × 150) + (0.6 × 130) = 138. Since the EMVs for the other two branches are 134 for immediately establishing a large platform and 141 for further appraisal before a final decision, the best decision will be to assess the two options before going ahead (EMV =141).

Proponents of utility theory therefore advocate for incorporation of either individual investor (or manager) preferences into the investment analysis or incorporation of shared organisational preferences into the investment appraisal. However, this is quite difficult to quantify and incorporate into decision-making though these so-called 'gut' feelings and preferences are indirectly incorporated into the investment decision-making processes of most investors.

11.5.3 Risk Analysis Based on Monte Carlo Simulation

Risk analysis using Monte Carlo simulation is also a very widely used investment appraisal technique in the oil and gas industry. According to Macmillan (2000), this method allows investors to assess risk and uncertainty surrounding the main project variables such as calculation of recoverable reserves of hydrocarbon in an acreage using probability distributions. Through a random sampling process among these distributions, the investor or manager is able to assess the effect of risk and uncertainty on the project results. This way, the analyst is presented with a holistic view of the risk-return profile of the project and is in a better position to make an informed decision (Domnikov et al., 2017).

For instance, consider a hypothetical oil field with the 163 million barrels of oil (MBO), and production is expected to plateau at 13% of total reserves per annum for 5 years and decline at 22% per annum thereafter. Assuming the firm needs five production wells, estimated at a cost of $17 million per well over 2 years and platforms/pipelines estimated at $763 million over 3 years while abandonment costs are estimated at $395 million post production; in addition, annual operating expenditure is estimated at $81 million per annum and the firm falls within the 30% corporate tax bracket while inflation rate is 6.3% over the investment period and capital is raised at 12% interest. Over the investment period, oil prices are expected to be $74 per barrel, rising at the inflation rate each year. Assuming a normal distribution for project drilling and operating capex, with a standard deviation (SD) of 10% of the mean for each, abandonment expenditure maintains an SD of 20% while the volume of production correlates positively with operating expenditure. If oil prices are lognormal with an SD of 12% of the mean and rises by 1.5% per annum, reaching 32% by the last year of production, 8,000 Monte Carlo simulations produce the following results:

Assuming the average NPV is $129m from the many possible outcomes, the results on Table 11.1 suggest that the project is viable, but 10% of the scenarios

Table 11.1 Monte Carlo Simulation Results

Percentile	*Value ($millions)*
0	−123
10	26
25	74
50	131
75	180
90	230
100	430

would result in outcomes less than \$26m and, indeed, about 5% of them would indeed result in negative NPVs while over 10% of them would produce values above \$230m, peaking at \$430m (Macmillan, 2000). By conducting the risk analysis, the investors are provided the broader picture of possible outcomes of the project under various risk scenarios, allowing them to make a more informed decision. Despite its advantages, this method is viewed by some firms as being cumbersome, and the choice of appropriate shape of the probability distributions to use for the simulation can affect the results of the simulation and predicted NPVs. This reduces its practical adoption rate for most oil and gas projects.

11.5.4 Option Analysis

Another capital appraisal tool used in the industry is option analysis. The standard discounted cash flow approaches to capital project appraisal have been criticised by some researchers (Dixit and Pindyck 1994 and Buckley, 2000) as failing to account for operating flexibility and the strategic option value of a project which usually arises from its interdependence with future and follow-up investments. These factors affect cash flows, and failing to account for them in cash flow projections makes the traditional DCF approaches such as the NPV method static. Option analysis, therefore, employs Black-Scholes' model for spot prices to value a project as a stochastic differential equation (Galli et al., 1999) of the form:

$$dP_{sp} = \delta p W_t + \mu P_{sp} dt \tag{11.2}$$

where P_{sp} denotes spot price, δ is the spot price volatility, p is the price, W_t is the Brownian motion, μ is the drift in spot prices, and t denotes time.

Applying Ito's Lemma, the explicit formula for the spot price becomes:

$$P_{sp} = P_0 e^{\{[(\mu - \sigma 2)/2] + \sigma W_t\}} \tag{11.3}$$

where *Psp*, δ, W_t, μ and t, all maintain the meanings from equation (2), and P_0 is oil price.

In the standard finance literature, an option allows buyer, to either exercise their right (not obligation) to buy or sell an asset at either a specific date in the future (European options) or any time up to that date (American options) at an agreed-upon strike price. The application of option analysis in oil and gas investments is due to the key similarities between standard financial options and oil and gas investments. For instance the owner of an undeveloped oil well, just like an investor in the stock market options, is faced with the decision between investing in a developed project with known value now (spot price) or a decision to incur development cost (exercise price) to receive production revenues. The investor has the right to develop the well and receive these revenues but is not obliged to do so. This managerial flexibility improves the value of the project as it allows management to undertake production when prices are high enough, temporarily stop production when prices drop or close the well, and permanently shut down when prices are too low and continue to drop.

The following contextual example from Macmillan (2000) helps explain the point. Assume that a firm is trying to value its license in a block. Paying for the license is equivalent to paying the premium for a call option, which gives the firm the right (not obligation) to invest in the block (at the exercise price or production cost) once the uncertainty about the value of the developed reserves (like stock price) has been resolved. For instance consider that the license is for 5 years and the block could produce 50 MBO which can be sold at \$10 per barrel. If the total cost of developing the field (in present value terms) is \$600m, using standard NPV method, the project has an NPV of −\$100m, which will lead to a rejection of the project. However, the NPV method failed to account for variability in the possible quantity of recoverable reserves, which can be estimated using historical data from geologically similar fields. It also fails to account for oil price volatility, which can also be estimated from historical oil price volatility.

Suppose these two sources of uncertainty account for 30% SD about the average growth rate of operating cash inflows and that holding the license obliges the firm to incur fixed reserve maintenance cost of \$15m. This represents a dividend-like payout of 3% (15/500) of the value of the asset. Thus, using the Black and Scholes' real option valuation equation:

$$ROV = Se^{-\delta t} * \left\{N(d_1)\right\} - Xe^{-rt} * \left\{N(d_2)\right\} \tag{11.4}$$

where $d_1 = \dfrac{\left\{ln\left(\dfrac{S}{X}\right) + \left(r - \delta + \dfrac{\sigma^2}{2}\right)t\right\}}{\sigma} * \sqrt{t}$ . . . $d_2 = d_1 - \sigma * \sqrt{t}$, S is the present value of expected cash flows, x is the value of fixed cost, δ is the value lost over the duration of the option, r is risk free interest rate, σ is the uncertainty of expected cash flows, and t is time to expiry.

Therefore,

$$ROV = 500e^{-0.03*5} * \left\{0.58\right\} - 600e^{-0.05*5} * \left\{0.32\right\}$$

$$= \$251m \; - \; \$151m \; = \$100m$$

This example shows that there is a \$200m difference between the NPV method and the real option valuation method, representing the value of the flexibility of having the option to wait and invest when the uncertainties are resolved. In this case, the project will be accepted.

Algorithms that employ option theory have become very popular, and its application in the oil and gas industry have become wide. It is based on the probability of variations in market variables such as price (or interest rates, exchange rates) or technical variables such as recoverable reserves of an oil field. Though values like initial capex in oil and gas projects are considered sunk cost and are unrecoverable, firms have the option to sell off a project's tangible and intangible assets, and the uncertainty in the industry must be accounted for during investment appraisal (Lima and Suslick, 2006).

11.5.5 Portfolio Analysis

In practice, a business or an investor usually invests in a portfolio of projects instead of one, and they have to rely on portfolio analysis to choose among competing projects under budget constraints. The use of portfolio theory allows firms to select projects that not only provide the greatest individual returns but also ensure that the overall performance of the basket of projects is not affected by risk factors. The fact that project returns are additive while risk is not makes it necessary for investors to choose project investment portfolios that ensure that adverse outcomes from one project does not affect the overall performance of the investor's business in a significant way as most of the diversifiable risk could be eliminated through optimal portfolio selection. Indeed, most oil and gas firms base their investment decisions on a combination rather than one investment appraisal technique, and they decide at what stage of the project each method is employed. This is because, while each technique has its own advantages over others, they all have their limitations. So, by combining different techniques in the project appraisal process, risk and uncertainty will be better evaluated. For instance while a firm may wish to know when the accumulated net revenues will equal the initial capex (payback period), it would also wish to know the overall expected monetary value (EMV) that the project will generate. Also, when using techniques like the NPV to evaluate a project, this is often tested for sensitivity to changes in underlying assumptions to see the effect of risk on the cash flow estimates.

11.6 Making Capital Investment Decisions in the Oil and Gas Industry

Oil and gas investment projects require a great deal of capital expenditure, and the complexity of oil and gas projects makes capital investment decision-making more complex in the sector than in most other industries. Meanwhile, the difference between success and failure in investment depends on the decisions an investor makes regarding the choice of projects, source, type and cost of financing for the project, cash flow management choices, and payout policies among others. However, there is a paucity of literature on the application of decision analysis in capital project appraisal in the oil and gas industry. This section reviews decision-making process used in the oil and gas industry for project selection, capex, project continuation, or abandonment decisions.

The investment decision process in the oil and gas industry follows several processes as shown in Figure 11.4. These processes range from exploration, bidding for a lease, drill or no drill decisions, project development, expansion, timing, contract legalities, and environmental considerations to marketing and other downstream activities (Macmillan, 2000). First, project proposals are generated and scrutinised for feasibility: hydrocarbon potential and availability of reserves, economic potential, firm capacity, etc. At this stage, a number of alternative ideas are identified which are subjected to scrutiny, evaluation, and testing. Once an idea is identified, technical feasibility is done to find out whether or not the firm has the needed technology, machinery and equipment, skills, and raw materials to be able to execute it. After this, further scrutiny is done to check the commercial viability of the idea. These are often done by technical experts (engineers, planners, and financial analysts) who study the geology, magnetics, gravity, commercial potential, among other technical facts to guide further decisions. In analysing the capital investment, these issues will have to be considered: the amount of capital needed for both fixed and working capital to be injected, selection of the sources of finance to be used, estimation of future cash flow, determination of project lifespan, residual value of the asset, rate of depreciation of assets, and the discounting rate of cash flows. The firm then selects the most promising project(s) and then subject them to authorisation and approval before further commitment of resources.

The second step in the decision-making process involves the formulation of the project idea into an operable venture. At this stage, the most effective investment decision is made from the alternatives, and it is then further evaluated to guide investors' drill or no drill decisions. This is often guided by the economic potential of the identified project. Also, decisions on project development and production infrastructure requirements, workflow, development, and reservoir engineering are all done to ensure smooth operation of the selected project(s). These involve detailed feasibility analysis, technical analysis, economic analysis, cost benefit analysis, input analysis, project appraisal, and project network analysis.

After project formulation is done, the management has to continue taking production and operation decisions, evaluating progress at each stage including issues related to pressure maintenance, well maintenance, infill drilling, ullage, cost and revenue management, among others as shown in Figure 11.5. At this point, procurement of plants, machinery, equipment, land and so on is done with the development of infrastructure taking place.

The last stage in the oil and gas investment decision-making process is to choose whether to maintain a project or abandon the project. This decision is taken very late into the project implementation. The decision to abandon a well or project is based on both environmental and economic factors ranging from possible effects of the oil and gas production process on the environment and the realities of economic potentials not meeting predicted expectations among others. When this decision is taken, it comes with cost implications which all affect the economic monetary value of the firm or investor.

11.7 Conclusion

Several significant issues emerge from the forgoing discussions. First, the chapter presents readers with a review of the capex requirements in the oil and gas industry and provides a broad scrutiny of the factors that influence oil and gas

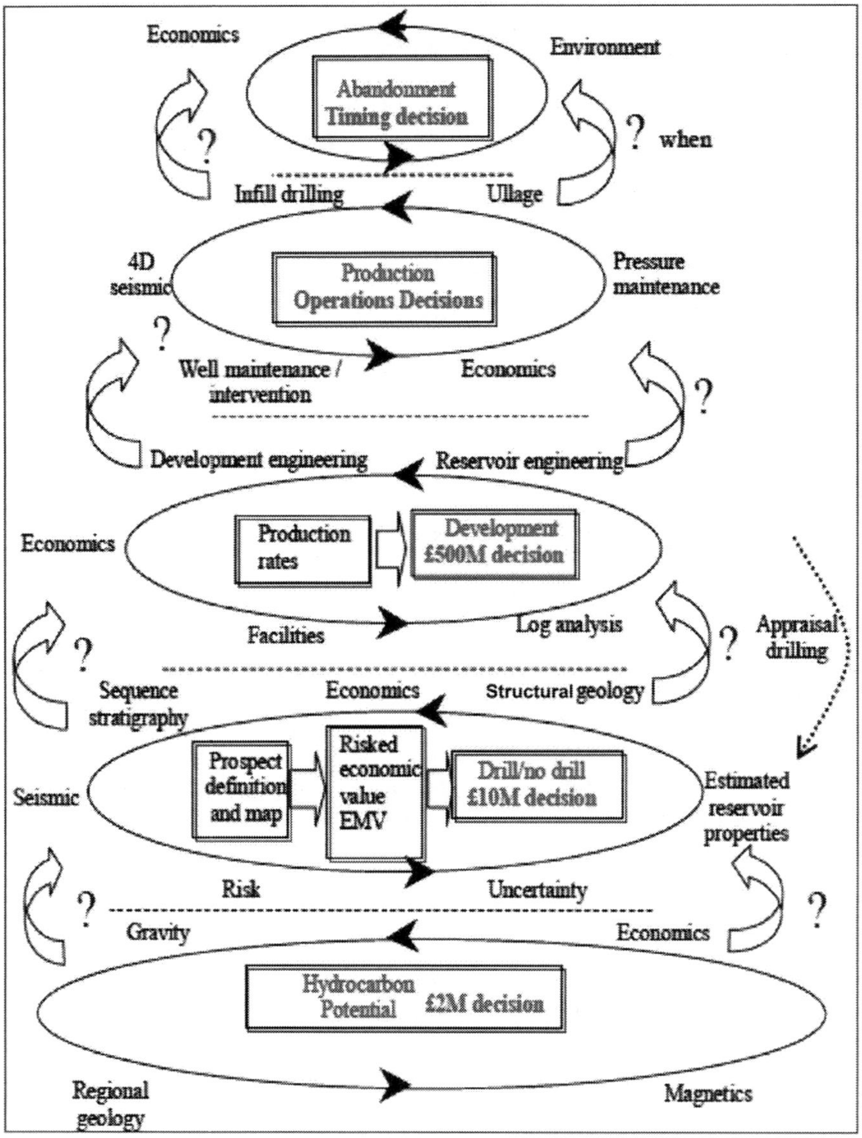

Figure 11.5 Oil and gas investment decision-making flow chart

Source: Macmillan (2000)

investment decisions. Also, the chapter provides a guide for writing investment proposals for oil and gas projects and blends generic investment appraisal techniques with decision theory to provide realistic project appraisal techniques used in the industry. In addition, the chapter outlines the processes involved in investment decision-making in the oil and gas industry. These details will guide appropriate methodology selection, decisions, and actions initiatives by policymakers, investors, oil and gas firms, managers, and other practitioners, which will ensure optimal allocation of oil and gas investment capital and the natural resource.

Notwithstanding the growing calls for greater investment in renewable energy, the global economy continues to depend largely on fossil fuels. This reliance on fossil fuel is expected to continue for decades to come at least in the developing countries where attempts to diversify away from fossil fuels remain slow or non-existent. Investment in the oil and gas sector comes at a great cost and risk. The risk tends to vary depending on the project phase under consideration. These risks may decline as one moves from the exploration phase through the construction to the production and processing phases. Given the huge cost involved in capital investment projects in this sector, related investment decisions must be passed through rigorous scrutiny. Among the range of factors that influence a firm's decision to invest in any of the project phases, the estimated project risk appears to be the most critical. Hence, firms should only consider investing in a given oil and gas project when the NPV remains positive after adjusting the projected cash flows to take care of all possible risks. It must be noted that a variety of investment appraisal techniques are used to evaluate oil and gas projects. Each technique is subject to some limitations. The best possible evaluation of a project can thus be achieved by combining a number of these techniques instead of relying on any of them in isolation. This act of combining techniques in the investment appraisal process helps firms overcome the limitations associated with individual techniques when used in isolation. The result is an investment decision that is more reliable and much easier to justify to shareholders.

Notes

1 The upstream sector involves exploration, development, production, and trading in crude oil and gas while the downstream sector involves transportation of crude, refining, storage, distribution, and marketing as well as gas marketing, transmission, storage, and distribution of gas.

2 The time it takes an oil and gas project to generate enough cash flows to cover the invested capex. The shorter this time period, the more time investors have to earn revenues in excess of their investment.

3 This is the ratio of the average annual profits over the initial investment, expressed as a percentage.

4 The IRR refers to the discount rate at which the project will generate an NPV of zero (NPV = 0). When a project's cost of capital is lower than the IRR, then the project is a positive NPV project and should be undertaken.

References

Abor, J. Y. (2017). Evaluating capital investment decisions: Capital budgeting. In *Entrepreneurial Finance for MSMEs* (pp. 293–320). Cham: Palgrave Macmillan.

Buckley, A. (2000). *Multinational finance*. 4th ed. London: Prentice Hall.

Coopersmith, E., Dean, G., McVean, J., and Storaune, E. (2000). Making decisions in the oil and gas industry. *Oilfield Review*, 12(4), 2–9.

CTI Private Financing Advisory Network (2014). *Guidelines for preparation of the initial project proposal*. https://www.icett.or.jp/kouryuu/h27/documents/ctipfan_projectproposal_guidelines_v07.pdf

Galli, A. G., Armstrong, M., and Jehl, B. (1999). Comparison of three methods for evaluating oil projects. *Journal of Petroleum Technology*, 44–50.

Dhochak, M., and Sharma, A. K. (2016). Identification and prioritisation of factors affecting venture capitalists' investment decision-making process: An analytical hierarchal process (AHP) approach. *Journal of Small Business and Enterprise Development.*

Dixit, A. K., and Pindyck, R. S. (1994). *Investment under uncertainty*. Princeton, NJ: Princeton University Press.

Domnikov, A., Chebotareva, G., Khomenko, P., and Khodorovskiy, M. (2015). Risk-oriented approach to long-term sustainability management for oil and gas companies in the course of implementation of investment projects. *WIT Transactions on Ecology and the Environment*, 192, 275–284.

Domnikov, A., Chebotareva, G., Khomenko, P., and Khodorovskiy, M. (2017). Risk-oriented investment in management of oil and gas company value. *International Journal of Sustainable Development and Planning*, 12(5), 946–955.

Fortune. (2022). *Global 500*. https://fortune.com/global500/

Kaiser, M. J., and Pulsipher, A. G. (2007). *Capital investment decisionmaking and trends: Implications on petroleum resource development*. Houston: US Gulf of Mexico.

Kuuskraa, V. A. (2008). *Investment decision-making in the oil and gas supply sectors*. A white paper submitted to Advanced Resources International, Paper No. JAF028029.DOC, 1–25.

Lima, G., and Suslick, S. (2006). Estimation of volatility of selected oil production project. *Journal of Petroleum Science and Engineering*, 54, 129–139.

Macmillan, F. (2000). *Risk, uncertainty and investment decision-making in the upstream oil and gas industry* (Doctoral thesis presented to the University of Aberdeen).

McMonigle, J., Thomson, A., van Agt, C., Fitz, R., and Webster, J. (2021). *Oil and gas investment in the new risk environment. An international energy forum report with Boston consulting group*. https://www.ief.org/investmentreport

Phan, D. T., and Nguyen, H. T. (2020). Factors affecting corporate investment decision: Evidence from Vietnamese economic groups. *The Journal of Asian Finance, Economics, and Business*, 7(11), 177–184.

Reynolds, D. (2005). Hubbert, hotelling and risk: The three causes behind peak oil. *USAEE Dialogue*, 13(2), 14–16.

US Energy Information Administration (2021). *International Energy Outlook*. https://www.eia.gov/todayinenergy/detail.php?id=41433

12 Financial Analysis of Oil and Gas Firms

Zangina Isshaq, Emmanuel Sarpong-Kumankoma, and Kemi Yekini

12.1 Introduction

Oil and gas companies operate in an industry that has a long value chain traditionally divided into upstream, midstream, and downstream. An oil and gas company may have operations in all three streams. Such companies are referred to as integrated companies. In this chapter, we provide the structure for analysis of financial statements of oil and gas firms. To facilitate the understanding of and gas financial statements, we first explore the components of financial reports, highlighting peculiar items in reports of oil and gas companies. We do so to facilitate the understanding of financial performance of oil and gas companies. Financial ratios are the indicators we use for the analysis of oil and gas firm financial statements.

12.2 Industry Economics and Dynamics

Oil and gas companies operate in an industry that has a worldwide market with many buyers. Many oil and gas companies are price-takers. So, to understand the performance of oil and gas companies, one also needs to understand the world economic situation and consider these in the financial performance evaluation of oil and gas companies. Figure 12.1 plots the quarterly prices of one of the benchmark oil price indicators – the Western Texas Intermediate Brent Crude oil price series. Crude oil prices, as the figures show, have been on quite a ride over the last two decades. This trend has implications for the fortunes of firms in the industry. This should be in the background in trying to understand the trends in the performance of an oil and gas firm over this period.

12.3 Components of Financial Statements

Financial statement components are determined by the International Accounting Standards Board (IASB) in the International Accounting Standard (IAS) 1 *Presentation of Financial Statements*. A complete set of financial statement includes:

DOI: 10.4324/9781003315056-15

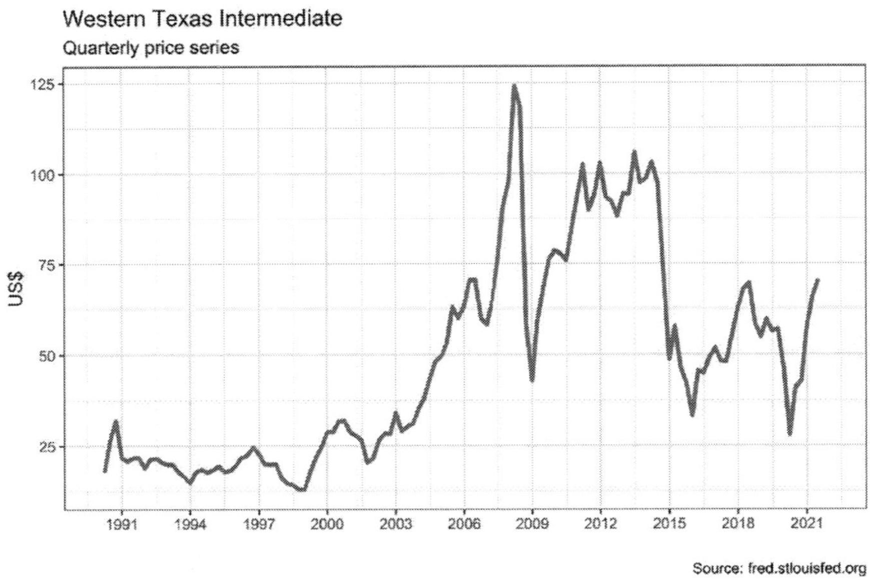

Figure 12.1 Quarterly crude oil prices using the Western Texas Intermediate price series

i Statement of income or statement of comprehensive income.
ii Statement of financial position.
iii Statement of cash flows.
iv Statement of changes in equity.
v Notes to the financial statements.

The statement of cash flows provides information about the movements of cash and cash equivalents of the reporting entity. The cash flow statement provides information on the cash generation ability of the business that is not made apparent in the financial statements because of the accruals basis of accounting that underlies the statements. Three key parts to the statement of cash flows are cash flow from operations, investment, and financing. Cash flow from a firm's ordinary business is called cash flow from operations. Cash flow from purchases of noncurrent assets and sales of noncurrent assets are cash flow from investing activities. Cash flows from financing activities are borrowing, raising equity, paying dividends, and paying interests on borrowings. The statement of changes in equity shows how, over the course of a financial year, equity has been impacted by transactions sanctioned by management. The notes provide further details to better understand how figures are arrived at and the composition of figures.

12.4 Statement of Financial of Position

The statement of financial position reports information on the values of assets, liabilities, and equity of a firm at a particular date. The statement of financial position gives shareholders information on the value of the assets their capital has been used to acquire and any obligations taken by management in the operations of the business. The appendix provides illustrative statement of financial position.

Assets and liabilities are reported in two categories – current and noncurrent. Noncurrent assets are those assets from which economic benefits are expected to accrue to the firm for more than one financial year after the reporting date. Noncurrent assets are either tangible or intangible. Tangible noncurrent assets have physical form – examples being property, plant, and equipment. Intangible noncurrent assets do not have a physical form – examples being exploration and evaluation cost. An example of intangible noncurrent assets is the *intangible exploration and evaluation assets* in Table 12.1. Upstream developments of oil and gas resources have a period of expenditure on prospecting until commercially viable quantities of reserves are discovered or nothing is found. Intangible exploration and evaluation assets represent such costs. The IASB consolidated financial reporting practices for the extractive industries in the IFRS 6 *Exploration and Evaluation of Mineral Resources* to provide guidance for reporting on expenditures incurred in exploration and evaluation. Exploration and evaluation expenditure includes costs of licenses, leases, concessions, geological and geophysical studies, and possible financing costs. Expenditures incurred prior to obtaining a legal right to explore are not included. There are two approaches to dealing with exploration and evaluation costs – full cost method and successful efforts method.

Exploration and evaluations costs are capitalised under the full cost method on the basis of large geographic cost centre or cost pool (PricewaterhouseCoopers, 2017). The cost centre is then depleted (depreciated) as production occurs. If all efforts in a cost pool or geographic formation are unsuccessful, then exploration and evaluation costs are expensed. With successful efforts, costs are capitalised field-by-field, and if a field is unsuccessful, the costs are expensed. The capitalised costs are allocated to commercially viable fields. A reporting entity will disclose their approach in the notes to the financial statements.

Noncurrent liabilities are liabilities that will be due for repayment in the future for a period in excess of the end of the next financial year. Provisions for decommissioning and restoration may be found under noncurrent liabilities of an oil and gas entity. Current liabilities are liabilities that will be due for repayment by the end of the next financial year. For example if the statement of financial position is prepared on 30 September 2020, any debt obligations due for payment before 30 September 2021 are current liabilities and those after that are noncurrent liabilities. Overlifts in a joint venture for oil and gas firm become a trade payable under current liabilities.

Current assets are assets whose benefits will be consumed by the end of the next financial year. Trade receivables are amounts due from credit customers. For oil and gas entities, this will include amounts due from joint venture partners and under lift and monies due from insurance claims. Held for sale assets are items that were previously accounted for as noncurrent assets, but a decision has been taken to sell these assets.

12.5 Statement of Income

We now highlight elements of the statement of income of a firm in the oil and gas sector. Illustrative statements in the appendix provides more detail.

12.5.1 Revenue

Sales revenue in the income statement represents the market value of products delivered to customers. Where production is done in a joint venture, sales revenue will include lifting that is within entitlements of the reporting entity. Revenue from the joint venture will include overlifting by the reporting entity's joint venture partners.

12.5.2 Expenses

Expense items of interest, for their uniqueness to oil and gas firms, are exploration costs written off, and provisions for onerous contracts and restructuring. Write-offs of exploration and evaluation costs to income statement reflects the approach to accounting for exploration and evaluation costs – full cost method or successful efforts. For a firm applying the successful efforts method, these write-offs imply efforts in a particular cost pool or field was not successful and the field or cost centre has been abandoned. The successful efforts method is considered more compatible with the *Conceptual Framework* (Pricewaterhouse-Coopers 2017; IASB, 2018).

Impairment of property, plant, and equity may be found in other financial statements, but it does have unique implications for oil and gas firms. Exploration and evaluation assets and other assets in the financial statements are subject to impairment testing within the general framework of financial reporting under IFRS (IASB, 2013). Impairment of exploration and evaluation assets occurs when certain triggers are in place under the impairment-testing regime of the IFRS 6. The indicators are factors that suggest that the incurred exploration and evaluation costs may not be recovered. Impairment indicators for exploration and evaluation assets under IFRS 6 include when no further explorations are planned or budgeted, expiration of exploration rights, not finding commercially viable discoveries of mineral resources, and sufficient data exists to show that the mineral resources found are not enough to recover the cost of exploration and evaluation (IASB, 2004).

12.6 Evaluating Oil and Gas Firm Performance

We will use pro-forma financial statements to demonstrate the computations and evaluation of the performance of oil and gas firms. The basic framework for assessing financial performance is the computation of ratios. Ratios relate one financial statement item to another. The choice of items is informed by the relations of interest to the analyst. Adequate interpretations of ratios require a comparator. Comparators can be prior year values, competitor firms, or an industry benchmark. We will use the prior year's approach. Past performance is best appreciated when a trend can be depicted. We compute ratios for a firm in the oil and gas sector for a 5-year period. A firm's financial performance can be assessed on dimensions of profitability, liquidity, productivity, and leverage (or solvency). We illustrate these dimensions with the pro forma financials. The formulas, we apply in the analysis closely follow formulas in Berk and De Marzo (2017).

12.6.1 Profitability

Profitability is measured as the net income of a venture over a financial year with respect to, most often, the capital invested by shareholders or the value of capital made available to management. Return on equity, ROE, is profits as a percentage of shareholders equity, and return on assets, ROA, measures profitability with respect to total assets. The difference between ROA and ROE is to show the impact of the use leverage (borrowed funds) to generate profits. The formulas for computing these ratios are as follows.

$$ROA = \frac{Net\ profit\ after\ taxes}{Total\ assets} \times 100$$

$$ROE = \frac{Net\ profit\ after\ taxes}{Shareholders'\ fund} \times 100$$

Profitability may also be measured with respect to pricing power and cost efficiency. Gross profit margin provides a measure of profitability that indicates the proportion of sales revenue that is in excess of direct cost of production. Firms in the oil and gas industry are price-takers, which implies that a high gross profit margin is indicative of control of cost of production. For firms operating in the upstream sector, this ratio reflects the control of cost of extraction and the efficiency of the firm's technology. Gross profit margin is,

$$\text{Gross profit margin} = \frac{\text{Gross profit}}{\text{Total revenue}} \times 100$$

Another profitability measure is the net profit margin. Net profit margin is net profit after tax as a percentage of revenue. This ratio may also be computed as net profit before interest and taxes as a percentage of revenue to give emphasis to the use of capital from all capital providers. Net profit margin, when

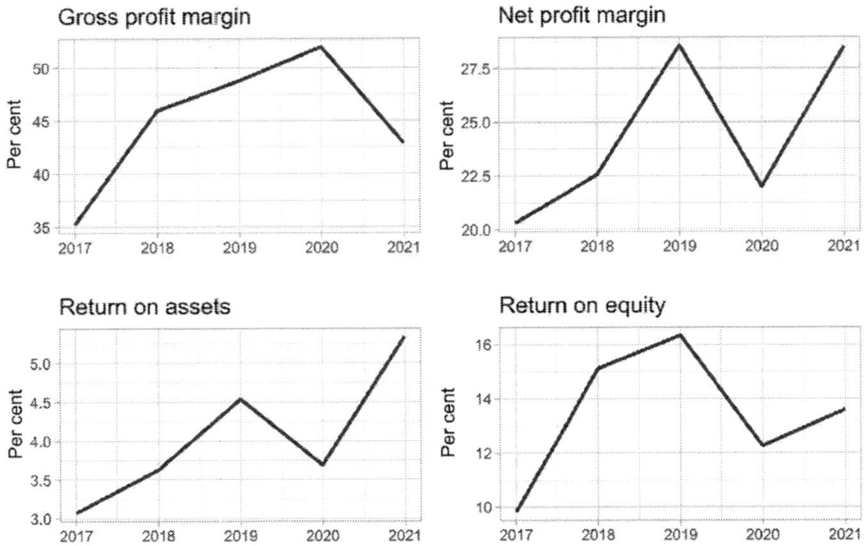

Figure 12.2 Profitability ratios

considered in relation to the gross profit margin, provides information on how operating expenses are eating into revenues.

$$\text{Net profit margin} = \frac{\text{Net profit after tax}}{\text{Total revenue}} \times 100$$

Figure 12.2 presents trends of the foregoing ratios for our illustrative company. We provide in the appendix the 5-year financial data used in the computation of these ratios.

From Figure 12.2, gross profit margin increased over the initial 4 years of the series from about 35% to 52% but fell sharply in the last year of the series to about 42%. Several factors can explain this trend. Compared to the Western Texas Intermediate quarterly price series, the sharp fall in the gross margin is likely attributable to the falling oil prices during that period. The net profit margin series has a trend similar to the gross profit margin except that a sharp decline occurs a year earlier than the fall in the gross profit margin. Investigating the financial statement for any jumps in expenditures and information on cost control considerations can explain this change. In the illustrative statements we find that the rise in exploration costs written off jumps in this year. Such write offs can be occasioned by exits, exploration licenses expiration, or decision to discontinue exploration at a site.

ROA and ROE have similar trends. Both increase in the initial year, drop in mid-way, and rise in the last year, like the net profit margin trend. We learn more by decomposing ROA and ROE into profitability and asset utilisation for ROA and profitability, asset utilisation, and leverage for ROE. Price inflation may lead to higher net profit margins when assets might not have been put to their best use. DuPont analysis is the framework to find drivers of ROA and ROE. ROA is decomposed into effect of net profit margin and asset utilisation.

$$ROA = \frac{Net\ profit\ after\ tax}{Sales\ revenue} \times \frac{Sales\ revenue}{Total\ assets}$$

Our analysis in the productivity section shows that asset utilisation was increasing throughout the 5 years. Our illustrative firm extracted more from assets in place. Falling global oil prices in 2020 means that managers were doing what was reasonable in a difficult year.

The decomposition of ROE leads to

$$ROE = \frac{Net\ profit\ after\ tax}{Sales\ revenue} \times \frac{Sales\ revenue}{Total\ assets} \times \frac{Total\ assets}{Shareholders'\ fund}$$

The ratio of assets to shareholders' fund (equity) is called the equity multiplier and indicates the effect of leverage on the returns generated for shareholders. Increasing ROE from increased leverage implies shareholders are getting higher returns from increasing financial risk.

12.6.2 Liquidity

Liquidity is the ability to raise cash when needed. Liquidity is, thus, measured in terms of the assets that can be converted into cash at a short notice with minimal or no loss in value. Current assets are the focus of liquidity management for any firm. Liquidity ratios measure ratio of liquid assets relative to their short-term obligations. We define the following liquidity ratios.

$$\text{Current ratio} = \frac{\text{Total current assets}}{\text{Total current liabilities}}$$

$$\text{Quick ratio} = \frac{\text{Total current assets} - \text{Inventory}}{\text{Total current liabilities}}$$

$$\text{Cash ratio} = \frac{\text{Cash and cash equivalents}}{\text{Total current liabilities}}$$

Figure 12.3 presents trends of these principal liquidity ratios.

The current ratio provides the answer to the question: how many times do our current assets cover our current liabilities? For the years 2017–2020, the current ratio of our illustrative firm is increasing and consistently greater than 1. Computation of current ratio includes inventory, which is not easily converted into cash like cash balances and other money market financial securities

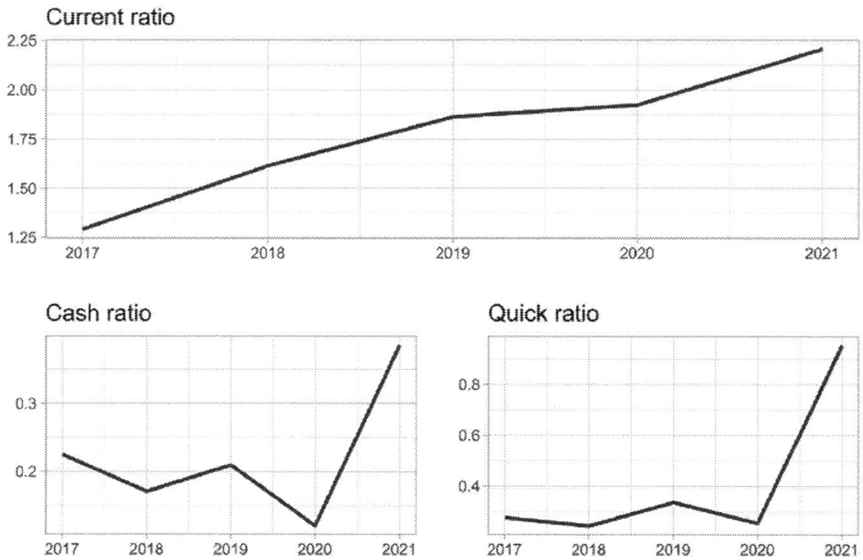

Figure 12.3 Working capital ratios

that can easily be sold at a short notice. Slow moving inventory can make this ratio higher. A more stringent liquidity measure is the quick ratio, which excludes inventory.

Quick ratio of our illustrative firm is below 1, and the years 2017–2020 do not show a similar upward trend like the current ratio. Inventory seems to have been the greater component of the current assets over these years. Cash ratio focuses on only cash and cash equivalents. Cash ratio is decreasing through the years 2016–2019 but makes a sharp increase in the year to 2020, like the quick ratio. These trends are better explained when the asset utilisation ratios are considered. Cash ratio increases may result from delays in paying current liabilities or more generous trade payables periods offered by trade partners. An oil and gas firm that owes much of its trade payables to joint venture partners through overlifting may have a leeway in how long it takes to repay. Borrowings on short-term basis add to liquidity and current liabilities, but borrowings on long-term basis increase liquid assets in the form of cash and this can boost the quick and cash ratios. So quick and cash ratios can provide insights on the financing strategy for current assets. Funding current assets with long-term debt offers liquidity, but it may not be the cheapest option.

12.6.3 Productivity

Our profitability analysis highlighted the importance of the asset utilisation in understanding the trends in profitability. This section elaborates on measures of asset utilisation (also termed efficiency). Others prefer productivity ratios. A firm's sales are generated from the operations of assets in place. We present four productivity ratios—asset turnover, inventory turnover, accounts receivable turnover, and accounts payable turnover. Asset turnover provides an answer to the question: how much in sales has been generated for each unit of investment in assets? Asset turnover is given by the following formula:

$$\text{Asset turnover} = \frac{\text{Total sales revenue}}{\text{Total assets}}$$

Another question to ask is how many times of our average inventory at the end of the financial year did we sell? To answer that we compute the inventory turnover ratio. A higher inventory turnover ratio indicates an ability to move inventory quickly. Slow moving has knock-on effects on liquidity as noted before in our analysis of liquidity indicators. Inventory turnover is computed as,

$$\text{Inventory turnover} = \frac{\text{Cost of sales}}{\text{Inventory}}$$

Accounts receivable turnover is the indicator of how many times of our receivables we have been able to collect, given credit sales over the year. A higher ratio means receivables are collected more quickly on average. A lower ratio indicates either cash-based sales or more extended credit periods for customers. Accounts receivable turnover is calculated as given here.

$$\text{Accounts receivable turnover} = \frac{\text{Sales revenue}}{\text{Trade receivables}}$$

Another question is how many times a firm has taken trade credits and repaid them over the year. This is the accounts payable turnover. Cost of sales is used as an indicator of how much inventory was acquired on credit. For oil and gas firms in the upstream sector, this is replaced with production costs. For downstream firms, the definition of the ratio does not change. Accounts receivable turnover is given as follows:

$$\text{Accounts payable turnover} = \frac{\text{Cost of sales}}{\text{Trade payables}}$$

Figure 12.4 presents the trends of the foregoing ratios computed from our example of financial statements.

Asset turnover indicates the amount of sales generated for each \$1 of investment in assets. While our computation of asset turnover divides total sales revenue by total assets that includes both current and noncurrent assets, an alternative is to divide total sales by total assets excluding current liabilities. With the alternative computation, the focus is on long-term funded assets. As Figure 12.4 shows, asset turnover is less than \$1 for each dollar of asset investment over the 5 years presented. But asset turnover is on an upward trend over the period. Asset turnover is depressed by new investments because some assets may take years to develop and for eventual sales to be generated. Exploration

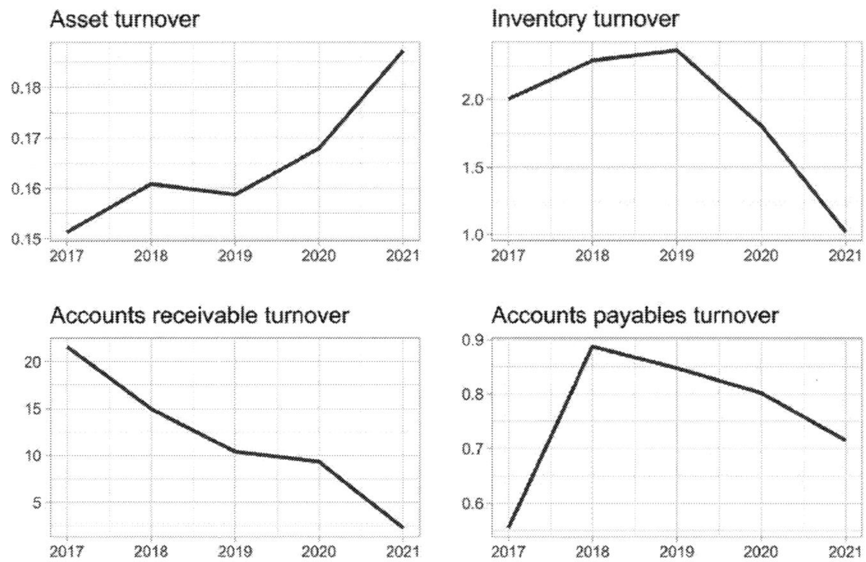

Figure 12.4 Productivity ratios

and evaluation expenditures for a period may be capitalised and form part of assets, but no revenue will be generated on these expenditures because no product has yet been sold on the basis of these investments. In our analysis of net profit margin, we noted that the drop in net profit margin coincided with increased write-offs of exploration and evaluation expenditures in 2020. Asset turnover for 2019–2020 shows the boost in the asset turnover ratio over this period, which in part can be attributed to the exploration and evaluation assets write-offs.

Inventory turnover in Figure 12.4 has a downward trend over the 5-year period. This may be a sign of slow-moving inventory. A downstream firm can signal bottlenecks in sales in the face of competition. An upstream firm can signal quality issues especially for crude oil from newer wells drawn from hard-to-reach reserves.

Figure 12.4 also shows declining accounts receivable turnover. This implies that receivables were taking increasingly longer to collect. Extended credit terms could be accountable, but the effect is that the less cash is generated from operations, which may increase the need for short-term borrowings or use of long-term debt to finance current assets.

Accounts payable turnover is also declining over the 5 years, although it started the period with an uptick. Accounts payable turnover decline means the firm is taking longer to pay trade payables, another sign of liquidity difficulties. Our analysis in this section helps make sense of liquidity trends we observed earlier. In Figure 12.3, current ratio was on an upward trajectory which can be attributed to slow moving inventory piling up. We also saw in Figure 12.3 an uptick in cash ratio and the quick ratio, both signalling borrowed funds shoring up cash balances.

12.6.4 Leverage Analysis

Leverage analysis is about the long-term sustainability of a firm, given its long-term debt obligations. Long-term debts have fixed commitments, which have implications for the firm's financial flexibility. Leverage analysis also evaluates the extent shareholders' capital is exposed to financial risk from leverage. We present three ratios next that provide an assessment of a firm's capacity to take on debt and a firm's ability to service its existing debt.

First, we compute the debt-to-equity ratio as

$$\text{Debt-to-equity ratio} = \frac{\text{Total debt}}{\text{Shareholders funds}}$$

Total debt in the formula includes both short-term and long-term borrowings. Only interest-bearing borrowings of any maturity are included in the figure for total debt. Increases in debt-to-equity ratio imply increasing financial risk.

Debt-to-total assets compare total debt to total assets of the firm to understand the portion of the firm's assets that is funded by external funds other than funds from shareholders. When debt-to-total asset is rising, it signals increasing financial risk. Uncertainty in the business environment means a sudden change in the normal business performance, which can lead to financial difficulty.

$$\text{Debt-to-total assets} = \frac{\text{Total debt}}{\text{Total assets}}$$

Debt-servicing ability is assessed through the interest coverage ratio. Interest coverage ratio shows how many times profits before interest and taxes can pay off current interest commitments. A lender will be interested in a trend of increasing interest coverage ratio, which indicates whether current profitability level is enough to service interest on debt.

$$\text{Interest coverage ratio} = \frac{\text{Net profit before interest and taxes}}{\text{Interest expense}}$$

While we use interest expense in the formula, the corresponding terminology in the financial statements we have presented before is finance costs. Figure 12.5 shows the trends of the leverage ratios from example financial statements.

Figure 12.5 shows that from 2018 to 2021, there is a continued effort to reduce the ratio of debt-to-equity. This mean either fresh capital from shareholders to pay down debt or profits are used. In the financial statements in the appendix, one will notice zero balances for short-term borrowings and decreases in long-term borrowings. This means financing arrangements are being rationalised. The trend of debt-to-total assets is like that of debt-to-equity, and the inferences about debt-to-equity apply. Interest coverage ratio shows an uptick between 2017 and 2018 but falls from there on. We can

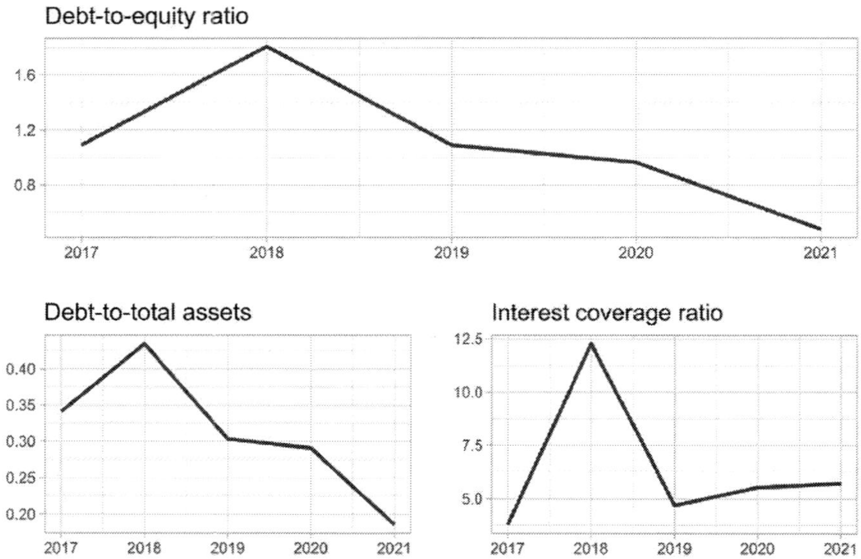

Figure 12.5 Leverage ratios

understand this change by referring to the profitability trends. The periods 2019 and 2021 had no consistent profitability growth, likewise asset turnover. But the crude oil prices in Figure 12.1 suggests that revenues were hampered by falling oil prices.

When the profitability, liquidity, and leverage ratios are put together, we see that price dynamics in the market led oil firms to cutbacks in leverage and paying down debts, which drained liquidity. If a firm's management rationalises its debt ahead of the price falls, the firm will have a better chance of withstanding liquidity challenges when the price falls bite.

12.7 Common Size Analysis

We have conducted the aforementioned analysis on the basis of relations between different elements in the financial statements – from the income statement to the statement of financial position. There is an alternative: common size analysis. Common size analysis involves comparing elements against one typical value in the financial statement of interest. Typically, income statement items are compared to revenue and all statements of financial position items are compared to total assets.

Common size analysis facilitates the evaluation of a firm's position in relation to its competitors. Common size analysis is also useful for trend analysis of a firm's performance. We now present the common size ratios for the income statement from our illustrative financial statements.

Table 12.1 Common Size Ratios of the Income Statement

Item	*2021*	*2020*	*2019*	*2018*	*2017*
Sales revenue	100.00	100.00	100.00	100.00	100.00
Other operating income, lost production insurance proceeds	2.22	9.20	8.34	4.84	2.61
Cost of sales	41.90	47.18	44.70	43.72	34.31
Gross profit	58.10	52.82	55.30	56.28	65.69
Administrative expenses	5.79	4.41	4.90	6.26	10.80
Restructuring costs	0.00	0.00	0.75	0.66	2.28
Gain/loss on disposal	0.34	1.04	0.08	0.18	3.15
Goodwill impairment	0.00	0.00	0.00	8.82	2.99
Exploration costs written off	13.16	14.42	7.37	6.61	8.30
Impairment of property, plant and equipment, net	5.26	0.89	7.15	9.01	3.68
Provisions for onerous contracts and restructuring	0.22	8.34	0.05	0.37	1.42
Operating (loss)/profit	33.55	32.07	35.04	24.74	34.49
(Loss)/gain on hedging instruments	0.08	0.12	0.61	0.98	3.28
Finance revenue	2.88	2.85	2.16	1.42	0.23
Finance costs	6.35	6.29	7.80	2.05	8.31
(Loss)/profit from continuing activities before tax	30.00	28.52	28.79	23.13	23.14
Income tax expense	2.11	8.55	2.60	1.67	3.37
(Loss)/profit for the year from continuing activities	27.89	19.96	26.19	21.46	19.77

Common size ratios are calculated by dividing each item in the income statement by the sum of sales revenue and other operating income. Table 12.1 shows that cost of sales as a percentage of revenue increased from 34.31% of sales in 2017 to 47.18% in 2020 and then dropped in 2021. This is mirrored by the gross profit margin moving in the opposite direction. Administrative expenses reduced from a high 10.80% of revenues in 2017 to 5.79% in 2021. But exploration costs written off increased as a percentage of gross revenues from 2017 to 2021. With common size analysis, we easily see the effects of expenses on reported net profit margin. Administrative cost was controlled, but write-offs of exploration expenditure hampered net profits.

We now consider common size ratios for the statement of financial position items. All items are expressed as a percentage of total assets. We highlight the portion of total assets financed by equity, noncurrent liabilities, and the trends in each of these.

Table 12.2 shows that intangible assets related to exploration and evaluation costs as a percentage of total assets decreased from 30% to 18% between 2017 and 2021. The income statement shows significant amount written off intangible assets, indicating that exploration efforts are coming on stream or write-off of unsuccessful efforts. Property, plant, and equipment as a percentage of assets decreased between 2018 and 2021, implying asset sales and decommissioning.

Table 12.2 Common Size Ratios of Statement of Financial Position

Non-Current Assets	*2021*	*2020*	*2019*	*2018*	*2017*
Goodwill	0.00	0.00	0.00	0.00	1.42
Intangible exploration and evaluation assets	17.55	17.14	17.22	18.42	29.45
Property, plant, and equipment	38.70	44.39	46.80	48.75	45.07
Other non-current assets	6.20	6.29	7.03	1.60	1.93
Derivative financial instruments	0.03	0.46	0.01	0.14	1.89
Deferred tax assets	5.15	5.86	6.45	6.90	2.56
Total noncurrent assets	67.62	74.15	77.52	75.81	82.32
Current assets					
Inventories	7.87	4.83	3.28	3.23	2.66
Trade receivables	8.34	1.80	1.53	1.08	0.70
Other current assets	9.24	8.75	6.84	7.63	6.61
Current tax assets	0.43	0.55	0.51	1.26	1.11
Derivative financial instruments	0.85	0.72	0.02	0.83	3.52
Cash and cash equivalents	5.66	1.62	2.53	2.56	3.08
Assets classified as held for sale	0.00	7.59	7.78	7.61	0.00
Total current assets	32.38	25.85	22.48	24.19	17.68
Total assets	100.00	100.00	100.00	100.00	100.00
Current liabilities					
Trade and other payables	11.21	10.87	9.13	8.33	9.62
Provisions	1.72	1.79	2.06	0.47	1.62
Borrowings	0.00	0.00	0.00	5.38	0.64
Current tax liabilities	1.59	0.75	0.40	0.76	1.80
Derivative financial instruments	0.15	0.02	0.47	0.05	0.02
Total current liabilities	14.67	13.44	12.06	14.99	13.70
Non-current liabilities					
Trade and other payables	12.06	11.58	12.67	1.02	2.25
Borrowings	18.61	29.07	30.30	38.06	33.45
Decommissioning and other provisions	7.49	6.11	7.14	10.06	9.25
Deferred tax liabilities	7.89	9.71	9.81	11.75	10.09
Derivative financial instruments	0.01	0.00	0.23	0.10	0.00

Non-Current Assets	*2021*	*2020*	*2019*	*2018*	*2017*
Total non-current liabilities	46.07	56.46	60.15	60.99	55.03
Total liabilities	60.73	69.90	72.21	75.98	68.73
Equity					
Called-up share capital	2.10	1.89	1.85	1.34	1.27
Share premium	13.72	12.14	11.82	5.63	5.28
Foreign currency translation reserve	2.41	2.15	1.99	2.11	2.16
Hedge reserve	0.05	1.18	0.02	1.17	4.94
Other reserves	7.51	6.82	6.60	6.74	6.42
Retained earnings	13.48	5.92	5.41	6.93	11.03
Equity attributable to equity holders of the company	39.27	30.10	27.69	23.91	31.10
Non-controlling interest	0.00	0.00	0.09	0.11	0.17
Total equity	39.27	30.10	27.79	24.02	31.27
Total equity and liabilities	100.00	100.00	100.00	100.00	100.00

Held for sale assets stayed at 8% of total assets between 2018 and 2020, implying a firm retreating from certain exploration activities or asset sales to pay down debts. Short-term and long-term borrowings to total assets ratios suggest efforts to reduce debt levels. Noncurrent borrowings declined from 38% in 2018 to 18.61% of total assets in 2021. One can infer a change in financial strategy. While borrowings were on decline, long-term trade and other payables were increasing as a percentage of total assets. These provide some explanations for the observations made about the debt-to-total assets ratio.

12.8 Non-Financial Information

The aforementioned analysis relies on financial data presented in the financial statements. A comprehensive understanding of a firm's performance needs to consider non-financial information. For an oil and gas firm, information on production is important. Natural resources are subject to depletion. Oil and gas reserves deplete with continued production. This means information on reserves and rate at which the reserves are being depleted is crucial to make informed decisions about future continued operations (Johnston and Johnston, 2006).

12.9 Summary and Conclusions

In this chapter, we have introduced a framework of analysing financial performance of oil and gas firms. We also highlighted financial statement items peculiar to the financial statements of oil and gas firms. We have shown, through financial ratios, how to evaluate the financial performance of an oil and gas firm. We proceed to give a few caveats about using ratios to evaluate performance. As noted earlier, non-financial information is crucial to get a complete picture. Financial ratios only provide insights about financial aspects of a firm's operations. For example production technology of an oil and gas firm is important to making decisions about the future sustainability of the firm. Financial ratios are affected by the accounting policies chosen in the measurement of financial statement items.

Appendices

Illustrative Financial Statements

Income Statement Items

Item	*2021*	*2020*	*2019*	*2018*	*2017*
Sales revenue	9,413.00	9,296.00	8,912.50	8,849.50	8,733.00
Other operating income, lost production insurance proceeds	213.50	942.00	810.50	450.50	234.00
Cost of sales	4,033.50	4,830.00	4,346.50	4,065.50	3,076.50
Gross profit	5,593.00	5,408.00	5,376.50	5,234.50	5,890.50
Administrative expenses	557.50	451.50	476.50	582.00	968.00
Restructuring costs			72.50	61.50	204.00
Gain/loss on disposal	33.00	106.50	8.00	17.00	282.50
Goodwill impairment				820.00	268.50
Exploration costs written off	1,267.00	1,476.00	717.00	615.00	744.50
Impairment of property, plant, and equipment, net	506.00	91.00	695.50	838.00	330.00
Provisions for onerous contracts and restructuring	21.00	854.00	5.00	34.00	127.50
Operating (loss)/profit	3,229.50	3,283.00	3,407.00	2,301.00	3,093.00
(Loss)/gain on hedging instruments	7.50	12.00	59.00	91.00	294.00
Finance revenue	277.50	292.00	210.00	132.00	21.00
Finance costs	611.50	643.50	758.50	191.00	745.00
(Loss)/profit from continuing activities before tax	2,888.00	2,919.50	2,799.50	2,151.00	2,075.00
Income tax expense	203.50	875.50	253.00	155.00	302.00
(Loss)/profit for the year from continuing activities	2,684.50	2,044.00	2,546.50	1,996.00	1,773.00
Basic	6.40	3.05	3.50	3.29	5.68
Diluted	5.67	2.95	3.15	2.70	3.68
(Loss)/profit for the year	2,684.50	2,044.00	2,546.50	1,996.00	1,773.00
Cash flow hedges					
(Loss)/gain arising in the year	593.00	503.50	33.50	676.50	565.00
(Loss)/gain arising in the year , time value	368.00	81.00			
Reclassification adjustments for items included in (loss)/profit on realisation	38.00	163.50	809.00	476.00	512.00
Reclassification adjustments for items included in loss on realisation, time value	305.00	263.50			
Exchange differences on translation of foreign operations	17.50	77.00	45.00	85.50	218.00
Other comprehensive (loss)/profit	2,414.00	1,881.00	2,558.00	1,405.00	1,426.00
Tax relating to components of other comprehensive loss			121.50	44.00	211.50

(*Continued*)

Income Statement Items

Item	*2021*	*2020*	*2019*	*2018*	*2017*
Net other comprehensive loss for the year			609.00	2,123.00	623.50
Total comprehensive (expense)/ income for the year	2,414.00	1,881.00	2,436.50	1,361.00	1,214.50
Statement of Financial Position Items					
Non-Current Assets					
Goodwill					820.00
Intangible exploration and evaluation assets	8,822.00	9,493.00	9,667.00	10,129.00	17,000.00
Property, plant and equipment	19,458.50	24,582.00	26,273.50	26,814.50	26,022.00
Other non-current assets	3,116.00	3,482.00	3,949.00	878.50	1,117.00
Derivative financial instruments	15.50	256.00	4.00	79.00	1,093.50
Deferred tax assets	2,587.50	3,247.00	3,622.50	3,794.50	1,476.50
Total noncurrent assets	33,999.50	41,060.00	43,516.00	41,695.50	47,529.00
Current assets					
Inventories	3,957.50	2,674.00	1,840.00	1,776.50	1,536.00
Trade receivables	4,193.50	997.00	857.00	592.00	404.00
Other current assets	4,643.50	4,845.00	3,841.50	4,194.50	3,816.00
Current tax assets	214.50	302.50	288.50	691.50	638.00
Derivative financial instruments	428.50	398.50	9.00	458.50	2,032.50
Cash and cash equivalents	2,844.00	899.00	1,420.00	1,409.50	1,778.50
Assets classified as held for sale		4,201.00	4,365.50	4,185.50	
Total current assets	16,281.50	14,317.00	12,621.50	13,308.00	10,205.00
Total assets	50,281.00	55,377.00	56,137.50	55,003.50	57,734.00
Current liabilities					
Trade and other payables	5,638.00	6,021.50	5,128.00	4,580.50	5,553.00
Provisions	864.00	992.50	1,154.00	259.50	935.00
Borrowings				2,957.50	369.00
Current tax liabilities	798.00	415.00	225.00	415.50	1,041.50
Derivative financial instruments	74.00	13.50	265.50	29.50	10.50
Total current liabilities	7,374.00	7,442.50	6,772.50	8,242.50	7,909.00
Non-current liabilities					
Trade and other payables	6,064.50	6,411.50	7,113.00	561.50	1,296.50
Borrowings	9,358.00	16,095.50	17,011.00	20,937.00	19,312.00
Decommissioning and other provisions	3,768.00	3,385.00	4,008.00	5,533.50	5,340.50
Deferred tax liabilities	3,967.00	5,376.50	5,506.00	6,462.00	5,822.50
Derivative financial instruments	6.00		129.00	54.50	
Total noncurrent liabilities	23,163.50	31,268.50	33,767.00	33,548.50	31,771.50
Total liabilities	30,537.50	38,711.00	40,539.50	41,791.00	39,680.50
EQUITY					
Called-up share capital	1,054.50	1,045.50	1,041.00	737.50	736.00
Share premium	6,900.00	6,721.00	6,634.00	3,096.50	3,049.00
Foreign currency translation reserve	1,210.50	1,193.00	1,116.00	1,161.00	1,246.50
Hedge reserve	23.00	654.00	13.00	641.00	2,849.50
Other reserves	3,776.00	3,776.00	3,704.50	3,704.50	3,704.50
Retained earnings	6,779.50	3,276.50	3,037.50	3,810.00	6,369.00

Income Statement Items					
Item	*2021*	*2020*	*2019*	*2018*	*2017*
Equity attributable to equity holders of the Company	19,743.50	16,666.00	15,546.00	13,150.50	17,954.50
Non-controlling interest			52.00	62.00	99.00
Total equity	19,743.50	16,666.00	15,598.00	13,212.50	18,053.50
Total equity and liabilities	50,281.00	55,377.00	56,137.50	55,003.50	57,734.00

References

Berk, J., and De Marzo, P. (2017). *Corporate finance*. 4th ed. Harlow: Pearson.

International Accounting Standards Board (IASB). (2004). *International financial reporting standard 6 exploration for and evaluation of mineral resources*. London: International Accounting Standards Board.

International Accounting Standards Board (IASB). (2013). *IAS 36 impairment of assets*. London: International Accounting Standards Board.

International Accounting Standards Board (IASB). (2018). *Conceptual framework for financial reporting*. London: International Accounting Standards Board.

Johnston, D. C., and Johnston, D. (2006). *Introduction to oil company financial analysis* (PennWell Nontechnical Series). Tulsa, OK: PennWell Corporation.

PricewaterhouseCoopers. (2017). *Financial reporting in the oil and gas industry: International financial reporting standards*. London: PricewaterhouseCoopers.

13 Financial Planning and Forecasting in the Oil and Gas Industry

Mohammed Aminu Sualihu, Mohammed Amidu, Tov Assogbavi, and Alex Donto

13.1 Introduction

The petroleum industry is an overwhelmingly capital-intensive industry, so companies operating in the industry require stable cash flows to succeed. The upstream, midstream, and downstream companies invest a lot in their operations to sustain themselves and provide stable returns to shareholders. These investment funds mostly come from external sources (debt or equity financing – both of which are difficult to raise because of the risk they are exposed to). Specifically, the upstream companies spend a lot on exploration, development, and production activities. The investments in exploration do not always lead to economically recoverable reserves, and, so, most of the wells are abandoned in the process and sunk costs in these activities are impaired (Deegan, 2016; Henderson et al., 2017).

Furthermore, the instability of oil and gas prices has made it extremely difficult for these companies to raise funds, further compounding the cash flow problems of most of the companies in the industry. Sönnichsen (2021) reports statistics that the 2021 annual average OPEC oil price stood at US$69.3 per barrel. This figure had increased from US$41.47 per barrel the previous year (higher than the average annual price during 2016 oil crisis). In 2014, oil price was above US$100 per barrel, which made the big oil and gas companies such as ExxonMobil, Chevron, and Royal Dutch-Shell to spend in excess of $30 billion per annum exploring for new oil and gas wells (Brown et al., 2017). However, by the end of January 2016, the oil price had dropped to as low as $27 per barrel – a precarious situation that resulted in layoffs and project delays. It is estimated that over $400 billion worth of projects were put on hold until oil prices recovered (Brown et al., 2017). Therefore, financial planning and forecasting, the most effective tools of financial policy, are very important for oil and gas companies.

Financial planning provides an avenue for these firms to plan their cash flows and to hedge effectively against periods of unstable oil and gas prices – especially, periods of significant drop in prices to maintain stable operations and performance. Financial planning is thus a process of designing financial policies in relation to, for example, procurement, investment, and the use of funds in a firm. It is a recurring process of forming and controlling a unified system of financial plans

DOI: 10.4324/9781003315056-16

(Mayorova et al., 2020). Evidence suggests that the oil and gas industry cannot be sustainable, given the current market conditions, without the use of modern methods of financial management (Daryanto and Nurfadilah, 2018; Mayorova et al., 2020). Financial planning and forecasting at the micro-level (or firm-level) are thus critical channels to increase the effectiveness of financial management.

Financial forecasting, on the other hand, involves making estimates about a company's future financial outcomes using available historical data—this allows firms to monitor cash inflows and outflows and their impact on the financial, sales, and operational plans of the firms (Harding and van der Ploeg, 2013). Given the uncertainty of oil and gas prices and the adverse effect that this has on the operating performance of oil and gas companies (Daryanto and Nurfadilah, 2018), financial forecasting is a crucial tool to help smooth out earnings and meet financial obligations in periods of revenue shortfalls. Thus, with financial forecasting, the companies can foresee periods where revenues are likely to increase (or decrease) and plan to shift or move funds around to maintain a smooth performance. There is, however, higher subjectivity in estimates from financial forecast due the higher risk, volatility, and uncertainty in the industry. Relying on only internally generated funds is unlikely to work well for the oil and gas companies, given the capital-intensive nature of their operations. For example in 2020, the total asset investments of downstream oil and gas marketing companies (OMCs) like Vivo Ghana Limited, Goil Ghana Limited, and Total Ghana Limited stood at GH¢3,514,702,000 (US$595,712,203) (2020 Annual Reports). The figures of upstream and midstream firms like Tullow Ghana are more likely to be greater because their exploration, development, and production activities require massive capital outlay in the region of US$3 billion.

The chapter proceeds as follows. In Section 13.2, we present a discussion on the definition, objectives, and importance of financial planning and financial risk. Section 13.3 discusses budgeting and financial forecasting, while Section 13.4 concludes the chapter.

13.2 Financial Planning

Financial planning typically involves the process of estimating future expenses and ensuring that funds are available to meet expected expenditures. It is the process of designing financial policies in relation to, for example, procurement, investment, and the use of funds. It also entails identifying the sources of funds and the use of the funds with respect to improving the financial future of the firm (Abor, 2017). According to Jalil et al. (2013), financial planning refers to the means by which cash is sourced (internally or externally) to cover future expenses. In short, financial planning is the task of establishing and determining how a firm can achieve its strategic goals and objectives. Designing a financial strategy is important for oil and gas companies because their activities are capital intensive and require stable funds for operational success. Financial turbulence or volatility resulting from abysmal financial planning of firms in the industry is likely to suffocate cash flows and stifle investment in capital expenditures. For instance Romanyuk et al. (2016) posit that in the midst of severe economic conditions, the companies in the petroleum industry are unable to raise funds to meet capital expenditure requirements and make efficient use of debt and equity capital. Daryanto and Nurfadilah (2018) argue that the cash flows of oil and gas companies are volatile due to the fluctuations in oil prices on the world market. Similarly, Sönnichsen (2021) notes that the 2021 annual average OPEC oil price stands at US$69.3 per barrel. This figure is increased from US$41.47 per barrel the previous year, slightly higher than the average annual price during 2016 oil crisis.

Abor (2017) outlined that financial planning process should include:

- Setting the firm's goals, involving setting long-term goals of the firm.
- Developing long-term financial plans to serve as the roadmap towards achieving the firm's long-term goals.
- Developing short-term financial plans, centred on short-term financial outcomes of the firm.
- Developing individual budgets, including sales, selling expenses, production, and administrative budgets.
- Developing a consolidated budget by putting the individual budgets together.

13.2.1 Objectives and Importance of Financial Planning

The objectives of financial planning include the following: (1) determining capital requirements; (2) determining capital structure; (3) designing financial policies with regards to cash control, lending, and borrowings; and (4) ensuring that the limited financial resources are optimally utilised in the best possible way to get maximum returns on investment (Juneja, 2021). Similarly, in their paper on mechanism of financial planning optimisation in corporations, Mayorova et al. (2020 at p. 847) identified the following objectives for financial planning in most organisations:

- Determining the estimated amount of financial support in the forecast period.
- Searching for the sources of their capital formation and the directions of the most effective use based on the analysis of emerging trends and considering the impact of various factors on them.
- Assessing the financial condition of the firm in the forecast period, depending on the possible options for its financial and economic activities.
- Giving recommendations regarding the selection of a rational financial strategy and tactics, ensuring the achievement of a stable market position and secure financial stability by the firm.

Given the cash flow volatility and performance turbulence of oil and gas companies and the capital-intensive nature of their activities as well as the difficulty they face in raising funds from external sources (Romanyuk et al., 2016; Daryanto and Nurfadilah, 2018), financial planning is arguably important for them. Accordingly, Juneja (2021) has generally identified the following, among others, as the benefits of financial planning to all companies regardless of the industry in which they operate:

- It helps to ensure that adequate funds are available for firms to execute projects and to meet operational requirements.
- It helps maintain financial stability by matching cash outflows against cash inflows.
- It attracts capital into the business as investors are more likely to invest in firms that exercise financial planning.
- The long-run survival of the firm is assured as financial planning helps in framing growth and expansion programmes.
- It lessens uncertainties regarding changing market trends which can be faced easily through enough funds.
- It helps in reducing the uncertainties which can stifle the growth of the company. This helps in ensuring stability and profitability of the firm.

13.2.2 Financial Risk

Financial planning is central in the petroleum industry due to the exposure of oil and gas companies to financial risk. Firms that have higher financial risk exposure are more likely to establish financial planning mechanisms to reduce that risk. Park and Yao (2016) find that financial planning has a profound and consistent impact on individual's financial risk attitude and behaviour. The upstream, midstream, and downstream petroleum companies all face enormous financial risk in their operations. Financial risk is the likelihood of losing funds on investments or business projects – companies facing financial risk may default in their financial obligations and, thus, are less likely to attract external funds. In the context of oil and gas industry, Awin (2018) defines financial risk as the likelihood that shareholders will lose funds if the firm has limited cash flows to meet its financial obligations. Hayes (2021) identifies more common and distinct financial risks as credit risk, liquidity risk, and operational risk. Credit risk is the risk of loss that may arise from the failure of a party in a financial contract to honour the terms and conditions of the contract. Brown and Moles (2014) note that credit risk is the probability that a contractual party will fail to meet their obligations in accordance with the agreed terms and conditions. This is likely in the oil and gas industry, given the uncertainty of operations as a result of volatile global oil prices and natural disasters.

Liquidity risk is the risk of loss incurrence as a result of inability to meet debt obligations when they are due – it is the risk that firms will not be able to meet the short-term and long-term financial obligations (Varotto, 2011; Kawaguchi, 2016; Awin, 2018). Firms experiencing liquidity challenges are sometimes unable to raise funds from the equity market and are more likely to rely on internally generated funds for their operational needs. Financial planning is thus very important for this category of firms to shore up their cash flows and to make them liquid at all times. This is largely to make the firms solvent. Operational risk is the risk of loss resulting from the failure of internal processes or exogenous events that potentially can disrupt the flow of business activities. According to the Basel Committee (2003), operational risk is literally the risk of loss resulting from failed internal processes, mechanisms, system and people, or from an external event that can adversely affect fortunes of the firm. Taken together, the occurrence of any of these types of risk can increase the financial risk of the firm, which. in turn, can stifle access to external funds.

13.3 Budgeting

Globally, there has been an increase in demand for oil and gas products, especially from the developing world despite the discovery of proven oil and gas reserves in these countries. This has, therefore, resulted in the focus-shift of world, leading energy companies from Europe and North America to the developing countries. This comes on the back of the current and future prospects these countries present. The focus-shift to the developing world, however, comes with the accompanying need to get access to huge finances to facilitate investments in such an industry. This has forced investors and project sponsors to engineer innovative financing structure involving partners from both private and public sectors (Bello et al., 2016). But the commercial and political risks associated with investments in the oil and gas industry have discouraged potential investors. It is for this reason that the World Bank has regularly revised its strategy in the oil and gas industry to provide a suitable platform for private investors and governments to manage and limit the impacts of such risks (Razavi, 1995). These arrangements have been innovative and have impacted the petroleum sector positively over two decades. As a consequence, private firms and governments have made significant strides in the oil and gas industry over the period.

In order to achieve operational excellence and stand the test of time, oil and gas firms like firms in other industries, as part of their planning process, prepare budgets for their impending projects as well as operational activities for specified periods of time. Budgets are generally estimations of financial inflows and outflows from an activity for specified periods of time (Ríos et al., 2018). Budgets are prepared to provide key stakeholders with a clear outlook of how their financial affairs would look like for a period of time. Assumptions in relation to the projected revenue and expenditure trends; estimates of the capital inflows and outflows; as well as the overall economic outlook of the market, industry, or country the activity relates to are made before the preparation of the budget for a specified period (Al-Ani, 2015). During the budgeting process, the key management personnel involved in the process seek to streamline all available data, conduct in-depth analysis of the data, and encourage other key staff to bring on board their opinions on how other issues can be taken into consideration and how best the entire budget can be implemented. In an industry where there are concerns about the security of crude oil and petroleum supplies, the consistent risk of price hikes, as well as the fact that supplies are made through cost-effective channels, budgeting is very important (Harding and van der Ploeg, 2013).

The budgeting in the oil and gas industry takes into consideration specific items, which are critical to both the financial and non-financial success of the firms in the industry. These items include the human resource and workforce, integrated business, production and capacity, sales and operational activities, capital and operating expenditure, profitability, strategic cash flow planning and allocations, as well as the other aspects of financial statements (Harding and van der Ploeg, 2013). The contemporary and emerging features of the budgeting system include self-service and analytics, technological integration, audit trail and workflow as well as unified corporate performance management system (CPM) (Bondarenko et al., 2018). The high profitability of the industry in general makes budgeting a critical aspect of business operations. The budgeting takes into consideration the management of production growth, reserves, fluctuating interest rates, and potential operational shifts after a sophisticated depth of analysis. Wolters Kluwer CCH Tagetik (2020) asserts that oil and gas firms plan for their budgets by aligning finance and operations with unified planning, deciding on the type of non-current assets to invest in, reducing cycle time to improve accuracy, analysing real-time key performance indicators for immediate action, optimizing the supply chain and production, as well as looking at ways to increase profitability and optimizing human resources (Wolters Kluwer CCH Tagetik, 2020). Further, the oil and gas firms are able to align their strategic, financial, and operational planning to ensure that tasks are completed faster when automated real-time and historical data are used during the budgeting period.

Some of the approaches used for budgeting in the oil and gas industry, especially in developing economies, take into consideration key capabilities including the custom oil and gas drivers, top down or bottom up approach, built-in financial intelligence, drilling down into details, modelling and what-if analysis, cash flow planning and forecasting, rolling forecasts, hierarchy management as well as some long-term planning (Harding and van der Ploeg, 2013). The most popular types of budgeting include operating budgets, cash budgets, investment budget, capital budget as well as performance budgets. Due the nature of the operations in the oil and gas industry, budgeting decisions are mostly centred on capital inflows and outflows. Capital budgeting involves evaluating the viability of a capital investment opportunity and making a decision to undertake or not to undertake a project. Firms in the oil and gas industry use cash flows instead of profit for their capital budgeting since cash flows are void of any accruals that may lead to inappropriate decisions (Abudu and Sai, 2020).

13.4 Financial Forecasting

Financial forecasting involves the process of analysing, estimating, and projecting the future financial performance of an entity (Kingdon, 2012). Forecasting helps oil and gas firms deal with the risk and uncertainty within their industry through the use of past information to predict trends in the future. Successes are achieved in the forecasting process when accurate assumptions are made on the basis of past experience, knowledge on current issues are applied, and excellent judgements are made. These assumptions are therefore put to use through estimation techniques including regression, trend analysis, exponential smoothing, and moving averages (Abor, 2017). The financial forecasting process therefore facilitates the projection of intended financial activities in the future, helps in the preparation of budgets, and serves as the basis of measuring performance in the future. Sales forecasts are usually the first aspects of the financial forecasting process for oil and gas firms as they project their revenues for specified future periods. The revenue projections from sales forecasts are critical to other aspects of the operations of oil and gas firms including asset and inventory management, risk management, human resources management, as well as financial planning and budgeting. There is a proper planning when oil and gas firms are able to anticipate price volatility and other uncertainties in the future and make suitable provisions for them through the sales forecast.

Financial forecasting also entails cash flow planning and forecasting, rolling forecasts, advanced hierarchy management, as well as long-term planning (Harding and van der Ploeg, 2013). The cash flow planning and forecasting involve making estimates about built-in functionality, which allows firms to monitor cash inflows and outflows, and their impact on the financial, sales, and operational plans of firms. If future financing requirements are not properly anticipated, there are serious problems whenever cash outflows exceed the inflows. The rolling forecasts involve quickly building short-term forecasts (13-months or 53-weeks forecast) that combine data from plans, budgets, and past performance (actuals) to automatically respond immediately to emerging market conditions. The advanced hierarchy management also involves the creation of unlimited hierarchies and roll-ups for any timeframe, adjusting charts of accounts, modifying business rules, and updating hierarchies without the intervention of information technology. The long-term planning entails developing long-range and top-down corporate strategies (up to 30 years) that include capital investments and huge revenue expenditures geared towards setting targets that drive short-term and bottom-up tactical decisions (Bierman and Smidt, 2012). Oil and gas firms can therefore be deemed to have adequately planned when they are able to identify future financing shortfalls and surpluses and make suitable provisions towards them through financial forecasts, especially since the financing needs for growth of firms usually out-muscle their cash generation abilities.

The budget forecast usually has four classifications: income statement items, cash flow items, statement of financial position items, and other items

Table 13.1 The Components of a Budget Forecast

Section 1	Income and costs
Section 2	Cash flow items
Section 3	Statement of financial position items
Section 4	Other items

(see Table 13.1). The income and costs involve the planning and gathering of actual data on revenue, expenditure, and other comprehensive incomes to form the budget forecast. The cash flow items entail the preparation of the budgeted cash flow statement directly and indirectly. The statement of financial position items also involves the planning and gathering of actual data on working capital items and forming items like non-current assets and prepayment of some expenditure for future periods. The other items focus on the preparation of reports on commodity flows, inventory (production and sales plan, gross output flows) as well as some additional items. The unified approach generally ensures the creation of budgeting packages for individual departments using similar unified data structure to facilitate the comparison of the budget and the actual data. It also simplifies the consolidation procedure for the full budget forecasts at all management levels for all the departments within the oil and gas company.

Some of the items which are central in the budgeting and forecasting processes for oil and gas industry include the expected revenue, expenditure, assets, liabilities, and capital injection into businesses. Some of the key expenditures include exploration expenses; dry hole costs; the acquisition, exploration, and evaluation assets as well as environmental expenditure. Natural resources from developing economies are constantly explored and exploited by oil and gas companies resulting in environmental consequences including hazardous waste, biodiversity loss (aqua and wildlife as well as agro reserves), and global warming (Onoja et al., 2021). Even though these resources are explored to achieve economic development, their non-renewable nature is subject to diminution. Environmental concerns from the operations of oil and gas companies in particular are now prominent due to the level of degradation caused by the hydrocarbon emissions (oil spills and gas leakages) from the downstream to the upstream operations of such firms. These concerns have also birthed the responsibility of these firms to make investments in projects geared towards preserving and restating the environment to its default state. The responsibility to incur expenditure in relation to the environment therefore necessitates its inclusion as a budget item. The budget forecasts reflecting the efficiency of production by individual units and departments are therefore approved by the responsible functional units.

Depending on whether a firm is in the upstream, midstream, or downstream sectors of petroleum, aspects of their financial planning will differ. For example, for firms in the upstream sector, their financial plans are centred on the identification, extraction, and production of raw materials for the petroleum industry since their activities are closer to the end users. They rely on past information on the identification of deposits and drill wells, as well as on the recovery of raw materials from underground to enable them plan for future periods. Cost of feasibility studies and research are some of the items taken into consideration in their forecasts. For the downstream sector, however, their budgets and forecasts are centred on post-production activities till petroleum products are supplied to customers. They also include costs on marketing and distribution of petroleum products like natural gas, diesel, gasoline, heating oil, lubricants, pesticides propane, and other pharmaceuticals. The midstream sector, on the other hand, serves as a link between the two sectors. Their financial planning and forecasting are, therefore, focused on processing, storage, and transportation of petroleum products. Some of the key personnel involved in the planning and forecasting in the oil and gas industry include management personnel, geologists, engineers, drilling contractors, storage officers, marketers, and distributors. Sensitivity analysis is therefore critical for the industry since it reflects how risk of errors in forecasts can be modelled to take risk into consideration when involved in an economic analysis (Ohnesorge, 2016). They help determine how the variations in prices (due to high volatility) affect the profitability of sustainable energy technologies.

13.4.1 Approaches to Forecasting

There are three major approaches to financial forecasting including experience, probability, and correlation (Abor, 2017). Under experience, oil and gas firms rely on past events and happenings to forecast their intended future activities in financial terms. Thus, future incomes and costs are predicted on the basis of experiences and trends from previous years. For probability, firms rely on the likelihood of certain events occurring to predict (forecast) future occurrence. Correlation is however used upon the realisation that there are correlations between some known and unknown variables. Forecasts are therefore made on unknown variables on the basis of their established relationships with known variables. How items like sales and financial statements are forecasted have been highlighted in the next paragraphs.

Sales are forecasted to reflect trends in sales from previous years which are not likely to change in future periods, as well as other events that can significantly affect such trends. The preparation of sales forecasts is not overly financial since they are usually based on the demand of oil and gas products and the competition on the market due to their high volatility. Demand assessments, production capacity estimates, and assessments of other constraints are made, since they help serve as a link between product–market performance and financial needs of oil and gas firms. Financial statements are also forecasted after sales forecasts to determine the extent to which they can be extended into future periods, with the assumption that organisational objectives are achieved and sales forecasts are met. This helps management to know whether there can be available funds to meet both short- and long-term obligations, and whether the return on investments will be rewarding enough and extra finances will be needed. This therefore necessitates the inclusion of cash and capital budgets aside the sales forecast.

An example of the financial forecasts of an oil and gas company is presented here.

Financial Forecast

ABC OIL & GAS COMPANY					
SALES FORECAST					
Expected Sales Volume: 2,000 units first quarter, 500-unit increases each quarter until 1,000 units increment in the fourth quarter					
For the Year Ending 31 December 2017					
	Quarter				
	1	**2**	**3**	**4**	**Total**
Expected barrel sales	2,000	2,500	3,000	4,000	11,500
Selling price	$55	$58	$62	$70	
Total sales	**$110,000**	**$145,000**	**$186,000**	**$280,000**	**$721,000**
PRODUCTION BUDGET					
This is made up of barrels requirements for oil, gas, and condensate production. Expectation: ABC can meet future sales needs with a closing inventory of 20% of next quarter's sales volume					
For the Year Ending 31 December 2017					
	Quarter				
	1	**2**	**3**	**4**	**Total**
Expected barrel sales	2,000	2,500	3,000	4,000	11,500
Add: Closing inventory	500	600	800	900	900
Total units requirements	2,500	3,100	3,800	4,900	12,400
Less: Opening inventory	(400)	(500)	(600)	(800)	(800)
Required production units	**2,100**	**2,600**	**3,200**	**4,100**	**11,600**

DIRECT MATERIALS BUDGET					
Expectation: ABC maintains closing raw material inventory, 10% of next quarter's requirements					
Processing of each product requires 2 kilograms of raw material, each kilogram expected to be $5					
An assumption that the closing inventory for the fourth quarter will be 920					
For the Year Ending 31 December 2017					
	Quarter				
	1	**2**	**3**	**4**	**Total**
Units to be produced (production budget)	2,100	2,600	3,200	4,100	12,000
Raw material per unit	2	2	2	2	2
Total kilograms required	4,200	5,200	6,400	8,200	24,000
Add: closing inventory	520	640	820	920	920
Total materials required	4,720	5,840	7,220	9,120	24,920
Less: Opening inventory	(420)	(520)	(640)	(820)	(420)
Direct materials purchases	4,300	5,320	6,580	8,300	24,500
Cost per kilogram	$4	$4	$4	$ 4	$4
Total direct material cost	**$17,200**	**$21,280**	**$26,320**	**$33,200**	**$98,000**

DIRECT LABOUR BUDGET					
Direct labour hours are determined based on the production budget					
For ABC, 2 direct labour hours are needed to produce barrels of oil and gas with an hourly rate of $8					
For the Year Ending 31 December 2017					
	Quarter				
	1	**2**	**3**	**4**	**Total**
Units to be produced (production budget)	2,100	2,600	3,200	4,100	12,000

Direct labour hours per unit	2	2	2	2	2
Total labour hours required	4,200	5,200	6,400	8,200	24,000
Direct labour cost per hour	$8	$8	$8	$8	$8
Total direct labour cost	**$33,600**	**$41,600**	**$51,200**	**$65,600**	**$192,000**

EXPLORATION AND REFINING OVERHEAD BUDGET

ABC expects variable costs to fluctuate with production volume on the basis of the following rates per direct labour hour:

Indirect material ($1.2), indirect labour ($2.0), utility ($0.8), and dry-hole Cost ($0.5).

Some of the overhead costs are fixed: $15,000 for supervisory salaries, $3,000 for depreciation, $8,000 for taxes and insurance, and $5,000 for maintenance.

For the Year Ending 31 December 2017

	Quarter				
	1	**2**	**3**	**4**	**Total**
Direct labour hours	4,200	5,200	6,400	8,200	24,000
Variable costs	**US$**	**US$**	**US$**	**US$**	**US$**
Indirect materials (1.2)	5,040	6,240	7,680	9,840	28,800
Indirect labour (2.0)	8,400	10,400	12,800	16,400	48,000
Utility (0.8)	3,360	4,160	5,120	6,560	19,200
Dry-hole cost (0.5)	2,100	2,600	3,200	4,100	12,000
Total variable costs	**18,900**	**23,400**	**28,800**	**36,900**	**108,000**
Fixed costs					
Supervisory salaries	15,000	15,000	15,000	15,000	60,000
Depreciation	3,000	3,000	3,000	3,000	12,000
Taxes and insurance	8,000	8,000	8,000	8,000	32,000
Maintenance	5,000	5,000	5,000	5,000	20,000
Total fixed costs	**31,000**	**31,000**	**31,000**	**31,000**	**124,000**
Total exploration and refinery overhead	**49,900**	**54,400**	**59,800**	**67,900**	**232,000**

Exploration and refinery overhead rate per direct labour hour			**10**		
SELLING AND ADMINISTRATIVE EXPENSE BUDGET					
This is variable (rates are based on unit sales from the sales budget) and fixed expenditure. Sales commissions are $2.5 per unit while freight is $1.5 per unit. Fixed expenses are $5,000 for advertising, $12,000 for salaries, $2,000 for depreciation, while $1,800 for taxes and insurance.					
For the Year Ending 31 December 2017					
	Quarter				
	1	**2**	**3**	**4**	**Total**
Sales units from sales budget	2,000	2,500	3,000	4,000	11,500
Variable expenses	**US$**	**US$**	**US$**	**US$**	**US$**
Sales commission ($2.5)	5,000	6,250	7,500	10,000	28,750
Freight ($1.5)	3,000	3,750	4,500	6,000	17,250
Total variable expenses	**8,000**	**10,000**	**12,000**	**16,000**	**46,000**
Fixed expenses					
Advertising	5,000	5,000	5,000	5,000	20,000
Salaries	12,000	12,000	12,000	12,000	48,000
Depreciation	2,000	2,000	2,000	2,000	8,000
Taxes and insurance	1,800	1,800	1,800	1,800	7,200
Total fixed expenses	**20,800**	**20,800**	**20,800**	**20,800**	**83,200**
Total selling and administrative expenses	**28,800**	**30,800**	**32,800**	**36,800**	**129,200**
Selling and administrative per sales unit			**11**		
BUDGETED INCOME STATEMENT					
To arrive at the cost of goods sold, it is necessary to determine the total unit cost of producing a barrel.					

Cost Element		**Units**	**Quantity**	**Unit Cost**	**Total**
Direct materials		kilograms	2	$ 4.00	$ 8.00
Direct labour		hours	2	$ 8.00	$ 16.00
Exploration and refining overhead		hours	2	$10.00	$ 20.00
Total unit cost					**$ 44.00**
To sell 12,000 barrels of oil and gas in 2017, the cost of goods sold is **12,000 × $44 = $528,000**					

ABC OIL & GAS COMPANY **BUDGETED INCOME STATEMENT** **For the Year Ending 31 December 2017**					
			US$		**US$**
Sales					721,000
Less: Cost of goods sold					*(528,000)*
Gross profit					**193,000**
Add: Interest income					4,700
					197,700
Less: Operating and administrative expenses					
Selling and administrative expenses			129,200		
Interest expense			7,500		
Licensing			*2,000*		*(138,700)*
Income before taxes					**59,000**
Income tax expense					*(17,700)*
Net income					**41,300**

Cash Budget

Cash receipts and cash payments for direct materials with these assumptions:

1 The opening cash balance as of 1 January 2017 is expected to be $45,000 with a plan to maintain a balance of $20,000.
2 Sales: Seventy-five per cent collected in the quarter of sale and the remaining 25% in the quarter thereafter. Accounts receivable as of 31 December 2016 was $50,000 and are expected to be collected in full in the first quarter of 2017.
3 Short-term investments are expected to be sold for $5,000 cash in the first quarter.
4 Direct materials Sixty per cent paid in the quarter purchased and the remaining 40% the following quarter. There was account payable of $25,000 as of 31 December 2016 and are expected to be paid in full in the first quarter of 2017.

5 Direct labour, exploration and refining overhead, selling and administrative overhead: full payment in the quarter incurred.
6 Management plans to purchase a truck in the second quarter at a cost of $12,500 and an exploratory machinery at a cost of $5,000 in the third quarter, all in cash.
7 ABC makes equal payments of its estimated annual income taxes quarterly.
8 Loans are repaid in the earliest quarter in which there is sufficient cash (i.e. when the minimum cash balance exceeds $20,000).

CASH COLLECTION SCHEDULE					
		Collections by Quarter			
	Sales Figure	**1**	**2**	**3**	**4**
	US$	**US$**	**US$**	**US$**	**US$**
Accounts receivable from 31/12/16		50,000			
First quarter	110,000	82,500	27,500		
Second quarter	145,000		108,750	36,250	
Third quarter	186,000			139,500	46,500
Fourth quarter	280,000				210,000
Total collections		**132,500**	**136,250**	**175,750**	**256,500**
CASH PAYMENT SCHEDULE (DIRECT MATERIAL)					
		Collections by Quarter			
	Purchases Figure	**1**	**2**	**3**	**4**
	US$	**US$**	**US$**	**US$**	**US$**
Accounts payable since 31/12/16		25,000			
First quarter	17,200	10,320	6,880		
Second quarter	21,280		12,768	8,512	
Third quarter	26,320			15,792	10,528
Fourth quarter	33,200				19,920
		35,320	**19,648**	**24,304**	**30,448**

ABC OIL & GAS COMPANY					
CASH BUDGET					
For the Year Ending 31 December 2017					
		Quarter			
	Assumption	**1**	**2**	**3**	**4**
		US$	**US$**	**US$**	**US$**
Opening cash balance	1	45,000	30,455	20,000	20,000
Add: Receipts					
Collection from customers	2	132,500	136,250	175,750	256,500
Sale of short-term investments	3	5,000	0	0	0
Total receipts		**137,500**	**136,250**	**175,750**	**256,500**
Total available cash		**182,500**	**166,705**	**195,750**	**276,500**
Less: Payments					
Direct materials	4	35,320	19,648	24,304	30,448
Direct labour	5	33,600	41,600	51,200	65,600
Exploration and refining overhead	5	49,900	54,400	59,800	67,900
Selling and administrative overhead	5	28,800	30,800	32,800	36,800
Purchase of non-current assets	6	0	12,500	5,000	0
Income tax expense	7	4,425	4,425	4,425	4,425
Total payments		**152,045**	**163,373**	**177,529**	**205,173**
Excess of receipts over payments		30,455	3,332	18,221	71,327
Financing					
Add: Borrowings	8	0	16,668	1,779	0
Less: Repayments including interest	8	0	0	0	(18,447)
Closing cash balance		**30,455**	**20,000**	**20,000**	**52,880**

ABC OIL & GAS COMPANY
BUDGETED STATEMENT OF FINANCIAL POSITION
As of 31st December 2017

Assets	**US$**	**US$**	**US$**
Non-Current Assets:			
Property, Plant and Equipment	167,500	(33,500)	134,000
Buildings	85,000	0	85,000
Exploration and Evaluation (Intangible)	*40,000*	*0*	*40,000*
	292,500	**(33,500)**	**259,000**
Current Assets:			
Accounts Receivables			70,000
Short-term investments			5,000
Closing Inventory: Finished Goods			39,600
Closing Inventory: Raw Materials			*3,680*
Total Assets			**377,280**
Financed by:			
Equity			
Stated Capital			250,000
Retained Earnings			*60,500*
			310,500
Non-Current Liabilities:			
Long-term Derivatives			45,000
Current Liabilities:			
Accounts Payables			13,280
Short-term lease liabilities			*8,500*
Total Equity and Liabilities			**377,280**

At the core of the budgeting and forecasting processes of oil and gas companies are comprehensive accounting systems which take into consideration the cost calculations for production/refining of oil and gas on the basis of primary documentation and inventory to facilitate financial forecasting (Bondarenko et al., 2018). These costs calculations help firms to timely and reliably ascertain the primary costs of oil and gas products and the actual production/refining costs. These processes also help monitor costs at all stages of the firms' operating activities. All these processes usually precede the set-up of comprehensive management accounting systems within the entities to determine the actual costs for each area of activity or subdivisions in comparable formats irrespective of the firm size or its production structure. These comprehensive systems facilitate the analysis of the costs incurred by the various business units within the oil and gas firms in relation to their unique technological process, cost units, and cost objects. Big oil and gas companies in both developed and developing economies usually have in place comprehensive practical solutions like PJSC 'LUKOIL' or 'OC Rosneft' which help them through their budgeting process and accounting set-up in general. Their medium- and small-sized contemporaries, however, resort to sub-standard solutions or outsource such functions to consulting firms at a fee. These limitations are usually due to resource constraints.

The practical solutions facilitate coordination between key divisions within oil and gas firms including finance and budgeting departments by segments (cost units and responsibility centres, internal audit, and legal and tax planning departments (Bondarenko et al., 2018). They also facilitate the development of algorithms for transition into a uniform standard of budgeting for firms. The solutions help account properly for costs associated with all technological links within the process chain, right from the production and refinery of the oil and gas to the identification of primary costs associated with each process within each division. The practical solutions also help obtain prompt and reliable information on each technological process to enhance current and future budgeting activities of organisations. The practical solutions are generally instituted through management reporting methodologies, as well as business, financial, and economic planning programmes, which are geared towards solving problems associated with the formalisation of the organisational financial structures and management reporting frameworks. Before the implementation of such practical solutions, the methodologies and programmes therefore ought to be adequately developed.

13.5 Conclusion

This chapter had identified the financial planning and forecasting as a conduit through which oil and gas companies project their financial and non-financial activities to facilitate quality short- and long-term decision-making. The oil and gas industry is a high capital-intensive industry requiring huge investments which usually come from external sources. The investments however do not result in economically recoverable reserves in all instances. The financing of such firms is therefore complex and requires massive investments in the budget planning and forecasting infrastructure of the firms within the industry. The financial planning and forecasting are crucial for them since they help the firms plan the timing of their revenues and expenditures to maintain stable cash flows and operating performance, especially due to the instability of oil and gas prices. Through financial forecasting, the firms are able to foresee periods of financial challenges and put in place corrective measures to help smooth out earnings and meet financial obligations in such periods. Effective financial planning and forecasting therefore help oil and gas firms achieve their strategic goals and objectives.

References

Abor, J. Y. (2017). Financial planning and forecasting. In *Entrepreneurial finance for MSMEs* (pp. 199–223). Cham: Palgrave Macmillan.

Abudu, H., and Sai, R. (2020). Examining prospects and challenges of Ghana's petroleum industry: A systematic review. *Energy Reports*, 6, 841–858.

Al-Ani, M. K. (2015). A strategic framework to use payback period in evaluating the capital budgeting in energy and oil and gas sectors in Oman. *International Journal of Economics and Financial Issues,* 5(2), 469–475.

Awin, E. (2018). *Liquidity risk and its determinants: A study on oil and gas industry in Tatneft.* https://ssrn.com/abstract=3181622

Basel Committee (20C3). *Operational risk transfer across financial sectors.* https://www.bis.org/publ/joint06.htm

Bello, U., Ahmad, H. S., and Aliyu, A. A. (2016). The impact of lease financing on the financial performance of Nigerian oil and gas industry. *Research Journal of Finance and Accounting*, 7(4), 28–34.

Bierman, J. R., and Smidt, S. (2012). *The capital budgeting decision: Economic analysis of investment projects.* Oxfordshire: Routledge.

Bondarenko, T. G., Ishkinina, G. S., and Arbievich, I. (2018). "Developing methodological approaches to financial and economic planning at oil and gas enterprises. *Espacios*, 39(19), 32–49.

Brown, D. K., Penkler, D. L., Sheik Amamuddy, O., Ross, C., and Atilgan, A. R. (2017). MD-TASK: A software suite for analyzing molecular dynamics trajectories *Bioinformatics,* 33(17), 2768–277.

Brown, K. and Moles, P. (2014). *Credit management.* Edinburgh: Edinburgh Business School, Heriot-Watt University.

Daryanto, W. M., and Nurfadilah, D. (2018). Financial performance analysis before and after the decline in oil production: Case study in Indonesian oil and gas industry. *International Journal of Engineering & Tourism*, 7(3.21), 10–15.

Deegan, C. (2016). *Financial accounting.* 8th ed. London: McGraw Hill: Australia.

Harding, T., and van der Ploeg, F. (2013). Official forecasts and management of oil windfalls. *International Tax and Public Finance*, 20(5), 827–866.

Hayes, A (2021). *Financial risk.* https://www.investopedia.com/terms/f/financialrisk.asp

Henderson, S., Peirson, G., Herbohn, K., and Artiach, T. (2017). *Issues in financial accounting.* 16th ed. Sydney: Pearson Australia.

Jalil, Md. A., Razak, D. A., and Ferdous, A. S. M. (2013). Exploring factors influencing financial planning after retirement: Structural equation modeling approach. *American Journal of Applied Sciences,* 10(3), 270–279.

Juneja, P. (2021). *Financial planning-definition, objectives and importance.* https://www.managementstudyguide.com/financial-planning.htm.

Kawaguchi, L. T. (2016). *Oil and gas: Process and liquidity optimization.* https://www.google.com/search?q=kawaguchi+(2016)+oil+and+gas+liquidity&rlz=1C1GCEB_enAE814AE814&oq=kawaguchi+(2016)+oil+and+gas+liquidity&aqs=chrome..69i57.41144j0j7&sourceid=chrome&ie=UTF-8 on 31/01/2022.

Kingdon, J. (2012). *Intelligent systems and financial forecasting.* New York City: Springer Science & Business Media.

Mayorova, V., Zabashtanskyi, M., Zhuk, O., Petrenko, I., Zveruk, L., and Babich, I. (2020). Mechanism of financial planning optimization in the corporations. *International Journal of Management,* 11(5), 846–857.

Ohnesorge, M. (2016). *A sensitivity analysis on oil and gas prices and how this affects sustainable energy implementation*. https://www.semanticscholar.org/paper/A-Sensitivity-Analysis-on-Oil-and-Gas-Prices-and-Ohnesorge/e100eb3b601a6162669f6f99edec302a55a9a219

Onoja, A. A., Okoye, E. I., and Nwoye, U. J. (2021). Global reporting initiative and sustainability reporting practices: A study of the Nigeria and South Africa oil and gas firms. *Research Journal of Management Practice*, 1(12), 1–25.

Park, E., and Yao, R. (2016). Financial risk attitude and behavior: Do planners help increase consistency. *Journal of Family and Economic,* 37(4), 624–638.

Razavi, H. (1995). Oil and gas financing by the World Bank. *Energy Policy,* 23(11), 1001–1007.

Ríos, A.-M., Guillamón, M.-D., Benito, B., and Bastida, F. (2018). The influence of transparency on budget forecast deviations in municipal governments. *Journal of Forecasting*, 37(4), 457–474.

Romanyuk, V., Karyakina, A., Vershkova, E., Grinkevish, L., and Pozdeeva, G. (2016). Financial planning as a policy tool in the petroleum industry: The case of OJCS Surgutneftegas. *Earth and environmental Science,* 43(2016), 1–6.

Sönnichsen, N. (2021). *Average annual OPEC crude oil price from 1960 to 2021*. https://www.statista.com/statistics/262858/change-in-opec-crude-oil-prices-since-1960/

Varotto, S. (2011). Liquidity risk, credit risk, market risk and bank capital. *International Journal of Managerial Finance,* 7(2), 134–152.

Wolters Kluwer CCH Tagetik. (2020). Budgeting, planning and forecast for oil and gas. *CCH Tagetik Budgeting and Planning*. https://www.wolterskluwer.com/en/solutions/cch-tagetik/budgeting-planning-forecasting

14 Oil and Gas Valuation

Isaac Otchere, Michael Adusei, Joshua Yindenaba Abor, and Thankom Arun

14.1 Introduction

The valuation of a company simply refers to the process of determining the present value of that company. To value a company, analysts typically look at how the company is managed, its future cash flows, the market value of its assets, and the composition of its capital structure. It is important to understand how to value a particular company on the basis of its cash flows and assets. This will prevent the situation of overpaying and that "you do not get caught up in the euphoria and unrealistic expectations that pervade the markets at various points in time" (Boisjoly et al., 2020). It is not easy to carry out valuation exercises, yet it is as important as raising capital for a business, and it must be done regularly (Abor, 2017). In order to determine the percentage of ownership or interest in a company for outside investors, the value of the company must be estimated. The "perceived value of the firm, as well as the capabilities of the initial investors to enhance the value of the firm, is critical to the external investor." On the other hand, the initial investors also anticipate the value addition to the firm by the external investors in terms of "financial resources and organisational capacity." For publicly listed companies, "the value of the firm is determined on per second basis by investors (buyers and sellers of the shares) on the stock exchange" (Abor, 2017).

There are several techniques available for determining the value of a company or its assets. Even though the valuation of oil and gas (O&G) assets is not generally different from the valuation of other assets, it is critical to fully understand the traditional valuation methods. The significance of valuing the oil and gas sector is more pronounced than any other sector, and the valuation analyses take a more complex and technical dimension. The oil and gas sector is completely different in the sense that its major assets are the reserves (as asset-intensive businesses). As soon as the reserves are completely extracted, the company is almost valueless notwithstanding the fact that there are some other properties such as vehicles and offices which have residual value. For this reason, it is very crucial to understand the dynamics of oil and gas firm's reserves vis-a-vis the costs of extraction in valuing the firm. More importantly, to be able to value the oil and gas assets of a company, the valuation needs to encompass a depleting asset base whose value keeps changing due to commodity price

DOI: 10.4324/9781003315056-17

changes. It is, therefore, important to engage the services of professionals who have a deep understanding of the technical areas of various techniques used in valuing O&G companies.

Valuing the reserves of O&G is important in determining how much an oil and gas producer will be willing to accept for the reserves in an arms-length transaction. For the purpose of financial reporting, a company's long-term assets or liabilities can be valued. Such valuations may also be required for reasons such as strategic planning, investment analysis, legal issues and litigation, capital budgeting, and transactions relating to mergers and acquisitions.

In this chapter, we discuss the valuation of oil and gas companies. The chapter starts with a discussion of oil and gas financial modelling. It then looks at valuation methods for oil and gas producers, valuation methods for oilfield services, and methods for determining the value of pipelines and finally concludes.

14.2 Oil and Gas Financial Modelling

The starting point for any model is to picture or understand the nature of the decision that model will support. A financial model needs to take account of a range of complex commercial and technical issues. In the energy sector, to build an effective financial model, you should be able to understand the intrinsic relationship between different stages of the value chain. Failure to understand the connections can create cash flow mismatches. Modelling in the oil and gas sector is about creating a "Net Asset Value (NAV) model for a project or energy asset." The model must, therefore, be able to predict cash flows for "all major projects in a company" to estimate the value of the affected segment. Most companies in the energy sector have a simple business model: "find and extract valuable stuff from the ground, turn it into something useful, and then sell it to customers." The market determines the prices of these commodities (e.g. gold, oil, or gas). The field is divided into three categories: "upstream (Exploration & Production), midstream (transporting oil, gas, and other commodities to companies), and downstream" (refine and market commodities). There are other supporting entities such as: Oil Field Services (e.g. "maintain their oil fields, repair broken spots, upgrade the technology, or even provide security for workers") and Integrated Majors (e.g. BP, Exxon Mobil).

14.2.1 Why Oil and Gas Modelling Is Different?

Oil and gas modelling is different due to the following reasons:

- **Accounting is different** – aside different line items, the system uses the "full cost and successful efforts" which are the two accounting methods.
- **Prices or revenue cannot be controlled** – the market determines the price of products, making it the major difference among the other differences. This makes it difficult to predict prices in the oil and gas industry with some reasonable degree of accuracy.

- **Cyclicality –** "O&G companies follow commodity price cycles." Investment in this sector is not different from investing in the underlying commodity, suggesting that investors must be comfortable with "giant price swings."
- **They are balance sheet-centric** – an exploration and production (E&P) company depends deeply on its balance sheet than companies in other sectors do. The reserves serve as the most important assets which will generate future cash, and profit is found on the balance sheet.
- **Depleting assets galore –** the assets of entities are supposed to increase generally, but that is exactly opposite in the context of O&G sector. There is negative relation between production (revenue generation) and reserves in the oil and gas sectors as more productions are made from the reserves and the quantity of the reserves declines.

Both insiders and outsiders use the results of a financial model to make decisions and to perform certain financial analysis. It should be noted that the management of the company largely depends on financial models to make critical decisions such as:

> [G]enerating capital either by debt and/or by equity), acquiring businesses and/or assets, allocating capitals by prioritizing the projects to invest in, organic business growth (e.g. opening new stores, entering new markets, etc.), selling or disposing of assets and business units, budgeting and forecasting (planning in the future), evaluating a company, analyzing financial statements and management accounting.

14.2.2 Types of Financial Models

Financial models exist in different forms, including "Three Statement Model, Discounted Cash Flow (DCF) Model, Merger Model (M&A), Initial Public Offering (IPO) Model, Leveraged Buyout (LBO) Model, Sum of the Parts Model, Consolidation Model, Budget Model, Forecasting Model, and Option Pricing Model." We discuss each briefly in turn.

Three-Statement Model – this is the "most basic setup" for financial modeling. Using Excel, the three annual financial statements (profit and loss account, balance sheet, and cash flow) are linked to formulas. Doing this will help obtain a model of which some assumptions can be used to bring changes in this model because all the accounts are linked together.

"Discounted Cash Flow (DCF) Model" – This model is based on the three-statement model. The DCF model values a company on the basis of the Net Present Value (NPV) of the company's future cash flows. The DCF model takes cash flows from the three-statement model and discounts those cash flows with some necessary adjustments to represent the firm's weighted average cost of capital (WACC) using the X–PV function in Excel.

Merger Model (M&A) – This model is a more advanced model used to assess the pro forma increase/dilution of a merger or acquisition. A "single tab template" is often used for each company. For instance the estimation of merging companies M and N can be expressed as: "Company M + Company N = Merged P–."

"Initial Public Offering (IPO) Model" – This model evaluates companies before going public. This model involves the analysis of comparable companies along with an assumption of how much investors would be willing to pay for the company in question. To ensure that the shares perform well in the markets, an "IPO discount" is included in the –PO model.

"Leveraged Buyout (LBO) Model" – This is an advanced form of financial modelling that models transactions of complex–debt schedules.

"Sum of the Parts Model" – This model is constructed by putting together a number of DCF models. The next step is to add any unit of the company that was not possible to be captured by the analysis of discounted cash flows (e.g. "marketable securities, which would be valued based on the market") so as to get the value of the entity. For example you would add the values of the P, Q, and R units and then subtract the X liabilities to get the company's–"net asset value."

"Consolidation Model" – This model combines multiple business units into a single model. It is similar to the Sum of Parts model, where two or more units are put together to form the main value. Naturally, there is tab for each business unit and with the sum of the various business units forming a consolidation tab.

"Budget Model" – The budget model is commonly used in financial planning and analysis. This helps companies to budget for the coming years. They are typically based on monthly or quarterly data, with a primary focus on the income statement.

"Forecasting Model" – This model was developed for forecasting and is also used in financial planning and analysis. It is normal to find this model and the budget model combined in one workbook, likewise having them separately sometimes.

Option Pricing Models – These models are based on mathematical formulas rather than subjective criteria and are, therefore, more or less a simple calculator built into Excel. The value of an option contract is calculated on the basis of appropriate variables in the actual contract. This model aims at working out mainly the probability of whether the option is in the money or out-of-the-money when it is exercised. Binomial tree and Black-Scholes are the two major option pricing model types normally used.

14.3 Valuation Methods of Oil and Gas

The basis upon which we measure value of a given firm is referred to as valuation approach. There exist different ways of valuing oil and gas firms, but three of these approaches are generally accepted. These are "Asset-based Approach"

(Net Asset Value), "Market Approach" (Trading Multiples), and "Income Approach" (Discounted Cash flow). Each valuation approach is associated with specific procedures and economic attributes which appropriately enhance the final value determination of a given entity.

14.3.1 The Asset-Based Approach (Net Asset Value)

This approach generally represents "the market value of a company's assets minus the market value of its liabilities" (Harkins, 2019). The net asset value (NAV) method of valuing an oil and gas company is perhaps the most common and widely accepted method. The cash flows associated with the assets (wells) are forecasted using the NAV approach on the basis of revenue projections from the sale of oil and gas products. These inflows of cash are adjusted to account for operating expenses, taxes, and working capital requirements. To estimate present value, these cash flows are discounted after taxes. As a result of accounting for both proven and probable reserves, the outcome is more reflective. Proven reserves are reserves with at least a 90% chance of commercial extraction. Probable reserves, on the other hand, are those whose commercial extraction likelihood lies between 50% and 90%.

14.3.2 The Market Approach (Trading Multiples)

The Market Approach uses market data from "comparable public companies or transactions of similar companies" (Harkins, 2019). In many ways, "this approach goes straight to the heart of value: a company is worth what someone is willing to pay for it." Trading multiples enable investors to compare the valuation of a company with that of other similar entities. It is critical to consider the selection of market multiples when using the Market Approach. The reserve life, the liquid–gas mix, the percentage of field/reserve developed, and the portion of upside excluded from the reserves should all be carefully considered. This approach is very helpful when investors want to compare the valuation of a company in relation to its peers. The following are some multiples that are commonly used:

Enterprise Value per Flowing Barrel – the value of the company is determined on the basis of "per barrel of production." This aids in determining the company's value by utilizing the volume of production (per barrel). It enables investors to compare the company's price/value with its production volumes.

Field Netback – this shows the margin generated from a barrel of oil after standard costs have been deducted. It indicates the profitability of the asset deducting taxes and interest.

Enterprise Value per Average Daily Production – this multiple compares the average production period of a firm to the production periods of similar firms to estimate its value. Non-producing assets within comparable or subject companies that have the potential to affect the implied multiple of daily production must be considered.

Enterprise Value per Acreage – this multiple compares the value of acreage of a firm to that of similar firms. It is a common method for determining the worth of non-producing assets.

Enterprise Value to Reserves – this multiple compares a company's price or value to its reserves (barrels still on the ground). This helps determine the potential of the company's assets in the future.

Enterprise Value per Earnings Before Interest, Taxes, Depreciation (or Depletion), Amortisation, and Exploration Costs (EBITDAX) – this approach attempts to align both successful efforts and full cost reporting.

Finding, Development, and Acquisition Costs – this multiple essentially depicts the cost of discovering barrel reserves. It also includes the cost of acquiring, developing, and producing the reserves.

Recycle Ratio – the recycle ratio as a multiple indicates the level of profitability of oil and gas asset.

Price Per Net Asset Value – this multiple determines "how much an investor is willing to pay for the present value of the company."

14.3.3 The "Income Approach" (Discounted Cash Flow)

This method estimates the value of a company by determining the present value of all relevant cash flows that the company expects to receive or generate in the future. These future cash flows are adjusted to account for inflation and other risks. The discount rate and future cash flows (FCF) are the two main components of the discounted cash flow (DCF) approach.

14.3.3.1 Future Cash Flow (FCF)

The FCF as used in the DCF approach comprises two parts: the cash flows over the forecast period and the terminal value. The forecast period is the time frame for which reliable and detailed estimates for the FCF can be obtained on the basis of certain assumptions. This period is usually longer for oil and gas firms than it is for manufacturing firms. The period for oil and gas firms is typically between 10 and 20 years. This period is adequate to make realistic assumptions about the future cash inflows. Typically, these cash flows are adjusted and brought to a certainty equivalent.

The terminal value of a firm is its value beyond the explicit forecast period. It typically accounts for a significant portion of the firm's value and thus necessitates scrutiny. When using the DCF approach, there are two main ways to calculate the terminal value. These are the perpetual growth assumption approach, which follows the going concern assumption but includes inherent firm growth, and the exit multiple.

The **Perpetual Growth Approach** method of estimating terminal value assumes that the company will continue to operate and generate FCF in a normalised manner for the foreseeable future or forever (i.e. the concept of perpetuity). The terminal growth is calculated as:

$$TV = \frac{FCF_n(1+g)}{WACC - g}$$

where

TV – terminal value
FCF – future cash flow
n – last year of the forecast period or the first year of the terminal period
g – annual growth rate for the terminal period
$WACC$ – weighted average cost of capital

The **Exit Multiple Approach** assumes that the firm is disposed of in multiples of a specific measure, such as "**Earnings before Interest, Taxes, Depreciation (or Depletion), and Amortisation** (EBITDA)," in the event of its disposal. This is done using comparable trading multiples of comparable businesses.

$$TV = \textit{Financial Metric} \times \textit{Trading Multiple}$$

(i.e. EBITDA × 50.0)

Professionals in the industry typically prefer the exit multiple, whereas academics prefer the perpetual growth model. However, in some cases, industry practitioners use both approaches and take an average of the results.

14.3.3.2 "Discount Rate"

In order to determine the present value of FCFs, an appropriate discount rate must be determined. In this case, the weighted average cost of capital (WACC) is most appropriate. The WACC is a weighted cost of capital that weights all sources of funding provided by investors and the associated costs. *The Capital Asset Pricing Model*, the *Accumulation Model*, or the *Gordon Growth Model* can be used to calculate the cost of equity. It is important to adjust the discount rate for the risk.

The value of a company can, therefore, be expressed as:

$$Value^1 = \frac{FCF_1}{(1+WACC)^1} + \frac{FCF_2}{(1+WACC)^2} + \frac{FCF_3}{(1+WACC)^3} + \cdots + \frac{FCF_n}{(1+WACC)^n} + \frac{TV}{(1+WACC)^n}$$

14.3.4 EV/EBITDA

The ratio that compares a company's enterprise value (EV) to its earnings before interest, taxes, depreciation, and amortisation (EBITDA) is known as EV/EBITDA. The "sum of book value (or market capitalisation) plus debt (or financial obligations) minus any cash (debt minus cash is called net debt)" is a company's EV. The EV/EBITDA ratio is commonly used as a valuation metric to compare the "relative value" of different companies (Gregory, 2021). "The EV/EBITDA ratio is used to compare a company's overall value with the EBITDA value it generates annually. This ratio tells investors how often they need to pay EBITDA if they want to acquire the entire company." EBITDAX, which is a company's EBITDA before exploration costs for successful efforts is added, is normally considered by analysts instead of using EBITDA.

14.3.5 "Price-to-Earnings (P/E) Ratio"

One of the tools commonly used to value stocks is "the price-to-earnings or P/E ratio" (Fernando, 2021). This tool helps determine if a company's stock price is "overvalued or undervalued" and can compare that assessment to its "industry group or a benchmark." Forward P/E divides a company's current stock price by that company's estimated future earnings per share (EPS). For valuation purposes, a future P/E ratio is preferable to a historical P/E ratio. We sometimes refer to P/E as a price multiple. Basically, the price-to-earnings ratio tells us "the dollar amount an investor can expect to put into a company to receive $1 of that company's earnings." The price-to-earnings ratio helps investors determine a stock's market value relative to the company's earnings. For example an investor is willing to pay $40 for $1 in current earnings, indicating that the company is currently trading at a P/E of 40. Simply put, the P/E shows what the market is willing to pay for a stock today based on its past or future earnings. When the stock price is higher than earnings, we have a high P/E ratio. On the other hand, a low current stock price relative to earnings means a low P/E ratio. We use the same formula to calculate direct P/E and regular P/E. However, instead of historical data, the formula uses estimated (or projected) earnings per share.

This is expressed as: **"Forward P/E formula** = Current Share Price/Estimated Future Earnings per Share."

14.3.5.1 Forward Price-to-Earnings

The forward P/E and the trailing P/E are the most common P/E ratios using both types of EPS metrics (Fernando, 2021). The third variation, which is not commonly used, uses "the sum of the last two actual quarters and the estimates of the next two quarters." Future earnings numbers are typically used when using the forward (or leading) P/E method. This indicator is very useful for comparing current earnings with future earnings. This helps provide a stronger representation of what earnings will look like – assuming there are no discrepancies or other accounting adjustments. However, there are specific problems associated with this metric. First, companies can understate earnings to exceed the estimated P/E when next quarter earnings are announced. Second, other companies initially overstate their estimates and then adjust them before the next earnings call. Third, the potential for confusion exists when the company's estimates differ from those provided by outside analysts.

14.3.5.1.1 TRAILING PRICE-TO-EARNINGS RATIO

This metric uses past performance, dividing current stock price by total earnings by EPS over the last 12 months. It provides objective reporting (as long as earnings are actually reported by the company), which makes it the most popular P/E metric. Apparently, some investors do not trust someone else's earnings estimates and, therefore, mostly trust the trailing P/E. Regardless, a company's past performance does not signal future behaviour, which becomes a detriment to this metric. Simply put, investors should invest money for future profitability, not for the past. Another issue is the fact that stock prices change while the EPS remains constant over a period of time. If a major corporate event significantly raises or lowers the stock price, the trailing P/E ratio will reflect less of these changes. Some investors prefer forward P/E because the trailing P/E continues to change on the basis of a company's stock price movements while earnings reports are released quarterly. If the forward P/E moves below the trailing P/E, profits are expected to increase. Likewise, when earnings are falling, there is an indication that the expected P/E is higher than the current P/E.

14.3.5.1.1.1 Absolute versus Relative P/E Analysts sometimes need to distinguish absolute P/E ratios from relative P/E ratios when performing certain analyses. **Absolute P/E** divides the current share price by "the trailing EPS, the estimated EPS for the next 12 months (forward P/E) or a mix of the trailing EPS for the last two quarters and the forward P/E for the next two quarters." Note that the absolute P/E represents the current period's P/E. Assuming today's stock price is $200 and final earnings are $5 per share, the P/E ratio is 40 = ($200/$5). **Relative P/E** compares current absolute P/E with a benchmark or a range of previous P/E's over a relevant time period, for example the last 10 years (Fernando, 2021). This metric indicates the level or percentage of the previous P/E that the current P/E has reached. It usually compares the current P/E value to the highest value in the range. Likewise, when looking for how close the current P/E is to the historical value, investors can also compare the current P/E to the lower side of the range. If the current P/E is less than the past value, then the relative P/E will have a value below 100%. If the relative P/E measures 100% or more, investors are confident that the current P/E is equal to or greater than the historical value. For example the current stock price of a particular company is $50, and given that its expected price per share for the next year is $5, that means the company's expected P/E ratio is 10x.

14.3.6 Sum of the Parts

This metric evaluates a company by evaluating the value of each business segment, division, or subsidiary separately and adding it to the total company value (implied total company value). This approach is flexible and, therefore, can be used in conjunction with other valuation methods such as discounted cash flow modelling can be used. This valuation approach is more applicable to companies with distinct divisions or segments, especially from a risk/return perspective. Valuing segments separately will make the valuation process more accurate. Once the sum of all segments of enterprise values has been determined, the remaining step is to subtract net debt and any non-operating assets or liabilities not related to shareholders to calculate book value.

Sum of the Parts Valuation (SOTP):

- $\text{SOTP}_{\text{Equity Value}} = \text{Enterprise Value}_{\text{Segment A}} + \text{Enterprise Value}_{\text{Segment B}} + \text{Enterprise Value}_{\text{Segment C}} - \text{Net Debt}$

Source: Authors' construction b ased on information from Wall Street Prep (https://www.wallstreetprep.com/knowledge/valuation-multiples/)

14.3.6.1 Sum-of-the Parts (SOTP) Application

While the most common reason to use SOTP analysis is for companies with business units in different industries, another scenario where SOTP can be useful is in restructuring. Often, one of the first steps for a struggling company that needs immediate restructuring is to identify underperforming non-core businesses that can be sold if a suitable buyer is found (e.g. distressed mergers and acquisitions). Another common use case for SOTP is spin-offs and related activities. Starting from SOTP in the given context, it tries to answer the question: "***Is the whole greater than the sum of its parts***?" If so, it would be better for the subsidiary to remain part of the parent company. However, if the answer is no, then the subsidiary may actually be in a more favourable position in a spin-off.

Box 14.1 Valuation Exercise

Eco Atlantic Oil and Gas Limited provides oil and gas exploration and development services. The company is focused on identifying, acquiring, and developing oil and natural gas and upstream shale properties. The company operates in Namibia, Guyana, and Ghana. Suppose you are a financial analyst at Eco Atlantic Oil and Gas Limited, reviewing the possible acquisition of JHI Associates Inc. through merger. The following data are available:

Particulars	*Eco Atlantic Oil and Gas Limited*	*JHI Associates Inc.*
Profits after tax	C$6,000,000	C$1,000,000
No. of equity shares	1,000,000	200,000
Market value per share	C$ 200	C$ 160

"If the merger goes through and the exchange ratio is based on current market prices, what is the new EPS for Eco Atlantic Oil and Gas Limited?"

After the acquisition, you prepared the company's financial statement and observed the following revenue for 5 years:

(C$ in million)	*Year 1*	*Year 2*	*Year 3*	*Year 4*	*Year 5*
Revenue	22,000	20,000	18,000	15,000	10,000

Given the following assumptions, what was the free cash flows to Eco Atlantic Oil and Gas Limited as well as the value of the company?

Assumptions	
EDITDA margin	25%
D&A% of revenue	5%
EBIT margin	20%
Tax rate	40%
Capex% revenue	5%
Change in NWC% revenue	2%
Project Financing	
Debt financing	15%
20-year AAA corporate bond yield	2.5%
Marginal tax rate	35%
Yield on 30-year treasury bond	2.34%
Risk premium	5%
Beta for the petroleum industry	1.45

Let us also assume that Eco Atlantic Oil and Gas Limited and two other O&G companies in the industry have the same financial data. How would you value the companies, using the multiples approach if "the value of operations is $10000 million while operating income (EBIT) in the last 12 months' value is 10% of the value of operations?" Assume Eco Atlantic Oil and Gas Limited is a low capital-intensity company with D&A C$400 million, the company with a base case has D&A of C$550 million, and the company with high capital intensity has D&A of C$800 million.

Solution to the Exercise:

Using an alternative approach used by professionals (i.e. the comparable company analysis approach) to estimate acquisition values, the following approach will be considered for the valuation:

"If the exchange ratio is based on market prices, it will be: 200/160.

This implies that, for every five shares of JHI Associates Inc, the target shareholders would receive four shares of Eco Atlantic Oil and Gas Limited."

Thus, for 200,000 shares of JHI Associates Inc., they will receive 160,000 [4/5 × 200,000] shares in Eco Atlantic Oil and Gas Limited.

Hence, the new EPS of Eco Atlantic Oil and Gas Limited will be

Particulars	
Combined PAT	C$ 7,000,000
No. of equity shares	1,160,000
Revised EPS	C$6.03

"Next, the free cash flow to the company is given as:

Free Cash Flow to Firm (FCFF) = NOPAT + Depreciation and Amortisation (D&A) − Change in Net Working Capital (NWC) − Capital Expenditure (Capex)"

Based on the assumptions listed, the EBITDA in the first year is C$5,500 million, from which we deduct C$1100 in D&A to get C$4400 million as the EBIT. And to calculate NOPAT, the analyst applies a 40% tax rate to the C$4400 million of EBIT, which comes out to be C$2640 million.

From C$2640 million in NOPAT, the analyst adds back the C$1100 million in D&A and then finishes the calculation by subtracting the C$1100 million in capex and C$440 in the change in NWC – for an FCFF of C$2200 million. The process is repeated for the subsequent 4 years.

($ in million)	*Year 1*	*Year 2*	*Year 3*	*Year 4*	*Year 5*
Revenue	22,000	20,000	18,000	15,000	10,000
EBITDA	**5,500**	**5,000**	**4,500**	**3,750**	**2,500**
Less: D&A	−1,100	−1,000	−900	−750	−500
EBIT	**4,400**	**4,000**	**3,600**	**3,000**	**2,000**
Less: Taxes	−1,760	−1,600	−1,440	−1,200	−800
NOPAT	**2,640**	**2,400**	**2,160**	**1,800**	**1,200**
Plus: D&A	1,100	1,000	900	750	500
Less: Capex	−1,100	−1,000	−900	−750	−500
Less: Change in NWC	−440	−400	−360	−300	−200
Free Cash Flow to Firm (FCFF)	2,200	2,000	1,800	1,500	1,000

The discounted rate of Eco Atlantic Oil and Gas Limited to be used in evaluating the company's project is equal to the company's weighted average cost of capital (WACC).

The analyst has to calculate the WACC of the company on the basis of the information given before.

This is expressed as:

"WACC = (Fraction financed by Debt) × (Cost of Debt) × (1 − Tax Rate) + (Fraction Financed by Equity) × (Cost of Equity)

First, the cost of debt financing would be expressed as: (Cost of Debt) × (1 − Tax Rate)

► [0.025 × (1− 0.35)] = 0.02

Second, the cost of equity financing using the CAPM would be expressed as:

Cost of Equity = Risk Free Return + Beta (Risk Premium)

► [0.0234 + (1.45 × 0.05)] = 0.1"

Given a 15% debt financing and 85% equity financing, the WACC for Eco Atlantic Oil and Gas Limited project would be:

► WACC = 0.15 × 0.02 + 0.85 × 0.10 = 0.095, or 9.5%

The value of a company can, therefore, be expressed as:

$$Value = \frac{FCF_1}{(1+WACC)^1} + \frac{FCF_2}{(1+WACC)^2} + \frac{FCF_3}{(1+WACC)^3} + \frac{FCF_n}{(1+WACC)^4} + \frac{TV}{(1+WACC)^5}$$

Year	*1*	*2*	*3*	*4*	*5*	
Free Cash Flow to Firm (FCFF)	2,200	2,000	1,800	1,500	1,000	
DCF Value	2009.13	1668.02	1370.97	1043.36	635.237	**C$ 6726.72**

Hence, the value of the company is C$6,726.72million.

Then the operating value of all three companies is CAD$10,000 while their operating income (EBIT) is C$1,000 million in the last twelve months (LTM). In practice, the EV/EBITDA multiple is often used in relative valuation to compare different companies in the same (or similar) sector.

Based on these information, we can calculate the EV/LTM EBIT using the simple formula of:

EV/LTM EBIT = C$10,000 EV/ C$1000 LTM EBIT
EV/LTM EBIT = 10.0x"

"All three companies have an EV/LTM EBIT multiple of 10.0x – but now, we must account for D&A."

Low Capital Intensity: D&A = C$400m
Base Case: D&A = C$550m
High Capital Intensity: D&A = $800m

"From the pattern above, we can recognise that the more capital intensive the company, the higher the D&A expense."

"Using those listed D&A figures, we can add the applicable amount to EBIT to calculate the EBITDA for each company."

- **"Company A (Low):** EBITDA" = $1000m + $400m = $1400m
- **"Company B (Base):** EBITDA" = $1000m + $550m = $1550m
- **"Company C (High):** EBITDA" = $1000m + $800m = $1800m

Now, we can calculate the EV/EBITDA multiples for each company on an LTM basis.

- **"Company A:** \$1000m EV / \$1400m = =7.14x"
- **"Company B:** \$1000m EV / \$1550m = 6.45x"
- **"Company C:** \$1000m EV / \$1800m = 5.56x"

	Capital Intensity		
	Low	Base	High
"Enterprise Value (EV)"	10,000	10,000	10,000
"LTM EBIT"	1000	1000	1000
"EV/LTM EBIT"	10.0×	10.0×	10.0×
"Enterprise Value (EV)	10,000	10,000	10,000
LTM EBIT"	1000	1000	1000
(+) Depreciation and Amortisation (D&A)	400	550	800
EBITDA	1400	1550	1800
EV/LTM EBITDA	7.1×	6.5×	5.6×

14.4 Methods for Determining the Value of Pipelines

Generally, pipelines can be categorised into two main types: liquid petroleum pipelines and natural gas pipelines. There have been instances of overpricing of pipelines by local tax authorities and target companies, as well as overpricing (and underpricing) of pipelines in M&A contexts and underpricing of pipelines in real estate comparisons. This required the development of specific assessment methods for pipelines. There are several reasons why there should be a valuation report for active or inactive pipelines, gas, or pipelines. For example pipeline rehabilitation, merger, and construction financing valuations may be required. Howell (2010) identified a number of reasons for pipeline evaluation. These are: liquidation of assets, preparing pipeline assets for sale or disposal, government re-regulation, local taxes, ad valorem/tax accounting, salvage valuation, termination of partnership, preparation for purchase or acquisition, preparation for conversion of pipeline use, and valuation for accurate accounting.

Howell (2010) suggests that there are over 40 methods (e.g. factors) that can be used to determine the value of pipelines. These factors are associated with the "technical aspects of business, physicality, property and commodity value, whether product is purchased at the wellhead and resold, whether and to what extent the product is compressed, enhanced, treated, cleaned, or processed, and by what procedures" (Howell, 2010). We discuss some of the methods for determining the value of pipelines.

14.4.1 Across the Fence Technique (ATF)

The "across-the-fence method of right-of-way" appraisal takes into account the value of surrounding land but does not include the value of the entity that uses it (Daniel, 2016). The midstream assets are calculated through an appraisal before sales. The ATF proposes that the "right of way" is worth what the surrounding land is worth. ATF is popular but only considers land value. Howell (2010) suggests that "right of way" accounts for between 5% and 7% of the total cost of constructing a pipeline, which is considered a small factor in determining value.

14.4.2 Seller-Determined Need Method

This method is primarily used when the seller wants to recognise a financial gain or loss from a sale use carrying amount. In practice, the property owner could generate the book value depending on the method that the company's accountant would use to determine the book value. For example it can be based on any method of determining value, such as construction costs, new or with discount, but such determination of the book value by the seller has no relevance to the buyer, as it is irrelevant to the present value.

14.4.3 The Income-Based or Cash-Flow Method

This is a popular method for valuing pipelines, which generates predicted cash flows. Forecasted income, which is based on "throughput volumes and rates of the commodity transported," is usually employed under this method. "Expenses based on a historical or projected income stream together with the revenues are used to estimate cash flows, which are then are discounted to arrive at the value." In addition, "a variation of this method uses multiples of current cash flow where the average annual cash flow is multiplied by a factor of 5 to 12." The factor, which reflects the discount rate, is called capitalisation multiple. The valuation can be done on a monthly or annual basis as it is done in the oil and gas royalties' value determination. The pipeline values of minerals and oil and gas can be compared by stakeholders since both have definite life (reserves) unless there are new discoveries of reserves. Stakeholders can also find the net present values or present values of the additional income by discounting these values.

Take for instance:

> Company A's future income after operating expenses of its gas pipeline is $500,000 per year. An amount of $2,500,000 might be a reasonable value based on a capitalisation multiple of 5.

14.4.4 The New-Construction or Replacement Cost Method

This is the most accurate or efficient way to determine the value of a pipeline. This is the cost of rebuilding the same pipeline with the same size, shape, and (comparable) easement (Crumbley and Cheng, 2014). A buyer considers this a key factor when evaluating a pipeline. We can also rule out this approach. Suppose Company A wants to value its pipeline that has been in operation for 10 years since it was installed, and that pipeline has an expected lifespan of 40 years. The company can get 3.5% per year of life or a total of 35% discount on the cost of new construction in the current market. Thus, the company specifies the replacement cost and deducts an amount for the loss in value due to deterioration, function, and economic obsolescence.

14.5 General Considerations in Valuing Oil and Gas Assets

Valuing oil and gas companies is crucial. A variety of factors affect the value of oil and gas companies. These factors include the company's reserves, production volume, and prevailing commodity prices. Company operations are critical in determining the value of oil and gas companies. Other factors that affect the value of oil and gas companies include the potential for higher cash flows and earnings, high capital investments, dividend policies, and the profitability of oil and gas companies. Some investors believe that the valuation of these companies is primarily driven by the current and estimated future value of oil producers' reserves, which are subject to commodity price risk.

Assessing the value of an oil and gas asset is complex. This explains why two analysts can place different values on one oil and gas asset. Valuation usually hinges on the analyst's experience as well as on the institutions and upstream operators' unique assumptions. Unlike other investments, oil and gas investments operate in longer time horizons. They are, therefore, exposed to the complex interaction of macroeconomic, technical, and geopolitical assumptions that may have some deep impact on perceptions of risk and value. In addition, two conditions exacerbate the complexity of the oil-and-gas-asset-valuation process: volatility of the global commodity markets and high levels of uncertainty associated with future energy demand.

Firms that engage in upstream activities or operate within that sector may adopt different strategies that affect the methodology used in valuing the business. Through acquisitions or development, some firms may replenish their reserves whereas others may cause a cessation of their operations or even exit when their reserves have fully matured. The preferred valuation techniques are the cost or NAV approach including the adjusted reserve values, DCF method (this must include all costs incurred at the corporate level), or the guideline public company method.

Regardless of the valuation method adopted, the valuation of an oil and gas firm follows three steps: data gathering, value assessment, and assets' screening. Data gathering involves the analyst gathering data on factors such as ownership structure, location, fiscal environment, economic conditions, tariff arrangements, and surrounding infrastructure of the firm. Data on existing production model that can be adjusted to reflect the views of the analyst may also be collected. The second step in the valuation process involves the analyst subjecting the data gathered in step one to some analysis. Here, the analyst adjusts price assumptions, conducts sensitivity analysis, and asks "what if" questions (What if operating costs is cut down by 5%? What if capital costs go up by 10%?, etc.). In the third step of the valuation process, the analyst relies on their experience to qualitatively and quantitatively assess the oil and gas assets, their value, and the risks and opportunities associated with them. The assets are screened to see those which satisfy the criteria of the client, creating a shortlist of recommended assets that are most likely to match corporate objectives.

14.6 Conclusion

In this chapter, we have covered oil and gas valuation. There exist different ways of valuing oil and gas firms, but three of these approaches are generally accepted: Asset-based Approach (Net Asset Value), Market Approach (Trading Multiples), and Income Approach (Discounted Cash Flow). The chapter discussed the valuation methods for oilfield services, including/EBITDA, P/E, and the Sum of the Parts. The methods for determining the value of pipelines include Across the Fence Technique (ATF), Seller-determined need Method, the Income Base or Cash-Flow Method, and the new-construction or replacement cost method. The chapter also identified a number of factors that tend to influence the value of oil and gas companies, and these are the firm's reserve levels, the volume of production, the prevailing commodity prices, the firm's operations, the potential to generate higher cash flows and earnings, high capital investments, dividend policies, and profitability. The last but not least issue discussed in this chapter relates to the general considerations in the oil and gas valuation process as well as the complexities inherent in the valuation process.

The aforementioned discussions support the conclusion that there is no single method for valuing oil and gas firms, oilfield firms, and pipelines. Depending on the analyst's experience, assumptions, and technical expertise coupled with the assumptions of the institutions and players in the industry, one or a combination of the methods discussed could be deployed to value oil and gas firms, oilfield service firms, and pipelines. Besides, it is evident that valuing firms in the oil and gas sector is complex, and two conditions add to this complexity: volatility of the global commodity markets and high levels of uncertainty associated with future energy demand.

References

Abor, J. Y. (2017). Valuation of new ventures and small businesses, In *Entrepreneurial finance for MSMEs* (pp. 321–355). Cham: Palgrave Macmillan.

Boisjoly, R. P., Conine Jr, T. E., and McDonald IV, M. B. (2020). Working capital management: Financial and valuation impacts. *Journal of Business Research*, 108, 1–8.

Crumbley, D. L., and Cheng, C. C. (2014). Avoid losing a Daubert challenge: Some best practices for expert witnesses. *ATA Journal of Legal Tax Research*, 12(1), 41–53.

Daniel, W. (2016, January 4). *Pipelines could affect property values*. http://catskillcitizens.org/news.cfm

Fernando, J. (2021). Price-to-earnings ratio–P/E ratio. *Investopedia, Investopedia*, 10.

Gregory, A. (2021). *Complete analysis*. London: Netflix, Inc.

Harkins, D. W. R. (2019). *How to value*. New York: Oilfield Services Company

Howell, D. (2010). Proper method boosts decommissioned pipe value. *Oil & Gas Journal*, 108(46), 144–144.

15 Mergers and Acquisitions in the Oil and Gas Sector

Anastacia C. Arko, Joshua Yindenaba Abor, Ali Sheikhbahaei, and Alfred Yawson

15.1 Introduction

Mergers and acquisitions (M&As) refer to the consolidation of two or more business entities or the combination of their assets to form a single legal and operating entity. Though typically used together, M&As differ in meaning. A merger refers to the amalgamation of two entities, usually of similar sizes, to form a different entity, with neither of the two entities surviving the other post-merger. An acquisition, on the other hand, refers to an outright purchase of one company by another. Typically, the smaller company in an acquisition is subsumed into the larger company, which survives post acquisition. Acquirers in M&As typically pay the target company's shareholders with cash, stock, or a combination of cash and stocks. It is therefore important for both parties to value the acquiree company to ensure that the right price is paid. Companies use valuation metrics, such as Enterprise Value to EBITDA, Price to Earnings (P/E) ratio, Price to Book (P/BV) ratio, and free cash flow valuation models to value the target company.

Mergers, acquisitions, and other business combinations are dominant within the oil and gas (O&G) industry, globally. As oil prices surged towards the fourth quarter of 2018 (Macrotrends.net), M&A deals in the sector increased concurrently, with deal size reaching over $500 billion in 2018 (Enverus Database). However, with COVID-19 and its associated plunge in oil prices during 2020, the industry recorded its lowest deal count (258 deals in 2020 compared to 433 in 2019) and value (approximately $30 billion within the first half of 2020) within the decade (Deloitte, 2021). Deal counts within the O&G industry fell sharply by 41% (year on year), as companies shifted focus to cash preservation and strengthening their balance sheet in the face of heightening liquidity challenges amidst industry revenue reduction (−54% in 2020) (PWC, 2018; Deloitte, 2021). The industry has recorded a turnaround in H2 2020, as deal value spiralled to $70 billion. The first half of 2021 saw the lowest level of O&G deal activity in the last 10 years. Overall, global O&G M&A deal value in 2021 rose by a modest 18% to $269 billion, compared to 2020 with recoveries in upstream and oilfield services offsetting weakness in midstream and downstream sectors (Deloitte, 2022). In addition, the industry M&A deal projections for 2021 are bullish as prices recover on

DOI: 10.4324/9781003315056-18

the back of improved economic fundamentals and as the industry positions itself to take advantage of its restructuring. While global deal valuations continue to rise in 2021, it is expected to rise further in 2022. For instance more than 80% of executives of the global deals expect valuations to climb by at least 10% in 2022 (KPMG, 2020).

In general, mergers and acquisition are driven by the need to take advantage of synergies to boost stakeholder value, redeploy assets, reduce cost, increase market share, restructure the business, and provide new operating plans and business strategies (Pazarskis et al., 2006). However, M&As in the O&G sector have traditionally been driven by industry-specific factors, rather than the standard economic factors (see Özgür and Wirl, 2020). This is mainly due to the extent to which political, institutional, and legal constraints weigh in on the production costs and profitability of O&G companies, especially those in exploration and production (E&P) (Özgür and Wirl, 2020). Specifically, infrastructural constraints, political challenges, and policy uncertainties affect O&G companies' ability to operate at full capacity, impacting revenue generation and thus profitability.

In this chapter, we explore the general forms of M&A within the sector, the factors that motivate M&A deals in the O&G sector, the top M&As that have occurred within the past years, and the causes of M&A failures in the O&G sector.

15.2 Types of Mergers and Acquisitions

Mergers and acquisitions are classified according to interrelationship of the merged entities, the forms of integration, the method of acquisition, or the mode of payment. We consider each classification and discuss the types of M&As that fall under each classification.

15.2.1 Interrelationship of Merged Entities

This classification of M&As include horizontal mergers, vertical merger, conglomerate M&As, circular M&As, lateral M&As, and diagonal M&As.

Horizontal Merger: This occurs when the merged entities operate within the same or similar industry. For instance the combination of two upstream or two downstream O&G companies. A typical example is the merger of SPAC Kayne Anderson Acquisition Corporation and Apache Corporation to form Altus Midstream Company in 2018. Because they operate within similar industries, the business combination is seamless. Horizontal mergers elicit cost synergies and boost economies of scale. However, the resultant reduction in competition and the creation of mega-monopolies could result in overcapitalisation, cartels, and associated unwarranted prize hikes. It may also be difficult managing such mega entities, leading to diseconomies of scale.

Vertical Merger: Vertical merger refers to the combination of businesses within the same value chain. This consists of downward integration and forward integration. In *backward integration*, a business acquires its supplier. Such is the case when a midstream O&G company acquires a company operating in the upstream space. A typical example is the 2020 transaction M&A deals of small- and medium-sized acquisitions by Perenco Company in Gabon and in Democratic Republic of Congo, as well as the acquisitions by Panoro Energy in Gabon and Equatorial Guinea, where these acquirers gained control over their distribution channels (i.e. refineries and gas stations). *Forward integration* refers to the acquisition of a distributor. Such is the case when a midstream participant acquires a company that operates in the downstream space. Backward combinations, for instance, allow a company to have control of and a consistent supply of raw materials, especially when its raw materials are scarce. This reduces the cost of inputs and allows for better pricing of the finished product. Forward integration eliminates middlemen within the distribution channel and allows for better pricing of the final product. However, managing businesses in different business lines may not augur well for economies of scale and synergies. Table 15.1 shows the differences between vertical and horizontal M&A of O&G companies.

Table 15.1 Differences between Vertical and Horizontal Mergers and Acquisitions[1]

M&A Type	*Advantages*	*Disadvantages*	*Examples*
Horizontal combination	Member units produce similar products.	Breakdown in one unit does not result in the stoppage of work in all other units.	SPAC Kayne Anderson Acquisition Corporation merged with Apache Corporation to create Altus Midstream Company
	Helps reduce competition	It may lead to the creation of mega monopolies and cartels	
	Economies of large-scale operations are available.	There is no specialisation and division of labour.	
Vertical combination	Member units do not produce similar products.	Breakdown in one unit interrupts work in other units.	Suncor gained control over Petro-Canada
	Helps secure regular supply of raw materials and control the price and distribution of final products.	Does not breed cartels since businesses do not operate in the same space	
	Every member unit specialises in a particular stage of production.	Economies of large scale may or may not be available.	

Source: Authors' construction based on data from: https://mymbaguide.com/kinds-business-combinations-advantages-disadvantages

Conglomerate Mergers and Acquisitions: This refers to the amalgamation of companies in unrelated businesses. The fundamental driving force behind conglomerate M&A is for diversification. A conglomerate merger occurs when a downstream O&G company acquires a company such as a convenience store and merges it into the operation of its service stations. An example is a transaction deal which occurred in 2020 between Decklar Resources and San Leon Energy in Nigeria, where these companies combined to control many other industries. The merits of conglomerate M&A are to improve the revenue diversification of the merged entity, reduce its reliance on a single industry, and manage the risk of revenue concentration. However, conglomerate M&As do not always offer synergistic benefits. Meanwhile, managing unrelated businesses may result in diseconomies of scale.

Independent and Integrated Mergers and Acquisitions: Independent M&A is an O&G industry that focuses on one segment of the industry or operates independently as an upstream (exploration and production companies), midstream (transportation and storage of oil and gas companies), and downstream (manage the refining and marketing of oil and gas), while integrated M&A refers to businesses that consist of a mix of upstream, midstream, and downstream activities. Examples of upstream O&G industry include Devon Energy and Occidental Company; examples of midstream include Enbridge, Kinder Morgan, SEACOR Holdings Inc., Teekay Shipping Corp., Western Gas Partners LP, and Enable Midstream Partners LP; and examples of downstream include Delek US Holdings, Marathon Petroleum, and Valero Energy. Examples of integrated O&G industry are BP, Chevron, ExxonMobil, and Royal Dutch Shell. Table 15.2 shows examples of M&A companies across the various segments.

Table 15.3 shows a summary of top 10 M&A deals, over 2016–2019 period, in the O&G industry. It also reveals the companies and the type of activities they undertake.

In Table 15.3, Occidental Petroleum and Anadarko were ranked first with a deal value of $57.00 billion, followed by Sunoco Logistics and Energy Transfer Partners ($51.00 billion), then Enbridge and Spectra Energy ($46.50 billion), Marathon Petroleum and Andeavor ($35.60 billion), GE Oil & Gas and Baker Hughes ($31.60 billion), Schlumberger and Cameron ($14.80 billion; Technip and FMC Technologies ($14.50 billion), and Rosneft and Trafigura and Essar Oil ($12.90 billion); BP acquired BHP Billiton ($10.35 billion), but Rosneft and Bashneft recorded the lowest rank corresponding to $8.20 billion.

Other forms of business combinations on the basis of the interrelationships of the merged entities are:

Circular Mergers and Acquisitions: This refers to the combination of different companies with dissimilar products to take advantage of the same distribution channel.

Table 15.2 Examples of M&A Companies across the Segments

Upstream	*Midstream*	*Downstream*	*Oilfield Services*
Rosneft acquired a majority stake in Bashneft; Pampa Energia SA, Statoil, and Total SA purchased assets off Petrobras in Brazil and Argentina; Diamondback Energy bought acreage in the Delaware Basin from Brigham Resources; Transocean acquired Songa Offshore; EQT acquired Rice Energy; Wood Group acquired Amec Foster; BP acquired BHP Billiton	Sunoco Logistics acquired Energy Transfer Partners; Enbridge acquired Spectra Energy; Pembina acquired Veresen; Enbridge acquired Spectra Energy Partners; Enbridge sold its non-core natural gas-processing plants to Brookfield Infrastructure Partners; SPAC Kayne Anderson Acquisition Corporation merged with Apache Corporation to create Altus Midstream Company	Canadian Government acquired Kinder Morgan's Trans Mountain pipeline; Shell sold its Argentinian gas station network to Raízen Energia; Motor Fuel Group acquired MRH GB; Marathon Petroleum acquired Andeavor; Andeavor Logistics acquired Western Refining Logistics; Sunoco divested its stake in its convenience stores; ONGC consolidated assets of Hindustan Refining; Aramco acquired ~50% stake in Petronas' RAPID project in Malaysia	Ensco acquired Atwood; Ensco acquired Rowan Companies; WorleyParsons acquired Jacobs Engineering; Transocean acquired Ocean Rig

Table 15.3 Top 10 M&As in Terms of Deal Value for the Period 2016–2019

Rank	*M&A Companies*	*Deal (Transaction Value) (US$)*	*Date of M&A*
1	Occidental Petroleum and Anadarko	57.00 billion	2019
2	Sunoco Logistics acquired Energy Transfer Partners	51.00 billion	2016
3	Enbridge acquired Spectra Energy	46.50 billion	2016
4	Marathon Petroleum acquired Andeavor	35.60 billion	2018

Rank	*M&A Companies*	*Deal (Transaction Value) (US$)*	*Date of M&A*
5	GE Oil & Gas acquired Baker Hughes	31.60 billion	2016
6	Schlumberger acquired Cameron	14.80 billion	2016
7	Technip acquired FMC Technologies	14.50 billion	2016
8	Rosneft and Trafigura acquired Essar Oil	12.90 billion	2016
9	BP acquired BHP Billiton	10.50 billion	2018
10	Rosneft acquired a majority stake in Bashneft	10.35 billion	2016

Lateral Mergers and Acquisitions: This is the amalgamation of businesses with allied products, which as a unit form the raw materials of a single product (convergent lateral combination), or allied products, which use the same raw materials in their production (divergent lateral integration).

Diagonal Mergers and Acquisitions: This is the merger of entities that produce ancillary products or services to an entity.

15.2.2 Forms of Integration

The classification according to forms of integration include statutory mergers and acquisition, subsidiary mergers and acquisition, and consolidation mergers and acquisition.

Statutory Mergers and Acquisition: This is a business combination in which one of the combining companies or entities continues as a legal entity. This occurs when the merging and acquiring entity survives the transaction. In statutory M&As, the target company ceases to exist after the business combination. For instance Wood Group's acquisition of Amec Foster Wheeler (both in the United Kingdom) in 2017 was a statutory merger.

Subsidiary Mergers and Acquisitions: In a subsidiary M&A, both the target and acquiring companies maintain their businesses after the consolidation. The target company continues to run its business as a subsidiary of the acquiring company, post-merger. O&G companies establish subsidiaries to allow them to expand into profitable new markets, increase revenue, and diversify their holdings to better manage risk. Example is the M&A case in Angola (Namibe and Kwanza), Namibia (Kavango, Walvis Bay, and Orange Basins), and South Africa (Orange Basin), which has one of the largest number of subsidiaries among the offshore oil and gas industry operations across developing oil markets.

Consolidation Mergers and Acquisition: Under this form of M&A, none of the companies involved survive post business combination. An entirely new company is formed post-merger to take up the businesses of both entities. The business combination between Eco (Atlantic) O&G and Azinam in a bid to enter Blocks 3B/4B and Block 2B within the Orange Basin offshore South Africa to consolidate its interests in its four existing licenses within the Walvis Basin offshore Namibia was a consolidation M&A.

15.3 Method of Acquisition and Mode of Payment

We now discuss the different methods of acquisition and modes of paying the purchase price.

15.3.1 Methods of Acquisition

Asset purchase and equity acquisition are the most popular methods of acquisitions in M&A transactions.

Asset Purchase: In an asset purchase, the acquiring company purchases specific assets of the target company, instead of an outright purchase of the entire company. By purchasing the assets of the business, the acquiring company is protected from liabilities and other encumbrances associated with the target company. In 2018, Enbridge sold its non-core natural-gas-processing plants in Canada to Brookfield Infrastructure Partners under an asset purchase agreement.

Equity Acquisition: Instead of an asset purchase acquisition, the acquirer can buy the shares of the target company. In 2018, French energy company Total acquired 74% stake in Direct Energie, under an Equity Acquisition arrangement. While the acquirer assumes the liabilities of the target company in an equity acquisition, the latter offers a smoother transaction as it eliminates the logistics associated with title changes and contract executions. In a cross-border acquisition, this is recorded as Foreign Direct Investment (FDI) transaction and reflected in the Balance of Payment (BoP) account of both countries.

15.3.2 Modes of Payment

The modes of settling the purchase price in M&As include cash payment, payments with shares, and payment with a combination of cash and shares.

Cash Payment: Acquiring companies typically pay for an acquisition with cash when they are cash rich and also when they expect the identified synergies of the target company to strongly drive up the price of the stock. Acquiring companies are therefore motivated to pay for an acquisition with cash if they perceive the stock of the target company to be undervalued.

Payment with Shares: Acquiring companies typically choose to pay for an acquisition with shares when they are less confident in the valuation of the target company and would therefore want to share the risk of the target company with the shareholders of the seller. Additionally, a company with high leverage and minimal cash would opt to pay for an acquisition with equity instead of cash.

Payment with a Combination of Cash and Shares: Sometimes, the acquiring companies pay for acquisitions with a combination of cash and shares in the acquiring entity or that of the merged entity.

15.4 The Role of Investment Banks in Mergers and Acquisitions

Investment banks play a major role in M&As, including the identification of potential companies that fit the transaction, structuring of the deal, leading the due diligence process, conducting valuation of companies, as well as pricing and negotiating the deal. We will segregate the role of investment banks by looking at it from the buy side and sell side of the transaction.

15.4.1 Role of Buy-Side Investment Banks

Investment banks on the buy side of the transaction advise the acquirers/buyers in the M&As. These roles are discussed as follows:

Evaluating Potential Target Companies and Determining Their Strategic Fit. At the initial stages of the M&A process, investment bankers identify several target companies and assess their synergy opportunities to determine their strategic fit into the business of the acquiring firm. M&As are costly, and so the assessment of the synergistic opportunities is important. Merging with a company which offers strong synergistic opportunities results in the generation of superior shareholder value.

Conducting Due Diligence. At the initial stages of the process, the lead investment bank (or the syndicate of book runners) conducts due diligence of the target company to examine the financials and ensure that there are no hidden liabilities (such as significant debt or off-balance sheet liabilities), which will eliminate the synergies identified.

Determining the Value of Potential Targets: Mergers are paid for with cash, stock, or a combination of the two. To enable the acquiring company to determine an appropriate price to pay to the shareholders of the target company, it is important to conduct a valuation of the target company. This valuation forms the basis for the negotiation process. Investment banks use free cash flow models such as free cash flow to firm and free cash flow to equity as well as multiples such as Enterprise Value to EBITDA, Price to Earnings Ratio, and Price to Book Value Ratio to determine the value of the target company.

The choice of models is driven by the availability of financial data and appropriateness of model for the business being valued. In addition to conducting a valuation of the target company, the buy-side investment bank conducts a valuation for the acquiring firm in the situation where the acquisition is paid for with stocks of the acquiring company or that of the new entity.

Determining the Appropriate Payment and Financing Method. Another role of buy-side investment bankers is to examine the capital structure of the acquiring firm to determine what payment method is efficient for the transaction. A company with significant debt may prefer to raise equity, instead of debt, to pay for a cash deal. Such a company may also opt to pay the target company shareholders with equity instead of cash. However, a cash-rich company with less debt can afford to pay for the transaction using internally generated funds.

Crafting a Bidding Strategy and Determining the Terms of the Transactions. The investment bank also designs a bidding strategy and determines the appropriate contract terms that will inure to the benefit of the acquiring company.

Negotiation. Being at the forefront of the valuation process as well as the due diligence process for the acquiring company, the investment bank leads the negotiation process and helps the acquiring firm to develop and deliver an appropriate offer. This ensures that the acquiring firm seals the deal at an attractive price to generate value to its shareholders.

Raising Funds. For clients who do not have sufficient internally generated funds, the investment bank also assists in raising the capital to fund the transaction. In addition to determining the appropriate security to issue, on the basis of the capital structure of the company, the investment bank also leads the fund-raising process. The fund-raising activities include valuing the business, designing the pitch book, seeking approval from the regulatory authorities, embarking on a road show, raising the funds, and listing the security.

15.4.2 Role of Sell-Side Investment Banks

Investment banks on the sell side of the transaction assist the sellers or the target companies, and these roles include:

Crafting a Bidding Strategy for Client. The investment bank monitors the market and advises the selling company about the appropriate timing for the sale as well as appropriate potential buyer.

Building the Investment Thesis. The investment bank builds a compelling investment thesis to pitch to potential buyers. The investment bank also prepares the deal deck (or online "data room") and pitch materials (Information Memorandum) and shares with interested buyers.

Acting as a Liaison between Seller and Potential Buyers. The investment bank contacts potential buyers and serves as a liaison between the seller and buyers, during the due diligence process.

Negotiation. The investment bank assists the buyer in negotiating the final terms of the deal.

15.5 Factors Influencing Mergers and Acquisitions in the Oil and Gas Sector

The M&A activity of the O&G industry has risen tremendously over the past few years. One of the major reasons that accounted for the massive growth is due to advancement in technology. However, the past 5 years have been challenging for the O&G sector. After oil prices hit a high of approximately \$110 per barrel around 2013 and 2014, prices have been plunging into the depths, influencing deal count and deal value within the sector. The industry had experienced a rise in M&A deals in the 2014–2016 period. However, the industry had witnessed a slowdown in the M&A deals towards the end of 2018 when the prices took a hit and dropped from \$85 to \$50 per barrel. Another reason for the slowdown was that most firms were moving towards more renewable resources in order to reduce their carbon footprint and move closer to achieving the global sustainability development goals. In addition, the M&A deals were softened due to the high price volatility in 2019, corresponding to a total value deal of \$92 billion (with respect to the United States). With an easy access to capital, low interest rates, and a recovering global economy, traders around the world announced \$5.1 trillion in M&A transactions in 2021, up from \$3.8 trillion in 2020 and later highest level since 2015 (Deloitte, 2021).

Global M&A activity in 2021 far surpassed pre-pandemic levels, nearing the peaks of 2015, and M&As are expected to increase even more over 2022 (Deloitte, 2021). Global oil and gas M&A activity grew by 16% in 2021 to \$335 billion. In terms of revenue, 2021 saw 1,799 deals versus 1,818 last year, down by a small 1%. In 2021, there were more than \$74 billion worth of M&A deals in the oil and gas sector, compared to \$40 billion the year before. Upstream contributed to the peak M&A transaction value of \$120 billion in 2021 and also saw the highest growth of 48% over 2020. However, in periods where sentiments in the sector are positive, the upstream leads M&A activities while during a bear run, the downstream sector records the highest transactions with the upstream sector lagging.

Recently, the EIA outlined that it expects the Brent crude oil to rise to \$116 per barrel for the second quarter of 2022, while gasoline prices are expected to average about \$4.10 per gallon during the same quarter and then decline thereafter. If realised, the average 2022 oil and gas prices would be the highest average price since 2014. The price volatility revealed the response of M&A activities in the O&G value chain to oil prices. However, the recent (2021–2022) high volatilities in O&G prices have been attributed to the war between the Russians and the Ukraine.

In the KPMG survey (2020), business leaders were with the view that their appetite for M&As could be dampened by a number of factors, including high valuations, inflation, and a lack of attractive targets to buy from. Another concern for some investors is the possibility of the increased cost of capital and potential tax increases. The global M&A patterns over the last 10 years are likely to be influenced by a combination of macroeconomic and microeconomic factors, including industry factors, price progression, and economic factors. We will discuss these factors in turn.

15.5.1 Industry-Specific Factors

Many empirical studies (e.g., Özgür and Wirl, 2020; Kviklys, 2013) rank industry-specific factors as the major driver of M&A activities in the O&G sector. This is mainly due to the extent to which political, institutional, and legal constraints weigh-in on the production costs and profitability of oil and gas companies, especially those in exploration and production (E&P) (Özgür and Wirl, 2020).

Constraints including infrastructure, political challenges, and policy uncertainties affect O&G companies' ability to operate at full capacity. In many oil-producing countries, where a government agency (such as the National Oil Company in Egypt and Libya) is the primary off taker of hydrocarbons, O&G exploration companies face political risk. Changes in political regime could lead to changes to the system in place. Additionally, transitional challenges could affect off-take agreements and expose companies to counterparty risk, having an effect on receivables, cash collections, and thus cash flows (Deloitte, 2021). Political uncertainties also emanate from uncertainties surrounding fiscal terms and royalties on offer from the local government, which also affect productivity, revenues, and, eventually, profitability (both at the initiation stage and renewal of contracts (Deloitte, 2021; KPMG, 2020). This in turn impacts the attractiveness of M&A deals in countries with such political risk exposures.

O&G industries are typically major drivers of economic growth and government revenue in oil- and gas-producing countries. O&G companies sometimes become easy targets for boosting government tax revenues. The uncertainties that surround the tax regime for oil companies are a major source of political risk for O&G companies. For instance following the introduction of the 2010 Oil and Gas Tax Law in Iraq over the past few years, the country has changed its tax regime for O&G companies to enable it to generate more tax revenues. Such uncertainties affect O&G companies' willingness to engage in M&A deals, even when the economic motivations of such deals are strong. Oil and gas companies generally face complex tax regimes due to the interaction of domestic tax laws and cross-border tax agreements, as well as the consistently changing tax regimes. O&G companies are also sometimes susceptible to different authorities such as the Ministry of Oil and Ministry of Finance, having different interpretations and approaches to applying tax on oil and gas contracts. That said, oil and

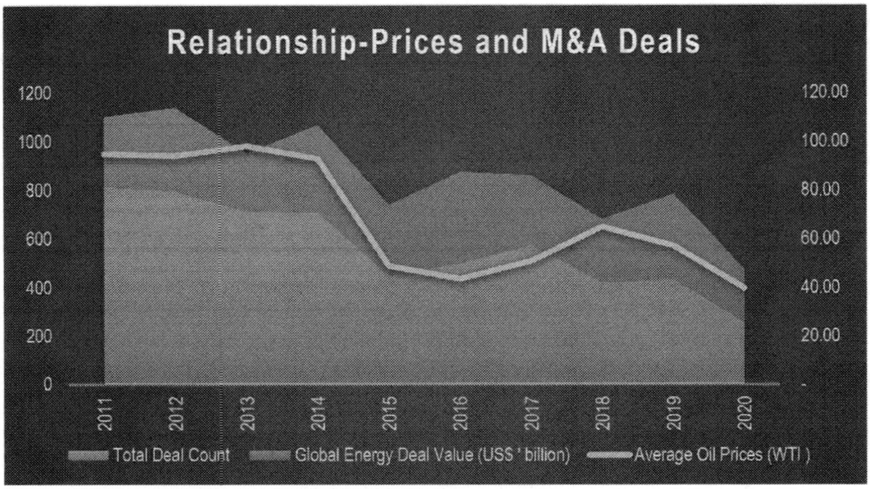

Figure 15.1 Relationship among oil prices, M&A deal count, and deal value in the O&G sector[1]

Source: Authors' construction based on KPMG Survey (2020) and Bos et al. (2018)

gas companies also benefit from some of wider tax exemptions which may also be available under certain government contracts, such as exemption from stamp duties, indirect taxes, withholding taxes, and customs duties.

15.5.2 Price Progression

By looking into past data, we find that spot prices and future price expectations of oil and gas affect M&A deals in the oil and gas sector (Bos et al., 2018). In the middle of the COVID-19 pandemic when prices plunged to approximately $20 per barrel, M&A activities dropped significantly by over 40% (in 2020). Figure 15.1, which compares price progression to M&A deals from 2011 to 2020, confirms the strong positive relationship between oil and gas prices and M&A deals within the sector.

When oil and gas prices fall below breakeven points, companies in the sector shift focus from acquisition and growth to preservation of free cash flow, capitalizing on cost synergies and strengthening the balance sheet in the face of heightening liquidity challenges and other disruptive forces. At the peak of the oil and gas crises in 2020, many O&G companies, including Tullow Oil, embarked on downsizing and other restructuring activities to enable them stay afloat and generate sufficient cash to meet their financial obligations and generate value to their shareholdings.

M&A activities during oil price bears are driven by other factors such as the existence of a sustainable strategy for profitable growth, the pursuit of cost efficiency, superior digital strategy to reduce R&D, and personnel costs and opportunities to divest distressed assets (IHS, 2019, PWC, 2018). Several empirical studies corroborate this position. For instance Ng and Donker (2013) conclude that energy reserves and prices cause and affect takeover activity, value, and performance. Acquirers are motivated to purchase reserves, while targets are motivated to sell on the basis of market timing. Additionally, Hsu et al. (2017) advance that industry-specific factors, such as oil prices, are the most important factors influencing M&A investments in the oil and gas industry.

15.5.3 Economic Motivations

The economic motivations include synergies, price consideration, and scale. The merged entity benefits from cost ***Synergies*** because it can operate more efficiently and exploit economies of scale. When companies within the same industry engage in horizontal combinations, they can eliminate redundant machinery and personnel, which enable the merged entity to operate near to, or at, capacity and thus benefit from economies of scale and reduced cost per unit of production. With respect to ***Price Considerations***, vertical forward integration offers synergies through the elimination of middlemen. This enables the company to avoid the extra layer of price middlemen add to the product and thus offer the product to clients at better prices. Backward integration allows for better supply and pricing of raw material, which help to constrain production cost. In terms of ***Scale***, business combinations result in larger companies than either of the original entities. In addition to the benefits of economies of scale as discussed earlier, scale affords a company visibility and enables it to have a stronger negotiation power with its suppliers, creditors, and buyers. This can boost a company's clientele base, reduce cost of inputs, and lead to greater profitability.

15.6 Causes of Failed Mergers and Acquisitions in the Oil and Gas Industry

The causes of failed mergers and acquisitions include limited owner involvement, overpaying for the transaction, integration problems, and unexpected external factors.

15.6.1 Limited Owner Involvement

Post-merger, the combined entity will be managed by the managers of the acquirer. Thus, it is important for the acquiring company to be actively involved in the entire transaction, from selecting a company with good fit to pricing and negotiating the deal. Managers often leave the M&A process to investment banks to handle. This leads to the failure of the merged entity, if the business selected is not a good fit and the synergies expected are not realised. Additionally, the failure of the managers to plan for the merged entity and design a post-merger strategy for the merged entity could result in a failed merger.

15.6.2 Overpaying for the Transaction

Bullish and overzealous investment banks may overestimate the synergies and assets of the target company, leading to extreme valuation and pricing of the deal. Additionally, failure to conduct effective due diligence may not expose hidden liabilities and thus lead to overpricing the assets of the target company. The fact that the acquirer depends on the target for information in the due diligence process also creates agency problems. Overpaying leads to value destruction which could lead the merger to fail.

15.6.3 Integration Problems

Differences in culture, geopolitical uncertainty, operational procedures and processes of the individual entities can create an avenue for integration problems, which may cause the merger to fail. For instance Russia's military invasion in Ukraine has made an already tight oil market even tighter and can cause integration problems. An integration plan, which identifies key employees, critical projects, core products and services, sensitive processes and designs a clear integration plan for them, is required to ensure a successful merger. Uncertainties surrounding the merger could also disrupt productivity and affect employee morale and efficiency. It is important for the management to clearly communicate their merger and integration strategy to deal with these problems. Failure to do these could result in a failed merger.

15.6.4 Unexpected External Factors

Adverse economic conditions, such as oil price crash, high financing costs, high unemployment costs, and pandemics such as COVID-19, could cause an otherwise successful merger to fail. It is important for managers to consider the worst-case scenario in designing the post-merger strategy for the merged entity. For instance the combination of geopolitical uncertainty, trade controls, inflationary pressures, and focus on shareholder returns can cause the merger to fail. For example the events of early 2022 have significantly affected the oil and gas industry as geopolitical uncertainty resulting from the Russian military invasion in Ukraine and Omicron-induced demand and investment declines – including supply-chain disruptions and inflation – may impede O&G M&A, leading to a failure of a merger.

Box 15.1 shows Savannah Energy signing deals to acquire key assets in Africa.

Box 15.2 shows an analysis of an M&A event that happened between Eco (Atlantic) Oil and Gas and the Azinam Group in South Africa and Namibia.

Box 15.1 Merger and Acquisition Deals: Case of Savannah Energy and Petroleum Companies in Chad and Cameroon

This is an analysis of an M&A event where Savannah laid the groundwork to complete the acquisition of ExxonMobil's and Petronas' entire upstream and midstream asset portfolios in Chad and Cameroon.

Savannah Energy Plc is an oil and gas company involved in the exploration, development, and production of crude oil and natural gas in Nigeria. The company focused on the acquisition and development of unique upstream petroleum opportunities, and the company holds a license interest in the Agadem Rift Basin field in South Eastern Niger. The company has an 80% interest in assets of Campo Uquo, 51% interest in the Stubb Creek field, and an 80% interest in Accuga midstream assets in Southern Nigeria. The company is classified into three categories, namely: upstream, integrated gas, and downstream. Basically, they search for oil by using technical and commercial expertise, transport the crude oil, refine it, and finally expand operations in Africa.

The company has signed share purchase agreements with Exxon and Petronas to acquire the asset portfolios in Chad and Cameroon for a total of $626 million. The deals with Exxon and Petronas have values of $360 million and $266 million, respectively. It plans to finance the deal through the combination of debt and equity securities. The deal is to provide Savannah Energy a 75% controlling interest in Doba oil project and a 70% indirect controlling interest in the Chad–Cameroon export transportation system.

The SHT Petroleum Chad company will hold the remaining 25% interest in the Doba oil project, while its affiliates will indirectly hold the remaining share in the transportation system.

The oil and gas reserve of Savannah is expected to generate positive free cash flows and fiscal revenue for Chad and Cameroon for more than 25 years from now. In addition, the deals are expected to more than double the production level and reserve base.

Box 15.2 Mergers and Acquisitions: Case of Eco (Atlantic) Oil and Gas and Azinam Group

This is an analysis of a merger and acquisition event where Eco (Atlantic) Oil and Gas laid the groundwork to complete the acquisition of the Azinam Group (AG). Eco Atlantic acquired AG's portfolio of assets and expanded its offshore in South Africa and Namibia.

Eco Atlantic is an oil and gas exploration company focused on the acquisition and development of unique upstream petroleum opportunities, and the company primarily has listed on Toronto Stock Exchange. The company is classified into three categories, namely: upstream, integrated gas, and downstream.

The targeted company is the Azinam Group, which is a multinational corporation that engages in the discovery and exploration of oil and focuses on leveraging its strengths in seismic acquisition, processing, interpretation, and geoscience to create value for shareholders and partners. By consistently demonstrating the successful management strategies of its operations, the corporation has built a strong footprint in the South Africa and Namibia O&G industry.

In January 2022, Eco Atlantic announced its intention to acquire the Azinam Group when it signed a Memorandum of Understanding to pursue its objective in South Africa as well as a purchasing agreement to add more operations off South Africa and Namibia in 2022. In the beginning of 2022, Eco Atlantic announced that it had final approval from the TSX Venture Exchange as the sole owner of Azinam. The company expects to be operating a number of prospective licenses in Guyana, Namibia, and South Africa. Upon the completion of the acquisition of Azinam, Eco will take over its operations with a 50% interest in the joint venture.

15.7 Conclusion

Business combinations within the O&G sector are classified according to interrelationship of the merged entities, the form of integration, the method of acquisition, or the mode of payment. In the O&G sector, industry-specific factors – oil price trends, uncertainties surrounding tax regimes, and political uncertainties – rather than the typical economic motivations are the key drivers of M&A deals. An analysis of the price progression in the past 10 years and the M&A deal count and deal value have shown a strong relationship between M&A activities and oil and gas prices. In the peak of the COVID-19 pandemic when oil prices fell to their lowest levels in the past decade, M&A deal counts and deal values also fell to their lowest levels, especially within the first half of the year. Since then, M&A activities have picked up on the back of optimistic outlook for the industry as economies recover and life returns to normalcy.

Investment banks play a critical role in the M&A process, at both the buy-side and sell-side of the transaction. They identify potential buyers and sellers, lead the due-diligence process, conduct valuation, and lead the negotiation process for both acquirers and target companies. These notwithstanding, M&As sometimes fail due to limited involvement of the acquiring firm, integration problems, and overpaying for the transaction. These factors often prevent the acquirer from realising the synergies originally identified in the target company. As such, it is necessary for the acquiring company to be actively involved in the entire M&A process. It is also important that the acquirer designs a strong post-merger strategy to ensure a smooth consolidation of the two entities, post-merger. Finally, M&A of O&G companies should prioritise capital discipline, strengthening of balance sheet, and shareholder distributions over price-led growth and spending.

Notes

1 Table adapted from https://mymbaguide.com/kinds-business-combinations-advantages-disadvantages/

2 Source: Deloitte, MacroTrends.

References

Bos, M., Demirer, R. G. R., and Tiwari, A. (2018). Oil returns and volatility: The role of mergers and acquisitions. *Journal of Energy Economics*, 71, 62–69.

Deloitte (2021). *2021 Oil and gas M&A Outlook*. https://www2.deloitte.com/content/dam/Deloitte/us/Documents/mergers-acqisitions/us-2021-Oil_And_Gas-MA_Outlook_3.6rev_02_22_21_FINAL.pdf

Deloitte (2022). 2022 oil and gas M&A outlook. Hsu, K, Wright, M., Zhu, Z (2017). What motivates mergers and acquisitions in the upstream oil and gas sectors in the US? *Energy Economics*, 65, 240–250.

IHS. (2019). IHS markit connect. https://connect.ihs.com/home.

KPMG. (2020). *The time has come. The KPMG survey of sustainability reporting 2020*. Amstelveen: KPMG International, pp. 1–64. https://home.kpmg/xx/en/home/insights/2020/11/the-time-has-come-survey-of-sustainability-reporting.html (accessed July 15, 2021).

Kviklys, D. (2013). Deloitte.com, *Journal of Business & Finance Librarianship*, 18(4), 343–35.

Ng. A, and Donker, H. (2013) Purchasing reserves and commodity market timing as takeover motivates in the oil and gas industry. *Journal of Energy Economics*, 37, pp. 167–181.

Özgür, S., and Wirl, F (2020). Cross-border mergers and acquisitions in the oil and gas industry: An overview. *Energies*, 13(21).

Pazarskis, M., Vogiatzogloy, M., Christodoulou, P., and Drogalas, G. (2006), Exploring the improvement of corporate performance after mergers – The case of Greece. *International Research Journal of Finance and Economics*, 6, 18–192.

PricewaterhouseCoopers (PWC) (2018). *The 21st annual global CEO survey*. https://www.pwc.com/gx/en/ceo-survey/2018/pwc-ceo-survey-report-2018.pdf (accessed 30 November, 2019).

16 Enterprise Risk Management in the Oil and Gas Industry

Evidence from a Developing Market

Elikplimi Komla Agbloyor, Emmanuel Joel Aikins Abakah, Susana Yamoah

16.1 Introduction

In the not-so-distant past (before the 1990s), companies used to manage risks on an 'individual' or 'silo' basis. For example market risks, operational risks, credit risks, and liquidity risk among others were seen as separate or stand-alone risks. These risks were therefore measured and managed separately without consideration of the organisation as a whole and the potential interaction of the various types of risk. Consequently, each risk had a separate head such as Head of Credit Risk, Head of Market Risk, and Head of Operational risk among others. However, there has been increasing recognition that such an approach is flawed. This is particularly so because various financial crises have shown that there can be malign interaction of risks. ERM takes into account that there are diversification effects, given that the correlation between different risks is usually less than 1. For example a market risk event can easily translate into a credit risk event. For example a fall in the stock price of a company can lead to it postponing investments and losing the confidence of its customers comprising its ability to repay its debt to a lender. As another example, an operational error can trigger a market risk event. For example inadvertently choosing a call option instead of a put option or failure to specify a correct stop loss order can easily trigger a market risk event. Organisations have therefore realised the need to manage risks in a holistic manner. Consequently, most organisations that practice enterprise risk management usually appoint a C-Suite level executive to oversee the management of risk. This executive works closely with management and the board to achieve the strategic goals of the firm. Due to the fact that ERM manages risks holistically, ERM may save costs as only the residual risks of the firm are hedged. Thus, it prevents the firm from over-hedging and using unnecessary or excessive risk cover.

The question that then arises is that what exactly is ERM and what are the benefits and challenges involved in adopting an ERM approach? Lam (2014) defines ERM as a comprehensive and integrated framework for managing key risks in order to achieve business objectives, minimise

DOI: 10.4324/9781003315056-19

unexpected earnings volatility, and maximise firm value. ERM has several benefits. These include enhancing the competitiveness of the firm, increasing shareholder value, reducing the cost of risk management due to, for example, identification of natural hedges (Eckles et al., 2014), increasing the likelihood of meeting strategic objectives, optimizing risk and return, reducing the likelihood and the average cost of financial distress, improving relations with regulators, and improving the credit ratings of the firm (Barbeau, 2019). Indeed, Florio and Leoni (2017) show that Italian firms that had advanced ERM systems achieved higher financial performance and market evaluation. Callahan and Soileau (2017) find similar results which indicate that ERM maturation has a positive effect on operational performance. In addition, Eckles et al. (2014) found that firms that adopted ERM had lower stock volatility and these effects were stronger over time. The effective implementation of ERM depends on the culture of the organisation. Indeed, ERM may not succeed or is not suitable for all organisations. Organisations that are not open and transparent may not benefit from ERM. Also, if the board and management are not committed to the implementation of ERM, it is unlikely to succeed (see e.g. Fraser et al., 2022). Further, when the focus of ERM is reporting/governance/control without focusing on problem solving, providing support and cultural change ERM is not likely to succeed.

Excluding the financial sector, the Oil and Gas industry is one of most risk-prone industries globally. Examples of risks that could occur in this sector include a major oil spillage, a breakdown of workplace safety leading to injury or death of employees, a fall in the price of oil and gas, a severe supply or demand shock (such as COVID-19), and geopolitical risks among others. Consequently, the application of ERM is germane and of primary importance in this industry. In this chapter, therefore, we examine the practice of ERM in a developing country context. The rest of this chapter is structured as follows: Section 16.2 sets the stage for the rest of the chapters by highlighting the essential aspects of the COSO ERM framework and how this may be applicable in the Oil and Gas industry. In Section 16.3, we discuss Corporate Philosophy and Culture. In Section 16.4, we present a country case study on Ghana to illustrate the practice of ERM in a developing country context. Finally, we conclude the chapter in Section 16.5.

16.2 The COSO ERM Framework

Enterprise risk management (ERM) which is highly strategic in nature (Ward, 2006) with an array of components (Psica, 2008) in recent decades has emerged as the ideal approach to managing business risk effectively and efficiently over time (Walker et al., 2002). In particular, ERM, which is purposefully broad in its definition (Quinn, 2006), enables organisations in making cognisant risk-based strategic decisions (Fadun, 2013). The seminal idea leading to the development of a new theory on managing business risk was propagated by the Committee of Sponsoring Organisation of the Treadway Commission (COSO), and the fundamental principles and concept of ERM framework are explained through the 'COSO Cube' (Beasley et al., 2010). The primary focus in this section is the 'COSO ERM Framework' which is the utmost commonly used starting point for implementing an ERM initiative (EuropeanCEO, 2001) and one of the two broadly accepted benchmarks used by organisations in their risk management agenda (Li, 2018).

The initial mission of COSO established in the United States in the mid-1980s by five major accounting institutes was to study financial reporting and propose recommendations to prevent fraud (Moeller, 2007; Anderson, 2017). This model which has become a preferred model (Muralidhar, 2010) released its first standard in 1992 as an *Internal Control Integrated Framework* with the primary goal of providing reasonable assurance of achieving organisational objectives in four areas, that is *strategy, compliance, operations, and reporting,* in the spirit of averting corporate disasters and maximising firm value (De Loach, 2003; Beasley and Hermanson, 2004; Quinn, 2006). Following that COSO's initial framework placed a strong emphasis on audit as the key driver of enterprise risk management, after its release, organisations shortly realised there was a gap in the internal control framework of 1992 even though it helped in reducing risks around regulatory compliance and fraudulent behaviour (COSO, 2004). In particular, there was no way to assess and identify the type of risks organisations had to put controls around. This recognition in alignment with demands for better risk management and corporate governance standards after the Enron scandal caused COSO to develop its *Enterprise Risk Management Integrated Framework in 2004* as shown in Figure 16.1.

The 2004 COSO ERM emerged as an expanded version of the internal control framework in that it goes beyond financial statements to include reports throughout the enterprise (Scott, 2004; COSO, 2004). In summary, the COSO ERM of 2004 which had eight interconnected components including *internal environment, objective setting, event identification, risk assessment, risk response, control activities, information and communication, and monitoring* focused mainly on what could be audited rather than uncovering opportunities and threats, which is where the real importance in ERM lies (Gramling and Myers, 2006). Consequently, the framework was a perfect fit for firms where business risk was promulgated by audit. Given that the 2004 COSO ERM retained a number of the features of the original framework with much emphasis on strategy, practitioners expounded that the COSO ERM focused mainly on internal controls.

To address this concern, COSO in 2017 updated the standard in partnership with PwC with the title *Enterprise Risk Management – Integrating with Strategy and Performance.* The 2017 COSO ERM framework incorporated some significant changes (COSO, 2017; Dias, 2017; Anderson, 2017). The updated 2017 framework placed a greater emphasis on the significance of integrating risk concerns when creating and implementing strategies to achieve the organisations' goals while the earlier framework focused mainly on the connection between risk management and strategy. Another key difference between the

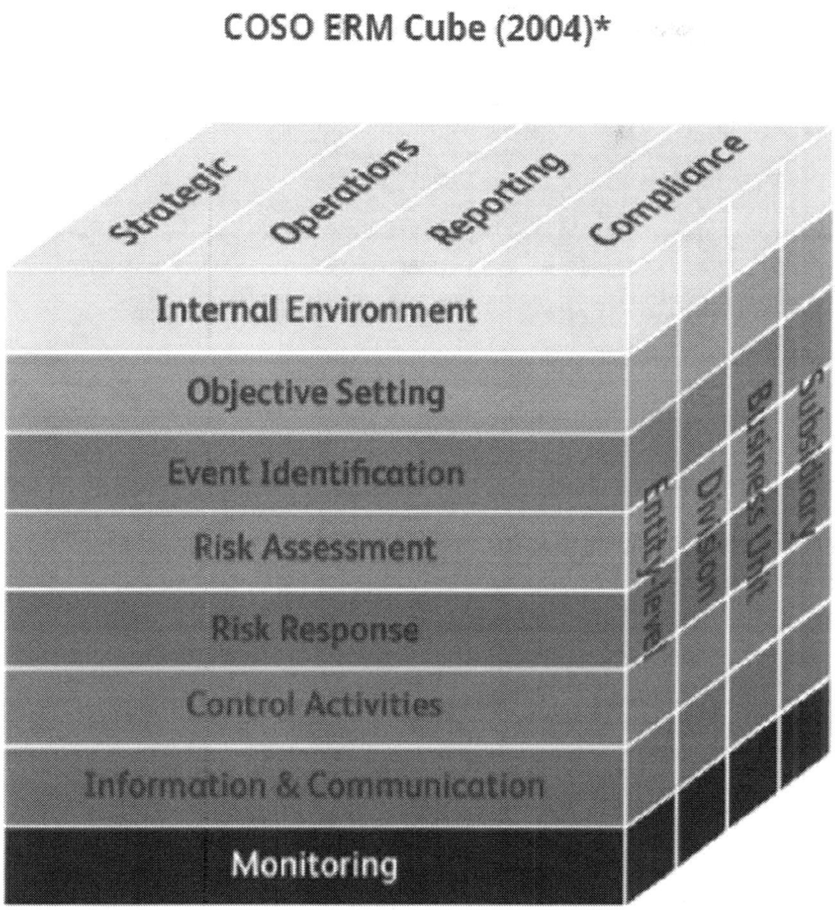

Figure 16.1 2004 COSO ERM cube

Source: COSO 2004

2004 and 2017 COSO ERM framework lies in the structure (Prewett and Terry, 2018). Rather than using a cube to demonstrate the linkage between the four categories and the eight components of business risk management approaches, the 2017 ERM framework used a ribbon-type diagram that links the now five categories throughout the lifecycle of an organisation as illustrated in Figure 16.2. The framework explains that the three ribbons denote common processes that 'run through the organisation' (including Strategy/Objective-Setting, Performance, and Review/Revision) while the remaining two ribbons depict the supportive mechanisms of ERM framework which includes Governance/Culture, Information and Communication, and Reporting). In summary, the COSO ERM framework of 2017 placed more emphasis on culture

Figure 16.2 2017 COSO ERM components

Source: COSO 2017

and dives more deeper into other concepts like risk appetite and integrating risk management in all areas of the organisation. As a result, the new framework currently includes 20 principles spread throughout the five components.

16.3 Corporate Philosophy and Culture

Philosophy has been defined in so many contexts. It is sometimes used to refer to the guide for action or guiding principle. Other times, it may refer to the logical basis, reason, or rationale for something. The word philosophy originated from two Greek words – *philos* (loving) and *sophia* (wisdom/thought). Therefore, philosophy means the love of wisdom or thought. In general, philosophy can be seen as the way of thinking which is strongly loved that it translates to action and a way of life. Corporate philosophy looks at the thoughts and ideas of individuals in an organisation, which translate into the reason and how they do what they do. It expresses and explains the organisation's values, beliefs, vision, and mission and determines its relationship with its stakeholders – employees, customers, shareholders, suppliers, government, and the public at large. Corporate philosophy describes the operations of the company, the products and services offered, and how organised the company is to meet its goals. It sets the roadmap for the organisation.

Culture is the way of life of a people. Culture encompasses the customs, beliefs, norms, and ethics of a particular group. It shapes the attitudes and behaviours and defines what is encouraged, accepted, or rejected within a group of people. Every organisation also has its way of doing things, and this forms the culture within the organisation. A corporate or organisation's culture consists of shared beliefs and values established by leaders and then communicated and reinforced through various methods, eventually shaping employee perceptions, behaviours and understanding. It is the personality and character of the organisation.

Corporate culture can manifest itself in a variety of ways, including leadership behaviours, communication styles, and corporate celebrations. Corporate culture may be influenced by varied factors including the organisation's values, traditions, and structure, the leadership styles adopted, the system and processes by which work is carried out, and the behaviour and attitudes of employees.

Corporate philosophy expresses the values and beliefs of the organisation. These values and beliefs are manifested in behaviour; and behaviour forms the culture of the organisation which includes the way it deals and adapts with its changing environment – how it addresses risk and uncertainty, explores new possibilities, and approaches new and challenging situations. Effective risk management can only be achieved if there are appropriately structured internal control systems and governance. A key element in the internal control system and governance is the risk management philosophy of the organisation. A risk management philosophy looks at how an organisation considers risk and their shared beliefs and attitudes towards dealing with it in their day-to-day activities. An organisation's risk management philosophy sets the tone of the top management regarding its views of risk control and creates an atmosphere that influences employees' decision-making. A clear and consistent risk management philosophy from the top must permeate the organisation till it becomes part of the culture of the organisation. This will enhance the proactivity of employees in risk management and influence employees' perception, attitude, motivation, and acceptance of an ERM programme.

16.4 Case Study: GOIL Company Limited (GOIL)

Fraser et al. (2022) document various questions that risk practitioners were interested in when setting up and operating a well-functioning ERM system. We adopted many of these questions in our interview guide and the questionnaires that we used to build our case study are outlined in Appendices 1 and 2. We carried out an interview with the Risk Officer at GOIL Company Limited, Accra, Ghana.

16.4.1 Company Background

GOIL Company Limited, known as GOIL, is a state-owned Ghanaian oil and gas company, formed on 14 June 1960. Currently, it holds the place of Ghana's top oil marketing company and is the only indigenous owned petroleum marketing company in Ghana. The Company's mission focuses on marketing quality petroleum and other energy products and services in a safe, ethical, healthy, environmentally friendly, and socially responsible manner. The Company is manned by a management team including the Managing Director/Group Chief Executive.

16.4.2 Why ERM Adoption Is Suitable for GOIL?

Risk management has been practiced for decades at GOIL on the silo basis. However, because GOIL suffered a couple of debacles coupled with increasing explosions in Accra (e.g. Circle and Dome) in recent years which cost the company fortunes and reputational damage, top management were forced to reconsider the risk management practices of the company. Like many organisations, an adverse event prompted the top management to move towards ERM, given that the environment and the context were opportune. So ERM was embraced because of the gaps top management may have envisaged in the silo approach of their risk management since the company was established. The executive board and the board of trustees endorsed the establishment of the ERM program and made the original decision to hire a risk management professional. In July 2018, a risk professional was hired to champion the ERM initiative at GOIL. The scope of the ERM implementation for GOIL is clearly defined. The ERM mission is to provide corporate leadership, methodology, and tools to support operational and strategic management with their responsibility to optimise risk-taking decisions. In principle, it leads a process for the management of all risks.

When the Risk Officer (RO) was hired to begin the process of rethinking risk management, there was limited information and literature about how one might consider and manage all of the critical risks GOIL does or could face. While the acute problem of these large vicarious catastrophes in the industry has substantially been mitigated by reforms, the enterprise risk management initiative has evolved over time as the external and internal risk profile changed. The maturation of GOIL's ERM program has been a dynamic process. However, even though there have been rough spots and learning curves, GOIL has been working within an ERM framework in the past 2 years. The RO noted that the ERM program is progressing steadily (about 50% to completion). As per the structure of the ERM programme at GOIL, the RO reports to the Chief Internal Auditor (CIA) who heads both the risk management department and audit department. The CIA is a member of the company's executive board. The risk department is headed by the RO who is the ERM champion. The RO feels that he has the full support of the executive teams, given that the board approves the risk management department to be autonomous and has adequate resources. GOIL has a clear strategic plan and an operational plan and sets up regular meetings to ensure the involvement of risk management in the process. In the risk register, the link between strategic objectives and risk is identified and managed. The risk register catalogues all major risks for every unit including operations, finance, legal, etc. When the RO arrived at GOIL, he had these goals: 'Tidy up' the risk register that contained 'non-risks' and 'risk controls' instead of just active risks; reduce the number of risks and bring more focus on risk mitigation and make sure that systematic project risk management is in place for major projects. The RO provides risk reports to the whole executive team every 6 months. The periodic risk report is well accepted by management who view it as an opportunity to enhance their performance.

16.4.3 ERM Process at GOIL

The risk management department which is independent from the audit department is developing the ERM framework on the basis of COSO framework. According to the RO, he is trying to sensitise the entire staff to be risk conscious, but it is a work-in-progress and as a result rates the ERM processes at 50% at this point because almost everybody knows that there is a risk department, but it must go beyond knowing a risk to the point where every department to the board room must also be risk conscious. On the progress and accomplishment of the ERM adoption, the RO opined that before he joined GOIL as their ERM champion, the structure had the IT, research, and planning sections of the company combined as a unit. However, through structural conversation with the executive board, the research department unit has conveniently been hived off over the last year. The next step according to the RO is to separate the IT from the planning unit. Additionally, in the case of strategy, he notes that only few heads of department, about two or three in most cases, get the opportunity to engage external consultants in developing the company's strategy historically. In effect, there is information overload when the strategy is done, and as a result most heads of department struggle to work with the strategy. With the adoption of ERM, the risk strategy is developed comprehensively with a broad-based strategy involving all heads of department. To alleviate explosions of buildings, the Health Safety Security and Environment (HSSE) units have been established through the ERM framework. In addition, to address security issues and not explosions and spillage alone, the company hired a trained retired army officer to be part of the HSSE units to account for the Quality part of the ERM framework. Hence, the unit is now known as the HSSEQ units. The RO noted that his strategy is to lead from behind and that too many things are happening as a result of GOIL's adoption of an ERM framework. The progress according to the RO was slowed by the outbreak of COVID-19. However, the ERM process is coming up excellently and yielding significant results, given that the ERM initiative at GOIL is deployed in the context of creating a culture of yes. For example budget impairment is a major risk to GOIL. The ERM budget changes worksheet and analysis tool not only helps determine the risks of budget cuts but also includes questions related to opportunities that could increase revenue or produce alternative revenue-generating opportunities. Many of the ERM tools also analyse processes to determine where things are over-controlled. By eliminating duplication, introducing mechanising processes, and streamlining operations, resources can be shifted from one area to another to increase opportunities and value.

16.4.4 The Challenges Associated with ERM Initiative at GOIL

Few of the major challenges is to maintain the attention of all involved, to keep the risk management process afloat and relevant to objectives, and to prevent it from being linked to the view that it is only about events/accidents. In management meetings, risks are managed but not necessarily consciously and systematically – this is the added benefit of a formalised risk management approach. However, sustaining ERM over time does not come naturally and requires a strong personal engagement, and engagement of everyone, especially the new employees. The quantification of results, or lack thereof, is not really an issue at GOIL as risk management has become a natural way of doing business. However, GOIL understands it still is in the learning curve for ERM. Also, the procurement process is reviewed and risk management is checked with the tender offer process (mostly IT due to the specific activity). The RO believes that, on the whole, the executive level is more aligned with risk management issues. However, culture and political environments appear to be a key hindrance to the ERM framework coupled with board busyness. Even though the board supports the ERM adoption, the pace is slow, given that board members sit on several boards in other companies and, as a result, are extremely busy most of the times to engage the RO extensively.

16.5 Conclusion

This chapter has discussed and presented results on ERM implementation within the oil and gas industry in Ghana using GOIL Company Limited (GOIL) as a case study. The chapter concludes on the basis of the interview with the RO of the company that ERM practices in the oil and gas industry in Ghana vary significantly between the cases and across the various units of the company. Interdisciplinary approach is key to the effectiveness and success of ERM adoption. ERM requires abilities not only to be a generalist in relation to the value chain, but also to be a specialist with a focus on risks to review, develop, and manage the risks portfolio of the company. In particular, it requires collaboration from all sections of the company including finance, legal, technical, IT, strategic, marketing, human resources, quality assurance, and plant security. ERM is essential in managing uncertainty and optimising performance – it is not a panacea, but all the same builds business resilience. The key findings in the chapter indicated that ERM initiative and implementation by the company, which commenced about 4 years ago have the full support of top management and that the company has an in-house department for ERM to identify risk factors and objectives of enterprise risk management. Additionally, results suggest that even though the ERM initiative of the company is evolving with about 50% of work done so far, the ERM initiative and adoption have improved the business outlook and performance of the company in terms of cost of capital, value of shareholders, and profitability. Thus, ERM is considered as a strategic instrument for the success of the company according to the RO. On the other hand, if properly implemented, ERM initiative at GOIL according to the RO will mature over time from being a tactical solution to a strategic imperative with the ultimate goal of improved performance. On the challenges, the findings revealed that the critical success factors for the effective implementation of ERM include top management commitment, culture, and risk appetite.

References

Anderson, D. (2017). COSO ERM: Getting risk management right: Strategy and organizational performance are the heart of the updated framework. *Internal Auditor*, 74(5), 38–43.

Barbeau, J. M. (2019). *Risk management in blood transfusion medicine*. London: Elsevier Health Sciences.

Beasley, M. S., Branson, B. C., Hancock, B. V. (2010). Current state of enterprise risk oversight and market perceptions of COSO's ERM framework. In *COSO's 2010 Report on ERM*. New York: Committee of Sponsoring Organizations of the Treadway Commission.

Beasley, M. S., and Hermanson, R. D. (2004). Going beyond Sarbanes-Oxley compliance: Five keys to creating value. *CPA Journal*, Vol. 74 No. 6, pp. 11–13.

Callahan, C., and Soileau, J. (2017). Does enterprise risk management enhance operating performance? *Advances in Accounting*, 37, 122–139.

Committee of Sponsoring Organizations of the Treadway Commission (COSO). (2004). *Enterprise risk management – Integrated framework*. https://www.coso.org/Publications/ERM/COSO_ERM_ExecutiveSummary.pdf.

Committee of Sponsoring Organizations of the Treadway Commission (COSO). (2017). *Enterprise risk management – Integrated framework*. https://www.coso.org/pages/erm.aspx (accessed 11 February, 2022).

Dias, A. A. D. S. P. (2017). A more effective audit after COSO ERM 2017 or after ISO 31000: 2009? *Revista Perspectiva Empresarial*, 4(2), 73–82.

Eckles, D. L., Hoyt, R. E., and Miller, S. M. (2014). Reprint of: The impact of enterprise risk management on the marginal cost of reducing risk: Evidence from the insurance industry. *Journal of Banking & Finance*, 49, 409–423.

European CEO. (2001). *Building shareholder value by building a culture of risk awareness*. New York: Risk Management, GARP Publication.

Fadun, O. S. (2013). Risk management and risk management failure: Lessons for business enterprises. *International Journal of Academic Research in Business and Social Sciences*, 3(2), 225.

Fraser, J. R., Quail, R., and Simkins, B. J. (2022). Questions that are asked about enterprise risk management by risk practitioners. *Business Horizons*, 65(3), 251–260.

Florio, C., and Leoni, G. (2017). Enterprise risk management and firm performance: The Italian case. *The British Accounting Review*, 49(1), 56–74.

Gramling, A. A., and Myers, P. M. (2006). Internal auditing's role in ERM: As organizations lay their enterprise risk groundwork, many auditors are taking on management's oversight responsibilities, new research finds. *Internal Auditor*, 63(2), 52–58.

Lam, J. (2014). *Enterprise risk management: From incentives to controls*. Hoboken, NJ: John Wiley & Sons.

Li, L. (2018). A study on enterprise risk management and business performance. *Journal of Financial Risk Management*, 7(1), 123.

Moeller, R. R. (2007). *COSO enterprise risk management: Understanding the new integrated ERM framework*. Hoboken, NJ: John Wiley & Sons.

Muralidhar, K. (2010). Enterprise risk management in the Middle East oil industry: An empirical investigation across GCC countries. *International Journal of Energy Sector Management*.

Prewett, K., and Terry, A. (2018). COSO's updated enterprise risk management framework—A quest for depth and clarity. *Journal of Corporate Accounting & Finance*, 29(3), 16–23.

Psica, A. (2008). The right fit: Auditing ERM frameworks; Enterprise risk management reviews provide assurance that the organization has a sound basis for assessing and mitigating risks. *Internal Auditor*, 65(2), 50–56.

Quinn, L. R. (2006). COSO at a crossroad: The folks who helped you weather SOX 404 now face their own moment of truth: Is COSO ERM just what the doctor ordered?. *Strategic Finance*, 42–50.

Scott, A. (2004). COSO ERM framework released. *Internal Auditor*, 61(5), 17–19.

Walker, P. L., Shenkir, W. G., and Barton, T. L. (2002). ERM: Pulling it all together. In *The IIA research foundation*. Altamonte Springs, FL.

Ward, J. (2006, August). ERM: Evolving, resonating and maturing down under. *RatingsDirect*. https://www.alacrastore.com/cgi-bin/alacraswitchISAPI.dll

Appendix 1

Interview Guide

- Do you know the difference between managing risk on a silo basis and ERM?
- Does your organisation use ERM?
- When did your organisation adopt an ERM approach?
- What were the reasons for adopting ERM?
- Were external consults involved in assisting the firm to develop an ERM system?
- Did your organisation have an ERM champion at the time of adoption? What was the position of this person and what role did they play?
- Can you explain the stages or process of ERM adoption at your organisation?
- Can you explain the ERM structure at your organisation?
- Can you highlight examples of how you have used ERM in your organisation and how it was beneficial? What were the challenges?
- Does your firm have a Chief Risk Officer (CRO)?
- If so, can you explain the reporting structure of the CRO?
- What are some of the benefits that your organisation has achieved from adopting ERM?
- What are some of the challenges that you have encountered in adopting or using ERM?

Appendix 2

No.	*Item*	*Response*	*Score (1–5)*
1	ERM adoption had the support of the board		
2	ERM adoption had the support of the CEO		
3	ERM adoption had the support of top management		
	The organisation has an ERM policy		
4	The board has established a risk appetite for the firm, and this is widely known		
5	The capital held by the firm is linked to its risk level		
6	The organisation has a risk register which catalogues the major risks		
7	The organisation has a Chief Risk Officer		
8	ERM focuses on	a. Strategic risks b. Operational risks c. Financial risks d. All of the above	
9	In quantifying and managing risks, the firm focuses on	a. Quantitative approach b. Qualitative approach c. Both quantitative and qualitative approaches	
10	The firm runs risk workshops at least once a year for	a. Major projects b. Specific risks c. Business planning	
11	The organisation employs the three lines of defence		
12	The lines of business are primarily responsible for identifying risk		

No.	*Item*	*Response*	*Score (1–5)*
13	The risk management function works with the business units to review their assumptions and to provide the necessary support		
14	Audit reviews the work done by risk management		
15	The enterprise risk function is separate from internal audit		
16	Enterprise risk management is seen as a support function		
17	Enterprise risk management is seen as a monitoring and control function		
18	In terms of the culture of the organisation, there is transparency and openness such that there is exchange of ideas from bottom of the organisation to the top and vice-versa		
19	How would you rate your ERM programme compared to your industry?		
20	How would you rate your ERM programme compared to global standards?		

17 Derivative Markets for Oil and Gas Transactions

Godfred Amewu, Joshua Yindenaba Abor, and Victor Murinde

17.1 Introduction

Businesses are faced with different types of risks, which include political, credit, operational, liquidity, and market risk. These risk exposures, if not properly managed, can immensely affect the earnings of the business and possibly lead to business termination. Firms operating in the oil and gas industry are highly prone to market risk, although the other risks cannot be ignored. Market risk is the risk exposure caused by unexpected changes in macroeconomic indicators such as exchange, interest rate, and commodity and equity prices. In dealing with such volatilities, investors and oil and gas companies have used various traditional tools such as diversification, inventory, insurance, and long-term contracts to manage the exposures. However, these tools have not been effective in dealing with price volatilities.

The Oil and Gas industry is one of the few industries that have highly interconnected with other sectors or industries. If risk exposures in the Oil and Gas sector are not well managed, a wide range of other investments such as stock and debt will be affected, resulting in immense consequences on local and global economies. Derivatives are one of the innovative, flexible, and popular tools in dealing with market risk exposures in the energy sector. Derivatives are financial securities that do not represent ownership but derive their existence on the basis of an underlying asset such as oil and gas prices. The most widely used derivative instruments in managing risk in the energy (oil and gas) sector are forwards contracts, futures contracts, options, and swaps. They allow firms or investors to transfer an identified risk to others who are willing to bear it and profit from taking the risk. These tools are most preferred because of their effectiveness and flexibility in managing market risk exposures. There is a wide range of variants of these derivative instruments designed for the specific needs of the investor.

This chapter seeks to provide a detailed understanding of trading and the use of financial risk management tools in the oil and gas sector. It also unearths the challenges, prospects, policy decisions, and the usefulness of derivations in hedging market risks.

DOI: 10.4324/9781003315056-20

17.2 Risk Exposure for Oil and Gas Companies

The oil and gas industry, just like any other industry, faces some risks. These risks include operational risk, liquidity risk, political risk, price risk, interest rate risk, foreign exchange risk, etc. Operational risk refers to the risks associated with the possible failure in the use of equipment, machines, or technology. This risk also concerns the risk of fraud. Liquidity risk, which is another form of risk, encompasses the risk that a firm may not be able to sell its commodities at the quoted price. A firm's inability to pay its utility bills or meet short-term obligations can also be classified as liquidity risk. Political risk is a type of risk faced by investors in the industry due to political changes, instability, or political decisions in a country. The political risk expands to the possible variations in returns due to the promulgation of new laws or regulations or the dispossession of properties by the government, otherwise known as expropriation.

However, commodity price risk, interest rate risk, foreign exchange risk, and credit/default risks are more common with transactions relating to the oil and gas industries. These risks are described in relation to the oil and gas transactions as follows.

Commodity price risk – This is a form of market risk. It is the most common form of risk in the oil and gas industries due to the high volatility in the prices of commodities offered by firms in the oil and gas industries such as crude oil and natural gas. Commodity price risk is the probability that the price of a commodity will change in a manner that leads to economic losses. This risk is driven by the activities on the external market, and it is therefore beyond the control of the entity. In the oil and gas industry, commodity price risk arises mostly in situations where an entity contracts to trade crude oil or natural gas sometime in the future. Determining the price at which the crude oil or natural gas will sell in future is also a difficult thing to do due to the uncertainties surrounding price volatility. Commodity price fluctuations can cause significant business challenges, influencing operation and production costs, the value of assets, product pricing, earnings, profitability, and credit availability. With the rapid fluctuations in crude oil prices, it is critical for entities to employ price management strategies and techniques across their value chain in order to ensure effective management of their financial performance. Firms in the oil and gas industries use a variety of derivatives instruments to mitigate price risks. This enables businesses to forecast or predict their cash flows and earnings for the purposes of planning, financial commitments, and the execution of profitable projects.

Interest rate risk – This risk refers to the volatility of the firm's value as a result of changes in interest rate. Interest rate risk encompasses interest rate fluctuations normally due to changes in monetary policies. These interest rate movements have a greater impact on long-term fixed-income securities such as bonds, costs associated with financing and hedging of forward contracts. In situations where the fluctuations in interest rates prolong over a significant time period, they could have a strong impact on the price an entity can realise from a new forward oil or gas contract. This is as a result of the possible differences that may arise from the forward and spot prices of the commodities.

Foreign exchange rate risk – One of the most significant types of risk exposure for oil companies is foreign exchange rate risk. This risk arises due to a change in the price of one currency in relation to another. It is also known as currency risk. In order to avoid the impact of price volatility, firms may hedge the oil/gas price risk. In doing so, an entity may face foreign exchange rate risk primarily because oil and gas contracts are mostly priced in US dollars. For oil and gas companies that operate across different countries, fluctuations in the foreign exchange rate may have severe consequences. This may be so because the firms may generate revenue and incur costs/expenditure in different countries which use different currencies. Therefore, the cash flows from the firm's operations can be greatly affected by foreign exchange risk.

Credit/counterparty risk – Credit or counterparty risk is the risk of a loss occurring as a result of a party's failure to comply with the terms and conditions of any financial contract, most especially the failure to make required loan payments. This risk is lower in oil and gas transactions conducted on organised trading exchanges (markets) than the less regulated over-the-counter (OTC) markets. In an organised market, contracts are well facilitated through the mark-to-market process, which requires margin deposits that are adjusted daily. This procedure increases the likelihood that derivative pricing will accurately reflect the current value. In oil and gas transactions, credit risk manifests in two forms: settlement risk and mark-to-market risk. The risk that the buyer of a commodity (oil or gas) will be unable to pay the required consideration despite taking physical delivery of the products is known as settlement risk. On the other hand, mark-to-market risk arises when the spot price of oil and gas is less than the fixed price agreed to in the swap contract. This may provide an incentive to the counterparty to renege on the contract and default on its obligations. Mark-to-market risk is, therefore, specific to contracts with a fixed price irrespective of whether it is settled financially or physically. Exposure to credit or counterparty risk can have a negative impact on an entity's financials. As a result, it is critical for firms in the oil and gas industries to take steps to mitigate credit or counterparty risks in the transactions they undertake.

17.3 Risk Management without Derivatives

Firms in the oil and gas industry have an incentive to act to reduce price risk because it has the potential to reduce the firm's value. Managers can still hedge against price risk without using derivative instruments by diversifying, entering into long-term fixed-price contracts, and purchasing insurance contracts and inventory maintenance (see Berger and Ofek, 1995; Energy Information Administration, 2002).

Diversification – Diversification is a risk-reduction strategy that entails investing in a variety of different businesses. Diversification is most effective when the portfolio of businesses invested in is unrelated and the amount invested is properly allocated. It can be an effective way for a company to reduce its reliance on the success of a single project or business for cash inflows. Theoretically, all risks associated with a project can be eliminated through diversification. In practice, however, diversification frequently fails due to the high cost and complexity of managing multiple businesses. Diversification is ineffective at mitigating price risk.

Long-term fixed-price contracts – Long-term fixed-price contracts can also be used to hedge against risk exposures due to volatility or movement in prices. For example a crude oil-producing firm can enter into a long term contract with another company for the supply of crude oil at a fixed price of $50 per barrel (bbl) in 2022, $55/bbl in 2023, and say $60/bbl in 2024. Even with such hedging, there would still be some risk. If, as in the example given before, the spot market price for crude oil in 2022 is $40/bbl, the buyer may default on the contract because buying at that price means the firm will be less competitive because other firms may buy at $40/bbl. In contrast, if the price of crude oil rose to $60 in 2022, the seller (oil-producing firm) may choose to default on the contract. It is important to note that a breach of contract has consequences or costs associated with it.

Insurance contracts – Risk management can also be accomplished through the use of insurance contracts. It is possible for a firm to run into a loss of revenue to a breakdown or due to some other specific reason. To hedge against such losses, the firm's management may purchase an insurance contract that will provide indemnity (claim payments) if the unexpected occurs. By purchasing the insurance contract, the risk is transferred from the company to the insurer (insurance provider). The insured (oil and gas company) will be required to pay insurance premiums to the insurance company.

Inventory maintenance – One other way to hedge against future fluctuations in the prices of oil and gas is through inventory maintenance. Using this strategy, a company buys crude oil at the current spot price (say, $50/bbl) and holds it as inventory and a hedge against future price increases. If prices fall in future to $40/bbl, the firm would buy the crude oil from the open market. However, if the price of crude oil rises to $60/bbl, the company will not make any new purchases and will instead rely on inventory purchased earlier at a lower price of $50/bbl. This strategy could be costly due to the cost of inventory holding.

It is important to note that while diversification, long-term contracts, insurance, and inventory maintenance are tools for risk management, such traditional approaches are ineffective for managing price risk.

17.4 Risk Management with Derivatives

A derivative is a contract or financial instrument whose value depends on (i.e. contingent) the value of some underlying variable, usually the price of some other financial asset. Derivatives are contracts or financial instruments, which derive their value from that of an underlying asset. A derivative contract in itself does not represent ownership of the underlying asset, as it is in the case of a stock or a securitised asset. That is even though the derivative derives its value from an asset, the ownership of a derivative does not constitute the ownership of the asset. Examples of commonly used derivatives include forward contracts, futures contracts, options, warrants, and swaps. The underlying instrument in a derivative contract can be commodities such as crude oil, natural gas, wheat; currencies; interest rates; debt instruments; stock indices; or market indices. To ensure clarity on what the value of a derivative is, the value of the underlying asset must be clearly defined. Derivatives are powerful tools for mitigating risk, particularly price risk, through hedging. It is also effective for managing foreign exchange risk, interest rate risk and other non-price risks (see Bodnar et al., 1996; Bodnar and Gebhardt, 1998; Energy Information Administration, 2002).

Derivatives, as used in hedging transactions, can be traded over-the-counter (OTC) or over an organised exchange. The risk profile of a company, its liquidity, the volume and value of expected future oil and gas production, the timing of production, and financing restrictions imposed by lenders or investors are all important factors in determining whether to conduct an OTC transaction or an exchange-traded transaction. **OTC derivative** is a financial contract that is privately negotiated between two parties. Such transactions allow the parties to customise or tailor the contract to meet their specific demands. Tailoring the contract to meet the specific risk strategy inhibits the parties' ability to transfer the contract to a third party. Forward contracts and swaps are examples of derivatives that are typically arranged over-the-counter. **Exchange-traded derivatives**, on the other hand, are contracts that are traded on public exchanges and have standardised contracts. Examples are options and futures contracts. As a result, the exchange determines, among other things, the expiration date, settlement process, and lot size through the contract. Through market-based pricing information, exchange-traded derivatives provide liquidity. Exchange-traded transactions provide greater transferability of the contract to a third party. However, because the parties cannot change the terms of the contract to meet their specific needs, a party's ability to hedge risk is limited.

For oil and gas producers, OTC transactions are especially useful since they allow producers to hedge their expected oil and gas production further into the future than may be practical with exchange-traded transactions. To a large extent, the OTC market exists to bridge the gap between exchange-traded products and the needs of individual traders so that the two markets in effect have a symbiotic relationship (Falloon and Turner, 1999). The various derivative instruments and how they transfer risk, particularly price risk, are now discussed.

17.4.1 Types of Derivatives

There are different types of derivatives, including futures, forwards, options, and swaps. These are discussed in turn with particular highlights on how they are used to minimise risk exposures.

17.4.1.1 Forward Contracts

A forward contract (or simply forward) is an agreement to buy or sell an underlying asset at an agreed price on a specified date in future. Forwards are used to lock in specific prices in order to avoid price volatility. Forwards are negotiated privately and customised to meet the specific needs of the parties involved and thus traded OTC. A basic forward contract must contain in clear terms, the specific underlying asset, the quantity, price, and the date of expiration or maturity. The buyer of a forward contract takes a long position, whereas the seller of the forward contract takes a short position. A party in a long position benefits if the price of the underlying asset increases and loses if the price falls. Similarly, the party in the short position benefits if the price decreases. Box 17.1 provides an illustration on a forward contract on natural gas.

Box 17.1 Illustration of Forward Contracts

To illustrate, let us assume that in January, an end user of natural gas signs a forward contract with an oil producer, which requires that the producer delivers 40,000 million British thermal units (mmBtu) on December 5th at a price of $10 per 10,000 mmBtu. If the spot price of natural gas on December 5th is $12 per 10,000 mmBtu, the contract benefits the end user (long position) because he has guaranteed his position at $10, which would have cost him $12 if he had not entered into the contract. In this case, the oil producer loses because if not for the contract, he could sell the gas at a higher price of $12 per 10,000 mmBtu.

However, if the spot price of natural gas is $7 per 10,000 mmBtu, the end user will lose because he is obligated by the contract to purchase the gas at $10 per 10,000 mmBtu even though it is currently available on the market for $7 per 10,000 mmBtu. In this case, the producer benefits because all he has to do is to buy the gas at $7 and sell it to the end user at $10. Clearly, the end user or producer has an incentive to renege on the contract depending on how the price moves. One major challenge with forward contracts is the risk of default or credit risk. To mitigate such risk, it is critical for the parties to conduct due diligence and assess each other's creditworthiness. Forward contracts are primarily used to protect against potential losses. They enable the parties to set a fixed future price for the commodities. This is critical in the oil and gas industries, where prices fluctuate. For example an entity may enter into a forward contract to sell a certain number of barrels of oil, which can be used to hedge against potential downward price swings in the oil market.

17.4.1.2 Futures

A futures contract is an agreement to buy or sell a specific commodity asset or security at a specified future date and price. Futures contracts are traded on a futures exchange and therefore, the contracts do not give room for customisation. In contrast to forward contracts, futures contracts are highly standardised in terms of the quantity and quality of the commodities involved. The contracts specify the specific locations for which the commodities must be delivered. Most of the oil and gas futures contracts are predominantly traded on the New York Mercantile Exchange (NYMEX) due to its high liquidity and price transparency. A party who has the right and obligation to buy the asset under the futures contract is said to have taken a 'long position', while the seller is said to have taken a 'short position'. Futures are used as tools to hedge against risks in the oil and gas industry.

Depending on the position (long or short) taken by an oil and gas firm in a futures contract, it has the right and obligation to make or take actual delivery of the oil and gas. However, it is unusual to come across an oil and gas futures contract that is settled through physical delivery. This is due to the fact that futures contracts specify where the physical commodity (oil and gas) underlying the contract will be delivered. As an example, the delivery point for the crude oil futures traded on the New York Mercantile Exchange (NYMEX) is the Cushing Hub in Oklahoma. A party with a long position whose wells are not situated close to this location may incur huge transportation costs to get it to their preferred locations. Thus, the party may not take physical delivery of the product. To address the credit risks associated with forward contracts, the exchange ensures that futures are settled daily.

17.4.1.3 Options

A financial option confers on the owner the right, but not the obligation, to buy or sell a financial asset at a specified date and for a specified price. There are two types of options – call option (an option to buy) and put option (option to sell). A call option gives the holder the right to buy an underlying asset in the future for a fixed price called the exercise or strike price. The contract may specify the date on which the right is exercisable as the last day of the given period. Such an option is called the European call option. If the right to acquire can be exercised anytime over the agreed period, then it is called an American call option. A put option, however, gives the holder the right to sell (but not under any obligation to do so) an underlying asset for a fixed price on a specific date. Options can be traded over-the-counter or through an exchange at a cost. There is always a cost to acquiring the option. Crude oil options are the most widely traded energy derivative on the NYMEX. The underlying asset, in this case, is not the crude oil itself but crude oil futures contracts. In spite of the name, crude oil options are actually options on futures. Options are used as hedging instruments against price fluctuations, and they are traded both on an organised exchange and over-the-counter.

With regards to exercising the option, there are two types of options – the American option and the European option. American options give the option holder the right to exercise at any time before the option expires, and European options give the option holder the right to exercise only on the expiration date. There is a unique variant of the American option known as the Bermudan option, which allows the option holder the right to exercise early but only at a specific date(s). This type of options affects the premium paid for the right. Obviously, American options cost more. Box 17.2 shows how options are used to hedge against price risk of crude oil.

Box 17.2 Illustration of Options

For example an end user acquires an option to buy 100,000 barrels of crude oil at $60 per barrel in June (assume a European call option). The cost of the option is $3 per 1,000 barrels. The acquisition of this option gives the end user the right to buy the underlying asset depending on how the price moves. If the spot price in June were to exceed $60 to say $80, the end user will exercise his right and buy the crude oil as the contract makes the price cheaper. However, if the spot price in June is $40 per barrel, then the buyer will not exercise the right since it will be expensive to do so. The buyer will allow the right to expire in which case he loses the cost of the option but is able to buy the crude oil at a reduced price of $40 in the open market.

Oil producers can also acquire put options, which give them the right to sell crude oil in future with the price agreed upon today but for delivery in future. When the price rises in excess of the price in the contract, the producer will not exercise the right. If not exercised, the producer can sell the crude oil in the open market for a higher revenue than it would have under the contract. If the price of crude oil were to fall, the producer would exercise the option to sell in order to rake in enough revenue from the contract, which has a higher selling price. Options are effective ways of managing price risk, but they can be costly. Options are very good financial instruments for hedging risk, and different trading strategies are used. Key among them are straddles, sprangles, and butterfly spread.

Straddle is an options trading strategy that allows the investor to simultaneously buy both call and put options with the same expiration date and same strike price for a given commodity. Straddles are employed when an investor anticipates a significant shift in the commodity price but is not sure whether the movement will go downward or upward. The potential profit on a straddle is limitless and can only be realised when there is a drop or rise in the price of the commodity that is significantly different from the strike price by a margin greater than the total cost of the option premium paid. A straddle could be long (buying) or short (selling). The long strategy involves limited risk, which is losing a maximum of the cost of the options, while the short straddle involves unlimited risk where the investor could lose the full value of the commodity.

Similar to straddles, **strangles** are options strategies that are designed to profit from significant movements in commodity prices, which involve purchasing an equal number of put and call options with the same expiration date. Unlike straddles, strangles have two different strike prices. They are best used when an investor is very sure of the direction of the commodity price and yet wishes to be covered in case of opposite directional movement.

A butterfly spread is an options strategy that involves a combination of four different options contracts with the same expiration date at three different strike prices. The strike prices (higher, at-the-money and lower) are selected in such a way that the options with the higher and lower strike are the same interval from the at-the-money options (which is the middle one). For example, if the at-the-money option has a strike price of $120, then the lower and upper option strike prices should be, $100 and $140, respectively. A technical combination of these options in various ways will form different kinds of butterfly spreads that create profit during a time of low or high commodity price volatility. Depending on the option strategy, a butterfly spread could be a short or long call butterfly spread, short or long put butterfly spread, iron or reverse iron butterfly spread.

Box 17.3 Illustration of Options Strategies

Straddles: For example on 11 April 2022, the trading activities on the commodity option market indicate that the price of crude oil will fall or rise by 20% from its strike price of $120 per barrel. An investor could purchase a $3 call and a $3 put at a strike of $120 that will expire on 25 April 2022. The net profit is $6. To determine the profit margin, the price of crude oil must rise or fall by at least 5% (thus: 6/120 = 0.05).

Strangles: Let us assume an investor believes that the price of crude oil will fall. That means the investor needs less protection against price increase. Instead of purchasing a call option at a strike of $120 for a cost of $3, the investor could possibly look for call option with lesser strike price (say $100) and cost (say $1.50). This strategy is less expensive, compared to the straddle as given before, and protects the investor against extreme drop in crude price and provides some gain if price rises.

Butterfly spread: Again, assume that an investor suspects the price of crude will remain unchanged for some few months and then buys two different call options with strike price of $100 and $140 which cost $4 and $2, respectively. At same time, the investor sells two call options at a strike of $120 which cost $3. At this point, the total cost is (4 + 2 − 2(3)) = $2 which will be the maximum loss for the investor if the strategy fails. However, if at expiration on 25 April 2022, crude oil trades at $120, then the two calls sold will be worthless while the call with strike above $120 will be out-of-the money, and the one with strike below $120 will be in-the-money. Thus, the profit (payoff minus initial cost) for this butterfly will be (120 − 100) − 2 = $18 per lot. Please note that this does not include exchange fees and commission charges.

17.4.1.4 Swaps

Swaps is one of the basic derivative instruments commonly used on the capital market. Swaps, which is also referred to as 'difference for difference', are individually negotiated transactions whereby each party agrees to exchange periodically a series of cash flows on the basis of differences over time in the state of one or more specific underlying assets (Carter et al., 2017). The underlying asset could be the interest rate, foreign exchange rate, equity, or commodity price. No physical assets are exchanged between the counterparties. Basically, swaps are a series of forward contracts. In other words, while cash flow exchange for forwards happens once at the end of the life of the agreement, a series of such cash flows are exchanged for swaps. Thus, swap features less credit risk because of the frequent settlements of cash flows between the parties involved. Unlike options or futures, swaps contracts are entered outside an organised market or exchange and are therefore considered as over-the-counter (OTC) transactions.

There are different types of swaps (such as basis, interest rate, currency, inflation, credit default subordinated risk, commodity swaps), but we will focus our attention on swaps that are used on the oil and gas markets which fall under commodity swaps. With a commodity swap, the underlying asset is a commodity such as oil or gas. Since swaps do not involve the physical exchange of an asset, a base amount, referred to as 'nominal amount', is always set to determine the cash flow that will be periodically swapped. The most common types of commodity swaps are the fixed-floating commodity swaps and the commodity-for-interest swaps. The fixed-floating commodity swap has two legs, namely – fixed-leg which is the agreed price of the commodity in the contract while the floating-leg is tied to the trading price of the commodity. Just as in fixed-floating swaps, one leg pays a return on the underlying commodity price while the other leg is tied to a predetermined fixed rate or a floating rate. This swap involves a nominal amount, predetermined payment timelines, and duration of the contract.

Commodity swaps are good hedging instruments in the oil and gas industry. Since they are OTC instruments and are individually negotiated, it allows users to customise them to suit specific risk exposures and investment needs. Besides, they can be used to hedge against price volatilities in the market. It allows commodity (oil and gas) producers and consumers to lock in an agreed price for a given product. For instance Kenya Airways has substantial aviation fuel consumption and is exposed to changes in fuel prices. Swaps are one of the tools to hedge their exposure by paying a fixed price. Box 17.4 provides an illustration on this.

Box 17.4 Illustration of Swaps

Let us assume Kenya Airways has entered into a swap contract to pay a fixed rate of $3.00/gallon for 500,000 gallons of jet fuel. If, at the agreed payment period, the cost of the fuel is $3.5/gallon, the airline would save a total of $250,000. Because of the swap, airline locks in the price at $3.00/gallon and pays only $3.00 × 500,000 = $1500,000 instead of paying $3.5 × 500,000 = $1,750,000. The difference ($250,000) is paid by the other party. Note that these payments are made periodically until the expiration of the contract.

Box 17.5 also illustrates crude oil swap contract between an oil producer and a refiner.

Box 17.5 Crude Oil Swap Contract Between an Oil Producer and a Refiner

Figure 17.1 presents a case of a standard crude oil swap. In the example, a refining company and an oil producer enter into a 10-year crude oil swap with a once-a-month exchange of payments. The refining company, hereafter known as Party A, agrees to pay the producer, hereafter known as Party B, a fixed price of $25 per barrel, while the producer agrees to pay the refiner the settlement price of a futures contract for

NYMEX light, sweet crude oil on the final day of trading for the contract. Working with a notional amount of 10,000 barrels, the contract requires the party owing the larger payment for the month to make a net payment to the party owing the lesser amount. To illustrate, assuming that the NYMEX settlement price on the final day of trading is $23 per barrel, Party A will pay $2 per barrel times 10,000, or $20,000, to Party B. If the price on the NYMEX is $28 per barrel, Party B will pay $30,000 to Party A. This decade-long swap thus sets up a package of 120 cash-settled forward contracts, one maturing each month for 10 years. As long as the two parties are able to buy and sell crude oil at the variable NYMEX settlement price, the swap guarantees a fixed price of $25 per barrel, because both the producer and the refiner can combine their financial swap with physical sales and purchases in the spot market in quantities that match the nominal contract size. What are required after the purchases and sales shown in the inner loop cancel each other, and out are the fixed payments for the producer and the refiner's purchase of crude oil. Interestingly, the producer never really delivers crude oil to the refiner, nor does the refiner directly purchase crude oil from the producer. All their physical purchases and sales are in the spot market, at the NYMEX price.

Source: Energy Information Administration, 2002

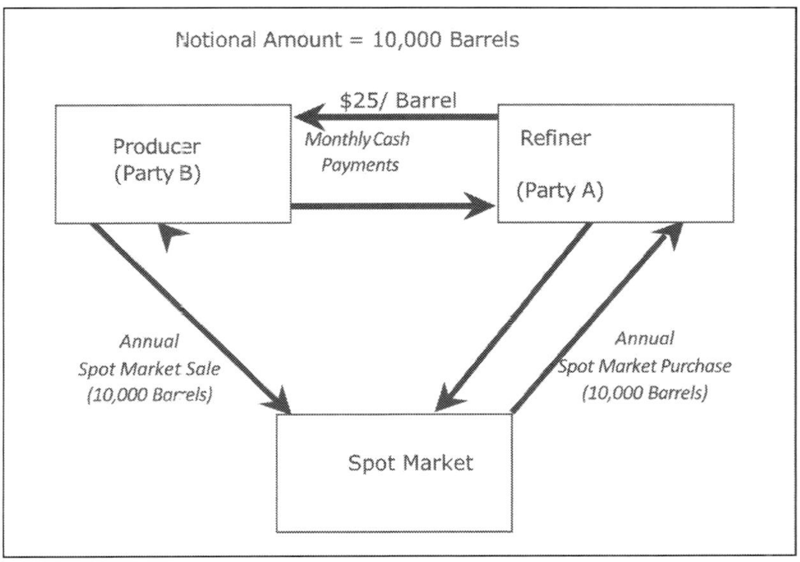

Figure 17.1 Illustration of crude oil swap contract between an oil producer and a refiner

Source: Energy Information Administration, 2002

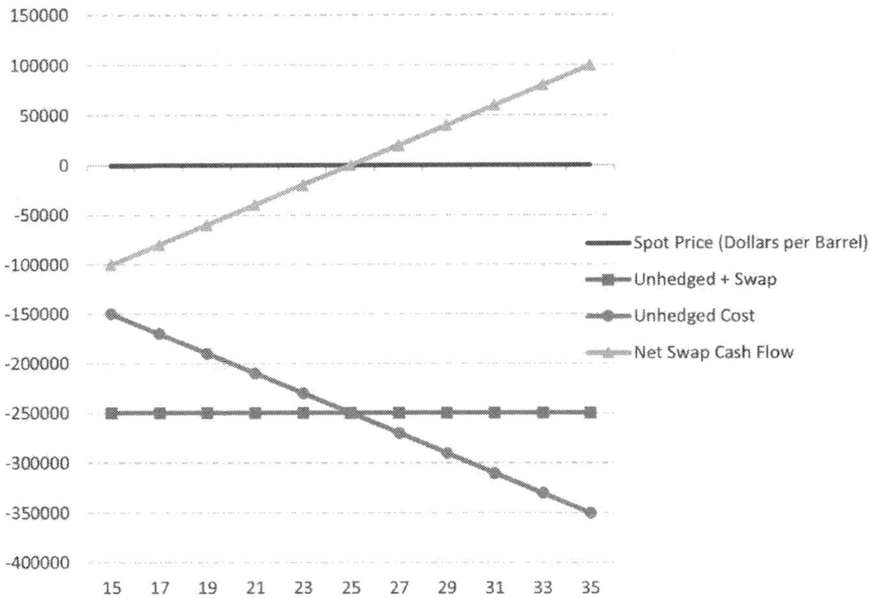

Figure 17.2 Crude oil acquisition cost with and without a swap contract

Figure 17.2 illustrates crude oil acquisition costs in a situation with a swap contract in place and also in another without a swap contract.

Many of the benefits in connection with swap contracts are similar to those associated with futures or options contracts (Hampton, 1999) in the sense that they allow users to manage price exposure risk without taking possession of the asset. They are, however, different from exchange-traded futures and options since they are customised to suit an entity's risk management activities to a large extent as compared to futures contracts or exchange-traded options, which are standardised. Despite the benefits of using commodity swaps, it is worth noting that, because swaps can be highly customised, they are less liquid and will require counterparties to renegotiate the contract terms before premature termination of the contract. In addition, the parties are exposed to credit default risk since the instrument is not guaranteed and supervised by an exchange or clearinghouse (Hale et al., 2002).

17.5 Conclusion

This chapter looks at oil and gas risk exposures and how they are managed using derivatives. These derivatives, in their form and functions, are designed to address specific lost exposures and have generally been considered as a more effective tool for managing risk in the oil and gas sector compared to the traditional approaches. Besides, these derivatives allow the acquisition of rights in the asset without actually owning it, and it gives room to the parties to remarkably leverage on the volatilities in the prices of the commodity. There is no limit to the variety and variants of hedging strategies that can be designed and entered. Although the review considered the functions and the trading strategies of these tools, investors can consider designing a specific product to meet their risk level, tolerance, and nominal amount. Subsequently, the oil and gas derivative market has seen significant growth in the digitalisation of trading, resulting in several online trading platforms for, especially, forwards and swaps. Most essentially, derivative tools permit oil and gas investors to effectively deal with their non-core business risks such as rising interest rates, a constant surge in commodity prices, and even undesirable currency exchange rates.

References

Berger, G., and Ofek, E. (1995). Diversification's effect on firm value. *Journal of Financial Economics*, 37 (1995), 39–65.

Bodnar, G. M., and Gebhardt, G. (1998). *Derivatives usage in risk management by U.S. and German non-financial firms: A comparative survey* (CFS Working Paper Nr. 98/17), Goethe University Frankfurt, Center for Financial Studies (CFS), Frankfurt a. M., https://nbn-resolving.de/urn:nbn:de:hebis:30-9545

Bodnar, G. M., Marston, R. C., and Gebhardt, G. (1996). Wharton 1995 survey of financial risk management by U.S. non-financial firms. *Financial Management*, 25(4), 113–133.

Carter, D. A., Rogers, D. A., Simkins, B. J., and Treanor, S. D. (2017). A review of the literature on commodity risk management. *Journal of Commodity Markets*, 8(1), 1–17.

Energy Information Administration. (2002). *Derivatives and risk management in the petroleum, natural gas, and electricity industries*. Washington, DC: U.S. Department of Energy

Falloon, W., and Turner, D. (1999). The evolution of a market. In *Managing energy price risk*, 2nd ed. London: Risk Books.

Hale, D. R., Lee, T., Zyren, J., Joosten, J., Kouserk, G., Rasmussen, J., and Hewlett, J. (2002). Derivatives and risk management in the petroleum, natural gas, and electricity industries (Report). Washington, DC: Energy Information Administration, U.S. Department of Energy.

Hampton, M. (1999). Energy options. In *Managing energy price risk* (p. 39), 2nd ed. London: Risk Books.

18 Petroleum Wealth Management in Emerging and Developing Countries

James Atambilla Abugre, Joshua Yindenaba Abor, Ruhul Salim, and Daniel Ofori-Sasu

18.1 Introduction

Natural resources and mineral wealth are extremely important to the economic transformation of many emerging countries across the globe. Minerals (including petroleum), for instance, accounted for 68% of the overall merchandise exports in the Middle East in 2009, 64% in Africa, 62.9% in the Commonwealth nations, and 38.9% in South and Central America in 2009 (Ross, 2013). Petroleum resources have significantly contributed to the infrastructure revolution in most emerging and developing countries that are endowed with oil and gas deposits to the extent that most of them virtually depend on the proceeds of these deposits to fund their national budgets and undertake developmental initiatives. Critical infrastructure such as transport, energy, and schools and hospitals and telecommunication among others, which are basic to improve the socio-economic needs of the citizens, are always nonexistent in the required mix in most emerging countries. Petroleum resources have therefore afforded these countries the opportunity to exploit the same to provide the needed infrastructure in these countries.

However, the exploitation of these petroleum resources by emerging countries and their quest to utilise the proceeds for the provision of the basic needs have been bedeviled with a myriad of internal and external challenges, including environmental and social issues, corruption and mismanagement, neglect of other critical sectors of the national economies, price volatilities, and capital flight among others. These factors have over the years rendered the management of petroleum wealth inefficient and turned the 'blessing of the resources into a curse' and counterproductive.

This chapter examines how petroleum wealth is managed in emerging and developing countries and the efficiency of same to the transformation of the economies. The chapter is in three parts: the first part examines the overview of petroleum resources and wealth management, second analyses the challenges of petroleum exploration and wealth management, and the last part looks at the challenges and proposed solutions to maximise petroleum wealth in emerging and developing countries.

DOI: 10.4324/9781003315056-21

18.2 An Overview of Petroleum Exploitation and Wealth Management in Emerging and Developing Countries

Natural resource discovery and exploration have a variety of socio-economic and environmental consequences for citizens in any country (Faria, 2020). In many emerging and developing countries, natural resources provide a solid economic foundation for long-term development. Extraction of petroleum in various emerging and developing countries provides foreign earnings into the countries, which, if properly harnessed and managed, should enhance the living standards of the populace. The cost of managing natural resources in less developed economies is high largely due to inadequate infrastructure, unskilled labour force, over-reliance on foreign-skilled professionals, managerial incompetence, and corruption. This has adversely affected and hamstrung the economic growth and development of most developing countries including that of Africa (Kalu and Ott, 2019).

The management of petroleum wealth across the globe has always been driven by a matter of policy decisions. One of such critical policy decisions is whether petroleum export earnings should be used to boost consumption, domestic capital formation, or foreign asset accumulation. Resource depletion becomes part of the larger problem of petroleum wealth management in this context. Oil-exporting countries' earnings are dominated by petroleum revenue. It is, without a doubt, one of the most stable sources of income for such economies. This throws a great deal of responsibility on the governments of these economies to wisely invest oil money in development. Many prosperous oil economies have discovered the necessity of putting accumulated income into dedicated accounts to fund development projects. These specially created funds, known as Sovereign Wealth Funds, are a type of investment set up by a government for the country's macroeconomic purposes as well as investment strategies in the exporting economy or are savings accumulated by the government over a long period as a result of prudent decision-making. These policy decisions and initiatives have yielded the needed economic impact in most developed countries such as Norway, Russia, and the United States.

However, the use and management of petroleum revenues in most emerging and developing countries have rather contributed to the continuous deprivation of the citizens of petroleum-producing nations. Conflicts and insecurity have characterised the exploitation of oil resources in economies like Sudan, Somalia, Northern Nigeria, and the Middle East among others. Insurgencies and militant groups have emerged in recent times from these conflicts to become one of the threats to global peace and security. Disagreements and discrimination in the use and management of the oil proceeds among the communities within which petroleum resources are extracted have become the norm in emerging and developing nations thereby depriving them of the needed investment climate to harness sustainable development.

The extraction process of oil and gas is characterised by few direct benefits on communities but with huge environmental and social issues and large sunk costs, making them vulnerable to extortion; and when produced in large quantities, natural resource wealth can affect a country's foreign earnings with the potential of reducing the size of the manufacturing and agricultural sectors, which can close economic opportunities for the unemployed youth and vulnerable people. This phenomenon has created the 'resource curse and the Dutch Disease' in most petroleum-producing countries. Corruption and mismanagement by political office holders and technocrats have been identified by literature as one of the factors that inhibit realising the potential benefits of petroleum wealth in emerging and developing countries. Weak institutional arrangements and low literacy rates in these resource-endowed countries have accounted for this.

18.3 Principles of Petroleum Wealth Management

Poor countries that rely on natural resource revenues are frequently impeded in their efforts to achieve long-term development due to a lack of effective institutional structures and governance. Regardless of the presence of natural resource richness, such institutional flaws may exist. However, bringing petroleum wealth into such an institutional context can lead to corruption, conflict, a rise in macro-financial inefficiencies, and environmental destruction, all of which contribute to economic deterioration and pollution of the natural ecosystem. Abundant petroleum wealth is typically regarded as a burden in many emerging and developing countries for these reasons. As a result of the issues generated by natural resource wealth endowment and extraction in emerging and developing nations, experience and expertise in natural resource revenue management techniques have evolved over the years to avert the inefficiencies that come with it.

Five principles are identified to be common in the management of natural resource wealth in emerging and developing countries to avoid the problems associated with utilisation and to achieve sustainable development. Each of the proposed five principles is discussed here.

18.3.1 Defined Institutional Responsibility on Petroleum Revenue Management

Emerging and developing countries endowed with petroleum wealth should have a well-established institutional arrangement defined by a petroleum fund management law to clearly outline the responsibility of each institution. The institutions with defined roles from prospecting, exploitation, sales, revenue management, investment, and expenditure controls to accountability and transparency would ensure prudent and efficient use of petroleum wealth that benefits the citizenry and ensures sustainable development. The case of Timor-Leste's Petroleum Fund Law and Ghana's Petroleum Revenue Management Act is in tandem with this principle which has clear functions for the various institutions set up in the laws and, at the same time, defines areas that oil revenues should be applied to and used on, contrary to which any other action will constitute a violation of the laws and attract spelt out sanctions and penalties to offenders. Accountability institutions such as Parliament, Auditor General, Human Rights and Administrative Justice and the Public Interest and Accountability Committee (PIAC), in the case of Ghana, are all strengthened to oversee the exploitation and utilisation of petroleum proceeds to promote sustainable and equitable development.

18.3.2 Establishment of a Natural Resource Fund by the State

This principle assumes that all revenues from natural resources such as petroleum wealth are received and managed by the state. A natural resource fund is an entity that separates the earnings of natural resources from other types of revenue. In theory, creating a natural resource fund demonstrates a country's commitment to administer proceeds from the exploitation of its natural resources separately, and it is the first step towards accounting for such money differently. It is more difficult to determine how much revenue is obtained from the exploitation of petroleum resources or how the revenue is utilised or misallocated when there is no natural resource fund, especially where institutions are weak. The natural resource fund serves as an earmarked receipt account that allows all proceeds of petroleum revenue to be deposited into it, and expenses are done electronically to identify areas in the national budget approved by parliament. However, the constitution of petroleum revenue must clearly be spelt out to prevent rent-seekers from exploiting the narrowness of the law to exploit the revenues as cited by Gary in the case of Chad's revenue management law.

18.3.3 Strategic and Prudent Investment of Petroleum Wealth

Another crucial part of prudent natural resource revenue management is how that revenue is invested financially. This principle argues that prudent and wise investment of petroleum wealth can be achieved in two ways: offshore and local investments. The offshore investment which is seen as a conservative principle requires that petroleum revenues are invested in foreign countries with low tax regimes and high returns. Offshore investments are done to achieve three main purposes: avoid creating opportunities for corruption and nepotism as is the case with other extractive resources such as gold, bauxite and timber; allay fears of bad and biased investment choices by political office holders; and reduce the tendency of the domestic economy to overheat due to huge volumes of investments in a limited infrastructure that always characterises emerging and developing countries. This type of conservative investment approach is practised by Timor-Leste and Ghana. The local investment approach of the prudent investment principle involves the identification of key sectors of the national economy that are seen as a national priority for both the present and future generations and, hence, allocated with percentages of the petroleum revenue for investment in the national budgets in annual basis. This principle argues that the investment of oil and gas proceeds in the domestic economy ensures that essential social infrastructures such as roads, railway, electricity, educational and health infrastructures among others are provided to trigger the take-off and transformation of economic development. In Ghana, the annual budgetary funds allocation (ABFA) that is invested in social infrastructures can contribute to expansion of the economies, creation of jobs, and enhance the living standards of the citizens. This investment principle is adopted and practised by Ghana since the production of commercial oil in 2010 through the ABFA. Further, establishing an offshore Sovereign Wealth Fund (SWF) in Ghana converts a temporary stream of resources revenues into a permanent stream of investment income. While there is a strong argument for using SWF to invest domestically, 70% of resource revenues were spent out of Ghana's SWF to embark on domestic investment (NRGI, 2015). However, the government channels this money back through the budget rather than spending or investing it outside the budget process.

18.3.4 Transparent Management of Petroleum Wealth

Without transparency, it is impossible to avoid the misappropriation of petroleum revenues. Transparency and open accounting are commonly viewed as keys to eliminating waste and corruption problems. Independent transaction reporting is now routinely sought out by countries with corruption issues. Governments and civil society organisations have also launched a variety of efforts aimed at improving accounting processes between energy corporations and governments and, therefore, increasing transparency. Such measures are intended to strengthen government accountability and encourage better budgetary management. The creation of relevant information by the responsible authority, the dissemination of that information, and the cognizant observation of that information are all required for transparent petroleum revenue administration in any emerging and developing country that seeks to achieve this principle. The establishment of the Public Interest and Accountability Committee in Ghana to monitor the administration and investment of oil revenues is a clear instance of enhancing the transparent management of petroleum wealth However, the committee is bereft of the needed authority to proffer sanctions in case of misappropriation by the government. This indirectly renders such bodies with oversight responsibilities on the management of petroleum revenues in emerging and developing countries ineffective and as mere advisory bodies.

18.3.5 Creation of Savings Fund for Future Generations

The creation of a 'savings fund' which is a natural resource fund, designed to assist a government in creating a store of wealth for future generations, is an important principle practised in most countries where petroleum resources are extracted. The justification for saving is that non-renewable resources such as petroleum are finite and a state must recognise this and plan for the inevitable decrease and exhaustion of this natural resource income for future generations.

For instance Ghana's Petroleum Revenue Management Act set up the Heritage and Stabilisation Funds which constitute the Ghana Petroleum Funds (30% of net revenue) to cater for future generations and as a buffer to cushion the economy in times of unanticipated petroleum revenue shortfalls. Countries such as Chile, Oman, and Norway are success stories with regard to savings funds for future generations. Although data restrictions have restricted investigations in this area, the effectiveness of saving funds appears to be limited empirically. Although it is difficult to isolate the benefits of the fund from the influence of cautious expenditure practices, time-series analysis reveals that in nations with such funds, fiscal spending is less linked with fluctuations in the price of the resource (Devlin and Lewin, 2004).

However, the extent to which these saving funds can compensate for the destructions of the environment and other nuisances created by the exploitation to cater for the needs of future generations in emerging and developing countries remains bleak. This stems from the fact that the savings rate and the investment diversifications of petroleum wealth in emerging and developing economies are insignificant and misdirected to guarantee a sustainable development. As a result, it is critical to expanding other economic sectors in order to generate more revenue. Over-reliance on natural resources, in this case oil, will not always foster progress, and it is a recipe for avoidable economic difficulties as has been witnessed in Nigeria, Somalia, and Kuwait among others.

18.4 Approaches to Petroleum Wealth Management and Utilisation

There are several approaches for petroleum wealth management and utilisation, and these include direct distribution of revenue to citizens, transfer of revenues to regional and subnational institutions, use of barter contracts and bundling, and deferment of petroleum wealth exploitation. These are discussed in the next section.

18.4.1 Direct Distribution of Revenue to Citizens

Direct distribution of money, according to scholars, could help emerging and developing countries avoid at least some aspects of the oil curse: a fund would retain at least some of the country's petroleum revenues out of the hands of political office holders, who might otherwise embezzle them or use them for political gain; it could help citizens hedge against price volatility if citizens are better at planning ahead than governments; and it could give citizens a powerful incentive to monitor their government's use of petroleum revenues thereby mounting pressures against corrupt practices and in favour of prudent governance. This reduces the government's financing for potentially worthwhile interventions; however, the government could, through fiscal policy, introduce taxes to indirectly retrieve portion of the monies allocated, which also prompts citizens to demand accountability from the government.

18.4.2 Transfer of Revenues to Regional and Subnational Institutions

Provincial and district authorities should be compensated for the social, environmental, and infrastructure costs they incur as a result of hosting petroleum projects. Revenue devolution, on the other hand, goes beyond cost reduction: it entails local authorities sharing the financial rewards of resource exploitation to also provide essential services and infrastructure within their jurisdictions. Developing countries such as Ecuador, Ghana, and Nigeria are a few of the countries that practice this approach of revenue sharing. There are two main approaches to this: countries can either enable local authorities to tax the petroleum industry directly, or they can send a portion of the central government's revenues to subnational governments based on a formula, either before or after smoothing out year-to-year revenue changes. Revenue localisation can be an efficient approach to minimise the extent of the central government's arbitrary windfall, and it may even lower the risk of separatist movements in the extractive region as experienced in Sudan in recent years. The localisation of petroleum wealth could better be used when various transparency mechanisms are instituted by national governments to check the use of the revenues for the provision of public goods by local authorities. The less bureaucratic nature of local governments makes them more efficient and transparent in the use of petroleum revenue.

18.4.3 Use of Barter Contracts and Bundling

Low-income countries can trade their oil directly for the public goods they eventually want instead of selling it for revenue. Several nations, notably Angola, Nigeria, Zambia, and Zimbabwe, have used barter-style deals to sell petroleum and other resource rights to Chinese-owned consortia; instead of royalties and taxes, these governments received assurances of future infrastructure and services. Petroleum firms have traditionally supported their activities in host countries by constructing additional infrastructures such as housing for workers, roads, railroads, and even ports. Barter arrangements go even farther, requiring corporations to compensate host governments in the form of unrelated projects and services rather than cash. Nigeria entered into agreements in 2006 to provide Chinese businesses exploration licenses to four offshore blocs in exchange for $4 billion in investment, which included commitments to construct a new hydropower plant, rebuild a dilapidated railway line, and create malaria and avian flu programmes. Similar oil deals have been exchanged for new roads, trains, bridges, schools, hospitals, and a cyber-optic network in Angola. Ghana entered into a similar agreement with Sinohydro to build infrastructure to the tune of $3 billion in 2018 for the exchange of bauxite in the Atiwa forest reserve.

Economists are naturally cautious of arrangements like this, which include a process known as "bundling", in which one transaction (the purchase of exploration or extraction rights) is linked to a second transaction (the sale of a product – the construction of roads and bridges). Bundling is sometimes used by businesses to obtain an advantage over competition. However, if the costs of doing the transaction sequentially are onerous, bundling can be advantageous. Barter contracts could help low-capacity countries avoid the process of collecting revenues (where leakages could occur), redistributing revenues across government agencies (where corruption is possible), and finally assigning revenues to government initiatives (where corruption, patronage, and inefficiencies are high). They may also alleviate governments of the need to smooth out revenue volatility because of revenue falls to the company; they can help attract foreign infrastructure corporations to low-income countries that might otherwise be avoided for the fear of not being paid to assist governments in making difficult-to-reverse commitments to long-term projects that might not otherwise be completed.

18.4.4 Deferment of Petroleum Wealth Exploitation

The first approach for low-income countries is to keep the oil underground. The exploitation of petroleum can be at a slower rate to ensure that revenues do not outpace the government's ability to spend them wisely or civil society's ability to supervise the operations of a rapidly expanding government. Because petroleum wealth is a non-renewable resource, exploiting it results in a one-time financial infusion. It can increase the living standards of future generations if judiciously invested, but it can equally be inimical to the economy if mismanaged. Deferring oil extraction for revenue has a large opportunity cost, especially in low-income countries where people desperately need basic services such as health care, education, and security. Hence, petroleum wealth provides a unique opportunity for rapid economic growth in the world's poorest countries to have these basic social services provided to the citizens. The challenge with deferment of petroleum wealth exploitation is that in this era of energy transition where price is not guaranteed as a result of shifting demand away from fossils, investors could lose value in the not-too-distant future. This approach may also not be plausible in this era of energy transition from fossils to other sources such as wind and solar energy which could cause the value of petroleum energy to depreciate in the near future.

18.5 Challenges of Petroleum Wealth Management

Petroleum wealth management is affected by several challenges. These include volatility of global oil prices, social and environmental problems, economic imbalances arising from excess petroleum revenue, collusion and corruption in extraction and management of petroleum wealth, over-dependence on petroleum revenue, and over-reliance on foreign labour and capital resources. These are discussed in detail.

18.5.1 Volatility of Global Oil Prices

The biggest issues with oil reliance are price volatility and the fact that oil reserves are finite. A one-standard-deviation shock to the price of oil indicates an income shock comparable to 6% of GDP in a country where oil accounts for around 20% of gross domestic product (GDP) (Hausmann and Rigobon, 2003). Oil prices fluctuate from month to month due to transient shifts in global economic and political situations that influence oil supply and demand. Political unrest between Russia and Ukraine in 2022, for example, has temporarily impacted oil supplies, pushing prices above $100 per barrel for the first time since 2014. Petroleum price volatilities produce large revenue fluctuations in petroleum-wealth-dependent countries which can saddle governments with revenue smoothing that emerging and developing countries are saddled with. The uncertainty of the revenue flows partly explains why oil-exporting countries in the emerging and developing world are faced with the challenge of productive investment of their petroleum wealth in other critical sectors of their economies to ameliorate the sufferings of their citizens. This is one of the factors that triggers conflict and insecurity in communities where petroleum products are extracted, such as the conflicts in Yemen in 1994, Sudan in 1983, and Indonesia in 1975. Again, the uncertainty about the future due to oil price instability affects the long-term investment plan of the government, discourages the private sector from investing in such economies, and reduces capital inflows which in the long run affect economic growth.

18.5.2 Social and Environmental Problems

The extraction process of petroleum resources such as oil and gas has limited direct benefits to the communities such as local content involvement including employment of local artisans and use of local materials due to the sophisticated nature of the same. However, the process has many devastating social and environmental problems for the local communities. A significant majority of petroleum deposit host communities in emerging and developing countries suffer from poor infrastructure and social amenities. Inhabitants in surrounding communities rely on fertile farmland and fresh waterways for their socio-economic well-being, which are badly harmed by crude oil processing, exploration, and transportation. Oil leaks from crude oil drilling have left the majority of communities without access to safe drinking water (Junger, 2007). The consequent effect of oil spills into water bodies poses a threat to aquatic life, exacerbating hunger and poverty. 'Due to runoffs from crude oil deposit sites, agricultural farmlands are also impacted in the process, turning once-fertile soils into wastelands'.

The economic effect is a decrease in agricultural yield and productivity, which have an impact on sales and, as a result, on the economic output from agriculture. The discharge of hazardous gases and particulates during gas flaring can endanger both humans' and animals' health. In flared gases, 'over 250 toxins have been detected, including polycyclic aromatic hydrocarbons (PAHs), hydrogen sulphide, toluene, benzene, sulphur dioxide, nitrogen dioxides, xylene, and others, some of which are responsible for acid rain, ozone depletion, global warming, cancer, and other harmful effects' (PAHs) (Junger, 2007). As a result, the widespread emission of particulate matter and precursor gases in the vicinity of oil-producing areas may be a cause for concern.

18.5.3 Economic Imbalances Arising from Excess Petroleum Revenue

The discovery of petroleum in emerging and developing economies which traditionally depended on rain-fed agriculture and low technology for their economic development naturally leaves them 'flooded' with unplanned and excess revenue from the sale and export of crude oil and gas. The excess windfall of revenue has economic implications if not managed well. Thus, it could lead to overheating of the economy, and, hence, the excess growth of the economy can plunge the economy into hyperinflationary pressures stemming from high government expenditure and income levels of individuals. Again, the inflows of the petroleum revenue have been identified as one of the reasons that have caused most emerging and developing countries to overly rely on petroleum wealth to the neglect of the traditional sources of revenue leading to limited diversification of the economies and high unemployment rates in Africa (Ali and Harvie, 2013). This makes the economic structure of countries weak and imbalanced and highly susceptible to global shocks such as price volatility and food insecurity.

18.5.4 Collusion and Corruption in Extraction and Management of Petroleum Wealth

The secrecy surrounding petroleum wealth exacerbates the numerous problems associated with its management. Governments frequently work with international energy firms to hide transactions, and they use their own state-owned businesses to conceal both revenues and expenditures. Secrecy is one of the main reasons why petroleum revenues are frequently lost to corruption, why resource-fuelled autocrats can stay in office by covering up evidence of their greed and mismanagement, and why insurgents are often hesitant to lay down their arms because they distrust others in the government to share their country's mineral revenues more equitably. This explains why emerging and developing countries' share of negotiated percentages of oil proceeds from the exploration averaged 8 and 20% in Africa: the tendency of African government officials to collude with foreign firms for their personal interest and benefit is undoubtedly high (Devlin and Lewin, 2004).

The diversion of petroleum wealth into private benefits has been attributed as one key reason why emerging and developing countries endowed with petroleum resources are still poor and undeveloped. For instance barely 1% of Nigeria's population gets a share of the overall wealth generated from crude oil exploration (Junger, 2007). It is further argued that from 1970 to 2020, given the average price of a barrel of oil for the timeframe under consideration, crude oil sales produced $669 billion in revenue. Nigeria is Africa's top crude oil producer, the world's seventh-largest oil and gas exporter, and home to the world's tenth-largest processed gas reserve (Amnesty International, 2006; Donwa et al., 2015). Notwithstanding its vast oil revenues, Nigeria is one of the world's poorest and most heavily indebted countries (Agbiboa, 2013). According to the corruption perception index (CPI), over 70% of its estimated 200 million people live on less than $2 US per day as a result of corruption, distortion, and mismanagement of petroleum wealth (Hope, 2017). The diversion of revenues from the national treasury to persons, as well as the awarding of oil blocks, contracts, licenses, and production rights to individuals, has hampered economic progress and resulted in the loss of jobs.

18.5.5 Over-Dependence on Petroleum Revenue

Most often than not, the discovery of crude oil and gas in most emerging and developing countries often leads to the neglect of other critical sectors of the national economy. Agriculture which is usually the mainstay of third-world economies, contributing nearly half of foreign earnings and employing close to 60% of the labour force, is affected by the adverse activities of the exploration leaving the previously employed labour force jobless, especially in the rural periphery where crude oil is always found. Other sectors such as manufacturing and industry, trade and commerce, service, and others are abandoned once oil deposits are found and extracted creating the phenomenon of the 'Dutch Disease'. This undoubtedly affects the income streams of the countries and the citizens and affects national development and standard of living.

The loss of economic diversity and total dependence on oil proceeds have been identified by many as two of the factors undermining socio-economic development and altering the economic structures of oil-producing nations in the emerging and developing world especially due to the high volatility associated with oil prices in the global market (Ali and Harvie, 2013). For instance until the discovery of oil in 1959, Libya was known for its agriculture. Crude oil has been Libya's main source of wealth since its discovery. forming 50% of GDP, 97% of exports, and 75% of government revenue and has played a significant part in the country's socio-economic growth (El-Sharif, 2005). Despite its contribution to the economic growth of the country, oil has reduced economic diversity and hampered the provision of various goods and services domestically, particularly amid the ongoing exogenous global oil price volatility (Ali and Harvie, 2013).

18.5.6 Over-Reliance on Foreign Labour and Capital Resources

Petroleum is primarily located in the rural areas. Because of the low level of education in such places, the technological competence required for its extraction and processing is frequently imported. The use of foreign expertise in the exploration of petroleum resources in emerging and developing nations of the world has largely contributed to the high deprivation and abject poverty and high urban–rural drift associated with communities of oil deposits. The income earned by these expatriates is repatriated to their home countries, which affects the economic activities of host nations, ultimately impacting on the domestic currency of the countries.

The discovery, exploration, storage, and management of oil and gas require a huge investment in research, machinery, and technology. Emerging developing countries endowed with petroleum resources are always bereft of the needed investment capital and would therefore rely on foreign investors to extract the oil and gas. This, coupled with collusion, corruption, and incompetence of government officials, leads to poorly negotiated deals and revenue-sharing agreements that leave the host countries and their citizens more improvised and disadvantaged. Tax exemptions and weak regulatory and enforcement regimes among others further worsen the economic and environmental fragilities of the emerging and developing nations, as profits of these foreign firms are expatriated home causing capital flight and its associated consequences and, finally, a devastated environment that cannot support human existence. The sophisticated nature of the machinery and technological know-how requirements in the extraction process of petroleum resources and the fact that these are mainly absent in emerging and developing countries are contributory factors to the problems experienced by petroleum-producing countries.

18.6 Factors That Petroleum Wealth Maximisation in Developing Countries

The discovery of petroleum and the management of its wealth present a major challenge to most emerging and developing countries. The excess revenue always leads to unplanned expenditure leading to structural imbalances in the economy and avenues for corrupt practices by political office holders. The absence of legal frameworks on the management of petroleum wealth and investment policies that characterise emerging and developing countries' response to oil and gas extraction do not lead to judicious maximisation of petroleum wealth. Factors suggested for the maximisation of petroleum resources are discussed here.

18.6.1 Legislation and Investment Policy on Petroleum Wealth Management

Like any other sector, petroleum resources and their revenue need to be guided by legislation and policy to direct its exploration, revenue management, savings

Box 18.1 Legislation and Regulatory Framework on Petroleum Revenue Management in Ghana

Following the oil find in Ghana in 2007, Parliament enacted the Petroleum Revenue Management Act (Act 815) in 2011 to serve as the guiding mechanism for oil revenue management. The Act is the exclusive authority on oil proceeds and offers fiscal guidelines on the allocations of the revenue to identified sectors and funds specified in the Act. The Petroleum Holdings Fund (PHF) was created to receive all revenues from the oil and through which all expenditures of the petroleum revenue shall be made to all the specified allocations by the law. The government is prohibited from borrowing from the Fund, neither can it be used as a guarantee for government debts. The Stabilisation and Heritage Funds receives 30% of net revenue after allocation to the Ghana National Petroleum Corporation. The remaining 70% is dedicated to support the annual national budget, mainly on four sectors identified by the government.

To ensure accountability and transparency on the use of oil revenue, Act 815, as amended, established the Public Interest and Accountability Committee consisting of various stakeholders from academia, traditional authority, religious bodies, civil society organisations, the media, professional bodies, and trade unions among others to oversee the utilisation of oil revenues and ensure compliance by government. The committee has since been producing semi-annual and annual reports on the use of oils revenue since 2012. The Investment Advisory Committee, Bank of Ghana, Ghana Revenue Authority, Ministry of Finance, and the Auditor-General all have identified and specified roles in the Act to carry out in a bid to promote accountability and transparency in the use of petroleum revenue in Ghana.

Source: Ghana Petroleum Revenue Management Act, (Act 815), 2011 as amended

and investment as well as utilisation of its proceeds. This allows for the establishment of a framework that prevents the mismanagement of the oil revenue and enhances accountability in the use of the same. Box 18.1 discusses the legislation and regulatory framework on revenue management of petroleum proceeds in the case of Ghana.

18.6.2 Development of Local Human Resources and Use of Domestic Capital

One fundamental challenge that bedevils emerging and developing countries extracting petroleum resources is the lack of technical expertise and knowhow. The petroleum industry is a highly sophisticated one that requires the use of highly professional skilled labour such as petrochemical engineers, mechanical engineers, geo-technical engineers, and energy experts. These calibres of human resources, according to Devlin and Titman (2004), are limited locally in emerging and developing countries. The academic world in emerging and developing nations must invest in research development to train these skilled professionals locally so as to reduce the amount of foreign currencies paid to imported labour which in the long run affects domestic spending to boost economic growth. The capital market of developing economies needs to be developed to provide the needed capital and promote financial intermediation. The development of the capital market will avail financial resources to both governments and the private sector to invest in technology, machinery, and capacity building and leverage on local resources that ensure that there is enough local expertise and capital to exploit petroleum resources and retain all wages in the local economy. This also ensures that the benefits of the petroleum resources are locally controlled for the collective development of the country unlike the practice of small stakes that are always negotiated by governments from foreign investors.

18.6.3 Equitable Distribution of Petroleum Wealth

Petroleum revenue and its distribution have served as a fertile source of conflict in many oil-exporting nations across both developed and developing countries. Corruption, nepotism, and patronage have characterised the ownership of oil contracts and blocs by the affluent in society to the neglect of the general well-being of the entire community. Patronage by political office holders squandering the wealth of petroleum resources on themselves to the disadvantage of the communal interest is a norm rather than an exception in many oil export countries. These have caused conflicts in many countries including Nigeria, Pakistan, Angola, Sudan, Chad, and Libya. To avoid conflicts and its attendant devastating effects on the economies of oil-producing countries, the stakeholders should be engaged openly and transparently on how the wealth of oil resources are used and distributed. Guidelines and legislations should be put in place, which ensures that no individual can engage in financial mismanagement with the proceeds of oil and that all geographical regions of the country are given their share and allocation of the wealth as prescribed in the guidelines or investment laws as it is the case in Ghana's Petroleum Revenue Management Act.

18.6.4 Transparency and Accountability in Petroleum Wealth Utilisation

In oil economies, transparency has been a major challenge because of the secrecy surrounding oil activities, rent-seeking, patronage, and corruption thrive. Many emerging and developing oil- exporting countries have performed petroleum exploration and monitoring without the awareness of the citizens they represent in government. Internal checks and balances among the major participants and monitoring institutions, as well as outward transparency where data is available for public consumption and investigation, constitute the main forms of transparency in petroleum wealth management. The type of political regime determines whether or not transparency is effective. Citizens will demand transparency and accountability from their government when public awareness is strong. As a result, transparent exploration procedures are entirely contingent on political will. Oil governance and revenue management, in particular, are frequently cloaked in secrecy. This is true in the majority of emerging and developing oil-exporting countries. The majority of information on the utilisation of oil wealth and production capacity, as well as contractual agreements, has been unavailable to the general public. This makes it impossible to implement accountability systems, whether by the people or by institutions, which have the constitutional responsibility of establishing checks and balances.

18.6.5 Development of Other Critical Sectors of the Economy

The over-reliance of governments of oil-producing countries on the revenue of petroleum resources after the discovery of oil to the neglect of other revenue streams creates the 'Dutch Disease' problem in most emerging and developing countries. Agriculture, trade and commerce, and manufacturing sectors have traditionally formed the engine of growth of most economies. In recent times, technology and the service sector, in general, has taken over the driving seat of every economy across the globe. However, there are ineffective policies by governments in emerging and developing countries to develop these sectors to contribute to the revenue streams of the countries and create employment for the teeming youth who may not have the required skills to work in the petroleum sector. Petroleum resources are exhaustive, and any reliance on the same to develop any economy cannot be sustained. Hence, the development of critical sectors such as agriculture, service, and manufacturing using the proceeds of oil and gas is one surest way to guarantee a robust local economy that can stand the shocks of global economic changes and create sustainable jobs to improve the living standards of the people in oil-producing nations.

18.6.6 Political Stability

No sustainable development thrives in an environment of insecurity and unrest. In this regard, so that emerging and developing countries maximise the resources of petroleum exploration, there must necessarily be political stability to provide the platform for various stakeholders including the media, civil society, and individuals to contribute to the utilisation and management of petroleum wealth. Uninterrupted democratic governance ensures that the relevant state institutions and monitoring frameworks are laid and strengthened over time to hold duty bearers accountable for the use and management of petroleum revenue. This ensures that investment projects yield the needed dividends to the citizens in the long run, and transparency on the use of the revenues is guaranteed.

18.7 Conclusion

Many petroleum-exporting countries in the emerging and developing world continue to depend heavily on revenues of their petroleum resources to run their economies and governance, and this will continue to linger on for some time. The contribution of petroleum wealth to the transformation of countries remains significant and a mystery. Thus, many nations have utilised petroleum wealth efficiently to remarkably improve the living conditions of their citizens while others mismanage the same to even retrogress in their quest to seek development. Maximisation of petroleum wealth in emerging and developing nations requires the adoption of best practices and the enactment of transparent and open laws that are inclusive and participatory. Slow exploration of petroleum resources to cater for future needs, diversification and investment in other critical economic sectors, fair and equitable distribution of petroleum revenue among communities and citizens, decentralisation of proceeds of oil sales to subnational bodies are practices that must be considered. Instituting transparency and accountability mechanisms through legislations and policy directions to check mismanagement by duty bearers is an important measure to adopt by emerging and developing countries to maximise their petroleum wealth.

References

Agbiboa, D. (2013). Corruption and economic crime in Nigeria: Social and economic perspectives. *African Sector Review*, 22(1), 47–66

Ali, I., and Harvie, C. (2013). Oil and economic development: Li bya in the post-Gaddafi era. Economic Model, 32, 273–285. https://doi.org/10.1016/j.econmod.2013.01.022

Amnesty International (2006). Nigeria: Oil, poverty and violence. https://web.archive.org/web/20070819155442 and http://www.web.amnesty.org/library

Devlin, J., and Lewin, M. (2004). Issues in oil revenue management. Presentation for the World Bank ESMAP Workshop on Petroleum Revenue Management, 2.

Devlin, J., and Titman, S. (2004). Managing oil price risk in developing countries. *The World Bank Research Observer*, 19, 119–13.

Donwa, P. A., Mgbame, C. O., and Ogbeide, O. L. (2015). Corruption in the Nigerian oil and gas industry and implication for economic growth. *International Journal of African Asian Studies*, 14, 29–41

EL-Sharif, I. A. A. (2005). An empirical investigation of the impact of oil price changes in disparate economic systems: Evidence from the UK and Libya (PhD thesis, Dundee University)

Faria, J. (2020). Main oil producing countries in Africa 2019. https://www.statista.com/statistics/1178514/main-oil-producing-countries-in-Africa

Hausmann, R., and Rigobon, R. (2003). An alternative explanation of the resource curse. In J. Davis, R. Ossowski and A. Fedelino (Eds.), *Fiscal policy formulation and implementation in oil-producing countries*. Washington, DC: International Monetary Fund

Hope, K. R. (2017). *Corruption in Nigeria. Corruption and governance in Africa* (pp 125–162). London: Palgrave Macmillan.

Junger, S. (2007). Blood oil. *African Sector Review* 2. http://www.vanityfair.com/politics/features/2007/02/junger200702

Kalu, K. and Ott, K. (2019). Ethical issues in environmental pollution: multinational corporations (MNCs) and oil industries in tropical regions—the Nigerian niger-delta case. In: Chemhuru M. (eds) *African environmental ethics. The international library of environmental, agricultural and food ethics*, Springer, Cham. https://doi.org/10.1007/978-3-030-18807-8_18

Natural Resource Governance Institute (NRGI) (2015). Six reasons why sovereign wealth funds should not invest or spend at home. https://resourcegovernance.org/blog/six-reasons-why-sovereign-wealth-funds-should-not-invest-or-spend-home-0

Ross, M. L. (2013). The political economy of petroleum wealth. *Middle East Development Journal*, 5(2), 1–23.

19 Oil Revenues, Finance, and Economic Development

Jabir Ibrahim Mohammed, Verah Ogeh Fiador, Amin Karimu, and Joshua Yindenaba Abor

19.1 Introduction

Oil is an important natural resource that nations all over the world derive from their energy sources. It takes close to two billion years to form and depletes within two centuries (Mohammed, 2020). Due to its long-time formation and high depletion rate, nations that discover oil put in strong mechanisms to maximise the gain from this natural resource. Oil is used for so many purposes, such as powering generators at home, vehicles, generating electricity, and industrial purposes.

Countries that have discovered oil in large commercial quantities are part of oil-producing countries. Oil-producing countries are either net exporters or net importers of oil depending on the quantity of oil the country consumes relative to its export. A country is a net exporting country if its consumption of oil products exceeds its export and verse versa. In most oil-producing countries, revenues from oil are the major source of income, and it is used to finance the country's budget. The revenues that accrue to governments of oil-producing countries come from different sources, which include royalties, income tax, resource rent, production sharing (contracts), import, and export duties and value-added tax, etc. International Oil Companies (IOCs) enter into an agreement with a host country with the oil resources for the purposes of exploration and extraction. The oil resources are shared according to a fiscal regime arrangement between the IOCs and the country that owns the oil-wealth. Due to the intensity of the capital invested, the IOCs receive a significant share of the oil revenues.

Consequently, oil revenues play an important role in the country where the oil is extracted. It facilitates the development of financial markets and also ensures economic growth. This is because oil revenues pass through the financial markets, making the market liquid. Ideally, revenues from oil are expected to pass through the financial system of most oil-producing countries thereby helping to develop the financial markets. However, it is always not the case for most oil-producing countries due to the financial curse experienced by most of these countries. Most of the IOCs take advantage of weak institutions from oil-producing countries to repatriate their income back to parent

DOI: 10.4324/9781003315056-22

companies instead of investing in the domestic economy (Mohammed et al., 2022). Empirical literature shows that IOCs enjoy investing in countries with weak political institutions but with relatively good banking systems where they can quickly transfer oil proceeds to their parent companies for re-investment (Mohammed et al., 2020).

Additionally, apart from the financial curse that is experienced by oil-rich countries, they also experience economic stagnation due to over-reliance on the oil revenues to the neglect of critical sectors of the economy. This is often referred to as the resource curse. Also, the consequence of the resource curse is often the Dutch Disease effect of the existence of oil abundance. Literature has shown that both the financial curse and resource curse stem from so many factors such as bad governance, rent-seeking behaviour of political actors, bad management of revenues, markets failures, and globalisation behaviour of Multinational Corporations' (MNCs') presence (Adam et al., 2019; Mohammed et al., 2022).

The rest of this chapter is organised as follows. Section 19.2 focuses on ownership of oil revenues and expected payments. Section 19.3 looks at revenue management models. Section 19.4 discusses oil revenues and financial markets. Section 19.5 is on oil revenues, growth, and economic development. Section 19.6 provides the concluding remarks.

19.2 Ownership of Oil Revenues and Expected Payments

The ownership structure of oil revenues is derived from fiscal regimes on the basis of the arrangement between the host country and the International Oil Companies. This is done through the structure of fiscal regimes. The fiscal regimes are the set of institutional arrangements such as royalties, taxes, and contractual agreements that give rise to the sharing of oil funds (Amoako-Tuffour and Owusu-Ayim, 2010). There are three main models of the ownership structure of oil revenues. These include:

- **Go-It-Alone Strategy:** This is a strategy where the oil-rich country discovers the hydrocarbon and forms its national oil company, extracts the resources on its own, and bears all the risks and benefits that come with petroleum exploitation. A typical example is Saudi Arabia which forms the Saudi Aramco to explore and extract oil resources.
- **State Grants Rights to IOCs:** Under this regime, the state grants the rights to an IOC who controls the entire industry. IOCs exploit, extract, and bear the entire risk and pay concessions to the state in the form of royalties, taxes, service rentals, etc. A typical example is the OCED countries that practice this ownership structure.
- **Mixed Structure:** this combines the features of the go-it-alone strategy and granting rights to IOCs. In the mixed structure, the host country's National Oil Company (NOCs) forms partnerships with the IOCs for exploration and production where the state has a stake in the oil

production. The percentage of the production sharing contract (PSC) is agreed upon by the hydrocarbon owner and the IOCs. This differs from country to country. The range for the PSC in most African countries is between 38% to 78% in most oil contracts.

19.2.1 Fiscal Regimes

According to energy economist Dr Carole Nakhle, the basic proposition of an oil and gas taxation regime is to 'acquire for the state in whose territory the resources lie, a fair share of the wealth accruing from their extraction, whilst encouraging investors to ensure optimal economic recovery of those resources'. Oil and gas activities are regulated by the hydrocarbon fiscal regimes of most countries. In this section, we discuss some of the fiscal regime features that are common among most oil-producing countries. They include taxes, royalties, resource rent tax, production-sharing contract agreements, state equity, indirect taxes, import duties, value-added tax, and other non-tax payments.

19.2.1.1 Royalties

Oil-producing countries generate taxes/royalties from International Oil Companies (IOCs) for the exploitation of the hydrocarbons in the host countries. The royalties are the sum paid on the total amount of oil and gas extracted by the IOCs. They are usually paid in kind to the host country as a percentage of the total oil and gas extracted. Globally, the average royalties rate stands at 7% due to the cost-recovering limit set by those IOCs. Some set a limit between 3% to 10% depending on the technical risk and the proactivity of the block concerned, measured by water depth and American Petroleum Institute (API) gravity (or crude sweetness). Some may even go as much as 20% depending on the type of agreement such as a service contract agreement or production-sharing agreement. Countries such as Cameroon's fiscal regime allows for the negotiable closing item after the investor has been guaranteed a minimum share of profit before tax. While in Ghana royalties are in ranges between 3% to 12.5%, and they are up to 15% in Congo. In Ghana, for instance, royalties' rates between 3% and 5% have been applied for deep water and marginal blocks, and 10% for shallow water operations respectively. Arguably, Ghana and Uganda discovered oil in commercial quantities within the same time frame, but they have differences in the arrangements of their fiscal regimes. While Ghana relies on a straightforward production volume, Uganda, on the other hand, relies on progressive sliding royalty between 5% and 12.5% which adjusts upward on the increments when production rises and vice versa. Similarly, Ghana's rate is lower than that of Nigeria which ranges between 8% and 20% for inland basin and offshore production, respectively.

19.2.1.2 Income Tax on Petroleum

Petroleum-producing countries generate income tax from IOCs after they have taken care of all their production cost. The rent received by the IOCs is known as profit before tax, and this amount is taxed by the host country. Globally, the average income tax on petroleum ranges from 30% to 35%. However, some countries receive income tax as low as 25% while others receive up to 85% of the profit made from oil in the case of production-sharing agreement contracts. The danger of higher income tax on petroleum income is that it leads to an overstatement of cost which leads to a substantial reduction in the profit before tax. Countries that charge higher income tax on petroleum risk losing substantial revenues because of cost overstatement.

19.2.1.3 Resource Rent Tax

Resource rent tax is an economic rent that is owned by the rightful owners of the natural resource following the extraction of the resources (Thampapillai et al., 2014). The rightful owners are the society that is endowed with the resources. This principle allows the state to tax only the rent of the resource and leave the rest to the IOCs to undertake their investment. This tax aims to stop distortion in investment decisions to prevent the altering of the pre-tax merits of an investment.

19.2.1.4 Production-Sharing Agreement

The Production-Sharing Agreement (PSA) is a contract between one or more investors and the government of a host country that owns the right to the oil reserves. The government hires the IOCs for prospection, exploration, and extraction of the oil resources from a specific area over a specified period which is determined. Under this contract, the investor is allowed to administer the business at their expense, and the risk is shared with the government as part of the production output by the agreement of the stake the government owns in the contract. The IOCs pay royalties under this contract and take away the covering cost and pay taxes, and the remaining profit is shared between the investor and the government on the basis of the PSA agreement. Most developing oil-producing countries such as Ghana, Uganda, Angola, and Nigeria have such contracts with IOCs. Other taxes that may be earned under this agreement besides what the government receives from its share include:

- **Indirect Oil Taxes:** The government also earns indirect taxes from oil extraction within the host country. Expatriates and their dependents in the host country engage in the buying of goods and services within the domestic economy, and therefore they pay taxes on these purchases. Also, personal income taxes are paid by workers of this sector, which are not directly coming from the oil but through the job done in the oil sector. These are all incomes that accrue to the government that are not coming directly from oil.

- **Import and Export Duties:** The IOC companies pay import duties on the equipment they import to be used in the sector. The Oil Marketing Companies also pay import duties for importing energy products into the country. Additionally, some governments such as Russia impose export duties on IOCs for the export of oil and gas products in the upstream sector. All these taxes increase the revenues of the government.
- **Value-Added Tax:** The government may also impose some VAT on petroleum products in the downstream sector. A host of those taxes in the case of Ghana may include sanitation tax (carbon tax), BOST margin levy, price stabilisation levy, special petroleum tax and the energy debt recovery levy, and a host of other taxes. These taxes increase the prices of petroleum products for consumers while they increase government revenues.
- **Other Non-tax Payments:** Both the upstream and downstream oil sectors make other non-tax payments such as corporate social responsibilities to the communities within which they operate. They go a long way to augment government effort in the provision of social amenities for those communities.

19.2.1.5 International Oil Companies (IOCs)

The international oil companies move to a host country for exploration, discovery, and extraction of oil and gas. They often agree with the resource owners. Those agreements are in the form of PSA and service contract agreements. In most cases, the IOCs bear 100% of the costs in the exploration and field development. In developing countries, the IOCs own a lion's share of the resource rent because they own the capital and bear significant risk. Mohammed et al. (2020) find that IOCs own close to 77% of the oil rent in oil-producing countries mainly because the sector is capital intensive and risky and the IOCs provide the required capital.

19.2.1.6 National Oil Companies (NOCs)

The NOCs manage the share of the state stake in any oil-producing country. State participation usually takes the form of initial carried interest and additional oil entitlement. The initial carried interest is free, and the state does not make any financial contribution towards exploration and development costs. The IOC bears all the risk and remains responsible for 100% of all costs. However, the state pays for its appropriate share of production costs on the commencement of production. The aim of this is to help the state recover its past expenditures in its exploration and promotional efforts on the block to help reduce government costs and risk and increase its share in the rewards of discoveries. The state may also obtain an additional participating interest after the discovery of the oil in commercial quantities. Usually, it ranges between 10% and 60% in oil-producing countries. Most countries in SSA have taken the advantage to ensure a certain degree of state ownership of NOCs, which manages their participating interest for them. For instance, in Ghana, have the Ghana National Petroleum Corporation (GNPC) and the Nigerian National Petroleum Corporation (NNPC). State participation is a major element of the fiscal regime.

19.3 Oil Revenue Management Models

This section discusses the oil revenue management models employed in the literature to manage windfall from oil wealth when nations discover oil. These models define the modalities under which developing oil-rich countries can manage their revenues via oil-rich countries. These are discussed as follows.

19.3.1 Permanent Income Hypothesis Model

The Permanent Income Hypothesis (PIH) was developed by Friedman in 1957. This theory forms the basis of Sovereign Wealth Funds (SWFs). The assumption is that countries can borrow and lend at the world interest rates. In this model, an optimal policy rule is set in such a way that the government spending can be constant according to the annuity value of natural resource wealth and non-natural resource wealth. Thus, government invests a proportion of the resource wealth in financial assets (foreign financial assets to dampen the 'Dutch Disease' effect which is associated with natural resource wealth). The return generated in the foreign asset is used to finance the government budget deficit in perpetuity when the natural resource wealth finally depletes. In this model, the natural resource-rich country benefits from the resource wealth forever, long after the resource wealth is deleted. It enables them to smoothen consumption for both current and future generations because the resource wealth remains permanent across the investment horizon.

19.3.2 Bird-in-Hand Model/Norwegian Model

The 'bird-in-hand' hypothesis is also known as the Norwegian model. In this strategy, all the wealth from the natural resource is invested into a diversifiable SWF, and the interest earned is used to support the country's budget. This can be attributed to the PIH, except that natural resource windfall is valued after it has been banked. Norway practices this kind of model. Norway has two Sovereign Wealth Funds. The Government Pension Fund Global (Oil Fund) was established in 1990. It is the largest SWF with an asset value of over US$1.4 trillion as of December 2020. The second is Government Pension Fund Norway established in 1967 as a type of National Insurance Fund. This is managed separately from the oil fund, and its revenues are used to purchase stocks within Norway and other neighbouring Scandinavian investments. The oil fund generates approximately 4% return on its investment, and this value is used to support the Norwegian government budget annually (Mohn, 2016). It is expected that with the current accumulation of the fund, Norway can benefit from it infinitely when the oil resources finally deplete.

19.3.3 Risk Premium and Capital Scarcity Model

Another model used in managing oil wealth is the recently developed capital scarcity and risk premium theory. This theory is proposed by van der Ploeg and Venables (2011) who opine that government can borrow and lend at the world interest rates by adjusting the debt component of the budget constraint to include risk premium using the foreign debt schedule. Their theory states that if a country has low indebtedness, the government can borrow at the world interest rates, but it can borrow at world interest rates plus a risk premium if the indebtedness is high for the country. Finally, the model was extended to include domestic investment in both public and domestic capital in addition to foreign assets. The conclusion from their extension is that in countries with a scarcity of capital, domestic investment should be geared towards scaling up their infrastructural investment rather than accumulating foreign assets for future generations. They argue that capital-scarce countries need to invest more in their infrastructure rather than financial assets since future generations are wealthier than the current generation.

19.3.4 Volatility Fund Management Model

The volatility fund oil revenue management model is proposed by Wills (2018). He built on the capital scarcity and risk premium model by van der Ploeg and Venables (2011). He argues that both developed and developing countries that extract oil need to build an offshore volatility fund and refrain from depleting such funds when oil prices fall. He developed a parsimonious model nested on certain principles for both capital-scarce and capital-abundance countries. He argues that capital-abundance countries' volatility management of oil revenues should be different from that of capital-scarce countries since both countries have differences in their capital needs and accumulation of capital for future generations through the investment of oil funds in financial assets. Wills notes that for capital abundance countries, the management of their oil funds is (i) smooth consumption using Future Generation Funds (FGF) and (ii) building a volatility fund and quickly leaving it alone. This advice to capital-abundance countries suggests that since those countries are already rich, they should smoothen their consumption with Future Generation Funds (FGF) such as the creation of Sovereign Wealth Funds. For example the Norwegian Pension Fund Global uses oil funds. This fund allows the Norway authorities to benefit from the oil funds long after the hydrocarbon has been depleted. This can be used to support their budget in critical spending areas. Second, part of Will's advice to developed countries is to build volatility funds and leave them alone. The crust of this advice is that oil prices are volatile and for that matter their revenues. So, during boom periods, oil-rich economies may be tempted to overspend thereby misusing the oil funds. Building volatility funds help the oil-rich countries to prevent the possibility of over-spending thereby curtailing the Dutch Disease effect. Leaving such funds even in a period of bust also helps the oil-rich countries to manage their expectations especially when the legal regimes are structured to favour that.

Wills' advice to capital-scarce (developing countries) is (i) consume, invest, and deleverage and (ii) invest part of volatility fund domestically then leave it alone. First, developing oil-rich countries should **consume** to meet their current budgetary needs. This means that part of the oil funds should be geared towards consumption because such countries need funds to finance major components of their budget such as education, health, agriculture, and infrastructure. Second, oil-rich developing countries should **invest**. The volatile nature of oil revenues requires investment for a rainy day against a non-rainy day. Developing countries need not treat a boom in oil revenues as a permanent shock and go on a higher consumption spree since this could have budgetary implications during periods of a burst. They should invest the excess revenues in stabilisation funds and future generations' funds. These funds will serve as a buffer for such countries against future shocks in oil prices leading to significant revenue shortfalls and when the oil reserves completely deplete. However, these investments should be protected by strong institutional quality, checks and balances, and strong civil society participation in the management of such funds. Third, oil-rich developing countries should **deleverage**. Against the backdrop of consumption and investment, oil-rich developing countries need to set part of the funds to settle their debt obligations in both the oil industry and the national budget. This is because investment in oil fields requires significant capital-intensive investment so most of the National Oil Companies (NOCs) usually borrow to take a stake in the production-sharing agreements of IOCs.

Box 19.1 Ghana's Oil Revenue Management Framework

Ghana discovered oil in commercial quantities in July 2007, and this presented a whole new potential for changing the economic dynamics and fortunes of the country. The country started commercial oil production in 2011 bringing in an additional revenue stream for the government. The economy grew by 14% in 2011, the highest growth recorded in the history of the country. The country is well endowed with natural resources – gold, cocoa, bauxite, and manganese. Revenues from these resources have not inured to the benefit of the ordinary Ghanaian in improved living standards. The government, faced with this reality and, of course, the experiences of other oil-rich countries, put in motion a process to safeguard proceeds from its oil find. The 'paradox of plenty' or the resource curse has rendered oil-rich developing countries poorer. In 2010, the government of Ghana presented the Petroleum Revenue Management Bill to parliament to pass into law. The Petroleum Revenue Management Act, 2011 (Act 815) and Petroleum Revenue Management Amendment Act, 2015 (Act 893) were passed and amended, respectively. The Act outlined governance and management of the proceeds from oil fields and ensured transparency and accountability.

Petroleum Revenues: Ghana's oil revenues come from different streams and include royalties (12.5%), income tax (35%), AOE, and state participation interest (10%). These form the building blocks of government oil revenues. The revenues are held in the petroleum fund and subsequently disbursed to other funds (Petroleum Funds).

Oil Revenue Collection: Revenues from petroleum resources are assessed and collected by the GRA for and on behalf of the government, and such monies are not treated as part of normal tax revenues. The receipts are paid into the petroleum holding fund.

Petroleum Holding Fund: All revenues received are lodged in the petroleum revenue fund for onward disbursement to other statutory funds on the basis of a sharing formula. The parliament of Ghana determines how much is paid to the various petroleum funds.

Allocation/Disbursement: The PRMA outlines and establishes various funds and their subsequent allocations to the Petroleum Funds (Stabilisation and Heritage funds).

Petroleum Funds:

Stabilisation Fund: The stabilisation fund is established to provide cost relief and mitigate the hardship of Ghanaians in times of rising petroleum cost pressures. The government sets aside monies from the petroleum revenues for future subsidies for Ghanaians.

The Heritage Fund: The heritage fund as established by the PRMA is to provide an endowment for future generations to support their development when the oil resource is depleted. This will ensure proper investment to give the unborn generation their due of the resource.

Annual Budget Funding Amount: Part of the revenues is used to support the annual government budget. The disbursement is determined by parliament on various budget support sectors.

Ghana Infrastructure Investment Fund (GIIF): Twenty-five per cent of the 70% allocation of the annual budget funding for public investment shall be transferred to the GIIF for infrastructure development.

Key Institutions

The key institutions in charge of the oil revenue management are the MOFEP which provides policy direction; the Bank of Ghana, which maintains the various funds, and releases and carries out internal audit of funds; and the Ghana Revenue Authority, which collects revenues for and on behalf of the government. Others include the Audit Service, which performs an external audit on the management of the oil funds.

Investment Advisory Committee (IAC): The Investment Advisory Committee (IAC) proffers advice to the minister of finance on the best financial instrument to buy.

The Public Interest Accountability Committee (PIAC): It monitors and evaluates compliance with the Act in managing and using petroleum revenues and investments.

Source: Authors' Construction of Ghana's Petroleum Management

19.4 Oil Revenues and Financial Markets

This section discusses how oil revenues facilitate financial markets' development in oil-producing countries. The extant literature demonstrates that oil plays two critical roles in the economy as a commodity and a financial asset (Venditti and Veronese, 2020). Venditti and Veronese (2020) argue that oil should not only be seen as a mere input into production but also as a barometer of economic activity and financial assets. Therefore, oil is assumed to be a financial asset and physical commodity. Thus, the use of oil as a financial asset and commodity to boosts equity markets, the derivatives market, the bond market, and the banking sector. This helps to promote the development of the financial markets in most oil-producing countries.

First, oil as a commodity is a very important financial derivative since most investors use it to hedge against risk. Due to this, the oil helps in facilitating productive investment in an advanced financial system (Erdoğan et al., 2020). Erdoğan et al. (2020) note that when the rate of financial deepening is 45%, the increase in oil exports does not have a statistical significant impact on economic growth; however, a financial deepening that is above 45% significantly increases economic growth by 7% with a unit increase in oil export.

In another development, Umar et al. (2021) study the impact of the resource curse on bank efficiency in 12 oil-producing countries. They find the presence of a resource curse. They argue that during the episode of oil price booms, banking efficiency declines, credit infection worsens, and the probability of default increases. Conclusively, countries that relied more on natural resource rent tend to have lower financial development. Their policy implication is that bank management, central banks, and policymakers should design robust lending policies to support both boom and burst counter-cyclical effects and tighter provisions for loan losses in oil-producing countries.

Li et al. (2020) document that the abundance of oil revenues validates the resource curse hypothesis on financial development in N-11 oil-producing countries. They argue that the presence of human capital and technological innovation validates their arguments. Therefore, N-11 countries should focus on improving the institutional framework which includes monitoring and assessment of capacities and management and budgeting procedures of public investments. When these inefficiencies are eliminated, they can help countries to fully benefit from the oil resources, and the wealth can be channelled into investment in human capital and technological innovation.

Mohammed et al. (2022) opine that in 82 oil-producing countries, government ownership of oil revenues undermines the efficiency of financial institutions at weak levels of political institutions but efficiency is strengthened when political institutions become stronger. The study equally finds private ownership of oil revenues reduces depth and access of financial institutions with weak level of political institutions quality but positive when political institution is positive. The study also observes a threshold effect on the depth and access of financial markets in the subsample of developing countries. The study concludes that oil-producing countries needs solid political economy to help boost the management of oil revenues to support financial markets development in oil-producing countries.

19.5 Oil Revenues, Economic Growth, and Development

This section discusses oil revenues, economic growth, and development. Oil revenues that flow to the government form part of the government fiscal policy in which the revenues are used in the budget to finance activities in the economy. The extant literature has argued that economies that have not managed their oil revenues very well have often played a limited role in stimulating economic growth. Sala-i-Martin and Subramanian (2013) show that oil revenues impact negatively on economic growth in Nigeria. They argue that this negative impact is occasioned by the delirious effect of institutional quality in Nigeria. In effect, they show that the effective way to manage the Nigeria oil money is to distribute the money to the general public. Globally, oil-producing countries also spend their oil money on promoting economic development. Some countries have apportioned their oil wealth into investment in physical spending, human capital development, health, and agricultural modernisation.

19.5.1 Oil Revenues and Economic Growth

This section discusses the implications of oil revenues on economic growth in oil-producing countries. Oil revenues and economic growth have been a contestable issue of discourse in the empirical literature. The literature has discussed the resource curse thesis where countries with an abundance of oil wealth have often led to volatile economic growth. However, countries with oil revenues are theoretically expected to experience positive outcomes in terms of growth in their economies. But in most cases, some of these countries have tended to have a dwindling economy. This section points out such studies and provides the needed advice for policymakers in oil-producing countries as to how to utilise their revenues.

Specifically, Mehrara (2008) studies the link between oil revenues and output growth in oil-exporting countries by applying a dynamic panel framework. Mehrara finds that oil revenue booms play a limited role in economic growth in oil-producing countries. This finding, he argues, has many macroeconomic implications for policy planning. The negative impact of oil revenues on growth can be mitigated through the use of stabilisation, savings funds, and the diversification of the real sector. Again, Hamdi and Sbia (2013) argue that oil revenues are the main source of revenues in financing government expenditure in Bahrain. They note that increases in government revenues have aided government financing of economic activities which have led to growth in Bahrain.

In a related development, Khanna (2017) underscores the impact of ownership of oil revenues on the economic growth of oil-producing countries. She finds that understate ownership and control of oil abundance reduce economic growth when institutional quality is poor, but growth increases with strong institutional quality. She also finds that under private ownership, oil abundance increases growth when institutional quality is poor and reduces growth when institutional quality is good. The policy effect of her finding is that ownership of oil matters, and countries can best manage their oil revenues by choosing good ownership of their oil. In conclusion with strong institutional quality in place, oil resources should be controlled by the state, while the private sector should own the oil sector when institutions are weak.

Furthermore, Mohammed et al. (2020) study the relationship between government and IOC investment of oil revenues on economic growth by considering the role of financial markets. They find akin to Khanna that government investment in oil revenues improves economic growth with strong banking sector development while private investment in oil revenues increases economic growth when the banking sector is weak. Their findings have policy implications on the role that government investment and private ownership and investment have on economic growth among oil-producing countries. Thus, oil revenue investment should be left with the government when the banking sector is strong, and the government should advise itself when the banking sector is weak.

19.5.2 Spending Oil Revenues for Economic Development

Oil revenues can either be spent directly into the economy or it may be saved in the international financial markets in the form of Sovereign Wealth Funds (SWFs). It may also be a mixture of SWF and direct expenditure in the economy. Some countries have a mixture of savings and spending directly into the economy depending on the kind of management model they adopt. Section 19.3 discusses the different management models and their implications for oil-producing countries. Spending of oil revenues can be done in two ways. These are direct spending into the government budget and spending into government defined priority areas such as infrastructure, agriculture, health and education. In Sub-Saharan African countries such as Ghana, the government has an allocation in the budget called Annual Budgetary Funding Amount (ABFA) which is determined by the Ghana petroleum revenue management Act. These priority areas are changed from time to time as prescribed by the Act. Currently, the ABFA funds are spent largely on education, health, agricultural modernisation, and others. Among these priority areas, education takes the lion's share of it which is occasioned by the government's Free-Senior High School Policy. The government of Ghana also apportions some of the oil funds for future generations called the Heritage Fund and Stabilisation Fund to cater for contingencies, distortion in oil prices, and when the oil reserves are completely depleted. Some of the funds are also allocated to GNPC for investment in the upstream sector on behalf of the government.

In general, some oil-producing countries use the windfall from the oil as a tax rebate for businesses, for investment within the economy, and for social spending. These help to support the economic development of the oil-producing country. First, the use of oil as a tax rebate in a form of lowering taxes for both individuals and businesses. This is put into the government budget directly, and it affects the beneficiaries uniformly (Segal and Sen, 2011).

Additionally, a certain number of oil-producing countries use the oil funds to increase fixed capital formation to reach a global average level. This is usually injected into state-sponsored enterprises to propel domestic growth and create jobs.

Finally, the use of oil revenues could be spent on social policy programmes, such as education, health care, women empowerment, and poverty reduction. In the case of Norway, they spend their oil funds as a form of investment for pensions for its citizens. Rajasthan's pension scheme is funded by the federal share of the oil revenues in India. These priority spending helps in facilitating economic development in these countries.

19.6 Concluding Remarks

The most crucial factor that can help in accelerating economic development in any country is a resilient and well-developed financial sector. However, the financial sector needs financial assets and commodities to translate the financial assets into real assets within the economy to propel the economic development needed. Interestingly, oil serves as a financial asset and physical commodity. Countries that are blessed with oil wealth can leverage this to enhance financial and economic development.

However, a plethora of literature has pontificated the oil curse on finance and economic growth in oil-producing countries. More importantly, the debate has surrounded the misuse of this natural wealth, leading to a curse in most of these countries. In this study, we document the fiscal regime that involves generating oil revenues and the models used in managing oil revenues. We also document the nexus between oil revenues and the financial market as well as oil revenues, growth, and economic development.

We pointed out that the fiscal regime a typical oil-producing country adopts facilitates the expected payments they will receive from the oil. We also noted that the management of the oil wealth is dependent on the country's consumption behaviour either by a full-blown budgetary allocation or by saving some as a financial asset. Some countries have a mixture of savings and allocating for present consumption. We further argue that the financial and economic growth curse exists in oil-producing countries by pointing out current existing studies. The argument is that this curse can be mitigated through proper management of oil funds and solid institutional quality. Finally, we document that with proper investment of oil funds, nations can achieve economic development through poverty reduction, human capital development, and good health.

The policy implication is that oil-producing countries should negotiate very well regarding new oil well contracts to increase their expected payments, and this could enable them to invest in productive sectors of the economy to enhance financial development and economic growth.

References

Adams, D., Ullah, S., Akhtar, P., Adams, K., and Saidi, S. (2019). The role of country-level institutional factors in escaping the natural resource curse: Insights from Ghana. *Resources Policy*, 61, 433–440.

Amoako-Tuffour, J., and Owusu-Ayim, J. (2010). An evaluation of Ghana's petroleum fiscal regime. *The Ghana Policy Journal*, 4, 7–34.

Erdoğan, S., Yıldırım, D. Ç., and Gedikli, A. (2020). Natural resource abundance, financial development and economic growth: An investigation on Next-11 countries. *Resources Policy*, 65, 101559.

Friedman, M. (1957). The permanent income hypothesis. In *A theory of the consumption function* (pp. 20–37). Princeton: Princeton University Press.

Hamdi, H., and Sbia, R. (2013). Dynamic relationships between oil revenues, government spending and economic growth in an oil-dependent economy. *Economic Modelling*, 35, 118–125.

Khanna, A. A. (2017). Revisiting the oil curse: Does ownership matter?. *World Development*, 99, 214–229.

Li, Y., Naqvi, B., Caglar, E., and Chu, C. C. (2020). N-11 countries: Are the new victims of the resource-curse?. *Resources Policy*, 67, 101697.

Mehrara, M. (2008). The asymmetric relationship between oil revenues and economic activities: The case of oil-exporting countries. *Energy Policy*, 36(3), 1164–1168.

Mohammed, J. I. (2020). Studies on oil revenue management in oil-producing countries: Implications for financial markets, economic growth and sustainable development goals (SDGs) (Unpublished PhD dissertation submitted to the University of Ghana), 1.

Mohammed, J. I., Fiador, V. O., Karimu, A., and Abor, J. Y. (2022). Ownership structure of oil revenues: Political institutions and financial markets in oil-producing countries. *Journal of Multinational Financial Management*, 100760.

Mohammed, J. I., Karimu, A., Fiador, V. O., and Abor, J. Y. (2020). Oil revenues and economic growth in oil-producing countries: The role of domestic financial markets. *Resources Policy*, 69, 101832.

Mohn, K. (2016). Resource revenue management and wealth neutrality in Norway. *Energy Policy*, 96, 446–457.

Sala-i-Martin, X., and Subramanian, A. (2013). Addressing the natural resource curse: An illustration from Nigeria. *Journal of African Economies*, 22(4), 570–615

Segal, P., and Sen, A. (2011). *Oil revenue and economic development: The case of Rajasthan, India* (No. 43, OIES Paper). WPM. https://www.econstor.eu/bitstream/10419/246511/1/978-1-907555-27-5.pdf

Thampapillai, D. J., Hansen, J., and Bolat, A. (2014). Resource rent taxes and sustainable development: A Mongolian case study. *Energy Policy*, 71, 169–179.

Umar, M., Ji, X., Mirza, N., and Rahat, B. (2021). The impact of resource curse on banking efficiency: Evidence from twelve oil-producing countries. *Resources Policy*, 72, 102080.

Van der Ploeg, F., and Venables, A. J. (2011). Harnessing windfall revenues: Optimal policies for resource-rich developing economies. *The Economic Journal*, 121(551), 1–30.

Venditti, F., and Veronese, G. (2020). Global financial markets and oil price shocks in real-time (Working Paper Series No. 2474/September 2020). https://www.econstor.eu/bitstream/10419/229086/1/ecb-wp2472.pdf.

Wills, S. (2018). Leave the volatility fund alone: Principles for managing oil wealth. *Journal of Macroeconomics*, 55, 332–352.

20 The Political Economy of the Oil and Gas Sector in Emerging and Developing Countries

Simplice A. Asongu, Gerald Emmanuel Arhin, Abdul-Gafaru Abdulai, and Justice Nyigmah Bawole

20.1 Introduction

Recent talks among the United States, the International Energy Agency (IEA) and European nations to release Western strategic petroleum reserves of between 60 and 75 million barrels in order to hedge rising fuel price following the Russia–Ukraine war have ignited conversations around the political economy of oil production (Blas, 2022). The narrative also maintains that even if only about 50% of the Russian oil is affected by corporate decisions or official sanctions, more still has to be done in an attempt to mitigate rising oil prices. This brings to the fore how hydrocarbon resources can be weaponised and used as a means to an end. Consequently, it is important to further understand the role of geopolitics, inter-party politics and institutional challenges in the management of oil and gas resources. Focusing on developing countries, the chapter seeks to survey the existing literature on the political economy of hydrocarbon governance.

In so doing, three main strands are emphasised: (i) the political economy of oil and gas exploration, (ii) the political economy of gas production, and (iii) the political economy of revenue sharing from oil and gas exports. The review shows how the interests and ideas of the major actors in the oil and gas sector, including the state, political actors, multinational companies, and the citizens relative to the power they wield, shape the governance of the sector at all levels. These interests and power of the actors also influence the emergence and performance of the institutions governing the sector.

After this introductory section, the chapter proceeds in four successive sections. The next section focuses on the political economy of oil and gas exploration. This is followed by a review on the political economy of oil and gas production. The penultimate section then surveys the literature on the political economy of hydrocarbon revenues. Concluding the chapter is a summary of the review, implications and suggestions for future studies.

DOI: 10.4324/9781003315056-23

20.2 The Political Economy of Oil and Gas Exploration

This section focuses on the political economy of "oil and gas exploration" prior to the production process, focusing particularly on local content issues in the legal frameworks of oil-producing countries. Local content requirements (LCRs) are relevant for understanding the political economy of oil and gas exploration because the content of LCRs as well as the approach adopted to consolidate LCRs should be clarified to all parties in order to mitigate contractual mismatches and misalignments between international companies and governments that can lead to responses from party politics, challenge institutional building and influence geopolitics in the sector. For instance while the first two externalities are self-evident because of domestic responses, the third involving geopolitics is apparent in the ongoing Russian–Ukraine conflict (Henn, 2022). Moreover, LCRs could engender positive externalities (e.g. securing jobs and improving the process of skills acquisition and technology transfer), and can also produce misalignments between investors and governments, especially for countries where party politics are fundamental in clarifying and adjusting the legal framework underpinning LCRs and minimizing risks and disputes. With the aforementioned clarifications, this section discusses (i) the drivers of LCRs in developing and emerging countries and (ii) governance and institutional challenges surrounding LCRs (Olawuyi, 2019).

20.2.1 Drivers of LCRs in Emerging and Developing Countries

Consistent with Olawuyi (2019), the drivers of LCRs are fivefold. The first relates to the desire of host governments to improve their domestic capability and competence levels with the unfolding of time. In essence, domestic governments usually desire that oil and gas exploration contracts should be tailored to enhance local skills, experience, and capacity in the attendant and/or future petroleum operations.

The second driver of LCR is related to the desire of citizens and residents to be included in potential production processes as well as the need for home-based companies to also participate in the underlying process. These positions have been substantiated with respect to oil and gas producers in the Middle East and North Africa (MENA) (Tagliapietra, 2019) and developing countries more broadly (Adams et al., 2019).

The third driver pertains to the need to improve the socio-economic well-being of citizens via employment creation. This builds from the growing evidence that most oil-rich developing and emerging countries are characterized by high levels of unemployment (Musa and Basir, 2019; Cheratian et al., 2020; Uduji et al., 2019a, 2019b). For instance there is a growing evidence that with the influence of opposition parties and elections in many African countries, agreements surrounding Chinese oil-exploration are tailored such that there is a local proportion of employment clearly articulated in the corresponding oil contracts (Asongu, 2016; Asongu and Ssozi, 2016).

The fourth determinant of LCRs in oil-producing countries is the overall need to improve technological capacity at the national level, and, within this remit, there are requirements to give priority to locally manufactured consumables, machinery, and equipment, especially when they are internationally competitive. This has been recently documented for countries such as Iran (Jahromi, 2021).

The fifth driver is the importance of mitigating socio-economic and political risks, especially as it pertains to the equitable distribution of the fruits of potential oil and gas production. This last determinant is consistent with the growing body of literature on the importance of improving economic governance at the national level as well as promoting corporate social responsibility at the level of multinational oil companies (Uduji et al., 2021a, 2021b).

20.2.2 Governance Challenges in LCRs

Consistent with Olawuyi (2019), there are obviously institutional challenges surrounding the nexus between governance and multinational oil companies, especially as it relates to procurement process.

While the concept and content of international best practices can be subject to debate and litigation in relation to compliance with LCRs, to limit and avoid such disputes, governments should be informed of standard practices on an annual basis. According to Olawuyi (2019), this is the case in countries such as Oman, Iran, Saudi Arabia and the United Arab Emirates (UAE). The narrative also maintains that some governments require such procurement plans to be submitted prior to oil and gas production (e.g. Iraq and Lebanon). In some countries like Egypt and Libya, beyond some financial limits, governments must take part in the procurement activities while in others such as Qatar, there is an advisory committee from the government. It is also important to clarify that while the direct participation of domestic governments in the procurement process is a way to ensure transparency and ensure that the interest of the country is upheld, such approaches can also lead to delays due to bureaucracy and disagreements from opposition political parties. It is in this light that several oil-exporting countries have put in place mechanisms aimed at navigating institutional challenges surrounding LCRs (Olawuyi, 2019).

20.3 The Political Economy of Oil and Gas Production

Beyond the drilling of petroleum, the processes characterizing the production of the discovered hydrocarbon cannot be detached from both political and economic reasoning (Hickey et al., 2020; Ngoasong, 2014). This section synthesises the literature on how hydrocarbon production in developing countries can be understood through a political economy lens. In so doing, two main areas are emphasised. The first subsection highlights how the nature of a country's political context, particularly the nature of inter-party politics, shapes production-sharing agreements and production contracts more broadly. It also briefly highlights the role of geopolitics in oil production on the global stage. The second focuses on local content policies (LCPs) at the stage of production. Emphasis is placed on how institutions are reformed to boost a state's share in oil and gas production through LCPs and how IOCs in turn respond to these institutional framing. This is distinct from the review in the earlier section, where LCRs were discussed at the stage of exploration.

20.3.1 Understanding the Politics of Hydrocarbon Production: The Role of Geopolitics, Interparty and Institutional Bargain

Political actors, through the use of different systems, may influence decisions around hydrocarbon governance that serve their personal interest of retaining power (Clark & Lee, 2016; Lomasky, 2004) at the expense of public interest. Prior studies (Zilliox and Smith, 2017; Bjorvatn et al., 2012; Briceno-Leon, 2006; Omgba, 2009; Watts, 2004) have documented several cases where oil and gas and political systems and actors have interplayed to influence the state of the economy. For instance Watts (2004) documents the evidence of how politics in the forms of chieftainship, ethnic minority and national politics influence the production of oil and gas in the Niger Delta of Nigeria.

The emergence of new hydrocarbon producers in sub-Saharan Africa, which was part of the "Africa rising" narrative, was deemed as an avenue for such countries to exert both political and economic control over the resources, and this included processes of negotiating production contracts (Hickey et al., 2015; Tordo, 2011). Vernon (1971) emphasised the role of economic dynamics in oil and gas governance, driven mainly by price volatility of hydrocarbons. At the exploration stage, firms take greater risks, giving them an upper hand in the design of contracts whereas states may have greater control when it comes to production, especially in cases of price appreciation (Vernon, 1971). Wilson (2015) argues that the underlining conditions that shape oil governance, including at the production stage, are political institutions.

Beyond the institutional approach to understanding resource governance, more recent research seeks to help us understand why and how institutions emerge and perform the way they do (Hickey and Izama, 2020; Hickey et al., 2020), and why similar institutions perform differently under different contexts (Rodrik, 2004). This has since seen several scholarships focusing on inter-elite bargaining and the power configuration underlining the emergence and actual functioning of institutions (Bebbington, 2013; Bebbington et al., 2018; Poteete, 2009). The differences in countries' political structures and the pursuance of different interest by actors relative to their bargaining strength have since been well captured by Khan's (2010) *Political Settlements* theory. Different forms of political settlements generate different incentives for ruling elites, leading to different approaches in negotiating and developing production contracts. As an illustration of this point, we draw on the work of Hickey et al. (2020) on the analysis of the production contracts by Ghana and Uganda: two countries with similar-sized hydrocarbon reserves but different political settlement dynamics.

Ghana's political settlement has been characterized as being competitively clientelistic (Oduro et al., 2014; Abdulai and Hickey, 2016) because of the increasingly fierce inter-party electoral competition that plays out in a clientelist political environment and where ruling elites remain highly vulnerable due to the strength of both excluded elite factions and lower-level factions within ruling coalitions. Though the country has experienced sustained economic growth, there has been little progress in achieving structural transformation in part because the nature of the country's political settlement undermines elite commitment towards long-term investments in the productive sectors of the economy (Whitfield, 2011). Uganda, on the other hand, can best be described as a dominant party settlement (Golooba-Mutebi and Hickey, 2013) where Yoweri Museveni and his National Resistance Movement (NRM) have been in power since 1986.

These differences in the political settlement of the two countries greatly shaped the negotiation of their oil and gas production contracts (Hickey et al., 2020). Whereas Ghana secured a profit share of 38–50% of its production share agreements with IOCs, Uganda managed 43.5–66% (Amoako-Tuffour and Owusu-Ayim, 2010). Hickey et al. (2020) argue that in Ghana, the vulnerability of the ruling elites due to a strong excluded faction compelled the then ruling National Democratic Congress (NDC) party to hasten the pace of the negotiations in order to secure revenues for purposes of sustaining power. Museveni of Uganda, on the other hand, had less threat from opposition parties and did not fear losing power. This enabled him to be patient in negotiating a better deal for the country (Hickey et al., 2020). This further emphasizes how the nature of a country's party politics shapes the negotiations around contracts on oil production. Deducing from the work of Hickey et al. (2020), a country with an intense party politics is likely to hasten the negotiation process, a tendency which may not yield the best deal for the country. In contrast, a country with weak or no opposition parties allows the ruling elites a longer time horizon, enabling them to have the patience to negotiate contractual terms that may better benefit the state in the long run (Hickey et al., 2020).

20.3.2 Reforming Institutions to Strengthen Local Content Policies (LCPs) in Petroleum Production Agreements

The role of the state in reshaping and reforming institutions through LCPs and LCRs, as an avenue to maximise the state's benefits in petroleum production is a field that has seen wider coverage in extant literature (Auty, 2012; Kazzazi and Nouri, 2012; Klueh et al., 2009). In recent times, oil-producing countries have engaged in institutional reforms around LCPs to regulate the activities of

IOCs, a move that has come under international scrutiny (Ngoasong, 2014). Although LCPs are not novelle, they gained renewed traction in petroleum production in developing countries through a revision of previous local content guidelines to boost domestic employment rate (Kazzazi and Nouri, 2012). Under these reformed LCPs, IOCs are required to prioritise locals in sourcing technical and human resources in petroleum production (Mendonça and de Oliveira, 2013).

Indeed, IOCs have long been under pressure to contribute to the economic and social development of host countries through the development of fiscal regimes, legal contracts and investments in corporate social responsibility (CSR) (Dongkun and Na, 2010; Auty, 2012). Despite the positives associated with LCPs, some scholars have cautioned that they have the potential to turn a country's natural resource wealth into a "curse" as stiff LCPs may circumscribe foreign direct investment (FDI) (Auty, 2012; Bakare, 2011; Dieck-Assad, 2006). This is against the backdrop that the form of some LCP/Rs has the potential of disrupting the operations of IOCs and even inhibiting their competitiveness (Ngoasong, 2014).

The state and IOCs are often the dominant actors in the political economy of oil production in developing countries (Ngoasong, 2014). It is therefore not uncommon for IOCs to negotiate with government, if the requirements of the LCPs are detrimental to their interest. For example a letter signed by 47 IOCs in Kazakhstan to the president criticized the LCRs of the country to be extremely stiff and a barrier to foreign direct investment in the country's petroleum sector (Ritchie, 2004). Although the concerns of these IOCs did not yield the expected results, it highlights how institutions around certain regulations in favour of national interest could harm the activities of IOCs. Assessing the operations of five IOCs in seven different developing countries, Ngoasong (2014) argues that the business activities adopted by IOCs in response to LCPs are a key determinant of socio-economic growth.

20.4 The Political Economy of Revenue Sharing from Oil and Gas Exports

Extractive resource revenues are a key source of income for resource-rich countries (Chang, 2007). However, the slow pace of development in resource-rich countries, partly as a consequence of greater rent seeking on the part of political elites, is regarded as a major manifestation of the resource curse thesis (Karl, 1997). The management and sharing of resource revenues, particularly, that of oil and gas have received substantial scholarly attention, mainly due to the material speciality of the resource: first, hydrocarbons are not infinite so they cannot be an everlasting source of revenue; second, prices of oil and gas fluctuate, exposing resource-rich countries to developmental fluctuations (Devlin and Titman, 2004) and third, petroleum resources are concentrated in specific geographical areas and are capital intensive (Chang, 2007; Shao and Yang,

2014). The delicate nature of hydrocarbon revenues has, therefore, necessitated the proposal of different mechanisms in sharing the revenues and the circumstances that shape such decision-making (Acosta, 2013; Hadna, 2017; Hjort, 2006; Körinek, 2015; Lebdioui, 2020).

This section begins with a review of some of the proposed mechanisms of sharing petroleum revenues. The section focuses on the citizens' fund and subnational sharing mechanisms and discusses the circumstances that shape the choice of particular approaches. The section ends with an analysis of how elite bargains shape the design of institutions that guide oil and gas revenue sharing.

20.4.1 The Citizens' Fund

Some states operate the "citizens' Fund" where portions of the resource revenues are directly shared among citizens (Agustina et al., 2012). It is also referred to as direct distribution. Mongolia and Alaska are examples of states that have such mode of distribution. This method is intended to make citizens feel a direct impact of the resource revenues. It is also argued that such method may serve as an incentive for citizens to pay their taxes to foster development (Acosta, 2013; Lebdioui, 2020). However, Acosta (2013) and Hjort (2006) argue that direct distribution is not an effective petroleum-revenue-sharing mechanism, neither is it an effective way of eliminating poverty especially in countries with weak institutions.

Since 1976, Alaska has been transferring 25% of their oil royalties into the Alaska Permanent fund (APF) and about half of the fund's dividend is transferred to citizens annually (Hjort, 2006). However, there has always been budget deficits and unfinished public works (Acosta, 2013). Also, in Africa where majority of the people do not save in banks, distributing such monies will be cumbersome. Direct distribution gives the individual a greater discretion in how to manage such revenues, and there is always a possibility of mismanagement at the individual level. Direct distribution as a way of social policy is therefore just a way of treating the symptoms rather than eliminating poverty (Lebdioui, 2020).

20.4.2 Subnational Sharing of Petroleum Revenues

The mechanism of sharing hydrocarbon receipts with subnational governments and taking into consideration oil- and gas-producing regions is not uncommon. Nigeria, Indonesia and Peru are examples of countries that operate such a system (Körinek, 2015). In Nigeria for instance the federal government is allocated 52.68%, states get 26.72%, and 20.60% of oil revenues are disbursed to local governments (Acosta, 2013). Prior to 2012, Columbia distributed 80% of mineral revenues to the mineral-producing regions. Peru's resource revenues are distributed among the three levels of government: the central government, the regions and the local areas (Körinek, 2015).

Consistent with the subnational mechanism of sharing petroleum revenues, using Indonesia as case study, Hadna (2017) argues that a just system of sharing oil and gas revenues is the adoption of the rights-based approach (RBA). The RBA framework is one that takes into account international norms and standards of a human right system into development processes (Boesen and Martin, 2007). To this end, Hadna (2017) contends that the relationship between duty bearers (government authorities) and right holders (the oil- and gas-producing regions) should be shaped by the RBA, where the indigens of the hydrocarbon-producing areas will be regarded as the rightful owners of the resources and gain a commensurate share of the revenues.

Such distribution has the purpose of making the resource-producing areas benefit from what they produce. It is also intended to compensate such regions for the environmental destruction that comes with natural resource extraction. Acosta (2013), however, argues that such mode of distribution brings about unequal development. Some regions of the country will receive more revenues for development at the expense of others. Again, subnational governments may not have the requisite technical know-how in the management of such funds. The result therefore is poor investments, embezzlement, corruption and misappropriation. Even with the justification of compensating for environmental pollution, it is difficult to determine areas or regions that are environmentally affected by the extractive activities. For instance some neighbouring towns may be directly or indirectly affected by the extraction of natural resources but will not be considered as the concession regions and as such will not benefit from such developments (Acosta, 2013).

20.4.3 The Political Economy of Hydrocarbon Revenue Sharing

The decision to opt for a particular form of revenue sharing is shaped by the political dynamics of a country, underpinned by both formal and informal structures, the interest and ideas held by the key stakeholders in line with their bargaining strength (Agustina et al., 2012; Asante, 2016; Bebbington, 2013). The externalities associated with the exploitation of extractives, such as petroleum, spark intense struggles between different social and political groups, which in turn shape the development of institutions and the subsequent sharing of the acquired revenues (Bebbington, 2013). The local dynamics of power is therefore crucial in shaping the decisions of national elites in the design of petroleum-revenue-sharing mechanisms (Asante, 2016).

As part of the local dynamics, spatial inequality is a key factor in negotiating the mechanisms guiding the distribution of petroleum revenues (Ewetan, 2012). This inequality could be either as a result of the deplorable nature of resource-rich regions or inadequate fiscal injection into non-resource-rich countries or both (Vande, 2021). The agitations and arguments by the people of the Delta region and northern sphere of Nigeria reflect the inter-regional bargain of petroleum revenue sharing, underscored by different reasons. As the main region for hydrocarbon production, people of the Niger Delta claim custody of the resources and contend that they should be the greater beneficiaries of the revenues (Ukpong and Obok, 2018). The northern regions, on the other hand, believe that the resources should be viewed as wealth of the whole country, and, as such, the revenues should be shared equally to benefit every Nigerian (Nzemeke, 2001). Similarly, interests of groups and individuals are vital in bargaining how much and how hydrocarbon revenues are shared. Thus, both political and economic reasonings shape the sharing of oil and gas revenues (Vande, 2021).

The discovery of oil and gas and the sharing of its revenues can be instrumentalized to gain political popularity and capture political power (Asante, 2016). For instance in the run up to Ghana's 2008 presidential elections, the NDC, which was the main opposition party, leveraged on the country's commercial discovery of hydrocarbons to promise 10% perpetual allocation of the petroleum revenues to the Western region (Ariweriokuma, 2009). The Western region, which harbours the country's petroleum resources, is seen as a swing voting region. Hence, winning the region boosts a party's victory in general elections. However, on winning power, the NDC did not fulfil its promise due to both political and economic reasons coupled with the idea of national unity and political stability. The NDC later resorted to informal means of compensating the region with the intention of repelling the wrath of the region (Asante, 2016).

The brief review of the literature and analysis in this section shows that developing countries resort to different forms of sharing petroleum revenues. The decision to settle on any form, however, depends on the social, economic and political contexts of countries. The discovery of oil and gas leads to the generation of different ideas and interests on their governance. Different strategies are, therefore, pursued by different actors, from the people in the region of oil and gas to political elites on how the revenues should be shared. The development and outcome of the institutional design guiding the sharing of these revenues are hence shaped by the interests of these actors relative to their bargaining strength.

20.5 Conclusion and Future Research Directions

This chapter has surveyed the existing literature on the political economy of the oil and gas sector in emerging and developing countries. The chapter has provided insights into understanding the politics of hydrocarbon production especially as it pertains to the role of interparty and institutional bargain and how the differential politics of countries shape the decision-making process in the production of hydrocarbons. These insights have been complemented with documented perspectives on reforming institutions to strengthen LCPs in petroleum production agreements. Relying on the Citizens Fund and subnational sharing of revenues as examples, the review explored the rationale underpinning the decision to adopt a certain mechanism of sharing oil and gas revenues. As argued earlier, the bargaining power of the relevant stakeholders cannot be downplayed in how hydrocarbon revenues are shared. For instance it is not uncommon for political actors to instrumentalise the sharing of hydrocarbon revenues to achieve their political and clientelist interests. Progressing on this review, future studies can focus on assessing how insights provided in this chapter are relevant to achieving the sustainable development goals (SDGs), especially given the importance of natural resource wealth in funding the socio-economic development of resource-rich developing and emerging economies.

References

Abdulai, A. G., and Hickey, S. (2016). The politics of development under competitive clientelism: Insights from Ghana's education sector. *African Affairs*, 115(458), 44–72.

Acosta, A. (2013). The impact and effectiveness of accountability and transparency initiatives: The governance of natural resources. *Development Policy Review*, 31, s89–s105.

Adams, D., Adams, K., Ullah, S., and Ullah, F. (2019). Globalisation, governance, accountability and the natural resource 'curse': Implications for socio-economic growth of oil-rich developing countries. *Resource Policy*, 61, 128–140.

Agustina, C. D., Ahmad, E., Nugroho, D., and Siagian, H. (2012). *Political economy of natural resource revenue sharing in Indonesia*. London: Asia Research Centre (ARC).

Amoako-Tuffour, J., and Owusu-Ayim, J. (2010). An evaluation of Ghana's petroleum fiscal regime. *AfricaPortal*. https://www.africaportal.org/publications/an-evaluation-of-ghanas-petroleum-fiscal-regime/

Ariweriokuma, S. (2009). *The political economy of oil and gas in Africa: The case of Nigeria*. London: Routledge.

Asante, E. P. (2016). *Pathway(s) to inclusive development in Ghana: Oil, subnational-national power relations and ideas* (PhD Thesis, University of Manchester).

Asongu, S. A. (2016). Sino-African relations: A review and reconciliation of dominant schools of thought. *Politics & Policy*, 44(2), 351–383.

Asongu, S. A., and Ssozi, J. (2016). Sino-African relations: Some solutions and strategies to the policy syndromes. *Journal of African Business*, 17(1), 33–51.

Auty, R. (2012). Causes, consequences, and policy implications. *Handbook of Oil Politics*, 2, 5–41.

Bakare, A. S. (2011). Local content policy in oil sector and the capacity utilization in Nigerian manufacturing industry. *Business and Management Review*, 1(6), 82–92.

Bebbington, A., Abdulai, A.-G., Hinfelaar, M., Humphreys Bebbington, D., and Sanborn, C. (2018). *Governing extractive industries: Politics, histories, ideas*. Oxford: Oxford University Press.

Bebbington, T. (2013). *Natural resource extraction and the possibilities of inclusive development: Politics across space and time*. ESID Working Paper No. 21, Manchester: The University of Manchester.

Bjorvatn, K., Farzanegan, M. R., and Schneider, F. (2012). Resource curse and power balance: Evidence from oil-rich countries. *World Development*, 40(7), 1308–1316.

Blas, J. (2022). Russia-Ukraine war: Pleas to stop buying Russian oil and gas go unheeded. *Business Standard*. https://www.business-standard.com/article/international/ukraine-conflict-pleas-to-stop-buying-russian-oil-and-gas-go-unheeded-122030100179_1.html

Boesen, J., and Martin, T. (2007). *Applying a rights-based approach/an inspirational guide for civil society*. The Danish Institute for Human.

Brennan, G., and Lomasky, L. (1997). *Democracy and decision: The pure theory of electoral preference*. Cambridge: Cambridge University Press.

Briceño-León, R. (2006). Violence in Venezuela: Oil rent and political crisis. *Ciência & Saúde Coletiva*, 11(2), 315–325.

Chang H.-J. (2007). State-owned enterprise reform. In *United Nations DESA National Development Strategies Policy Notes*, New York: United Nations Department of Economic and Social Affairs.

Cheratian, I., Golpe, A., Goltabar, S., and Iglesias, J. (2020). The unemployment-entrepreneurship nexus: New evidence from 30 Iranian provinces. *International Journal of Emerging Markets*, 15(3), 469–489.

Clark, J. R., and Lee, D. R. (2016). Higher costs appeal to voters: Implications of expressive voting. *Public Choice*, 167(1), 37–45.

Devlin, J., and Titman, S. (2004). Managing oil price risk in developing countries. *The World Bank Research Observer*, 19(1), 119–139.

Dieck-Assad, F. A. (2006). Energy resources: A blessing or a curse?. *Journal of Canadian Petroleum Technology*, 45(8). DOI: 10.2118/06–08-GE.

Dongkun, L., and Na, Y. (2010). Assessment of fiscal terms of international petroleum contracts. *Petroleum Exploration and Development*, 37(6), 756–762.

Ewetan, O. O. (2012). Fiscal federalism in Nigeria: Theory and practice. *International Journal of Development and Sustainability*, 1(3), 1075–1086.

Golooba-Mutebi, F., and Hickey, S. (2013). *Investigating the links between political settlements and inclusive development in Uganda: Towards a research agenda*. ESID Working Paper 20. Manchester, UK: Effective States and Inclusive Development Research Centre (ESID).

Hadna, A. H. (2017). Formulating an oil and gas revenue sharing fund based on rights based approach. *BISNIS & BIROKRASI: Jurnal Ilmu Administrasi dan Organisasi*, 23(1), 16–27.

Henn, J. (2022). Fossil fuel companies are trying to exploit this war for their gain. We can't let them. *The Guardian*. https://www.theguardian.com/commentisfree/2022/feb/26/big-oil-ukraine-russia-putin.

Hickey, S., Abdulai, A. G., Izama, A., and Mohan, G. (2020). Responding to the commodity boom with varieties of resource nationalism: A political economy explanation for the different routes taken by Africa's new oil producers. *The Extractive Industries and Society*, 7(4), 1246–1256.

Hickey, S., and Izama, A. (2020). 'The politics of governing oil after 'best-practice' reforms: Can 'pockets of effectiveness' survive within Uganda's political settlement? *The Extractive Industries and Society*, 7(4), 1200–1210.

Hjort, J. (2006). Citizen funds and Dutch disease in developing countries. *Resources Policy*, 31(3), 183–191.

Jahromi, F. S. (2021). An appraisal of local content requirements in the Iranian oil and gas industry. *Resources Policy*, 73, 102151.

Karl, T. L. (1997). *The paradox of plenty*. Berkeley: University of California Press.

Karl, T. L. (2007). *Ensuring fairness: The case for a transparent fiscal social contract escaping the resource curse* (Eds. M. Humphreys, J. Sachs and JE Stiglitz). New York: Columbia University Press.

Kazzazi, A., and Nouri, B. (2012). A conceptual model for local content development in petroleum industry. *Management Science Letters*, 2(6), 2165–2174.

Khan, M. (2010). *Political settlements and the governance of growth-enhancing institutions*. https://eprints.soas.ac.uk/9968/1/Political_Settlements_internet.pdf

Klueh, U. H., Pastor, G., and Segura, A. (2009). Policies to improve the local impact from hydrocarbon extraction: Observations on West Africa and possible lessons for Central Asia. *Energy Policy*, 37(3), 1128–1144.

Körinek, J. (2015). *Managing the minerals sector: Implications for trade from Peru and Colombia (OECD Trade Policy Papers, 186)*. Paris: OECD Publishing.

Lebdioui, A. A. (2020). *Economic diversification and development in resource-dependent economies: Lessons from Chile and Malaysia* (Doctoral thesis, Chapter 4). Cambridge: University of Cambridge.

Lomasky, L. E. (2004). When hard heads collide: A philosopher encounters public choice. *American Journal of Economics and Sociology*, 63(1), 189–205.

Mendonça, R. W., and de Oliveira, L. G. (2013). Local content policy in the Brazilian oil and gas sectoral system of innovation. *Latin American Business Review*, 14(3–4), 271–287.

Musa, S. F. P., and Basir, K. H. (2019). Youth unemployment and the rentier economy in Brunei: Lessons from Norway. *AL-ABQARI: Journal of Islamic Social Sciences and Humanities*. https://oarep.usim.edu.my/jspui/handle/123456789/5158.

Ngoasong, M. Z. (2014). How international oil and gas companies respond to local content policies in petroleum-producing developing countries: A narrative enquiry. *Energy Policy*, 73, 471–479.

Nzemeke, R. (2001). Resource control not feasible. *National Interest*, 4.

Oduro, F., Mohammed, A., and Ashon, M. (2014). A dynamic mapping of the political settlement in Ghana (SSRN Working Paper) https://papers.ssrn.com/sol3/papers.cfm?abstract_id=2386788.

Omgba, L. D. (2009). On the duration of political power in Africa: The role of oil rents. *Comparative Political Studies*, 42(3), 416–436.

Olawuyi, D. S. (2019). Local content requirements in oil and gas contracts: Regional trends in the Middle East and North Africa. *Journal of Energy & Natural Resources Law*, 37(1), 93–117.

Portes, A. (2006). Institutions and development: A conceptual reanalysis. *Population and Development Review*, 32(2), 233–262.

Poteete, A. R. (2009). Is development path dependent or political? A reinterpretation of mineral-dependent development in Botswana. *The Journal of Development Studies*, 45(4), 544–571.

Ritchie, M. (2004). Kazakhstan: Investors call on Kazakhs to rethink legal changes. *NEFTE Compass*. https://www.energyintel.com/0000017b-a7a4-de4c-a17b-e7e64a310001?_amp=true

Rodrik, D. (2004). Institutions and economic performance-getting institutions right. *CESIfo DICE Report*, 2(2), 10–15.

Shao, S., and Yang, L. (2014). Natural resource dependence, human capital accumulation, and economic growth: A combined explanation for the resource curse and the resource blessing. *Energy Policy*, 74, 632–642.

Tagliapietra, S. (2019). The impact of the global energy transition on MENA oil and gas producers. *Energy Strategy Reviews*, 26, 100397.

Tordo, S. (2011). *National Oil Companies and Value Creation*. New York: World Bank Publications.

Uduji, J. I., Okolo-Obasi, E. N., and Asongu, S. A. (2019a). Does CSR contribute to the development of rural young people in cultural tourism of sub-Saharan Africa? Evidence from the Niger Delta in Nigeria. *Journal of Tourism and Cultural Change*, 17(6), 725–757.

Uduji, J. I., Okolo-Obasi, E. N., and Asongu, S. A. (2019b). Corporate social responsibility in Nigeria and multinational corporations in the fight against human trafficking in oil-producing communities. *Local Environment*, 24(12), 1097–1118.

Uduji, J. I., Okolo-Obasi, E. N., and Asongu, S. A. (2021a). Sustainable peacebuilding and development in Nigeria's post-amnesty programme: The role of corporate social responsibility in oil host communities. *Journal of Public Affairs*, 21(2), e2200.

Uduji, J. I., Okolo-Obasi, E. N., and Asongu, S. A. (2021b). Does corporate social responsibility initiative dissuade the increasing electoral violence in Sub-Saharan Africa? Evidence from Nigeria's oil producing region. *Journal of Global Responsibility*. https://doi.org/10.1108/JGR-05-2021-0052

Ukpong, I. G., and Obok, E. (2018). Implications of crude oil extraction on agriculture and livelihood in oil producing rural communities in Nigeria. *Review of Agricultural and Applied Economics (RAAE)*, 21, 71–77.

Vande, P. T. (2021). Fiscal federalism and the politics of revenue allocation in Nigeria. *Zamfara Journal of Politics and Development*, 2(1), 19–19.

Vernon, R. (1971). Sovereignty at bay: The multinational spread of US enterprises. *The International Executive*, 13(4), 1–3.

Vivoda, V. (2009). Resource nationalism, bargaining and international oil companies: Challenges and change in the new millennium. *New Political Economy*, 14(4), 517–534.

Watts, M. (2004). Resource curse? Governmentality, oil and power in the Niger Delta, Nigeria. *Geopolitics*, *9*(1), 50–80.

Whitfield, L. (2011). *Growth without economic transformation: Economic impacts of Ghana's political settlement* (DIIS Working Paper No. 2011: 28). Copenhagen: Danish Institute of International Studies.

Wilson, J. D. (2015). Understanding resource nationalism: Economic dynamics and political institutions. *Contemporary Politics*, 21(4), 399–416.

Zilliox, S., and Smith, J. M. (2017). Memorandums of understanding and public trust in local government for Colorado's unconventional energy industry. *Energy Policy*, 107, 72–81.

Index

Note: Page numbers in *italics* indicate a figure and page numbers in **bold** indicate a table on the corresponding page.

Made in the USA
Las Vegas, NV
19 September 2026

aebefc72-29c6-4a5d-8222-a6988f57ad3fR01